CompTIA® Cloud+ CV0-001 In Depth

Ron Gilster

Cengage Learning PTR

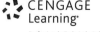

CENGAGE
Learning®

Professional • Technical • Reference

Australia, Brazil, Japan, Korea, Mexico, Singapore, Spain, United Kingdom, United States

CENGAGE
Learning·

Professional • Technical • Reference

**CompTIA® Cloud+
CV0-001 In Depth**
Ron Gilster

**Publisher and General Manager,
Cengage Learning PTR:**
Stacy L. Hiquet

Associate Director of Marketing:
Sarah Panella

Manager of Editorial Services:
Heather Talbot

Senior Marketing Manager:
Mark Hughes

Product Manager:
Heather Hurley

Project and Copy Editor:
Karen A. Gill

Technical Reviewers:
Serge Palladino, Ashlee Welz Smith

Interior Layout:
Shawn Morningstar

Cover Designer:
Mike Tanamachi

Indexer:
Larry Sweazy

Proofreader:
Sue Boshers

CompTIA is a registered trademark of CompTIA, Inc. Microsoft, Windows, and Internet Explorer are either registered trademarks or trademarks of Microsoft Corporation in the United States and/or other countries. All other trademarks are the property of their respective owners.

All images © Cengage Learning unless otherwise noted.

Library of Congress Control Number: 2014937099

ISBN-13: 978-1-305-09735-3

ISBN-10: 1-305-09735-1

Cengage Learning PTR
20 Channel Center Street
Boston, MA 02210
USA

Cengage Learning is a leading provider of customized learning solutions with office locations around the globe, including Singapore, the United Kingdom, Australia, Mexico, Brazil, and Japan. Locate your local office at: **international.cengage.com/region.**

Cengage Learning products are represented in Canada by Nelson Education, Ltd.

For your lifelong learning solutions, visit **cengageptr.com.**

Visit our corporate Web site at **cengage.com.**

Printed in the United States of America
1 2 3 4 5 6 7 16 15 14

This book is dedicated to my beautiful, caring, and supportive wife.
May God bless her.

Acknowledgments

I am deeply indebted to the wonderful people at Cengage Learning for the opportunity to write this book. I wish to especially acknowledge the contributions (and patience) of Heather Hurley, the product manager, Karen Gill, the project and copy editor, and Serge Palladino and Ashlee Welz Smith, the technical editors. I would also like to express my gratitude to Shawn Morningstar, Sue Boshers, and Larry Sweazy, all of whom have made this book look so good.

I also wish to acknowledge the companies that provided technical expertise, subject matter, and art for this book. In alphabetical order, they are:

Acronis International GmbH

Intel Corporation

Margaret Rouse/Whatis.com

Microsoft Corporation

QNAP, Inc.

Seagate Technology LLC

SOASTA

SolarWinds

Tenable Network Security

VMware, Inc.

Zabbix SIA

In addition, my gratitude and appreciation go out to the developers who have contributed to the following open source programs:

PuTTY

UNetbootin

Virt-p2v

About the Author

Ron Gilster has worked in data processing, computing, networking, computer technology, and information technology (IT) fields since 1966. He has performed just about every job in IT during that time, including operator, programmer, systems analyst, database manager, project manager, instructor, professor, and executive. Ron has a long list of IT certifications from CompTIA, Cisco, and others. He is best known as a bestselling author, having written more than 40 books on a variety of IT certification and business topics.

Table of Contents

Chapter 1 Cloud Architecture   1

Chapter 2 Cloud Computing Service Models   17

Chapter 7 Virtual Resource Migration   105

Chapter 8 Storage Technologies   125

Chapter 9 Storage Configuration   141

Chapter 10 Protocols   167

Chapter 11 Virtual Environment Planning   203

Chapter 12 Implementation   221

Chapter 13 Monitoring   251

Chapter 14 Physical Resource Allocation   267

Chapter 15 Security   287

Chapter 16 System Management   311

Introduction

As the number of vendors offering cloud computing software, services, and support continues to grow, so does the need for qualified, certified technicians. The Cloud+ certification from the Computer Technical Industry Association (CompTIA) provides a vendor-neutral certification that verifies the knowledge of the holder to a robust set of objectives. A Cloud+ certified professional knows the infrastructure, communication, delivery, and storage systems that come together to create a cloud service data or service center. This certification also verifies that the certified professional has the equivalent of 2 to 3 years of work experience in information technology (IT), with knowledge of networking, storage systems, data center administration, and the major virtualization systems and operations of their hypervisor technologies.

Because many of the concepts and technical topics can be difficult to grasp, this book explains concepts and technical topics logically using plain language and relatable examples. In addition, it offers numerous photographs, illustrations, tables, and lists along with a glossary, appendixes, chapter summaries, and review questions to prepare you for the Cloud+ certification exam and give you a reference to use in your new career as a Cloud+ certified professional.

Intended Audience

This book is intended for career IT professionals looking to earn the Cloud+ certification, students, and anyone interested in gaining knowledge of computing in a cloud service environment. Some networking knowledge and experience will greatly enhance your learning experience from this book. However, even without that background, you should be able to learn the concepts included in the book, because each concept is in an easy-to-understand presentation. This book follows the exam objectives of the Cloud+ (CV0-001) exam closely and keeps its focus on the exam, without limiting the information to only the exam questions.

Chapter Descriptions

The following list summarizes the topics covered in each chapter of the book:

> **Chapter 1, "Cloud Architecture,"** introduces you to the various cloud delivery models and services and the structures of the different cloud service models: private, public, and hybrid. The chapter goes on to explain the security differences of the various models and services and lists the primary laws and regulations governing cloud computing.

> **Chapter 2, "Cloud Computing Service Models,"** provides a more in-depth look at cloud service models and the software, platform, infrastructure (SPI) model of the National Institute for Standards and Technology (NIST). The chapter also explains the purpose and application of each of the NIST cloud service models.

➤ **Chapter 3, "Object Storage,"** discusses object-based storage and the role and purpose of the various object storage elements, including object IDs, containers, metadata, and the storage policies that define the use of object storage. This chapter also discusses the interactions of storage service application programming interfaces (APIs) with the storage system.

➤ **Chapter 4, "The Benefits of Virtualization,"** introduces you to the concepts of shared resources, resource elasticity, the creation of a virtualized data center, network and application isolation, and the methods used in infrastructure consolidation.

➤ **Chapter 5, "Virtual Components of a Cloud Environment,"** continues the discussion of virtualization with an explanation of virtual network concepts and the differences between the various virtual network types. Also discussed in this chapter are the roles and purposes of virtual network components, including virtual networking devices, virtual resource sharing, and the use of tunneling protocols.

➤ **Chapter 6, "Management of a Virtual Environment,"** explains the processes used to create, import, and export virtual machines, the reasons for and the procedures used to create snapshots and clones, and the difference between image backups and traditional file backups. The chapter concludes with a discussion of the processes used to manage virtual devices.

➤ **Chapter 7, "Virtual Resource Migration,"** describes the process, tools, and reasons for the migration of a physical environment to a virtual environment, a virtual environment to another virtual environment, and a virtual environment to a physical environment. This chapter also explains the use of maintenance mode in a virtual environment.

➤ **Chapter 8, "Storage Technologies,"** expands on the information presented in Chapter 3 by describing the architecture and functions of network-enabled storage systems, including direct attached storage (DAS), network attached storage (NAS), and storage area network (SAN). This chapter explains the different storage system topologies and communication techniques of these storage systems.

➤ **Chapter 9, "Storage Configuration,"** continues the discussion of Chapter 8 by detailing the purpose and use of RAID storage systems, the more common file types, and the difference between hard disk drive (HDD) storage and solid state drive (SSD) storage technology.

➤ **Chapter 10, "Protocols,"** describes the purpose and application of the protocols commonly used in virtualized environments and cloud services, as well as the various management requirements of these protocols. The chapter also lists and identifies the usage of the common Transmission Control Protocol/User Datagram Protocol (TCP/UDP) ports used in cloud computing.

➤ **Chapter 11, "Virtual Environment Planning,"** looks at the planning processes involved with planning for and implementing a virtualized environment. The areas covered in this chapter include a discussion on the role of hardware, technology, and software considerations in the planning process for a virtualized environment. This chapter also discusses the process of capacity planning for a virtualized system.

➤ **Chapter 12, "Implementation,"** covers the use and purpose of a variety of technologies implemented into a virtualized environment or a cloud service to ensure its functionality. The technologies discussed in this chapter include routing and switching, network ports, classful and classless networking, virtual local area networks (VLANs), and system documentation.

➤ **Chapter 13, "Monitoring,"** explains the concept and purpose of network and system performance monitoring, including TCP/IP system management and monitoring protocols. The chapter also discusses the configuration and use of performance monitoring alert notifications and the possible need for resource pooling in a cloud service environment.

➤ **Chapter 14, "Physical Resource Allocation,"** discusses the processes used to allocate physical and logical devices and other resources in a virtualized environment. The chapter also includes discussions on physical resource redirection and mapping, along with an explanation of the various types of remote access tools for networking, virtualization, and cloud service environments.

➤ **Chapter 15, "Security,"** covers the security concepts and methods for storage systems and access control. It also discusses and compares the various encryption technologies and methods used to secure network storage systems. This chapter concludes with a discussion of the hardening techniques that can be applied to both guest and host computer systems.

➤ **Chapter 16, "System Management,"** provides an in-depth look at network planning, including IP address planning for IPv4 and IPv6 and configuration standardization. Included in this chapter are an explanation of the system life cycle and its management, the need for and the implementation of change management, and the actions performed in capacity management.

➤ **Chapter 17, "Optimization,"** describes the processes used in optimizing data storage devices, the configuration of a virtualized environment's hypervisor, and the concepts and metrics of measuring and monitoring network and system performance.

➤ **Chapter 18, "Deployment,"** explains the testing procedures of each level of system deployment, the responsibilities and duties in system testing, and the processes used to perform vulnerability assessment.

➤ **Chapter 19, "Availability and Disaster Recovery,"** provides an in-depth discussion and explanation of the different solutions that provide system availability. The chapter also includes coverage of the concepts, terminology, and methods used in disaster recovery planning and execution.

The appendixes at the end of this book should help you in your studies for the Cloud+ exam. The Glossary in Appendix C should also help you understand the terminology and concepts included in this book.

➤ **Appendix A, "Cloud+ Examination Objectives,"** provides the complete list of the exam objectives for the Cloud+ CV0-001 exam cross-referenced to the chapters in the book in which each is explained, used in context, or illustrated.

> ➤ **Appendix B, "Cloud+ Practice Exam,"** provides 100 practice questions that cover all the exam objectives in the Cloud+ CV0-001 exam in proportion with the percentage of the exam that each domain provides.

> ➤ **Appendix C, "Glossary,"** is an alphabetical listing of the key terms identified in each chapter with a brief explanation of their meaning or usage.

> ➤ **Appendix D, "Cloud+ Practice Exam Answers,"** provides the answers to the 100 practice exam questions in Appendix B.

Features

To aid you in fully understanding the concepts of cloud computing and virtualization, this book includes many features designed to enhance your learning experience:

Chapter Objectives—Each chapter begins with a list of the concepts discussed within that chapter. This list is a quick reference to the chapter's content and coverage so you can study only the material you want to study.

Illustrations and Tables—Numerous figures, photographs, and illustrations depict a range of concepts, functions, actions, and outcomes to help you visualize technical material for a better understanding. In addition, many tables are included to provide both a quick study list for related material and a means for displaying comparative data.

Chapter Summaries—At the end of each chapter, the key concepts, points, and terms are summarized to review the material in that chapter after you've read the chapter or as a quick refresher before sitting down for the exam.

Review Questions—The end-of-chapter review questions are designed to reinforce your knowledge of the concepts, ideas, and technologies discussed in the chapter. These questions are similar to those you may encounter on the Cloud+ exam, but only in content and coverage. The automated Cloud+ exam includes some matching, drag and drop, and labeling exercise questions, which are a bit tough to replicate in print.

Text and Graphic Conventions

Additional information is included throughout the book, where appropriate, to provide you with a different viewpoint, related information, or just something of interest. The intent of this information is to help you understand a certain topic or concept or to consider a different viewpoint.

This book uses two icons to highlight these insertions:

Note

The Note icon draws your attention to helpful or interesting material related to the concept, topic, or process under discussion in a specific section of a chapter.

Tip

The Tip icon highlights helpful pointers on particular topics and actions.

In addition, the key terms, listed at the end of each chapter, are in italic the first time each appears in the chapter.

State of the Information Technology (IT) Field

Organizations depend on computers and IT to thrive and grow. Globalization and the opportunity for cloud services to provide IT services to virtually anyone around the world have meant an explosion in big data and application services heretofore beyond the reach of many small to medium businesses and organizations. Along with the expansion of cloud and enterprise services comes the need for trained, knowledgeable, certified cloud computing and virtualization professionals.

The trends in the IT world, while involving computers and information processing, are moving away from the data centers of yesterday into the "Internet of Everything" of tomorrow. Although the Internet has been largely about personal computers and mobile devices, it is moving toward the interconnection of household appliances, factory equipment, services, assets, and virtually any electronically powered and communications-capable device. Soon all these devices will interconnect to process data and information in the four realms of the Internet: people, things, information, and places.

To facilitate these evolutions of information processing, large, centralized, cloud-based data centers will also evolve to provide people and information with Software as a Service (SaaS), things with Infrastructure as a Service (IaaS), and places with Platform as a Service (PaaS). The shift is away from devices and toward services. Devices become less important to the business, even though devices of some kind remain in use. When the particular type of device becomes unimportant, the service and its information reign supreme. The client/server world of the local area network (LAN) and the wide area network (WAN), as they exist today, gives way to personal, private, and public clouds.

If the cloud is the future, then certified cloud professionals must be as well. In reality, the change from private enterprise networking to globally connected cloud services is really one of scale. The processes won't be that different in general, but the characteristics of the service centers must move to the highest capabilities possible: high availability (HA), high reliability, and nearly zero-fault. As a newly certified cloud professional, this is your world and future! Aren't you excited?

Certifications

Different levels of education and experience are required for the myriad jobs in the field of IT. The complicating factor in this is that the levels of education and experience vary greatly from employer to employer. Some employers aren't sure what to request in a professional being hired to take on new challenges facing the business, so they copy what a competitor is asking for, and on it goes.

Certifications, in any professional field or area of expertise, establish a baseline of skills and knowledge in a particular area. Certification provides employers with the capability to place not only their job requirements, but the qualifications of their applicants, on a level playing field. A candidate holding a certification in a particular field can confidently attest to her qualifications. Likewise, the employers know that the holder of that particular certification has demonstrated through a rigorous examination that she meets or exceeds a determined standard in that field, as defined by a specific set of exam objectives.

Certifications fall into two general categories: vendor specific and vendor neutral. Vendor-specific certifications qualify their holders with skills and knowledge in that vendor's products, processes, or services. Certified professionals holding a vendor-specific certification may have broad or narrow employment opportunities depending on the expansive or limited presence of the sponsoring vendor. For example, Microsoft certifications provide relatively broad employment opportunities, but only in Microsoft installations—not that that is a problem, necessarily. However, someone holding a certification as a Brocade Accredited Data Center Specialist may have fewer employment opportunities than a Cisco Certified Networking Associate (CCNA), just because of the size of the two companies' market shares.

A vendor-neutral certification, on the other hand, qualifies the certification holder across the width of a particular segment of the IT industry. The CompTIA Cloud+ CV0-001 exam, officially the "Cloud Essentials" certification, tells employers that the cloud professional who holds this certification has a solid, adaptable, flexible knowledge of cloud and virtualization concepts, technologies, and processes. It may not matter to the employer exactly what type of equipment it has when the need of the organization is to move its IT operations into the cloud.

Cloud+ is more than a ground-floor certification, but as this information processing technology grows, it is almost certain that specific higher-level certifications will follow. Earning the Cloud+ certification can give you a foot in the door and the springboard of your new career.

How to Become CompTIA Certified

To become CompTIA Cloud+ certified, follow these steps:

1. Visit either the Pearson Vue website at www.pearsonvue.com or Prometric at www.prometric.com to register and choose a testing center, date, and time for your exam.

    Both of these testing services have contracted testing centers in virtually all large cities and at least one in every region of the country (and overseas).

2. When you register, you will pay the testing fee. The fee changes from time to time, so verify the fee on the testing service or on CompTIA's certification website at www.comptia.org/certification. There are discounted test fees for CompTIA members.

3. Show up at the testing center on time and ready to take an online interactive exam.

CHAPTER 1

Cloud Architecture

After reading this chapter and completing the exercises, you will be able to:

- Discuss the various cloud delivery models and services

- Differentiate among private, public, and hybrid models

- Explain the security differences of the various models and services

- List the primary laws and regulations governing cloud computing

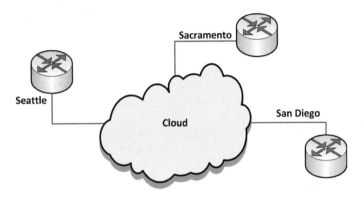

A lthough *cloud computing* is considered a relatively new concept in networking, it has, in fact, been around longer than you might think. The cloud image, as illustrated in Figure 1-1, represents the Internet and all the mysterious goings-on that occur between one network and another.

Figure 1-1 A cloud image represents the networking beyond or in between networks.
© 2015 Cengage Learning®.

Up front, you should understand that cloud computing is not a revolution seeking to replace the current means and manner of computing and information technology (IT). Rather, it represents an evolution of how hardware and software are used to provide enhanced efficiency and utility to networking resources. In fact, cloud computing is just an extension of client/server computing using the Internet as a bridge to internal and external computing resources.

In this chapter, you learn the fundamentals of cloud computing, including its different service types and delivery models. For the Cloud+ exam, this information is vital. You absolutely need to know the foundation and fundamental definitions and applications of these elements.

Cloud Architectures

Cloud services can be set up for private or public use. In addition, a cloud can provide some hybrid (a little of both) service, being available for just about anyone anytime. A cloud can be constructed to be a private, public, hybrid, or community service.

Private Cloud

As you'll see with nearly everything cloud, the names and descriptors are mostly marketing terms given to each particular type of service or delivery model to differentiate one from another to business and the public. To this end, a *private cloud*, which is also known as an internal cloud or a corporate cloud, is a completely proprietary computing architecture to a specific network and its users, all of which are located behind a specific firewall (see Figure 1-2).

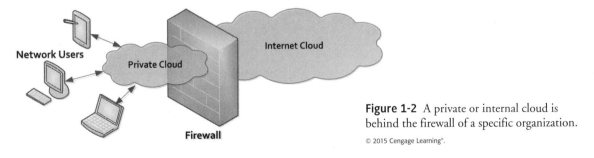

Figure 1-2 A private or internal cloud is behind the firewall of a specific organization.
© 2015 Cengage Learning®.

A private cloud is actually not a cloud at all, in the sense that a "cloud" is external to an organization's computing resources. The best example of a private cloud is the IT department of a company creating and maintaining a computing resource environment, virtualized or not, that is available only to its internal users.

For example, a corporation implements centralized servers that host a primary application. The corporate users, regardless of where they are located, access the centralized service via the Internet and a virtual private network (VPN). In the past, this was known as an enterprise network. However, in the current vernacular, it's a private cloud.

A private cloud provides storage and computing capabilities to specific subscribers. It's a virtualized environment that exists for exclusive use by a single company or organization that is made up of multiple entities and users. A private cloud can be owned as a proprietary structure, it can be provided by a service provider, or both. It can be on the company's premises or accessed via the Internet.

Don't confuse a private cloud with a personal cloud. A personal cloud is a limited form of a private cloud. However, unlike a private cloud, a personal cloud may or may not include a firewall or any other security devices. A personal cloud, which is also called MiFi (the short form of My Wi-Fi), is a wireless network router that serves as a mobile hotspot. A MiFi device is commonly a dedicated wireless appliance, but many smartphones also have this capability.

Public Cloud

Whereas a private cloud essentially provides only access to the Internet, a *public cloud* provides services over the Internet. A public cloud allows a company or organization to purchase one or a set of services that are accessed and delivered via the Internet from a third-party vendor. Table 1-1 compares the attributes of a public cloud to those of a private cloud.

When using a public cloud service, the company or organization doesn't own the computing resources involved in the delivery of a service. Any storage capacity or computing hardware required in the delivery of the service is owned and managed by the cloud services vendor or its partners.

Table 1-1 Public Versus Private Cloud

Attribute	Public Cloud	Private Cloud
Hosted by	Service provider	Organization
Available to	Multiple entities	Single entity
Environment	Shared	Unshared
Connectivity	Internet	Private network or Internet
Sensitive data	Unsuited for sensitive data	Suited for sensitive data
Cost	Subscription cost may be less than private cloud	Cost borne by organization

BENEFITS OF A PUBLIC CLOUD

As a company or organization outgrows its local area network (LAN) or perhaps even its private cloud or its ability or desire to install and maintain sophisticated software systems, a public cloud service may be the answer to its dilemma. Sophisticated systems—meaning those enterprise-wide applications that focus on one or more business functions—are typically expensive and may require costly maintenance agreements, specialized staff, and a large investment in additional computing and network resources.

The benefits of a public cloud service are many, but the primary benefits to any company or organization are these:

> **Availability**: This refers to the reliability of a cloud service and how much it is available when it's needed. This benefit is typically expressed as a percentage of uptime, such as 99.99 percent availability (four-nines availability). However, availability can also refer to the fact that wherever an Internet connection is available, so are the public cloud services.

> **Reduced investment**: Some of the more sophisticated systems, such as a customer relationship management (CRM) system, can run into the hundreds of thousands of dollars and possibly more. This amount doesn't include the additional hardware and support staff typically required to support such a system. By using a public cloud service, you can avoid a large investment but still have the same application system available by paying a much smaller subscription fee. Using a public cloud service not only reduces the investment required to gain software-based functionality, but lowers the organization's risk of making a bad software choice and having to live with it.

> **Reduced maintenance**: The cloud provider performs all the system maintenance, including hardware and software. This means that the company has access to the latest versions of the software applications to which they subscribe. This also means that any hardware capacity requirement increases or replacements are automatically scalable and handled by the provider, often with transparency to the cloud users. The *cloud service provider (CSP)* is responsible for backups, disaster planning and recovery, and staffing and staff training.

PUBLIC CLOUD APPLICATIONS

Not all public cloud applications are large, expensive applications, but in the business world, this is the most common form of a public cloud. However, there are also public cloud applications for personal use. This is where the personal cloud term can be applied to your use of the public cloud.

If you use an email client that is connected or related to a browser or portal, such as Gmail, Hotmail, Outlook.com, or Yahoo, you are using a public cloud application. Saving documents to SkyDrive, iCloud, Dropbox, or Google Drive; enjoying music from Pandora, Grooveshark, or Amazon's Cloud Player; or backing up your personal hard drive or a company's network storage to an Internet-based data security service is using a public cloud service.

Hybrid Cloud

With the wealth of services available in the public cloud, a company could be at a disadvantage if it limits its computing capabilities to a private cloud. Not all computing functions can, or should be, served through public cloud services. The company's private cloud (intranet) services may be unique to the company. However, this doesn't mean that neither the company, nor you personally, is limited to an either-or choice.

A *hybrid cloud* contains at least one private cloud service and at least one public cloud service. The result is that some computing resources are provided and managed in-house, and some are obtained from an external source. For example, a company might use a service such as Amazon's S3 to store or archive its general data but choose to manage its mission-critical or sensitive data in-house.

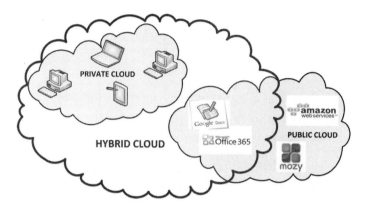

Figure 1-3 A hybrid cloud combines private cloud and public cloud services into a single infrastructure.

© 2015 Cengage Learning®; Google, Inc.; Microsoft®; Amazon.com, Inc.; Mozy®. Used with permission from Microsoft.

SCALABILITY VERSUS ELASTICITY

Two of the most marketed and often confused terms in cloud computing are scalability and elasticity. *Scalability* refers to the capability to quickly increase or decrease available resources as needed. As a company's volumes, needs, or strategic direction changes, a scalable system—whether hardware, software, or both—can grow or shrink as needed. Scalability typically requires adjusted configuration, added or removed equipment or software, and some form of a provisioning action, which implies a system disruption.

On the other hand, *elasticity* is used to mean the automatic reprovisioning or configuring of an infrastructure to meet the storage and computing resource needs of a subscriber. The automatic adjustment of the resources to meet current and possibly temporary requirements can avoid the cost of overprovisioning a scalable environment.

Community Cloud

A *community cloud* is a shared environment in which several companies, or even individuals, gain the benefits of a public cloud but with private cloud control and security. Community clouds are multitenancy environments.

A community cloud is an excellent way for several individuals or companies to collaborate on a joint project, regulatory issues, or other common issues. One or more of the cloud members or a third-party service provider can manage a community cloud.

Accountability in Cloud Computing

Recent surveys and studies continue to find that nearly 80 percent of potential cloud subscribers have concerns over the privacy and security of their data and activities in the cloud. The lack of complete trust by potential cloud customers continues to slow the expansion of cloud computing, much like it did in the early days of networking.

DIVIDED RESPONSIBILITIES

The cloud computing environment requires *accountability* from all participants. The lines of responsibility must be clearly defined in case something goes wrong. At its most basic, the share of accountability is split between the cloud subscriber and the CSP. However, the CSP may also be using cloud services from other CSPs in its service delivery. The potential for a domino effect in the cloud services of a cloud consumer exists.

Each party in a cluster or chain of cloud services has certain areas of responsibility. If each of these participants upholds its responsibilities, the cloud environment is trustworthy for the cloud consumer or its end user. Following are the responsibilities of the various parties:

> **End user**: The end user must ensure that all user equipment is configured and operating properly. The end user must also be properly trained in the appropriate use of the cloud applications.

> **Cloud consumer**: The IT department of the cloud service subscriber and the subscriber's end users must configure, maintain, and properly use their subscribed applications.

> **Application providers**: The companies that produce and provide software applications must ensure that their software applications are current, free of errors, and reliable.

> **Infrastructure providers**: The companies that provide computing, storage, networking, and security hardware and system software must ensure the robustness and reliability of their devices.

> **Network service providers**: The companies that provide network services must ensure that the network is available, reliable, and secure.

> **Cloud service providers**: CSPs must ensure that the subscribed services are available and that the services that make up the cloud computing environment are reliable and robust.

Note

In most cloud computing environments, it is common for one service provider to be responsible for more than one of the responsibilities listed.

ON-PREMISES VERSUS OFF-PREMISES HOSTING

Of course, to whom the responsibilities in the preceding section belong varies with where a service or application is hosted. Essentially, two basic hosting options are available:

> **On-premises**: Services or applications are provided from the local network through either a physical server or appliance or a virtualized environment.

➤ **Off-premises**: Services or applications are provided by a third-party hosting or through a cloud service. Third-party hosting can range from rack space rental or a shared hardware environment.

The decision of where a service is hosted also involves determining whether resources or services are to be physical or virtual in nature. The hosting choice is an integral part of the division of responsibilities discussed in the preceding section.

Cloud Security Essentials

As discussed earlier in this chapter (see "Accountability in Cloud Computing"), cloud computing subscribers have concerns about the security of their data and resources in the cloud environment. These concerns include, but are not limited to, network availability, disaster recovery, loss of physical control, and transparency. (See Chapter 15 for a detailed discussion on cloud security.)

Each of the delivery models discussed in this chapter has its own set of security issues. In the sections that follow, the security issues of private and public clouds are discussed. Understand that the security concerns of hybrid and community clouds are essentially a composite of those of private and public clouds.

> **Note**
>
> Chapter 15 discusses cloud security from the prevention and detection level. The discussion here provides a brief overview of the security risks and vulnerabilities that may be present in a cloud environment.

Private Cloud Security Issues

The security issues in a private cloud are essentially those that should be present on a secure local or enterprise network. These security services and features include the following:

➤ **Authentication and authorization**: *Authentication* is the verification of at least one type of identifying information, such as a username or a passcode. Is the user who she says she is? Authorization is allowing or denying access to a computing or network resource based on authentication. What is the user allowed to do or not do based on who she is? These two steps are typically tied together in a login process.

➤ **Identity and access control**: Identity verification is typically accomplished through authentication, but it can also be applied as a second (higher) layer of security that requires specific and unique identification to gain access, such as a fingerprint, retinal scan, or one-time password. If the probability of the identity verification is high enough, the user is allowed access.

➤ **Data integrity**: Maintaining the integrity of the data to which users may have access is primarily done by limiting access to those who really need access to it (principle of least privilege).

In addition to the items in the preceding list, the security infrastructure should provide for the monitoring and auditing of cloud transactions, requests, and services provided.

However, in the cloud environment, including private, public, and hybrid clouds, the nature of these security elements changes from local or discrete vertical services (silos) to one in which every user and all communication must independently pass through the security measures in place. In effect, each component, element, and action in the cloud environment is enclosed by a security shield, or *wrapper*. A private cloud must be designed, configured, and implemented so that every interaction that takes place in the cloud, whether physical or logical, is secured.

A public cloud has its share of security issues in addition to those of any networked or virtualized environment or private cloud. The characteristics and components of a public cloud bring their own security issues.

MULTITENANCY ISSUES

Multitenancy means multiple consumers occupy or share a computing resource, like an apartment building. Multitenancy is an inherent component of many private and public cloud services and is the core structure of a community cloud service. The security concerns for such an environment should be obvious and apparent. Using the apartment house analogy, users in a multitenant cloud are likely to worry about "locked doors," "strong walls," and privacy.

The most common form of a multitenant environment is *virtualization.* A recent study by the Gartner Group found that less than 20 percent of the computing environments that could be virtualized actually had been. In most cases, the reason for not virtualizing their computing environment was the perceived lack of security in a virtualized environment. This concern naturally extends to multitenancy environments.

The two primary fears consumers have of multitenant environments are data exposure and a failure in the virtualized infrastructure. The risk that data could be inadvertently exposed to other users because of poor access management or any other software failure is a major issue to some consumers. Data from every consumer is essentially stored in the same structures, and in many instances, they share a common application. A minor glitch could direct a consumer to another user's data. In addition, if this exposure exists, it is also a potential vulnerability for exploitation. To prevent and avoid this type of risk, service providers go to great lengths to ensure these types of risks don't exist or are under robust prevention and detection systems.

Commonly in a virtualized environment, regardless of whether it supports a private, public, or community cloud, a single server or cluster of servers supports a number of virtual machines (VMs). If one of the VMs was able to trace what one or more of the other VMs were doing, a potentially severe breach would result. Understand that service providers are way ahead of this sort of thing happening for real, but the risk from the consumer's perspective is there nonetheless. This is more likely to occur in a private virtualized structure than in one of the service infrastructures you'll learn about in Chapter 2.

LIMITED CONTROL ON TECHNOLOGY

When you subscribe to a public cloud, you give up control over the type of virtualization and management software and the control processes in use in the cloud. Your view of the cloud may as well be an actual cloud because there is typically no transparency to what is in the cloud other than the functions, applications, and services to which you are subscribed. For most consumers, this isn't an issue, but it could yield security issues caused by incompatibility.

DATA ENCRYPTION AND COMPLIANCE ISSUES

For many public cloud subscribers, data security and data management can be huge concerns. *Data integrity* is universally important, so data encryption, storage management, and in many cases, storage location can be major issues. It's virtually a given that data stored in a public cloud must be encrypted. In addition, the encryption must be a highly secure method that cannot be easily defeated should unauthorized access occur.

Tip
If the public cloud provider shares private keys with other users, it should raise a red flag.

In addition to encryption, data retention, storage processes, and where the data is physically stored can be compliance issues to many governmental and industry regulators. Regulators and auditors are increasingly more concerned over how companies manage their data resources and are applying increased scrutiny to these practices. Although your data may be in a cloud, to the regulators and auditors, it may as well be on your premises, and you should know everything about its security, management, and storage.

ISOLATION

The basic concepts of *isolation* on a network aren't new. In fact, the idea of isolating a server, node, or network is as old as network switching and routing. Network and security administrators have considered isolation a key part of their security policies.

You've likely heard the old saw that to be truly secure, a computer needs to be locked in a room to which access is extremely limited, and it must have no network connections whatsoever. If the computer isn't plugged in or turned on, its security is enhanced all the more. Although this approach, known as a clean room, definitely isolates and secures the computer, the result is that the computer has limited value as a resource.

In a cloud environment, consumers share the same physical infrastructure. Unless some form of network isolation is present, consumers may, either intentionally or unintentionally, access another consumer's data or perhaps initiate side-channel security events. To prevent these risks, cloud providers implement resource control and security methods that isolate consumers to their own virtual environments.

For the most part, the isolation techniques used in a cloud environment are essentially the same as those used on any network. A virtualized environment isolates its nodes as an inherent element of its design. However, in a virtualized environment, there are different ways to implement isolation and a variety of reasons to do so. The two most basic approaches to isolation are network traffic isolation and network security isolation.

Network Traffic Isolation

The network traffic from each cloud service consumer, almost by definition, should be isolated in the cloud. Different consumers may subscribe to varying bandwidth commitments, levels of data backup processes, or pricing or chargeback schedules. In addition, to control the environment, a cloud provider must monitor and control the environment's bandwidth to prevent network congestion and possible downtime, ensure that it is meeting its Service Level Agreement (SLA) and

Quality of Service (QoS) commitments to consumers, and protect both the physical and the logical infrastructure from exploitation or attack.

Physical Isolation   Network traffic isolation can be accomplished either physically or logically. At its lowest level, physical network isolation is created by dedicating network interface controllers (NICs), through their Media Access Control (MAC) addresses, to one or a group of applications or services, separating the nodes in which the NICs are installed into physically addressed network segments.

Logical Isolation   Logical network isolation is accomplished through software-based virtual local area networks (VLANs), virtualized NICs (vNICs), or a service listening for multiple logical endpoints. Although network traffic, directed to different applications and services, shares the same physical infrastructure, the separate applications see only their own unique traffic, creating a logical isolation of network traffic.

> **Note**
>
> Although an endpoint device, service, or application has a physical address, it may also have one or more unique logical addresses. An endpoint "listens" for requests sent to either its physical or its logical addresses, captures these messages, and then acts on them.

> **Note**
>
> A physical network interface controller (also known as a network interface card or network adapter) can host multiple virtual NICs (vNICs) to allow the host computer to belong to several VLANs over vNICs. Each of the different virtual environments available implements vNICs in its own way, but the usage is essentially the same.

Network Security Isolation

Along with network traffic isolation, network security isolation has become an essential part of any cloud environment. Governmental regulation and other governance and compliance mandates have increased the need for security and data integrity in general, but specifically in a cloud.

Because network traffic isolation doesn't prevent security events that can occur from external networks or side channels, cloud service providers must ensure that other security measures are in place, such as operating system and database system security, consumer account isolation, and VLANs created from vNICs.

A VLAN created from vNICs creates an extra layer of security. A VLAN created in a nonvirtualized environment allows multiple logically isolated networks to occupy the same physical transmission medium without the capability of the separate VLANs to see one another (unless a router or another Layer 3 device is involved). A VLAN that is built on vNICs restricts the vNICs from communicating with each other. In addition, broadcast traffic is sent only to the vNICs on the VLAN.

Cloud Laws and Regulations

In addition to the security and integrity issues that are important to a company or organization, the appropriate cloud environment, national and state laws, and regulations may also be important criteria. Several laws govern and regulate where data can be stored, how it's protected, how long it must be retained, and who has the legal right to intercept or view it. Here are the major U.S. laws and standards affecting data stored in the cloud:

> *Family Educational Rights and Privacy Act (FERPA)*: A federal law administered by the U.S. Department of Education that governs the privacy and distribution of student data.

> *Gramm-Leach-Bliley Act (GLBA)*: A mandatory compliance regulation in the banking industry that requires protection for financial information from threats to data integrity and security breaches.

> *Health Insurance Portability and Accountability Act (HIPAA)*: Under Title II of this law, insurance companies, hospitals, and all other keepers of medical records must comply with the national data storage, security, and privacy standards of electronic health care transactions.

> *Payment Card Industry Data Security Standard (PCI DSS)*: Standard that defines the secure data storage requirements for all companies that process, store, or transmit credit card information

> *Sarbanes-Oxley Act (SOX)*: Establishes management, reporting, and data accuracy standards for U.S. public company boards of directors, company management, and public accounting firms.

> *Uniting and Strengthening America by Providing Appropriate Tools Required to Intercept and Obstruct Terrorism Act of 2001 (USA PATRIOT Act)*: Enacted into law in 2001 and extended in 2011, defines the standards for roving wiretaps, business record searches, and counterterrorism surveillance.

Each of these laws and standards stipulates where and how sensitive data is stored, protected, and retained, which in turn sets the standard for where and with whom a company can do business for cloud computing. In addition to the national laws just listed, most U.S. states have data security and data breach laws. Any company looking to move into the cloud should thoroughly research the laws, regulations, and standards that are applicable to its business or products on both the national and state levels. In fact, it may also be a good idea to check out international laws as well.

Cloud Orchestration

Like just about all things cloud, *cloud orchestration* is a marketing buzzword that has come to mean different things to different vendors and writers. It is defined by some as an automated process that brings together private, public, and even hybrid clouds into a single environment that ensures scalability, elasticity, and operations at the "speed of the cloud." Another definition describes it as facilitating the automated provisioning of resources in a cloud infrastructure.

Simply stated, though, cloud orchestration provides the capability to manage, apply, and facilitate the elements in a cloud infrastructure, in real time, to meet the computing needs of a consumer, business, or organization. The conductor of an orchestra brings together just the right instruments at just the right time with just the right volume on just the right beat to play classical concertos. This concept is likely the origin of the term cloud orchestration as it applies to cloud computing. Think of the consumer as the audience in this case.

In summary, cloud orchestration provides the capability to manage and control all the resources in a cloud, including its physical, logical, and virtual resources. Cloud orchestration software is available from a number of companies, including Flexient, Tier 3, Cisco Systems, and Hewlett-Packard.

Chapter Summary

> A cloud environment may be a private, public, hybrid, or community service.

> A private cloud is a proprietary computing architecture specific to an internal network and its users. A private cloud is commonly located behind a specific firewall.

> A public cloud allows a company or organization to subscribe to one or more services from cloud service providers that are accessed via the Internet. The benefits of a public cloud service include availability, reduced investment, and reduced maintenance. There are public cloud applications for personal use as a "personal cloud."

> A hybrid cloud contains at least one private cloud service and at least one public cloud service.

> A community cloud is a shared environment in which several companies, or even individuals, gain the benefits of a public cloud, but with private cloud control and security. Community clouds are multitenancy environments.

> The cloud computing environment requires that the lines of responsibility are clearly defined. Accountability is split between the cloud subscriber and the cloud service provider. Each of the following participants in a cloud has defined responsibilities, including the end user, the cloud subscriber, the application provider, the infrastructure provider, the network service provider, and the cloud service provider.

> Cloud infrastructures use one of two hosting options: on-premises hosting or off-premises hosting: Where a service is hosted defines whether resources or services are physical or virtual in nature.

> The security issues of a private cloud are authentication and authorization, identity and access control, and data integrity. The security infrastructure should provide for monitoring and auditing of cloud transactions, requests, and services.

> Multitenancy is an inherent component of many private and public cloud services and is the core structure of a community cloud service. The most common form of a multitenant environment is virtualization.

> Data protection measures, such as encryption, data retention, storage processes, and storage location may be security concerns with governmental and industry regulators.

➤ The two most basic approaches to isolation are network traffic isolation and network security isolation. Network traffic isolation includes physical and logical isolation. Network security isolation is an essential part of a cloud environment.

➤ The major U.S. laws and standards affecting data stored in the cloud are FERPA, GLBA, HIPAA, PCI DSS, SOX, and USA PATRIOT.

➤ Cloud orchestration provides the capability to manage, apply, and facilitate the elements in a cloud infrastructure, in real time, to meet the computing needs of a consumer, business, or organization.

Key Terms

Accountability

Authentication

Cloud computing

Cloud orchestration

Cloud service provider (CSP)

Community cloud

Data integrity

Elasticity

Family Educational Rights and Privacy Act (FERPA)

Gramm-Leach-Bliley Act (GLBA)

Health Insurance Portability and Accountability Act (HIPAA)

Hybrid cloud

Isolation

Multitenancy

Payment Card Industry Data Security Standard (PCI DSS)

Private cloud

Public cloud

Sarbanes-Oxley Act (SOX)

Scalability

Uniting and Strengthening America by Providing Appropriate Tools Required to Intercept and Obstruct Terrorism Act of 2001 (USA PATRIOT Act)

Virtualization

Wrapper

Review Questions

1. True or False? A private cloud is configured to support only a single end user.

2. A cloud that provides both private and public cloud services is a

   a. Private cloud

   b. Public cloud

   c. Hybrid cloud

   d. Personal cloud

3. In a cloud environment, _____ is split between the cloud service provider and the cloud service subscriber.

4. What cloud environment is shared by several subscribers with public cloud services, yet with private cloud control and security?

   a. Hybrid cloud

   b. Community cloud

   c. Personal cloud

   d. Virtualized cloud

5. True or False? Network security isolation is an essential part of a cloud environment.

6. The two hosting methods used in cloud environments are _____ and _____.

7. Multitenancy is a characteristic of what cloud environment?

   a. Public cloud

   b. Private cloud

   c. Community cloud

   d. Hybrid cloud

8. True or False? Authentication and authorization are primary security issues in a private cloud.

9. _____ automates the management, application, and facilitation of the elements in a cloud infrastructure to meet the computing needs of a business or organization.

10. Which of the following is NOT a network isolation method implemented in a cloud environment?

    a. Network traffic isolation

    b. Network security isolation

    c. Logical isolation

    d. Physical isolation

11. True or False? Virtualization is an instance of a multitenant environment.

12. In a(n) _____ environment, a subscriber typically doesn't own the computing resources involved in the delivery of service.

13. Which of the following laws or standards impacts the method, security, and possibly the location of data stored in a cloud environment?

    a. HIPAA

    b. FERPA

    c. USA PATRIOT

    d. SOX

    e. All of the above

    f. None of the above

14. A _____ environment should ensure that every interaction that takes place in the cloud, whether physical or logical, is secured.

15. True or False? A physical NIC can host only a single vNIC, limiting a host to a single VLAN.

Answers to Review Questions

1. False

2. c

3. Accountability

4. a

5. True

6. On-premises, off-premises

7. c

8. True

9. Orchestration

10. d

11. True

12. Public cloud

13. e

14. Private cloud

15. False

CHAPTER 2

Cloud Computing Service Models

After reading this chapter and completing the exercises, you will be able to:

- Explain the NIST SPI model

- Discuss the purpose and application of the NIST cloud service models

The *National Institute for Standards and Technology (NIST)* publishes the authoritative and definitive standard for cloud computing in a document titled, "NIST Cloud Computing Reference Architecture." Many blog postings, and even vendor whitepapers, typically describe cloud computing in vague or broad terms; it's great to have the NIST as a standard for reaching a common understanding. The NIST standard for cloud computing is the primary reference for the Cloud+ exam, especially for service models.

> **Note**
>
> To access the NIST Cloud Computing Reference Architecture document, visit www.nist.gov/customcf/ get_pdf.cfm?pub_id=909505.

Cloud computing, like nearly all computing resources, is defined by NIST in three service delivery models: software, *platform*, and infrastructure. NIST refers to these three delivery types collectively as the *Security Parameter Index (SPI) model* (see Figure 2-1).

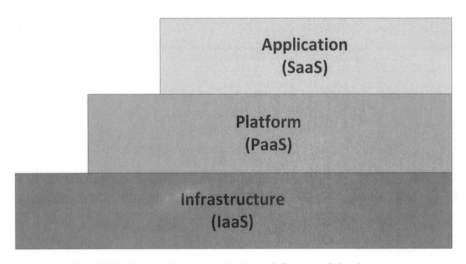

Figure 2-1 The NIST SPI model provides the basic definition of cloud computing.
© 2015 Cengage Learning®.

SPI Service Models

If you use your superhero x-ray vision to penetrate the cloud, you will see that the SPI model defines the use of hardware and software to provide client/server services via the Internet. The magic of the cloud enables hardware and software to work together to deliver services.

In this context, a *"service,"* as defined by NIST, is available on demand and for a fee. As general as this may sound, this use of service should be familiar to you. When you go to a fast food joint for a burger, you only pay for the items you want to consume; you don't buy the building or the cooking equipment, nor do you hire the workers. Just like in cloud computing, a direct relationship exists between the amount of food and beverage you consume and the price you pay. As you eat and drink more, it costs you more.

The same goes for cloud computing services. As you use more services, the accumulative cost of those services goes up, which can be the bad news. However, the good news is that when you stop using the cloud services, you also stop paying.

As stated earlier, the NIST SPI model consists of three service elements: software, platform, and infrastructure. Each of these elements is grouped into a variety of particular forms of service delivery, with each focused on a particular service type.

In the sections that follow, you learn about the three major service models: *Software as a Service (SaaS), Platform as a Service (PaaS)*, and *Infrastructure as a Service (IaaS)*. In addition, you learn about four specialty service models included on the Cloud+ exam: *Communications as a Service (CaaS), Desktop as a Service (DaaS), Everything as a Service (XaaS)*, and *Business Process as a Service (BPaaS)*. With the exception of the BPaaS, the NIST standard defines each of these service models.

Software as a Service (SaaS)

Figure 2-2 shows a simplified depiction of SaaS cloud computing, in which your personal computer (PC) or a company's network directly connects to the cloud for a variety of application-based services. The services in the cloud can be anything from your Gmail or Yahoo email account to your Facebook or Twitter account to your company's customer relationship management (CRM) system hosted by a CRM software service provider.

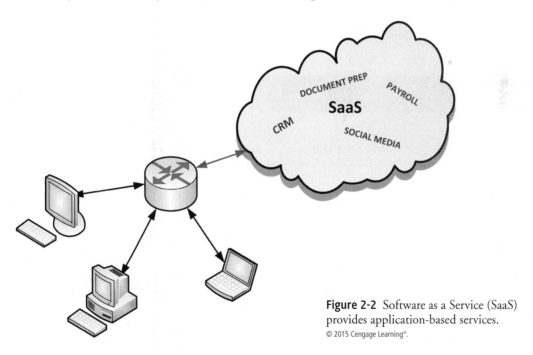

Figure 2-2 Software as a Service (SaaS) provides application-based services.
© 2015 Cengage Learning®.

SaaS (pronounced as *sass*) encompasses any cloud-based service that provides access via the Internet to software applications hosted in the cloud. SaaS is essentially software-on-demand for consumers who rent usage of an application. The SaaS model eliminates the need for a consumer, whether an individual or an organization, to purchase the software and install it on owned equipment. SaaS consumers subscribe to a service on a monthly or per-use basis. This saves the cost of a private software license and any hardware or resources necessary if the application was installed on their premises.

SaaS has a variety of benefits to consumers, including

> **Scalability**: The use of a SaaS service typically doesn't require additional hardware or software locally, beyond perhaps a software client or the like. To add services via a SaaS, the consumer just has to subscribe and start using the application.

> **No installation or setup costs**: SaaS applications are generally ready to go after the consumer subscribes.

> **No software maintenance**: All maintenance and upgrade activities are the responsibility of the SaaS provider and available immediately to the consumer.

> **Platform and location independence**: In a majority of instances, just about any Internet-capable device can access a SaaS application. This allows the consumer to use existing equipment for a new application. It also frees users from having to use the same device or be in the same location every time they access the service.

> **Customization**: Some SaaS services allow for customization or modifications to suit the needs of a particular consumer. Consumers may also be able to white-label some SaaS services.

> **Pay-as-you-go**: Consumers only pay for what they use. SaaS providers measure usage in a variety of ways, depending on the application. Some measure the volume of transactions, the data transmitted, the amount of disk storage space, or some combination of all three, as well as other measurements. Regardless of the cost accounting in use, the consumer pays only for its specific usage.

SERVICE-ORIENTED ARCHITECTURE (SOA)

An emerging concept that relates to SaaS services is *service-oriented architecture (SOA)*. SOA (pronounced as *ess-oh-ay*) is the structure that supports the communications between cloud-based services. SOA establishes how two computing resources, such as applications, interact so that one of the resources is able to perform tasks for the benefit of the other.

Margaret Rouse, writing on Whatis.com, explains the use of SOA very well:

Whether you realize it or not, you've probably relied upon SOA, perhaps when you made a purchase online. Let's use Land's End as an example. You look at their catalog and choose a number of items. You specify your order through one service, which communicates with an inventory service to find out if the items you've requested are available in the sizes and colors that you want. Your order and shipping details are submitted to another service, which calculates your total, tells you when your order should arrive, and furnishes a tracking number that, through another service, will allow you to keep track of your order's status and location en route to your door. The entire process, from the initial order to its delivery, is managed by communications between the web services—programs talking to other programs, all made possible by the underlying framework that SOA provides. © Whatis.com

Platform as a Service (PaaS)

PaaS (pronounced as *pass*) is essentially middleware that is in the middle of the cloud layers. PaaS provides virtual or cloud servers and an array of operating systems, integrated development environments (IDEs), and mashup tools. PaaS provides cloud services that support the creation, testing, deployment, and management of applications.

> **Note**
>
> A *mashup* is a web application created by combining existing coding, web applications, or other blocks of programming.

"Wait a minute," you may be saying, "I thought that application software was in the SaaS service model." And you're mostly right. However, in the SaaS service model, the consumer only wants to manipulate software applications without worrying about who developed them or who may maintain them. In the PaaS service model, the cloud platform provider manages, and likely owns, the servers, storage, networking devices, runtime environment, operating system, and middleware and controls for the virtualized environment. PaaS consumers manage only their applications and data, using the service provider's platform. The alternative to PaaS services is to develop applications on local resources, in Java, PHP, Ruby on Rails, or Visual Studio, among others, and then manually deploy the application to a SaaS service center.

Perhaps the major advantage a PaaS development platform has over the more traditional development environment is that multiple developers can have access to the platform at the same time, as opposed to the old one-at-a-time method.

The most common services available from a PaaS provider are platforms that provide business intelligence, database service, development and testing, application integration, and application deployment. Examples of PaaS implementations are Engine Yard, Force.com, Google App Engine, Heroku, Microsoft Windows Azure, OrangeScape, Red Hat OpenShift, VMware Cloud Foundry, and Wolf Frameworks. You should visit the websites of a few of these PaaS vendors to understand fully just what they do and what PaaS is.

Infrastructure as a Service (IaaS)

Perhaps the easiest way to think of IaaS (pronounced as *eye-as*) is Hardware as a Service (HaaS), although it's a bit more than that. The traditional approach to organizational computing services is to purchase, install, manage, and maintain servers, networking devices (firewalls, routers, switches, and the like), operating systems, Internet Protodol (IP) addresses, and virtualized environments in-house through an in-house Information Technology (IT) department. IaaS frees the organization of the majority of this by providing a complete computing infrastructure on-demand.

Figure 2-3 shows the hierarchy of the three primary service models. Depending on the consumer's needs, penetration into the cloud (service models) is as deep as necessary. In many ways, none of which you need to memorize for the exam, the PaaS and the SaaS depend on the IaaS layer for support; similarly, the SaaS layer depends on the PaaS.

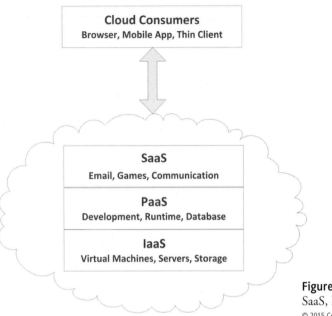

Figure 2-3 The relationship of the SaaS, PaaS, and IaaS service models.
© 2015 Cengage Learning®.

The IaaS service provider is responsible for both the physical equipment and the logical resources available. The IaaS consumer pays only for the use of the infrastructure on a per-use basis. Common IaaS services include backup and recovery, content delivery networks (CDNs), services management, and mass data storage.

Communications as a Service (CaaS)

In several different applications, you use CaaS (pronounced as *cass*) services almost every day. As illustrated in Figure 2-4, if Joan places a call from her notebook computer to Jeff's cell phone, the telephone services companies involved may need to convert the in-bound voice signals from the computer to outbound signals for the cell phone.

Figure 2-4 You use CaaS service every day.
© 2015 Cengage Learning®.

The situation shown in Figure 2-4 is a simple example of CaaS services. For the most part, CaaS services are a means for a company or organization to outsource a communications solution that best fits its needs. The services desired can be *Voice over IP (VoIP)*, instant messaging, teleconferencing or videoconferencing for meetings or collaborations, and integrated voice and email. The system may also need to integrate both fixed and mobile devices. Like a SaaS consumer, a CaaS subscriber uses only the services to which it has subscribed. The hardware and software necessary to deliver the desired services are the responsibility of the CaaS provider.

The benefit to the subscriber is the same as other cloud services: elimination of the need for a large capital outlay, avoidance of the overhead required to maintain the system, and flexibility and *scalability* to change the subscribed service almost immediately. Another benefit to a CaaS service is that the subscriber is free of the risk that the system may become obsolete or require periodic updates, upgrades, or perhaps replacement.

Desktop as a Service (DaaS)

DaaS (pronounced as *dass*), which is also known as "hosted virtual desktop" or "hosted desktop services," allows a *virtual desktop infrastructure (VDI)* to be outsourced to a cloud service provider. A DaaS service manages the personalization and the decoupling of the operating system from the desktop and the applications from the operating system in the virtualized environment. DaaS also allows the subscriber users to connect to the service from any device in any location. The VDI manager copies data to and from the virtual desktop during login and logout. Figure 2-5 illustrates the relationship of the users to the VDI environment through a DaaS service.

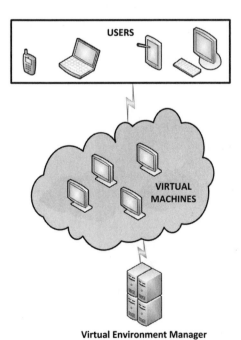

Figure 2-5 DaaS creates a virtualized environment in the cloud.
© 2015 Cengage Learning®.

By definition, DaaS must be multitenant because it is likely that a DaaS subscriber wants to access a number of VDI clients. The DaaS service provider is responsible for data storage, backup, network and data security, and the implementation of system upgrades.

> **Note**
>
> Chapters 4 through 7 specifically cover the various topics of virtualization.

> **Note**
>
> Don't confuse Desktop as a Service (DaaS) with Data as a Service (DaaS), which is not covered in this book or on the CompTIA Cloud+ exam. Data as a Service is essentially data storage as a service (also referred to as SaaS, which can be a part of the real DaaS.

Everything as a Service (XaaS)

XaaS (pronounced as *zhas*; sounds like *sauce* only with a *z*) is just about what it sounds like. This cloud service model may combine SaaS, PaaS, IaaS, and possibly CaaS, DaaS, and *Network as a Service (NaaS)*. [See "Network as a Service (NaaS)" later in this section.]

XaaS, which is also called X as a Service or Anything as a Service, is a collective term used to describe a cloud service that combines two or more of the NIST-defined cloud service models. Essentially XaaS is cloud computing.

Non-NIST Cloud Service Models

Two additional cloud service models that you may encounter on the Cloud+ exam are BPaaS and NaaS. The NIST standards omit these two in the current version, but you should be aware of them. The following sections give a brief look at each of these models.

BUSINESS PROCESS AS A SERVICE (BPAAS)

A business process is an event in a sequence of prescribed business activities required by the organization to conduct its business operations. This includes such activities as placing orders, receiving goods, hiring employees, selling products, budgeting, and more.

Business processes, the activities performed in the process of doing business, fall into three general categories:

> ➤ **Managerial processes**: This business process category includes the activities that support the general governance and strategic management of a business. In terms of applications, information retrieval, business intelligence, and dashboards are commonly used.

> ➤ **Operational processes**: This business process category includes the activities that constitute the core business functions, such as selling, purchasing, inventory, manufacturing, and human resources.

> ➤ **Supportive processes**: This business process category includes the activities and automated systems that support, record, and report on the operational processes, such as accounting, call center operations, technical support, and CRM.

Should a business choose to outsource its business processes to a business process outsourcing (BPO) vendor, it's likely in today's world that the BPO is a cloud service. Business processes performed or supported in the cloud are in the form of a Business Process as a Service (BPaaS), pronounced as *bee-pass*.

Like all of its "aaS" cousins, the primary aim of a BPaaS is to reduce the cost of operations and to make its resources available on-demand. A business may decide to outsource only a few of its business processes, such as payroll or its CRM, or it could outsource its more strategic processes like business intelligence and dashboards. BPaaS can also approach the levels of XaaS, depending on the types and requirements of the business processes outsourced.

Network as a Service (NaaS)

Most likely, you're able to guess what service a NaaS vendor provides. Just in case, a NaaS vendor provides a service that makes network, transport, and cloud service model connectivity available on-demand to a consumer via the Internet.

All a consumer needs to have to create a networked environment for himself is essentially a single, network, and Internet-ready computer. And, of course, the consumer needs a subscription to a NaaS portal. With the NaaS access, the consumer is able to access a virtualized network environment, use only the elements needed, and pay on an as-you-go basis. In addition to the virtualized network, common offerings in NaaS are virtual private network (VPN) and bandwidth on-demand.

Service Model Accountability

Should a cloud service become unavailable, who is responsible? In cloud computing, accountability, or who's responsible for what, falls on the consumer, the infrastructure provider, and the cloud service provider, but not always equally and certainly not in that order.

In the case of the cloud being unavailable due to a natural disaster or some other severe catastrophe, what the lawyers call *force majeure,* the consumer and the provider may share the accountability. However, in most cases, Gilster's Law applies: you never can tell, and it all depends.

In cloud computing, accountability dictates that the service provider will be responsible for protecting and managing the private information of its consumers, including its security, integrity, and appropriate usage. At the present, this statement is essentially a notion of good intentions. The complexity of cloud computing, especially in the deeper levels of service, has made a true definition of accountability difficult on both a legal and a technical basis.

The problem with accountability and responsibility in cloud computing is that it hasn't yet been clearly defined. A cloud service provider may provide a *Service Level Agreement (SLA)* that commits to a certain uptime percentage, bandwidth availability, or other quantifiable operating metrics. However, issues like throughput, response time, and other subjective measurements are hard to pin down because, between the consumer and the cloud service provider, there may be one or two other service providers who may be causing a service problem.

NIST publishes a document accepted as the nearest thing the cloud computing industry has as a standard. However, this document doesn't define performance standards and, in the various service models, who has what responsibility. Until this occurs, consumers and service providers must depend on SLAs and service contracts to define who has what responsibility in the case of a disruptive event.

Chapter Summary

> NIST publishes the authoritative and definitive standard for cloud computing in a document titled "NIST Cloud Computing Reference Architecture," which is the primary reference for the Cloud+ exam for service models.

> Cloud computing is defined by NIST in three service delivery models of the SPI model: software, platform, and infrastructure.

> NIST defines a service model as being available on-demand and for a fee.

> SaaS provides access via the Internet to on-demand software applications hosted in the cloud. Benefits of SaaS include scalability, elimination of installation, setup costs, software maintenance, platform independence, and pay-as-you-go.

> PaaS is middleware that provides virtual or cloud servers and an array of operating systems, integrated development environments (IDEs), and mashup tools.

> IaaS provides a complete computing infrastructure on-demand. The IaaS consumer pays only for the use of the infrastructure on a per-use basis.

> CaaS services allow a consumer to outsource communications solutions to a cloud service provider.

> DaaS allows a VDI to be outsourced to a cloud service provider.

> XaaS may combine SaaS, PaaS, IaaS, and possibly CaaS, DaaS, and NaaS. XaaS is essentially cloud computing.

> A business process is an event in a sequence of prescribed business activities required by the organization to conduct its business operations. Business processes fall into three general categories: managerial processes, operational processes, and supportive processes.

> The objective of BPaaS is to reduce the cost of operations and to make its resources available on-demand.

> A NaaS service provides a network, transport, and cloud service model connectivity on-demand to a consumer via the Internet. A NaaS service is typically a virtualized network environment.

> In cloud computing, accountability dictates that the service provider is responsible for protecting and managing the private information of its consumers, including its security, integrity, and appropriate usage. A cloud service provider may provide an SLA that commits to a certain uptime percentage, bandwidth availability, or other quantifiable operating metrics.

Key Terms

Business Process as a Service (BPaaS)

Communications as a Service (CaaS)

Desktop as a Service (DaaS)

Everything as a Service (XaaS)

Infrastructure as a Service (IaaS)

Mashup

National Institute for Standards and Technology (NIST)

Network as a Service (NaaS)

Platform

Platform as a Service (PaaS)

Scalability

Security Parameter Index (SPI) model

Service

Service Level Agreement (SLA)

Service-oriented architecture (SOA)

Software as a Service (SaaS)

Virtual desktop infrastructure (VDI)

Voice over IP (VoIP)

Review Questions

1. Which U.S. agency publishes the accepted standard on cloud computing?

    a. NASA

    b. ICANN

    c. NIST

    d. ANSI

2. The _____ model includes the three primary cloud computing service models.

3. True or False? All levels of cloud computing can be completely contained inside a single organization.

4. Which of the following is NOT a primary cloud computing service model?

    a. SaaS

    b. PaaS

    c. VPaas

    d. IaaS

5. The cloud computing service model that provides a complete computing infrastructure on-demand is _____.

6. True or False? The DaaS cloud computing service model provides for desktop virtualization on-demand.

7. The cloud computing service model used to access on-demand software applications via the Internet is _____.

    a. SaaS

    b. PaaS

    c. DaaS

    d. IaaS

8. The _____ cloud computing service model combines two or more service models into a single on-demand service.

9. True or False? A cloud service provider should be responsible for protecting and managing the private information of its consumers, including its security, integrity, and appropriate usage.

10. Cloud computing provides a consumer with what primary benefits? (Choose all that apply.)

    A. Scalability

    B. On-demand availability

    C. High installation costs

    D. Flexibility

      a. A and D only

      b. B and C only

      c. A, B, and D only

      d. All of the above

      e. None of the above

11.   The primary objective of _____ is to reduce business process operating costs.

12.   True or False? Although an organization may subscribe all of its IT services from a cloud service provider, it must retain a highly skilled and well-trained IT department.

13.   What is the cloud computing model that is primarily middleware and provides for a variety of development tools and environments?

   a. SaaS

   b. PaaS

   c. XaaS

   d. IaaS

14.   The cloud computing service model that provides a virtualized networking environment is _____.

15.   True or False? In general, accountability in cloud computing is solely the responsibility of the consumer.

Answers to Review Questions

   1. c
   2. SPI
   3. False
   4. c
   5. IaaS
   6. True
   7. a
   8. XaaS
   9. True
   10. c
   11. BPaaS
   12. False
   13. b
   14. DaaS
   15. False

CHAPTER 3

Object Storage

After reading this chapter and completing the exercises, you will be able to:

- Explain the concepts of object-based storage
- Discuss the role and purpose of object storage elements, including:

    Object identifiers

    Containers

    Metadata

    Storage policies

    Access control

- Describe the interactions with storage service APIs

There's one thing about data in relation to computing: you have to store it somewhere so you can use it again. Don't confuse data with information. Data is static at any one time, consisting of facts, codes, measurements, and any other quantifiable entity expressed as a number, alphabetic character, symbol, or value. In computing, data must be convertible to binary for storage. And, for all this, data by itself doesn't tell you anything. You can store the number 4 on the computer, and you have a 4 expressed in binary digitally and electronically. A four is just that: a 4.

However, when you give the 4 a context, or meaning, it becomes information, which may answer a question or make a statement. This 4 can now be the number of legs on a camel, the number of tent pegs in a pack, or just about anything else you can express as a number, as long as it holds credibility. Information is essentially contextual data or processed data that has a meaning.

Whether computing on a local computer or computing in the cloud, data must be stored to be of use in producing information. This chapter looks at data storage in the cloud and the concept of object-based storage or object storage.

Object-Based Storage

The Internet-connected world creates more and more data every day. Some of the data is just plain old data, but data that was once stored on paper, film, CDs, DVDs, and other portable media is now being stored on the net and in the cloud. Just like the 4 in the preceding section, most of the data stored on the net and in the cloud is unstructured, unrelated, and in a variety of formats. This data comes from email, instant messages, documents, images, drawings, audio, and video sources.

The need to store these entities comes from the need to retrieve this data rapidly—almost instantaneously—whenever and wherever a business, regulatory, compliance, or strategic necessity demands. Forecasters project that this data growth will continue almost exponentially, as much as 60 percent a year, for the foreseeable future.

As cloud computing continues to evolve, several new capabilities have emerged to improve not only processing efficiencies, but the way data, in its traditional definition, is stored, shared, and secured. The new paradigm for storage in the cloud is object-based storage. The Cloud+ exam refers to object-based storage as just object storage, so that's the term used in the remainder of this chapter.

Before you learn about object storage, you should review traditional storage just a bit to understand fully how and why this new technology has emerged. Like many cloud technologies, the methodologies aren't that much different than what you've been doing, but the approach to data storage has changed significantly.

Traditional Storage

Traditional storage methods treat and store data as clumps, clusters, groups, and entities such as fields, records, or files along with image, audio, and video objects. At one time, sharing data meant either giving other users permission on a peer-to-peer network or storing the data on a server to which those wanting to share the data had access.

> **Note**
>
> An important concept to keep in mind is that data is universally the most important resource an organization or individual trusts to the cloud.

Locally, data can be stored on backup tapes, universal serial bus (USB) and hard disk drives, memory cards, and a variety of other fixed and removable media. Although generally reliable, these storage media share one common potential problem: security. *High availability (HA)* systems, such as hot-swap, HA clusters, and failover systems, remove some of the risk of data loss from mechanical or electrical failure, but there is still a risk. Reliability and security are possible, but typically at a prohibitive cost to a single organization.

Data is stored in either an unstructured or a structured form. A key weakness with *unstructured data*, when stored in traditional file systems, is that it can lose its context. *Structured data*, associated with an event, such as a transaction, is stored in groups of related data, commonly in a database system.

Traditional data storage systems have a foundation file system based on *storage area network (SAN)* or *network attached storage (NAS)* protocols, like the *Common Internet File System (CIFS)* or the *Network File System (NFS)*. These network file systems arrange data in a method to which humans can relate. However, if the amount of data (entities) to store rises up into the billions or trillions, a human-friendly hierarchical storage method loses its speed, scalability, and reliability.

Traditional storage methods are typically some form of a *Redundant Array of Independent Disks (RAID)*. RAID-based storage is not easily scalable, should the amount of data or data entities suddenly balloon. There is a growing direct relationship between moving to cloud computing and an expansion of the amount of data to be stored.

Although this chapter is about object storage, you should understand that it will not likely replace all traditional NAS storage. There are in-house systems and smaller data storage needs that NAS accommodates well. Object storage is not a universal replacement for all forms of data storage.

> **Note**
>
> In late 2013, the Simple Storage Service (S3) from Amazon Web Services, one of the largest cloud storage services, was storing just over 2 trillion data objects. That's not 2 trillion bits of data, but 2 trillion objects, each of which could be a small number of bits or some multiple of megabits.

Object Storage

Recall that one of the primary principles of cloud computing is sharing: sharing hardware, sharing software, and, more to the point, sharing storage. Your organization may not require the same storage capacity of companies like Amazon, Facebook, and Google, all of which designed their own *object storage* systems. However, cloud storage providers, looking to provide a scalable solution to multiple consumers, have had to move to object storage solutions to provide for ample capacity, flexibility, and scalability.

Object storage relieves storage administrators from traditional tasks like formatting, creating and managing logical storage volumes, and managing RAID levels in case of storage device failures. Object storage also provides for the addressing and identification of objects with multiple "file-names" on multiple "file pathnames." You'll learn more about how object identification works in the sections that follow.

OBJECT STORAGE DEVICES

Traditional hard disk drive (HDD) or *block storage device*s read and write data in fixed-length blocks, regardless of what your application or database software leads you to believe. In contrast, an *object storage device (OSD)* arranges data into variable-length objects or containers. An OSD *object* contains the data (in whatever form it exists) and all related metadata. Figure 3-1 illustrates a simplified comparison of fixed-block or file systems placed end to end on an HDD volume on the left with the concept of objects stored in a partition on an OSD on the right.

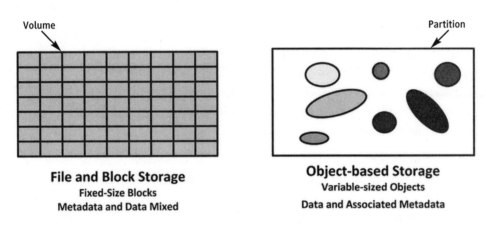

Figure 3-1 A conceptual comparison of fixed-block storage and object storage.
© 2015 Cengage Learning®.

THE OSD STANDARD

The *Storage Networking Industry Association (SNIA)* developed the object storage devices (OSD) standard in conjunction with the International Committee for Information Technology Standards (INCITS) in 2004. This standard defines a command set, based on the Small Computer System Interface (SCSI) command set, for interfacing with OSD.

The OSD standard's command set includes commands to read and write objects, as well as a number of commands to access and manipulate data attributes and metadata. This standard also allows object commands to be stacked to reduce the interactions on the media to accomplish a task.

The OSD-2 standard (2009) added support for a storage function called snapshot. A snapshot takes a point-in-time copy of the contents in a partition and places it in a new partition. A snapshot is read-only. Another OSD function is cloning. A clone is similar to a snapshot, but a clone is a writeable copy of a partition. OSD-2 also added support for object collections, which are objects that contain only the object IDs of other objects.

OBJECT IDs

The OSD standard identifies an object with the combination of a 64-bit (8-byte) partition identifier and a 64-bit object ID. A partition on an OSD holds numerous objects, each with its own unique object ID. Objects exist within partitions. Objects and the partitions may grow independently without a physical size limit besides the size limitation of the OSD.

An object is something like a file, but you should visualize an object as a *container*. This storage container holds the data, metadata, and even some associated files of the entity. Traditional file systems store data in a hierarchical structure of directories, subdirectories, or folders and subfolders. Object storage assigns each object a unique identification number (object ID) and associates it with a partition ID. You can view a partition as just a larger container, as illustrated earlier in Figure 3-1.

METADATA

At one time, *metadata* referred to "data about the data," but several different definitions now exist. In the context of object storage, metadata refers to descriptive data that describes a number of characteristics of a stored object.

As shown in Figure 3-2, any item that describes or defines a data entity, whether file or object, is metadata. This includes such descriptors as filename, creation date, file size, thumbnail image of a printed version of the file, and perhaps even who has permission to access it. Not all file systems or storage methodologies keep this metadata for every file or object. However, some keep even more.

The term metadata isn't new with object storage. If you're familiar with the *Hypertext Markup Language (HTML)* and the creation of webpages, you know that metadata included in the page coding is bait hoping to attract search engine bots to catalog a webpage or website. In the context of object storage, metadata is still data about the data, only with a bit more information about the content and context of an object. The metadata of an object defines attributes, both performance and appearance, of the object.

Metadata is not exclusive to object storage. Traditional file systems also create metadata, but it is typically limited to the filename, the file creation date, the creator, and the file type. If you look at the Info option on the File tab of a Microsoft Word document, you'll see the file metadata for the open document file.

Figure 3-2 The metadata of a traditional structured data file.

Object storage adds metadata to the object, as controlled by the interface in use, when it creates or rewrites it as an object. Figure 3-3 shows an example of some of the metadata stored with the object.

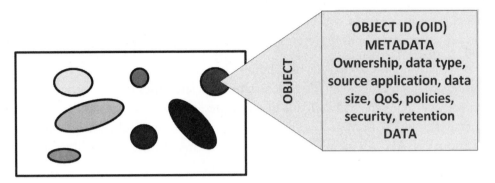

Figure 3-3 A short example of the metadata stored with a document in object storage.
© 2015 Cengage Learning®.

As illustrated in Figure 3-3, the metadata stored with the object includes its object ID, descriptive data about the object itself, and a set of attributes required by the interface that will get and list the object. Of course, the actual data is also in the object.

Object BLOBs

When you hear the word "BLOB," you may think of the old Steve McQueen horror movie in which a gelatinous outer space creature oozes all over a town. Well, in the context of object storage, a *BLOB* isn't anything as sinister as that big slime ball of the movie. The term "BLOB," which came from IBM and its database system DB2 back in the 1980s, stands for binary large object (or basic large object) and is a group of binary data stored as a single entity, such as images, audio, and multimedia objects. A BLOB can also be a large binary executable program (and yes, this includes viruses and other malware).

> **Note**
>
> Large objects aren't limited to binary data, though. A collection of character data stored as a single large object is a character large object or a CLOB.

Object Storage Policies

Generically, a policy, in the context of business and information technology, is a rule or guideline that states the intended outcome for an application of resources or assets. A policy can also set the boundaries of business decisions, actions, or initiatives. A business policy, which can include security policies, data integrity policies, or even outbound sales calls policies, usually derives from the strategic objectives of the organization.

Data Storage Policies

The data storage policies of an organization may be generic or very detailed, with the latter the more preferred among IT professionals. A generic policy leaves too much to chance and doesn't really give IT justification for the cost of "doing it right." In the extreme, a detailed *data storage policy* defines specifically the how, when, and where of data collection, storage, access, retention, integrity, and security.

An example of a generic data storage policy is similar to the guidelines in Table 3-1.

Table 3-1 General Data Storage Policy		
Sensitivity Level	**Covered Data**	**Usage and Storage Policy**
General	All data not covered in any of the policies below	Open usage and storage
Confidential	All data related to customers, employees, and vendors	Password access required; least privilege principle applied
Restricted	All product, engineering, and R&D data, drawings, and specifications	Stored as encrypted data; access restricted by department and position rank

© 2015 Cengage Learning®.

Table 3-1 is pointedly understated. To the IT professional who has the responsibility for data storage, the information in this data storage policy is extremely vague on many of the issues that ensure the security, integrity, and access of the data meets the organization's overall policies.

In contrast, a robust data storage policy addresses all possible considerations, processes, storage media, handling, retention, and disposal, among other characteristics and processes. A data storage policy defines data storage methods and media, such as online, SAN/NAS, offline, tape, disk, fixed, removable, off-site, onsite, archiving, and disposal. A strong data storage policy addresses at least four specific areas:

> **Risk assessment**: What is the true worth of the data in terms of business interruption and continuity? This analysis helps to set up the relationship between the data's value and the cost to protect it.

> **Data availability requirements**: When and to whom should data be available? This policy section may also address response time, high-availability requirements, and the methods for accessing data.

> **Data integrity requirements**: What measures should be in place to protect the reliability and integrity of the data? This policy section may also include backup and restoration procedures and testing schedules, encryption, authorization, and other protective measures.

> **Disaster recovery**: What steps will ensure that the time to restore business operations and data is as short as possible? This policy section should address any catastrophic event that could reasonably occur, as well as a scenario for a complete disaster.

Data Storage Policies in the Cloud

Policies generally express internal controls. However, having an organization's policies control or dictate the services of an object storage provider, who, remember, is in the multitenant business, isn't likely to work well—that is, unless the object storage service supports only one customer or is an in-house operation. This is a common barrier for organizations considering storing data in the cloud, let alone on an object storage service.

For a company or organization with well-defined and executed policies in use, the unknown can be a risky venture. The upshot is that the object storage provider must have data storage policies in place to meet the needs of a consumer's own business and data policies.

Object Storage Operations

Interfacing with an object storage system in the cloud is essentially transparent to the user. The user uses a web browser and the Uniform Resource Locator (URL) address of the object storage server. Behind the scenes, web services provide the actual interface and control the interaction. In the sections that follow, you'll get an overview of the operational components of an object storage system and the web services that interface with it.

Web Services

To a consumer, object storage is an application service accessed via an Internet browser through one or more web services. A web service provides communication control and management between two devices or applications over the Internet and World Wide Web (WWW). The two most commonly used web services are the *Simple Object Access Protocol (SOAP)* and the *Representational State Transfer (REST)*. Understand that in the context of object storage systems, these two transport protocols differ in that SOAP defines a stateful transfer, and REST creates a stateless endpoint-to-endpoint communication.

Simple Object Access Protocol (SOAP)

The SOAP web service standard defines the rules for the transfer of *Extensible Markup Language (XML)* messages, using the *Web Services Description Language (WSDL)* standard. SOAP relies primarily on *Hypertext Transfer Protocol (HTTP)* but can use other transport protocols, like *Simple Mail Transfer Protocol (SMTP)* or the *Java Message Service (JMS)*. SOAP is especially useful when one platform, such as a Windows device, needs to communicate with a device running a different platform, such as Linux. SOAP can penetrate firewalls and proxy services typically because of its HTTP standard base.

Representational State Transfer (REST)

On the web, there are literally thousands upon thousands of points of content. A point of content can be a page of text, a video, a picture, an animated image, or a block of executable code. Each point of content has a *Uniform Resource Identifier (URI)*. You are most likely familiar with a type of URI: a webpage address or a URL.

REST defines a set of structure rules that allows the transmission of data over a standard transport protocol, typically HTTP. Unlike SOAP, REST doesn't add additional messaging parameters. It merely allows the interface client to use a URI to access the point of content (and its content) and receive a representation of the content in return. The webpage address (URI/URL) provides the resource identifier. The HTTP commands GET, PUT, DELETE, POST, and HEAD define the action desired on the object.

SOAP Versus REST

When should you SOAP, and when should you REST? Although that distinction sounds like something your junior high PE teacher might have told you, there are a number of considerations for choosing which web service to use. Here are some of the benefits of SOAP:

> ➤ WSDL describes the messages, bindings, operations, and location of the web service endpoints.

> ➤ SOAP maintains conversational states and contextual information. REST requires that any transmission controls desired be programmed into the application layer.

> ➤ SOAP supports asynchronous processing.

> ➤ SOAP is flexible and works with several protocols and technologies.

> ➤ When using REST-ful web services, the service provider and the consumer must have a common knowledge of the transmitted content because REST doesn't contain a standard rule set to define the web service.

REST has these benefits:

> ➤ REST-ful Web services are stateless.

> ➤ REST provides a caching infrastructure over the plain vanilla HTTP methods, such as GET.

> ➤ REST is useful for applications interfacing with mobile devices, such as smartphones and personal digital assistant (PDA) devices. SOAP web services require additional message parameters, such as headers and other elements.

> ➤ REST integrates easily with existing websites.

> ➤ REST-ful services are simpler to implement than SOAP.

Because of, or in spite of, the benefits listed here, the choice between SOAP and REST boils down to the complexity of the application and the web service it requires. A more complex API (see the next section) will likely find SOAP better suited to its needs. Uncomplicated APIs that support simple transactions or interactions generally choose REST. Believe it or not, most object-based storage interfaces use REST-ful web services.

Application Programming Interface (API)

In general, an *application programming interface (API)* defines the interactions between software components. An API is a standard coding block that provides interfaces between application programs and other components, such as device drivers, database systems, and video/graphics cards. An API can also provide the standard interface between a program and the graphical user interface (GUI). APIs eliminate the need to "reinvent the wheel" each time a developer wants to work with a common system component.

In the context of object-based storage systems, the OSD manufacturer, the operating system developer, or a third-part utility developer may supply the API used to interface and carry out commands to access, store, or delete objects from the object store. OpenStack, SoftLayer, Hewlett-Packard, Microsoft, Sun Microsystems, and several others offer object storage APIs.

Object Storage Web Service Operations

As stated earlier, subscribers to an object storage service interface to the service through an object storage API. The descriptions of the functions and interactions of the user to the service through an API that follow use the *OpenStack Object Storage API* from the OpenStack Foundation (www.openstack.org) as its basis. The OpenStack API and components are open source products that serve as the base for many of the current cloud and object storage products available.

API Core Components

A cloud services API that contains object storage services typically has several active components, all of which interface with one another to accomplish the actions directed by the user. For example, the OpenStack Object Storage API includes five core components or functions, each of which provides a specific function or set of functions that provide support for user interactions. These components follow:

> **Accounts and account servers**: Object storage systems are multitenant, and a unique account code identifies each user. The user enters this code to authenticate the user account.

> **Authentication and access permissions**: A user must authenticate its account ID to gain its permissions and an object storage *authentication token*. The token, which is a digital code, must accompany all requests for object storage actions.

> **Containers**: As discussed earlier, a container is something like a folder in Windows or a Linux directory, but unlike folders and directories, a container cannot be nested one within another. In essence, a container creates the location of an object and serves as a receptacle for data. Within an account, there is no practical limit on the number of containers, but an account must have at least one container.

> **Objects**: As you might suspect, objects are the basic storage unit in an object storage system. Data uploaded to a container is stored raw (as-is) without compression or encryption. An object has three parts: its container (location), the object ID or name, and any object metadata.

Object Storage API Requests

The object storage API makes creating, modifying, and removing objects and containers relatively simple. As mentioned earlier, there are only five standard HTTP requests to use:

> **GET**: This request lists containers or objects in an account.

> **PUT**: This request creates object containers, objects, or metadata in an account.

> **DELETE**: This request removes containers, objects, and their metadata.

> **POST**: This request writes new objects or updated metadata.

> **HEAD**: This request retrieves metadata for a container or object.

> **Note**
>
> Once created, an object is immutable, which is to say, it's unchangeable. Remember that for redundancy and availability, snapshots are made constantly. If an object requires modification, a new object must be created.

In each use of these commands, a URI indicates the target for the implicit action. For example, the following code shows an OpenStack Object Storage API PUT request to create a new container:

```
PUT HTTP://object.storage.com/v1.1/AUTH_321456/certifications/cloud+
```

This request applies the PUT request with the following elements, which are common to most OpenStack Object Storage API requests:

> ➤ **Base object.storage.com/v1.1**: The URL of the object storage service interface

> ➤ **Account AUTH_321456**: The account ID for the subscriber accessing the service

> ➤ **Container certifications**: The user assigned name of a container in the account

> ➤ **Object cloud+**: The user-assigned name of an object in the container

Here are a few examples of common request statements:

> ➤ List all the containers in an account:
>
> ```
> GET HTTP://object.storage.com/v1.1/AUTH_321456/
> ```

> ➤ Create a new container in an account:
>
> ```
> PUT HTTP://object.storage.com/v1.1/AUTH_321456/new_container_name
> ```

> ➤ List all the objects in a container:
>
> ```
> GET HTTP://object.storage.com/v1.1/AUTH_321456/certifications
> ```

> ➤ Create a new object in a container:
>
> ```
> PUT HTTP://object.storage.com/v1.1/AUTH_321456/certifications/study_guide
> ```

Chapter Summary

> ➤ Data storage in the cloud will continue to grow at an increasing rate into the future.

> ➤ Traditional storage methods treat and store data in files and directories or folders.

> ➤ Data is stored as unstructured or structured.

> ➤ Object storage relieves storage administrators from tasks like formatting, creating, and managing logical storage volumes or managing RAID levels.

> ➤ An object storage device (OSD) arranges data into variable-length objects or containers. Objects and containers may grow independently without a physical size limit.

➤ An object holds the data, metadata, and even some associated files of the entity. Object storage assigns each object a unique identification number (object ID) and associates it with a container ID.

➤ Metadata refers to descriptive data that describes a number of characteristics of a stored object.

➤ A BLOB is a binary large object or a group of binary data stored as a single entity, such as an image, audio, multimedia, or executable object.

➤ A policy is a rule or guideline that states the intended outcome for an application of resources or assets. A business policy derives from the strategic objectives of the organization.

➤ Data storage policies define the specifics of the how, when, and where of data collection, storage, access, retention, integrity, and security. A strong data storage policy addresses at least four specific areas: risk assessment, data availability requirements, data integrity requirements, and disaster recovery.

➤ A web service provides communication control and management between two devices or applications over the Internet and the World Wide Web.

➤ SOAP defines the rules for the transfer of XML-encoded messages using the WSDL standard. SOAP relies primarily on HTTP. SOAP is useful when one platform needs to communicate with a different platform.

➤ A URI identifies each point of content on the Internet and the web.

➤ REST defines a set of structure rules that allow the transmission of data over HTTP. REST doesn't add messaging parameters.

➤ An API defines the interactions between software components.

➤ Subscribers to an object storage service will interface with the service through an object storage API.

➤ A cloud services API contains addresses for four core components: accounts and account servers, authentication and access permissions, containers, and objects.

➤ An object storage API references five standard HTTP requests: `GET`, `PUT`, `DELETE`, `POST`, and `HEAD`.

➤ Object storage addressing references two required and two optional components. Required are the base and account ID. The optional components are the container ID and the object ID.

Key Terms

Application programming interface (API)

Authentication token

Binary large object (BLOB)

Block storage device

Common Internet File System (CIFS)

Container

Data storage policy

Extensible Markup Language (XML)

High-availability (HA)

Hypertext Markup Language (HTML)

Hypertext Transfer Protocol (HTTP)

Java Message Service (JMS)

Metadata

Network attached storage (NAS)

Network File System (NFS)

Object

Object storage

Object storage device (OSD)

OpenStack Object Storage

Redundant Array of Independent Disks (RAID)

Representational State Transfer (REST)

Simple Mail Transfer Protocol (SMTP)

Simple Object Access Protocol (SOAP)

Storage area network (SAN)

Storage Networking Industry Association (SNIA)

Structured data

Uniform Resource Identifier (URI)

Unstructured data

Web Services Description Language (WSDL)

Review Questions

1. True or False? Object storage and traditional file and block technologies use the same methodologies and data structures to store data.

2. What is perhaps the largest difference between a traditional HDD and an OSD?

   a. OSD uses fixed-length data blocks.

   b. HDD allows for variable-length objects and containers with no physical size limitations.

   c. OSD allows for variable-length objects and containers with no physical size limitations.

   d. Operationally, there are no differences between these two storage technologies.

3. Each object or container on an OSD has a unique _____.

4. The data that describes characteristics of a stored object is _____.

5. A large object of binary data that is stored as a single entity is a

   a. BLOB

   b. CLOB

   c. GLOB

   d. SLOB

6. True or False? A business policy derives from the strategic objectives of the organization.

7. A data storage policy should address all of the following except

   a. Data availability requirements

   b. Data integrity requirements

   c. Disaster recovery

   d. Maximum file sizes

8. The logical interface that provides communication control and management between two devices or applications over the Internet and World Wide Web is a(n) _____.

9. SOAP defines the rules for the transfer of what data type?

    a. HTML

    b. JavaScript

    c. REST

    d. XML

10. True or False? The primary transport protocol for SOAP is UDP.

11. True or False? A URI identifies each point of content on the web.

12. REST defines a set of structure rules that allow for a(n) _____ transmission of data.

13. A(n) _____ defines the interactions between software components.

14. Which of the following are required components of a REST-ful API request?

    a. Account ID

    b. Base

    c. Container ID

    d. Object ID

    e. All of the above

    f. None of the above

15. True or False? READ is a standard HTTP request in an object storage API.

Answers to Review Questions

1. False

2. c

3. Identifier or ID code

4. Metadata

5. a

6. True

7. d

8. Web service

9. d

10. False

11. True

12. Stateless

13. API

14. e

15. False

CHAPTER 4

The Benefits of Virtualization

After reading this chapter and completing the exercises, you will be able to:

- Explain the general use and application of a virtualized environment
- List the different component-based virtualizations
- Discuss backup and recovery techniques for a virtualized environment

Though benefits of virtualizing the internal information technology (IT) resources of a major-ity of company and enterprise data centers are myriad, as this chapter discusses. A study conducted at the end of 2012 stated that nearly 70 percent of all companies had imple-mented some form of virtualization on which to process their application workloads.

Virtualization is the process for creating a virtual version of IT resources. This includes the virtual-ization of hardware, operating systems, storage devices, and other network resources. The concept of virtualization originated in the 1960s to describe the partitioning of main memory on main-frame computers into discrete processing environments that could support multiple instances of a single application.

Today's virtualization systems, through hypervisors and virtual machine (VM) management systems, allow a company to employ fewer physical servers to support its application workload. In doing so, a company with a virtualized environment is able to realize several benefits. In this chapter (along with Chapters 5, 6, 7, and 11), you will learn the fundamentals of virtualization and its link to cloud computing.

Virtualization

As is often the case, the benefits of virtualization vary depending on whether you are in business management or IT. While essentially the benefits are the same for both points of view, the man-agers look at the savings and costs avoided, and the IT people look at the savings in terms of time, effort, schedule, and maintenance. Because time is money, as is computer hardware and software you didn't have to buy, it ultimately comes down to efficiency and effectiveness.

Nonetheless, this section discusses the benefits of virtualization under each viewpoint. First is an overview of the benefits of virtualization from the IT perspective, followed by a business manage-ment view.

Virtualized Environments

Creating a virtual (as opposed to a physical) environment in which virtual versions of devices, resources, and operating systems convert into shareable elements and one or more execution spaces is virtualization. The concept of virtualization isn't all that new to traditional computing envi-ronments. Partitioning a hard disk drive into volumes is a form of virtualization. A *virtualized environment* is such that users, applications, and even devices see virtualized resources as one log-ical resource.

The term virtualization applies to a variety of computing technologies: hardware virtualization, storage virtualization, network virtualization, and application virtualization. The sections that follow discuss these virtualized technologies.

SERVER VIRTUALIZATION

In general, *server virtualization*, also known as hardware virtualization and platform virtualization, creates one or more logically isolated execution partitions on a single physical server. There are several forms of server virtualization: full virtualization, para-virtualization, and operating system virtualization.

Full Virtualization

This virtualization approach fully virtualizes a physical server to provide distinct execution spaces. Applications function as if they were the only software running on the physical device, when, in fact, other instances of the application or other applications are running in separate virtualized spaces. In addition, each application can be running with a completely different operating system.

Full virtualization, also called platform virtualization, requires the use of host software or a control program, generally called a virtual machine monitor (VMM) or a hypervisor, to create and control the simulated virtual environment. Each of the virtual execution spaces it creates is a virtual machine (VM) in which guest software executes. Guest software is typically an application, but VMs can also support completely different operating systems, even from the operating system running on the physical computer. Figure 4-1 illustrates a fully virtualized environment.

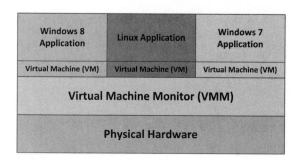

Figure 4-1 A fully virtualized computing environment runs applications in virtual machines.
© 2015 Cengage Learning®.

Guest software may have limited access to certain system peripherals, such as the network, keyboard, display, and disk storage. The access rights and privileges of the VM and its guest software depend on the host software in use and its guest software access policies.

Para-Virtualization

The prefix "para" comes from the Greek word for "with" or "beside." Its use in the term *para-virtualization* means that the guest operating system must work in conjunction with the VMM for many nonvirtualizable instructions native to the guest operating system. To accomplish this, the guest operating system's kernel must be modified so that the nonvirtualizable instructions are removed and replaced with compatible system call instructions, called hypercalls, to a VMM application programming interface (API). Hypercalls are common for memory management, interrupt handling, and clock functions. Figure 4-2 shows the modifications made to the guest operating systems to provide the required hypercalls.

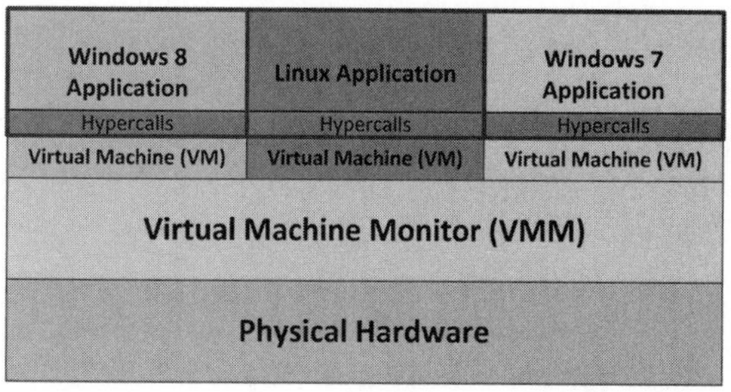

Figure 4-2 Para-virtualization requires hypercall modifications to the guest operating system.
© 2015 Cengage Learning®.

Operating System Virtualization

Operating system-level virtualization creates multiple, independent, and isolated virtual servers, which are also known as virtual containers or virtual private servers. Each of the guest servers shares the same operating system kernel as the host system. Figure 4-3 illustrates this environment.

Application	Application	Application
Shared Operating System	Shared Operating System	Shared Operating System
Shared Operating System		
Physical Hardware		

Figure 4-3 Operating system virtualization creates stand-alone virtual servers.
© 2015 Cengage Learning®.

Operating system virtualization is common for virtual hosting environments, multiple virtual web servers, and load balancing. Unlike other virtualization models, operating system-level virtualization relies on the operating system for scheduling, allocation, and device control, eliminating the need for a hypervisor or VMM.

STORAGE VIRTUALIZATION

Storage virtualization consolidates multiple network storage devices into a single virtual device. Storage virtualization is common in *storage area network (SAN)* implementations to make tasks like backups, archiving, and restoration or recovery more efficient. Storage virtualization is implemented through software.

Figure 4-4 shows a simplistic view of how storage virtualization works in concept. Users or applications make input/output (I/O) requests to the storage virtualization controller software, which maps the logical data block to its physical location on the storage medium. The virtualization controller returns the requested data block to the user or application.

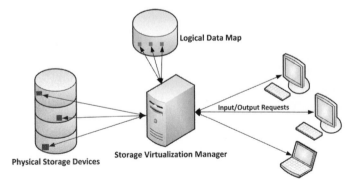

Figure 4-4 Storage virtualization creates a mapping between the logical and physical storage.
© 2015 Cengage Learning®.

There are two different approaches for storage virtualization:

> ➤ ***Block virtualization***: This creates a logical structure of the physical storage that is transparent to applications and users (as illustrated in Figure 4-4) at the data block level. The software that controls the virtualization intercepts all requests for data and maps the request to the physical location of the block that contains the data. This approach isolates users from administrative activities performed on the storage devices, such as maintenance, the addition of new storage devices, and data protection services.

> ➤ ***File virtualization***: This method of storage virtualization works similarly to block virtualization, except the logical mapping occurs at the file level.

Application Virtualization

Application virtualization is a software technology that creates application software encapsulation under the control of the native operating system. In a virtualized environment, an application still runs as if it is in direct contact with the operating system, but in an isolated partition with virtual support services.

In a nonvirtualized environment, the operating system directly supports running applications on a one-on-one basis. Figure 4-5 illustrates this relationship in a nonvirtualized environment.

In a virtualized environment, the application partition also contains system service interfaces along with the running application. These emulators accept requests from the application and then interface with their associated system services and the operating system. Figure 4-6 shows the differences created by application virtualization. Compare Figure 4-6 to Figure 4-1 earlier in the chapter for the subtle differences between hardware virtualization and application virtualization.

Under application virtualization, when the operating system loads an application, it also loads some system services, such as configuration files, registry keys, and local data, into the execution partition, as illustrated in Figure 4-6. These system services run in conjunction with the application in the virtual environment, which creates a sort of bubble or cocoon for each executing application.

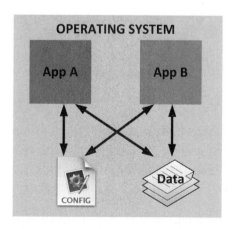

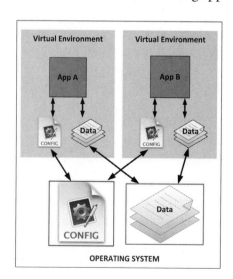

Figure 4-5 In a nonvirtualized environment, applications interface directly with system resources.
© 2015 Cengage Learning®.

Figure 4-6 Application virtualization separates applications into their own application partitions.
© 2015 Cengage Learning®.

This allows different software or multiple instances of the same software to run simultaneously without contention on the system services. When the application run finishes, the bubble is broken and the space is available to another application instance.

Many of the modern operating systems support application virtualization, at least on a limited basis. This includes Microsoft Windows and virtually all Linux versions. For example, Windows 8 includes a service called Virtual PC that allows you to run older versions of Windows as well as a few other operating systems. There are also third-party packages like AppZero, Citrix XenApp, and VMware ThinApp that provide application virtualization on a Windows platform.

In addition to true application virtualization, there are other technologies that generally fit into this category, specifically application streaming, desktop virtualization, and remote desktop services.

Application Streaming

Application streaming may sound something like Software as a Service (SaaS), but there is a major difference. For one thing, application streaming actually downloads some or all of an application to your desktop and you run the application locally. You only access the application in the cloud to begin streaming (downloading) it to your desktop.

Application streaming is on-demand software that works off the fact that nearly all application software requires only a small portion of the total programming to run. You're familiar with streaming audio and video. Well, application streaming works along the same lines. The host server communicates with a local desktop client and sends only enough of the programming for the application to start (as little as 10 percent for many applications). The remainder of the application's programming transmits to the client in the background, while the user goes ahead and begins working with the application. Like many streaming services, application streaming uses *Real Time Streaming Protocol (RTSP)*, Hypertext Transfer Protocol (HTTP), or *Common Internet File System (CIFS)* to send the application programming to the desktop client.

From a desktop point of view, application streaming is almost transparent, allowing for communication hiccups. However, the packaging for a streaming application is specific. Developers of a streaming application divide the programming into a sequence of four-byte blocks that are one of three types: starter blocks, predictive blocks, or on-demand blocks.

If you are using a streaming application, you click the shortcut on your desktop to begin the transmission of a stream of starter blocks. When the starter blocks arrive at the local computer, the application starts, and a sequence of predictive blocks, the blocks that the streaming system believes you will probably need first, transmits. The streaming service sends only on-demand blocks, like when you choose a function outside of the already received programming.

Remote Desktop Services (RDS)

Remote Desktop Services (RDS) creates a form of virtualization in which remote clients are able to access and run server-based applications on a session host server. This type of system extends the capability of a virtual machine to applications outside the virtualized environment.

RDS, formerly known as Terminal Services, is a Microsoft service available on Windows Server from its 2003 version through and including the 2012 version. It was on earlier releases of Windows Server. RDS allows a Windows server to host multiple client sessions simultaneously. RDS runs on the server, which then becomes a remote desktop session host server (formerly a terminal server).

A remote computer, one that is not inside the server itself, connects to the session host server using the *Remote Desktop Protocol (RDP)* and the *Remote Desktop Connection (RDC) client* or the *Remote Desktop Web Connection (RDWC)*. Once connected to the session host, the client computer can remotely run applications made available to it, regardless of what operating system the client is running. Although RDS is a Microsoft product, other third-party RDP products are available, including VMware PC-over-IP and Citrix's HDX.

Desktop Virtualization

Chapter 2 introduced you to *virtual desktop infrastructure (VDI)* in the "Desktop as a Service (DaaS)" section. Desktop virtualization and VDI are essentially interchangeable terms. However, in contrast to how DaaS implements VDI, on a local network (not in the cloud), *desktop virtualization* has a slightly different approach.

In a virtualized desktop environment, a hypervisor or VMM can control multiple desktop operating system instances on a single server platform. This approach separates some or a desktop's entire environment and any associated applications from the physical server the client would normally access. Okay, so this is about the same as DaaS, only without the cloud.

Performance in the Cloud

One of the key benefits to virtualization is that an organization can get more from its IT resources. Add the cloud to the picture, and these benefits increase through Infrastructure as a Service (IaaS) and other service models. The cloud is all about capacity, and virtualization is about increased usage and efficiency in that capacity.

The scalability and flexibility of cloud resources allow organizations to expand or contract as needed to optimize their computing capacity to their immediate needs. Although virtualization does extend the realized capacity of an in-house system, at some point it's likely that the organization may need more IT resources. The cloud eliminates or at least puts off the acquisition of additional IT resources, providing both cost avoidance and cost efficiency at the same time. At the end of the day, the cloud and virtualization are partners in success.

However, organizations should carefully consider the critical nature of their applications and use that information when comparing the available cloud services and cloud service providers. Some applications may do better if kept in-house, and others may be a perfect fit for the cloud. Security, data protection, availability, elasticity, and reliability must be part of the evaluation of a cloud service provider and its services.

At this point in this book, you have yet to learn about two of the topics in the list of evaluation criteria just mentioned: elasticity and reliability. Although the former is a relatively simple concept, the latter has several aspects you should know, not only for your future career, but for the Cloud+ exam.

Elasticity

Computing resources, whether in the cloud or in-house, should be ideally like the elastic in your favorite sweatpants, pajamas, or whatever pants you wear to lounge around. Over the time you've worn these pants, the elastic waistband has had to stretch at times to accommodate the expansion of your body. On other occasions, the elastic relaxed to fit your smaller hold-up-my-pants demand.

Computing resources in an in-house situation can expand or contract as needed, but typically not without considerable cost or idling expensive equipment. Cloud services, virtually all the service models, can contract when your needs are low and, to a certain extent, expand as your needs grow. In some cases, service providers may need some proactive notice should your needs really jump up quickly. Remember that cloud services are on-demand for the most part, and you only pay for what you use. Unfortunately, the cloud isn't an all-you-can-eat buffet; rather, it's more like a delicatessen where you pay by the pound.

Elasticity also includes flexibility. For example, the capability to move a VM from one server to another without interrupting the application is an example of both flexibility and availability, two very important criteria when evaluating service providers.

RELIABILITY

The reliability of a VMM or a cloud service should be an important consideration for most organizations in either case, but it's especially important in the cloud. In the next few sections, you learn about the reliability measures and standards that can provide important data for consideration in your evaluation of a cloud service.

Whether it's your equipment or systems or a cloud service provider's equipment, certain metrics should be known as indicators of quality and the reliability of the system. Here are a few of the service quality metrics you should know for the Cloud+ exam:

> **Mean time between failures (MTBF)**: MTBF is a common system and component indicator in computing (and other technical areas). It represents the average time a service or component should operate before failing (again or for the first time). Figure 4-7 illustrates MTBF.

> **Mean time to failure (MTTF)**: MTTF represents the average time a service remains operational. In other words, how long can you count on the service being available before it fails? Figure 4-7 illustrates what MTTF measures.

> **Mean time to implement (MTTI)**: MTTI gives the average (mean) time consumers experience to bring a service fully operational for themselves. MTTI can also be mean time to install.

> **Time to service (TTS)**: TTS can have two different, yet similar, meanings. It can denote the amount of time it takes to start up a new implementation (see also MTTI), and it can mean, more commonly, the amount of time required to restore service after a system failure that causes a service outage, also called mean time to restore service (MTRS).

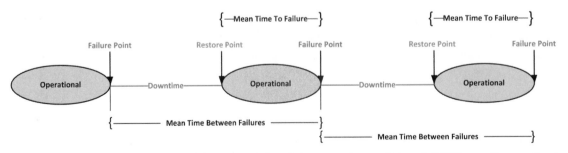

Figure 4-7 The mean time between failures (MTBF) and the mean time to failure (MTTF) are often confused.
© 2015 Cengage Learning®.

A lengthy amount of time in any of these service indicators should be a red flag on a service's reliability.

RESOURCE POOLING

Resource pooling is one of the five essential attributes of cloud computing. The five essential attributes are on-demand/self-service, anywhere network access, location transparent resource pooling, rapid elasticity (see "Elasticity" earlier in the chapter), and pay-per-use service.

The National Institute for Standards and Technology (NIST) Cloud Computing Standard defines these attributes as part of the *5-3-2 principle of cloud computing*. The "3" refers to the three basic service models: SaaS, Platform as a Service (PaaS), and IaaS. As discussed in Chapter 2, these three service models provide the base for all the service models in use in the cloud. The "2" represents the two primary deployment methods for cloud computing: private cloud and public cloud. You've learned about the other parts of this principle and the essential attributes, with the exception of resource pooling. The next few sections introduce you to this attribute.

Essentially, all cloud computing data center resources fall into one of three resource categories: computing, networking, and storage. This may seem relatively obvious, but consider that these resource categories form the foundation of all cloud computing methods and services.

> ➤ *Computing resources*: This category includes all central processing unit (CPU)-related functions of a data service center. Data center servers, including those supporting virtualization and those directly running SaaS functions, are the primary resources of this category. A computing resource pool represents all the computing (execution and virtualization) capacity of a cloud service center.

> ➤ *Networking resources*: This category includes the pooling of the physical network devices and software services that connect, segment, and isolate network services performed at the Open Systems Interconnection (OSI) model's Network layer (Layer 3) and below. Pooling these resources increases the visibility and manageability of these resources.

> ➤ *Storage resources*: This resource category, of course, includes the storage devices, but it also includes the physical and logical resources that enable resource availability, security, and elasticity.

The NIST standard refers to "location transparency" of pooled resources. It's easy in a virtualized and remotely accessed environment to take this to mean that you don't know or care about the physical location of network storage devices or services. Although this definition may be somewhat relevant, location transparency, as defined by NIST, means that consumers access physically stored data using a logical name, such as container ID or object ID.

INFRASTRUCTURE CONSOLIDATION

Infrastructure consolidation (or data center consolidation or information technology consolidation) has been a hot IT topic for more than 10 years in the computing world. As IT budgets have shrunk, the need to gain more "bang for the buck" has caused technology managers to look for ways to gain efficiency in both the cost of their operations and the effective utilization of the computing resources.

Physical consolidation has been the first attempt in consolidating an organization's computing infrastructure. Moving remote servers and networking resources to a centralized facility and service has gained organizations more effective and efficient use of fewer resources, including physical, logical, and human resources.

Virtualization has proven to be a valuable approach to further improving on the objectives and outcomes of infrastructure consolidation. Converting an organization's network into a virtualized environment increases resource utilization, availability, and, in many cases, reliability. Virtualization as an approach to infrastructure consolidation provides benefits to cloud service providers in multitenancy services.

VIRTUAL DATA CENTER

Cloud service providers must provide an infrastructure that supports service models that are both scalable and elastic enough to operate efficiently and to meet increased demand. The creation of a *virtual data center* is one way to provide these services at a profit. A virtual data center allows the service provider to construct a virtual environment for a new consumer that optimally meets the existing needs of the consumer as well as any demand that arises as the consumer's computing needs grow.

If the cloud service provider attempts to offer consumers computing, networking, and storage in silos, expanding to meet increasing demand of a single consumer and to meet the requirements of new consumers, the provider's TTS will also increase. Virtualizing the data center environment allows the provider to avoid delays in implementation, the installation of new resources, or a limit to its multitenancy capabilities.

A virtualized data center offers the provider two primary benefits:

> ➤ **Multitenancy**: Virtualized environments are able to support as many as 20 or more VMs on a single physical server, which might mean one computer can support 20 different consumers.

> ➤ **VM mobility**: In a virtualized data center, the provider can move a VM to a different server transparently without service interruption. Achieving this capability requires a virtualized Internet Protocol (IP) domain, but all OSI Layer 2 functions as well, so that they span the entire virtual data center.

However, a virtualized data center is not without its issues. Here are a few of the issues the service provider must resolve:

> ➤ **Scalable infrastructure**: Multitenancy means a data center must manage a large number of logical nodes. For example, if you are a cloud service provider with a single rack of 64 servers that each provides 20 VMs, you are ready for multitenancy. However, this infrastructure could require up to 1,200 subnets and virtual local area networks (VLANs) just on that one rack. Add to this the capability of each VM to support as many as 10 virtual interfaces, and the support requirement grows even larger. Remember that these numbers are for a single rack. A cloud service provider with additional identical server racks may soon run into the limitation in the Institute of Electrical and Electronics Engineers (IEEE) 802.1Q standard of 4094 VLANs.

> **Storage transport**: Because a consumer's VM can be moved from one server to the next, communications to the storage system must move with it. This can require storage mobility between servers in the virtualized environment.

> **Bandwidth**: Many of the services provided in the cloud, such as SaaS, unified communications, and DaaS, require high bandwidth with low latency. This can mean that these services may need network priority rather than processing priority.

UNIFIED COMMUNICATIONS

Unified communications (UC) integrates two or more real-time communication services, including instant messaging (IM) or chat, presence information (the status or availability of a communication client), Voice over IP (VoIP), video conferencing, data sharing, and unified messaging (the integration of voicemail, email, Short Message Service [SMS], and fax).

UC is typically a combination of products that interact to provide a unified user interface across a variety of media and device types. Cisco Systems, ShoreTel, and Avaya, to name only a few, have UC product lines.

Virtualization Recovery Plans

Whether the computing resources of a business, organization, or enterprise include virtualization, contingency and action plans for service interruptions that can range from minor disruptions to major catastrophes must exist. These plans, most commonly called disaster recovery plans, are a key part of good IT management. Disaster recovery plans are a must in a virtualized environment.

Restoring a virtualized computing and network environment requires more than simply rebooting a server. The more severe the event causing the interruption of service, the more detailed the recovery plan must be.

Virtualization can be an effective part of a disaster recovery plan. An organization can realize a lower cost to recovery because there are fewer physical servers required at both the production and the recovery sites. Virtualization also eliminates any hardware dependencies typical in a non-virtualized recovery. Perhaps most importantly, restoring virtualized server images is rapid and, if applicable, deployment can be across more than one physical infrastructure.

However, for all its benefits for disaster recovery, virtualization also requires some day-to-day commitments to be truly effective.

> **Data integrity and protection**: No recovery plan, whether in a virtualized environment or not, can be effective without valid, up-to-date, and immediately usable data. Without this, no recovery can effective. Virtualization, on its own, cannot guarantee good recoverable data.

> **VM image recovery**: In a virtualized environment, you have a choice between traditional file and data backup procedures and an image-level backup. A traditional backup scheme captures all or only modified data as it exists in granular (file-level) form. A VM image-level backup scheme uses either the VMware Virtual Machine Disk (VMDK) format or the Microsoft Virtual Hard Disk (VHD) format.

- ➤ **Restoration issues**: Something to consider when creating or restoring a virtual image backup is that either requires a high number of I/O operations. For example, if a physical environment contains 20 virtual servers, during a disaster recovery operation, limited I/O capabilities can create serious contention for the I/O channels.

- ➤ **RPO/RTO**: An effective disaster recovery plan must define the *recovery point objective (RPO)* and the *recovery time objective (RTO)*. An RPO specifies the specific business operation point to which systems are to be restored, such as beginning of day (BOD) on the day of the interrupting event or end of day (EOD) on the day preceding the interrupting event. The RTO specifies the minimally accepted time duration for the system recovery. In other words, the RPO defines the restart point of business operations, and the RTO defines the amount of time it should take to recover the system.

VM Backup and Recovery

The creation of system backups in a virtualized environment changes the approach to recovery from a knowledge-based process to more of a process-based procedure. Virtual system backups capture the entire contents—data, applications, and operating system—of a VM.

REPLICATION

One approach to creating a recoverable backup for a virtual environment is to replicate the virtualized environment to a remote server and storage environment, typically offsite, at regular, predefined intervals, via the network. The replicated system is then ready to roll should a failover become necessary.

Of course, when a failover becomes necessary, the *replication* process must stop when the remote/failover system becomes live. When the failover system becomes active, the hypervisor or VMM scans for logical unit numbers (LUNs—identifiers for storage devices sharing a common channel), pulls the VMs into its inventory, and activates them in a predefined order.

VM SNAPSHOTS

VM snapshots are point-in-time captures of the state, data, and configuration of a VM while it's running and stored in a file. The state refers to the run status of a VM (powered-on, powered-off, or suspended). Data includes the files that constitute the VM, including data from storage devices, data in memory, and data from any other devices, like virtual network interface (VNI) cards.

Many files make up a VM. Table 4-1 lists the primary files of a VMware VM by their extensions and briefly describes each one.

A VM may have other files associated with it, some of which exist only when the VM is running.

> **Note**
>
> A *virtual disk drive* consists of one or more `.vmdk` files (see Table 4-1). However, if a VM links to a physical disk instead of a virtual disk, the `.vmdk` files contain addressing and access information of the partitions the VM can access.

	Table 4-1 Key VM Files	

File Extension	Description
.log	Contains a log of key VM activities for troubleshooting.
.nvram	Contains the state of the VM's Basic Input-Output System (BIOS).
.vmdk	Contains the contents of the VM hard disk drive.
###.vmdk	Contains changes made to the virtual machine while the VM is running should redo operations be necessary. The ### is a unique serial number assigned by the VM to prevent duplication.
.vmem	Contains a backup of the memory allocated to the VM on the host system. This file exists only while a VM is running or has crashed.
snapshot.vmem	Contains the memory contents of the memory allocated to the VM. This file is created as part of a snapshot.
.vmsd	Contains information and metadata about a snapshot.
snapshot.vmsn	Contains the state of a snapshot.
.vmsn	Contains the running state of a VM as part of a snapshot.
.vmss	Contains the state of a suspended VM.
.vmtm	Contains the configuration file of a VM.
.vmx	Contains the primary configuration created through the New VM Wizard.
.vmxf	Contains a supplemental configuration file of a VM.

© 2015 Cengage Learning®.

You should understand that a snapshot is not a backup. When the hypervisor or VMM creates a snapshot, only the log files and state files change. You really can't use a snapshot recovery process. VM snapshots create a point-in-time copy of the files listed in Table 4-1 (and possibly others). Snapshots typically slow a system down, and they are often not taken in critical response situations or in a production environment.

Chapter Summary

> Virtualization is the process for creating a virtual version of IT resources.

> Virtualization applies to a variety of computing technologies: hardware virtualization, storage virtualization, network virtualization, and application virtualization.

> Server virtualization creates one or more logically isolated execution partitions on a single physical server. There are several forms of server virtualization: full virtualization, para-virtualization, and operating system virtualization.

> Full virtualization, also called platform virtualization, requires the use of a VMM or a hypervisor.

- ➤ In para-virtualization, the guest operating system must work in conjunction with the VMM for many nonvirtualizable instructions native to the guest operating system. The nonvirtualizable instructions are replaced with hypercalls.

- ➤ Operating system-level virtualization creates multiple, independent, and isolated virtual servers, also known as virtual containers or virtual private servers.

- ➤ Storage virtualization consolidates multiple network storage devices into a single virtual device.

- ➤ Application virtualization creates application software encapsulation under the control of the native operating system.

- ➤ Application streaming is on-demand service that loads only enough of the programming for the application to start.

- ➤ Remote Desktop Services (RDS) creates a form of virtualization in which remote clients are able to access and run server-based applications on a session host server.

- ➤ In desktop virtualization, a VMM controls multiple desktop operating system instances on a single server platform.

- ➤ The reliability of a cloud service is an important consideration. Important performance and reliability indicators are MTBF, MTTF, MTTI, and TTS.

- ➤ The five essential attributes of cloud computing are on-demand/self-service, anywhere network access, location transparent resource pooling, rapid elasticity, and pay-per-use service.

- ➤ The NIST Cloud Computing Standard defines the 5-3-2 principle of cloud computing.

- ➤ Cloud computing data center resources fall into one of three resource categories: computing, networking, and storage.

- ➤ Infrastructure consolidation may be accomplished through physical consolidation or through virtualization.

- ➤ Virtualization can be an effective part of a disaster recovery plan.

- ➤ An effective disaster recovery plan must define an RPO and an RTO.

- ➤ Replication and VM snapshots are approaches used for backing up a virtualized environment.

Key Terms

5-3-2 principle of cloud computing

Application streaming

Application virtualization

Block virtualization

Common Internet File System (CIFS)

Computing resources

Desktop virtualization

Elasticity

File virtualization

Full virtualization

Infrastructure consolidation

Mean time between failures (MTBF)

Mean time to failure (MTTF)

Mean time to implement (MTTI)

Networking resources

Operating system virtualization

Para-virtualization

Physical consolidation

Real Time Streaming Protocol (RTSP)

Recovery point objective (RPO)

Recovery time objective (RTO)

Remote Desktop Connection (RDC) client

Remote Desktop Protocol (RDP)

Remote Desktop Services (RDS)

Remote Desktop Web Connection (RDWC)

Replication

Resource pooling

Server virtualization

Storage area network (SAN)

Storage resources

Storage virtualization

> **Time to service (TTS)**
>
> **Unified communications (UC)**
>
> **Virtual data center**
>
> **Virtual desktop infrastructure (VDI)**
>
> **Virtual disk drive**
>
> **Virtualization**
>
> **Virtualized environment**
>
> **VM snapshots**

Review Questions

1. True or False? Virtualization does not apply to networking.

2. Which of the server virtualization methods may require some operating system instructions to be removed and replaced with hypercalls?

    a. Full virtualization

    b. Para-virtualization

    c. Operating system virtualization

    d. Application virtualization

3. Full virtualization requires a _____.

4. Which of the following is an efficiency feature of application streaming?

    a. Applications are downloaded completely before starting.

    b. Applications are encapsulated in a virtual server container.

    c. Applications start running after downloading only required blocks.

    d. Application streaming cannot run in a virtual environment.

5. _____ is a form of virtualization in which remote clients are able to access and run server-based applications on a session host server.

6. True or False? In desktop virtualization, a VMM controls multiple desktop operating system instances on a single server platform.

7. What reliability indicator could you use to predict when a service may fail based on your knowledge of the last failure?

    a. MTBF

    b. MTTF

    c. MTTI

    d. TTS

8. All of the following are essential attributes of cloud computing, according to the NIST, except

    a. A service must be shareware or freeware.

    b. A service must be on-demand/self-service to consumers.

    c. A service must include location-transparent resource pooling.

    d. A service must provide for rapid elasticity.

9. True or False? Virtualization can be an effective part of a disaster recovery plan.

10. The NIST Cloud Computing standard defines the _____ principle of cloud computing.

11. True or False? Replication and VM snapshots are approaches that can be used for creating a restorable image of a virtualized environment.

12. In an effective disaster recovery plan, the amount of time allowed to restore service is defined by the _____.

13. True or False? Cloud computing data center resources fall into one of three resource categories: computing, networking, and software.

14. _____ may be accomplished through physical consolidation or through virtualization.

15. The state attribute of a VM snapshot indicates the run status of a VM. Which of the following is NOT a run status for a VM?

    a. Powered-on

    b. Powered-off

    c. Suspended

    d. Idled

Answers to Review Questions

1. False

2. b

3. Hypervisor or VMM

4. c

5. Remote Desktop Services, or RDS

6. True

7. a or b

8. a

9. True

10. 5-3-2

11. True

12. RTO, or recovery time objective

13. False

14. Infrastructure consolidation

15. d

CHAPTER 5

Virtual Components of a Cloud Environment

After reading this chapter and completing the exercises, you will be able to:

- Explain the concepts of virtual networks
- Differentiate the types of virtual networks
- Discuss the role and purpose of virtual network components, including:

    Virtual devices

    Tunneling protocols

    Virtual resource sharing

I n the previous chapter, you learned about the different methods of virtualization and a few of the technologies employed by a virtualized environment. In this chapter, you learn about how a virtual environment integrates hardware, software, and system components, both real and virtual.

This chapter discusses a variety of the components a virtualized cloud service employs to meet its service agreements and its consumer expectations. You learn about virtual network components like *virtual network interface cards (vNICs)*, virtual host base adapters (vHBAs), virtual CPUs (vCPUs), virtual switches (vswitches), and virtual routers (vrouters). The chapter also expands on the discussions in Chapters 3 and 4 on memory and storage virtualization.

Virtual Network Components

For the Cloud+ exam, you need to be familiar with virtual networking components, but especially with vNICs, vHBAs, vCPUs, vswitches, and vrouters. In the next few sections, you'll learn about each of these components. However, you should first understand the basic concepts of a virtual network.

Virtual Network Concepts

First, if it's virtual, it's software. A *virtual network* is a computer network that doesn't use physical wire (or wireless) communication media to create a connection between two or more virtual devices. A virtual network can be one of two forms: protocol based or virtual device based. Protocol-based virtual networks have been around for a while, and you are likely familiar with the more common types—*virtual local area networks (VLANs)*, *virtual private networks (VPNs)*, and *virtual private LAN services (VPLS)*. Virtual device-based virtual networks interconnect virtual machines (VMs) and the virtual machine monitor (VMM) or hypervisor. Figure 5-1 illustrates a simple virtual network layout.

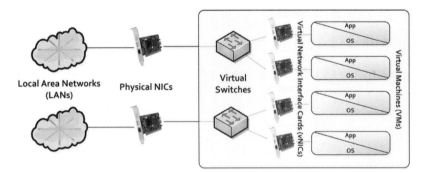

Figure 5-1 The layout of a simple virtual network that extends the capabilities of the physical devices to connect with virtual devices. © 2015 Cengage Learning®.

VIRTUAL LOCAL AREA NETWORKS (VLANS)

Virtual can also mean logical, in the sense that anything software based is a logical element, and any physical device is, well, physical. In this context, a VLAN is a logical LAN that is set up in a physical network switch or Layer 2-capable router by partitioning the physical LAN into two or more logical LANs.

The most common use of a VLAN is to group workstations that share a common profile, security settings, or permission set together for ease of administration, regardless of the physical location of the workstations. Figure 5-2 illustrates this point. Here we have 20 computers, five to a floor in a building. Station 1 (the leftmost) on each floor is assigned to the floor manager. Unless you want to string cable to link the four floor managers together physically, a VLAN allows you to group these four stations together and assign a common set of permissions, security settings, and other configuration data. In Figure 5-2, also notice that three other VLANs exist, with one workstation belonging to two VLANs.

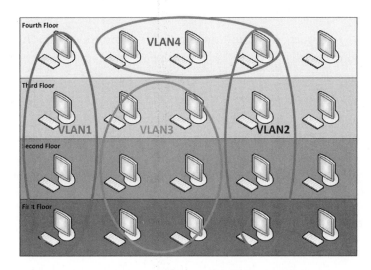

Figure 5-2 A VLAN can create logical groupings within a physical network.
© 2015 Cengage Learning®.

VIRTUAL PRIVATE NETWORKS (VPNS)

If your company has employees who work outside the main office, where all the servers and IT resources are, they don't have to be remote to the company's applications, data, or other resources. Using the Internet for what it was largely intended to do, remote users can use a VPN to connect securely to the head office network or beyond.

VPN Types

A VPN is "nailed up," as the telecom folks say to mean created, between a VPN controller at the head office end and a VPN client running on a remote computer. A *tunneling protocol* protects the private communication stream between the two endpoints. Tunneling protocols encapsulate and encrypt the transmitted data at one end and decrypt and remove the encapsulation at the other end. Theoretically, this creates a "tunnel" through the Internet and perhaps a cloud. The encryption of the data creates a "pipe" that other data on the transmission media cannot penetrate.

Nearly all VPNs fall into one of the following two categories:

➤ **Remote-access VPN**: This type of VPN connects a user to a LAN from a remote location. Anywhere a user can connect to the Internet can be the remote endpoint. A *remote access VPN* establishes a secure, encrypted connection between a private network and a remote user over third-party communication lines. VPNs are not limited to desktop and notebook computers; just about any computing device with Internet connectivity can be a VPN remote device. Depending on the system in use, such as a hardware VPN appliance or a software VPN controller, the remote device may require a VPN client.

> ➤ **Site-to-site VPN**: The basic function of a *site-to-site VPN* is essentially the same as the remote-access VPN. The major differences are that a site-to-site VPN communicates over dedicated, often leased, lines applying large-scale encryption. Site-to-site VPNs are common within large companies or enterprises to permit geographically separate offices to communicate over a common internal network. This application of a site-to-site VPN is an intranet VPN. Should the site-to-site VPN allow external contacts, such as customers, vendors, or partners, it becomes an extranet VPN.

VPN Methods

A VPN has several characteristics that make it a common choice for communicating private and sensitive data. The major characteristics of a VPN are data confidentiality, data integrity, data origin authentication, data tunneling, and user *authentication, authorization, and accounting (AAA)*.

Data Confidentiality Data confidentiality may be the single largest reason for anyone using a VPN in the first place. Think about it: you're sending your private, possibly sensitive, data over the public network. Data confidentiality is the result of encryption. VPN encrypts all the data sent from one computer to another, encoding the data so only the receiving computer is able to decrypt it.

Typically, a VPN implementation uses one of four protocols to encrypt the data, which then creates the "tunnel." Here are the four protocols:

> ➤ **Internet Protocol Security Protocol (IPsec)**: IPsec provides an encryption method that uses stronger algorithms and provides a robust authentication. IPsec contains two encryption methods: tunnel and transport.
>
>> **Tunnel encryption**: This encryption mode encrypts the header and payload of each data packet.
>>
>> **Transport encryption**: This encryption mode encrypts only the payload in each data packet.
>
> ➤ **Point-to-Point Tunneling Protocol (PPTP)**: PPTP, by itself, doesn't encrypt or authenticate data traffic. It depends on Transmission Control Protocol (TCP), Generic Routing Encapsulation (GRE), and Microsoft Point-to-Point Encryption (MPPE) to provide the control, encapsulation, and encryption that the VPN needs.
>
> ➤ **Layer 2 Tunneling Protocol (L2TP)/IPsec**: L2TP is the result of combining PPTP with the Cisco Systems Layer 2 Forwarding (L2F) technology. The Point-to-Point Protocol (PPP) portion of PPTP encapsulates data packets and L2TP and then encapsulates the PPP frames with an L2TP header. L2TP then transmits this package across the Internet. The sending end of an L2TP tunnel is the L2TP Access Concentrator (LAC), and the receiving end is the L2TP Network Server (LNS). The LNS terminates the communication session, removes the encapsulation, and passes on the original IP packets to the network. Because of its foundation on PPTP, L2TP doesn't include encryption and must rely on IPsec to provide secure VPN connections to the endpoints.

> ➤ *Secure Sockets Layer/Transport Layer Security (SSL/TLS)*: Although you'll likely see these two protocols linked (as in the title of this bullet point), actually SSL has become a part of the TLS protocol. Developed by Netscape, SSL has been in use as the public-key encryption method common to Internet browsers for some time. SSL/TLS (also TLS/SSL) provides three services: validating website identity, creating an encrypted connection (tunnel), and ensuring the transmitted data is error free.

Data Integrity Whether data is in transit or recorded to a storage device, it is important that protection methods are in use to prevent or detect changes or loss. Even though VPN protocols encrypt data before transmission, verification that the data hasn't changed in transit is essential. IPsec checks a received packet to ensure that its encrypted portion of the packet hasn't changed during transmission. Authentication of the endpoints, included in nearly all VPN protocols, adds to data integrity as well.

By protecting data against interception or modification, the endpoints of a VPN channel can be reasonably sure that data is reliably true. VPN protocols use *hashing* to protect data before and after transmission. Using a *one-way hashing* algorithm, even a one-bit change indicates a change to the packet. A one-way hashing algorithm converts data, even variable-length data, into a fixed-length hash value, which is appended to the message as a *message authentication code (MAC)*. Once converted, the transmitting protocol appends the hash value to the packet prior to transmission. The receiver calculates the hash value for the packet and compares it to the value sent with the packet. If the two don't match exactly, the protocol drops the packet. If the hash values do match, the packet is intact and true.

ONE-WAY HASHING

A hashing function is an algorithm (mathematical formula) that converts text and data into a fixed-length string of digits, typically much shorter than the original data's length. Hashing, and especially one-way hashing, provides for data security, data integrity, and, to a certain level, authentication of the transmitting endpoint. One-way hashing creates a hash value that is virtually impossible to undo, hence the "one-way." What it does produce is a value, a message digest, used for comparison purposes only.

The two primary hash functions in VPN are hmac-md5 and hmac-sha1. The "hmac" portion of their names refers to hash message authentication code (hmac). A MAC is another name for the hash value appended to the VPN message by IPsec. The second part of the hash function names refers to the actual hash function that calculated the MAC. MD5 (message digest 5) and SHA1 (secure hash algorithm 1) are standard encryption and hashing functions.

In addition to their use in VPN operations, the creation of digital signatures in messaging and email is another use of one-way hash functions. One-way hashing is also part of public-key encryption.

Data Origin Authentication When data travels across the Internet from a web service to the requester or vice versa, it travels through any number of intermediary routers, switches, or other networking devices. If someone is able to intercept a message and alter its data, the web service may not be able to perform the requested function, or it may have its behaviors changed for a while. In the previous section, you learned about message data integrity; in this section you learn about verifying the origin of a message.

Attackers capture and alter network messages to perform malicious activities. Although it may be extremely difficult to alter some protocol-encrypted messages, it's not impossible. Once an attacker alters a message, he wants to spoof (pose) as a legitimate and authorized sender in an attempt to pass off the altered data as valid. Should the altered message exploit vulnerability on the receiving system, a search for the culprit identifies the spoofed identity—someone the attacker has managed to frame.

The solution, in addition to maintaining strict data integrity, is *data origin authentication*. Data origin authentication further verifies that no alterations occurred to a message in transit and that the message originated from an expected or accepted sender. It may be somewhat redundant, but data origin authentication involves two parties: a sender and a receiver.

A sender originates a message, including all the formatting, encryption, and encoding of the message, before transmitting it. The sender sends a request message to a web service and, if the message is valid and gets through the security and screening of the web service, the web service responds with the requested information.

On the other end of the transmission, a receiver accepts a request message from a sender. As stated in the previous paragraph, if all is well with the message, the receiver prepares a response and transforms into a sender to transmit the response. Likewise, the sender of the original request message becomes the receiver for the response.

Digital signatures identify the originator of a transmitted message. The receiver can verify the originator and its integrity from the *digital signature* on the message. The digital signature provides a "proof of origin" that also provides proof against tampering. Any type of electronic message, encrypted or not, can have a digital signature applied.

> **Note**
>
> A digital signature and a digital certificate are two different things, although they are relatively close cousins. A digital certificate provides a digital signature from the certificate authority that issued the certificate. A digital certificate lets the world know that the certificate is valid and can be verified.

The digital signature algorithm (DSA), defined by the Digital Signature Standard (DSS), generates and verifies the digital signature of a message at either end of its transmission. The DSA generates a digital signature using a private key. The verification of a private key is with a public key. The basis of the digital signature is a private key (known only to an authorized sender), so its corresponding public key (known to the world) can verify the validity of the digital signature.

The MAC you learned about in the preceding section is essentially a symmetric form of digital signature. However, the digital signature discussed in this section is an asymmetric signature. Symmetric signatures use a single shared key to both encrypt and decrypt a message. An asymmetrical signature uses two keys: a private key and a public key.

Data Tunneling Tunneling through the Internet is one of the better images you can see with your mind's eye. The idea that messages can flow from point to point inside a solid, protective, enclosing tunnel or pipe is a security person's dream. In reality, data tunneling is the process of encapsulating one packet inside another before it is sent out on a network. This double-bagging, of a sort, hides the original message and creates an almost impenetrable shell around it.

A tunneling protocol, like L2TP and IPsec (see "Data Confidentiality" earlier in the chapter), encrypts the original packet and its header and places them inside a new encrypted packet and adds a Layer 3 header. Only trusted peer gateways, like the ones shown in Figure 5-3, at each end of the "tunnel" are able to peel away the added layer and decrypt the original message. Visualize the original packet as a large piece of scientific equipment placed inside the space shuttle for transportation.

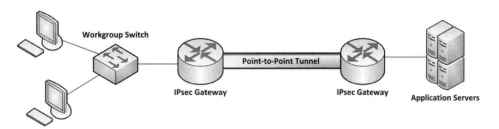

Figure 5-3 An encapsulating protocol creates the effect of a tunnel across a network.
© 2015 Cengage Learning®.

Tunneling requires three types of protocols, characterized based on their functions:

> ***Originating protocol***: This protocol, also referred to as a passenger protocol, provides the formatting of the original data packet. Typically, this is IP, Internetwork Packet Exchange (IPX), or the like.

> ***Encapsulating protocol***: This protocol encrypts the original packet and encapsulates it in a second packet. Protocols of this type are IPsec, L2TP, PPTP, and GRE. Site-to-site tunneling commonly uses IPsec or GRE as encapsulating protocols. Remote access tunneling uses PPTP as the encapsulating protocol.

> ***Transport protocol***: This protocol, also called a carrier protocol, carries the encapsulated packet across the network, such as TCP or User Datagram Protocol (UDP).

Authentication, Authorization, and Accounting Part security, data protection, and business, the AAA functions of a VPN service add another layer of security and verification to user access. This is especially true in remote access VPNs where, because PPTP is typically in use, there is no user authentication in the tunneling protocols. Adding AAA functions to the tunneling and encapsulation functions can help to protect system resources from exploitation.

For the most part, authentication consists of a username and password, but it could also require some form of biological check, such as a fingerprint, eye scan, and other body part verifications. Once authentication establishes the user's identity, authorization identifies the access permissions and rights of the user. Associating the username with an account, the accounting function can begin to track system usage, access, bandwidth, and other utilization-based charging systems.

Simply put, authentication establishes who you are; authorization establishes what you can do; and accounting tracks and possibly charges you for what you actually do.

VIRTUAL NETWORK DEVICES

A hypervisor can create a virtual network based on virtual devices inside its sphere of control. The hypervisor routes network traffic between virtual servers through vNICs, vHBAs, vCPUs, vswitches, vrouters, and perhaps virtual firewalls. You should know the purpose and function of each of these virtual devices for the Cloud+ exam.

Virtual NIC (vNIC)

A vNIC is a software program that creates a network interface card that the host operating system sees as a physical NIC (pNIC) installed on the physical server. Because the operating system believes the vNIC to be hardware, it manages and interfaces with the virtual device in the same manner it does with all network adapters, physical or virtual. See Figure 5-4 for an illustration of where vNICs fit into a virtualized network.

A vNIC connects to a VM in one of two standard ways:

> ➤ *Virtual machine connection*: A VM can connect to multiple vNICs through a port group (connection). In a VM connection, many vNICs can associate with one port group.

> ➤ *VM kernel (VMKernel) connection*: Only a single VMKernel vNIC (VMK) associates with a connection (port group).

Virtual Switch

Like all virtual devices, a *virtual switch (vswitch)* is a software program through which one VM communicates with another. In most virtualization environments, vswitches are part of the virtualization software, but they can also be in the firmware of a physical server. Like a physical Open Systems Interconnection (OSI) Layer 2 switch, a vswitch forwards packets on its (virtual) network.

A vswitch can connect to one or more port groups or connections. (See "Virtual NIC (vNIC)" for more on port groups or connections.) Each port group has a network identifier associated with the host server. The vswitch detects which port groups connect to a VM and forwards network traffic using that information either internally between VMs or to a link that connects to an external network.

Virtual HBA

A *host bus adapter (HBA)*—also a host controller or a host adapter, depending on its use or system) connects the physical host server to either a storage device or other devices in a network. In a virtualized environment, HBA most commonly refers to connections to Small Computer System Interface (SCSI—pronounced as *scuzzy*), Fibre Channel, or external Serial Advanced Technology Attachment (eSATA—pronounced as *eee-sayta*).

Typically, an HBA is a physical expansion board inserted into a computer or an integrated adapter that provides input/output (I/O) operations and physical connectivity between a host system and a storage system or device.

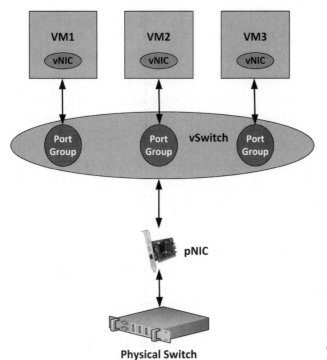

Figure 5-4 Virtual NICs and virtual switches can be part of a virtual network.
© 2015 Cengage Learning®.

Note

Although it's unlikely that you'll encounter eSATA on the Cloud+ exam, you might want to know what it is, just in case. eSATA is a derivative of the Serial ATA storage device interface common to many PCs. The eSATA interface allows SATA devices to attach externally to computers. It is faster than USB 2.0 and FireWire, but unlike these two interfaces, eSATA requires its own external power source.

A *virtual HBA*, patterned after the physical Fibre Channel HBA, has the responsibility of limiting virtual servers and VMs to only its assigned virtual data storage. Virtual HBA incorporates the feature *N_Port_ID Virtualization (NPIV)* that permits each virtual server to have a unique World Wide Name (WWN). Access to the virtual data storage is by WWN, and virtual devices may access only that data assigned to it.

NPIV makes it possible for several virtual servers to share a single physical Fibre Channel port identifier. Multiple World Wide Port Names (WWPNs) and NPIV identifiers can be associated with a single virtual HBA or interface in a storage array or Fibre Channel loop. Each virtual server can then use its unique WWN to access the physical or virtual storage area network (SAN) and see only its own storage space.

Virtual Router

A *virtual router (vrouter)* is a software program that provides its host with the capability to route network traffic over a LAN in the same way as a hardware router. Typically, a vrouter has most of or the same capabilities as a fully featured OSI Layer 3 router. The difference is software versus hardware.

WWN, WWID, WWPN, AND WWNN

Perhaps you think all that could possibly be missing from the mnemonics in the title is WWW, because you'd know what that means at least. You might know more than you may realize. The "WW" in each of these abbreviations does stand for "World Wide." However, the world wide that applies to these terms is storage.

> *World Wide Name (WWN)*: Also World Wide Identifier (WWID), this is a completely unique identification code used in certain storage technologies, including ATA, SCSI, Serial Attached SCSI (SAS), and Fibre Channel. Typically, a WWN is a serial number or an addressable locator code, such as a WWPN or a WWNN.

> *World Wide Port Name (WWPN)*: A WWN assigned to a Fibre Channel port is much like a Media Access Control (MAC) address in Ethernet to identify an interface uniquely.

> *World Wide Node Name (WWNN)*: A WWNN assigned to an endpoint device on a Fibre Channel system. Unlike WWNs and WWPNs, a WWNN may be assigned to multiple ports, provided each port has a unique WWPN, to identify the ports as interfaces to a single WWNN.

The *Virtual Router Redundancy Protocol (VRRP)* can implement one or more vrouters on a network to improve its reliability. The vrouter assumes the role of the default gateway of the network, and any physical routers on the network, typically two physical routers, become logical parts of the vrouter and serve as its backups. Within the vrouter, one of the physical routers continues to route data packets on the network or internetwork, and the other takes the role of a redundant router by keeping its routing data current. The redundant router provides failover capability in the event that the routing physical router fails.

A variety of different software virtual router programs are available, most free as open source. Many of the virtual router applications available are primarily for Wi-Fi networks, but there are Ethernet network virtual routers as well.

Virtual CPU

A *virtual central processing unit (vCPU)*, also a virtual processor, is a component of a CPU with a *symmetric multiprocessing (SMP)*, multithreaded, and multicore design. Virtualized software applications depend on these CPU capabilities. A multicore CPU is able to support several vCPUs on each of its physical or logical cores. SMP processors provide parallel processing of virtualized tasks by distributing threads over multiple cores.

Virtual Bridge

A *virtual bridge (vbridge)* connects a VM to the physical LAN of the host server. If implemented, it provides a connection between a VM's vNIC and the pNIC of the host computer. A vbridge is not a substitute for a vswitch because bridges, physical or virtual, are strictly forwarding devices.

Shared Memory

Memory sharing isn't unique to a virtualized environment. *Shared memory* is accessible by several programs and provides *inter-process communication (IPC)*. Shared memory also helps to avoid redundant memory pages. Programs, running on a single CPU or on several separate CPUs (and vCPUs), are able to pass data to one another. Shared memory also provides the capability for communication between multiple threads of a single program.

In a virtualized environment, shared memory can support multiple VMs. This is especially true when two or more VMs are running on the same guest operating system and have the same application, components, or data loaded into memory. For example, VMware Workstation can eliminate redundant memory pages. Figure 5-5 illustrates this configuration in a virtualized environment.

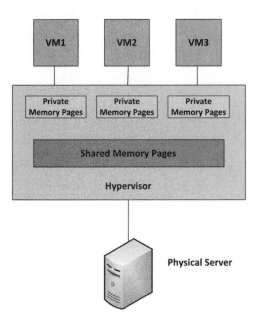

Figure 5-5 A hypervisor can share memory for common or duplicated data among VMs.
© 2015 Cengage Learning®.

Underneath all virtualized environments is the host operating system. The host operating system cannot perform efficiently if it doesn't have enough free memory for its own usage. When an operating system runs low on memory, it begins to thrash, meaning that it must begin moving "idle" memory pages in and out of Random Access Memory (RAM) to and from its paging files on a disk storage device, including its virtual memory space. To avoid this condition, hypervisors or VMMs limit the amount of memory space a VM can use and maintain a memory reserve for the host operating system. The memory allocated to the VMs and reserved for the operating system depends on the operating system and the amount of memory available on the host server.

Hypervisor Systems

One important part of any virtualized environment is a hypervisor or a *virtual machine manager (VMM)*. These two terms are generally interchangeable, but you may also see hypervisors referred to by their brand names: Hyper-V, Xen, ESX Server, Padded Cell, VLX, TRANGO, Virtage, or KVM, just to name a few of the more common. Regardless, hypervisor is the more commonly used general reference.

> **Note**
>
> You should be careful with the term VMM because it also represents a virtual machine monitor, which is actually a component of a hypervisor.

The term hypervisor really doesn't represent anything other than it is higher (hyper) than a machine supervisor. This term came out of IBM in the 1960s as an earlier name for what would later become an operating system. So, if the word means anything, it is a higher-level supervisor. The concept of today's implementation of hypervisors more directly grew out of UNIX and Linux systems starting around 2005.

A hypervisor is software that manages a virtual environment made up of several VMs on one server/computer. In a cloud environment, you access a VM to utilize your contracted services, especially on a Software as a Service (SaaS) platform. The hypervisor on the service provider's server manages the VM you're using, plus those of the other subscribers on the server or cluster.

Although your interface with the VM gives the impression that you are alone on the server and have free access to its resources, the hypervisor is managing, monitoring, and allocating resources to the VMs running in its virtual environment, including all other virtualized elements in the environment.

Hypervisors are one of two types, based on their implementation, their dependencies, their tasks, and their methods. In the sections that follow, you learn about Type I or "bare metal" hypervisors and Type II or "hosted" hypervisors.

Type I Hypervisor

Type I hypervisors, which are also known as *bare-metal hypervisors*, are installed on a server's bare metal. This means that no other software is on the computer—specifically no operating system. The hypervisor is to be the operating system. Figure 5-6 illustrates the relationship of a Type I hypervisor and its environment.

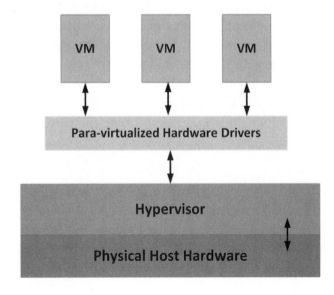

Figure 5-6 The hypervisor serves as the operating system in a Type I or bare metal virtual environment.
© 2015 Cengage Learning®.

Type I hypervisors communicate directly with the physical server hardware through their device drivers or adapters. The hypervisor para-virtualizes each device and makes the device available to the VMs under its control.

> **Note**
>
> Recall from Chapter 4 that para-virtualization refers to communications between the guest operating system of the VM and the hypervisor.

Type II Hypervisor

Type II hypervisors, also known as *hosted hypervisors*, operate on top of the host operating system instead of replacing it. Like the Type I hypervisor, a Type II hypervisor creates and manages virtual machines, but it must interact with the host operating system for CPU, memory, disk, network, and any other resource requirements. Figure 5-7 illustrates a Type II hypervisor installed on top of a host operating system.

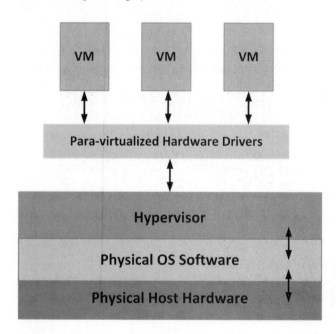

Figure 5-7 A Type II hypervisor interacts with the host system operating system for resource access.
© 2015 Cengage Learning®.

Which hypervisor type is right for any particular implementation depends on several factors: efficiency, diversity of hardware resources, and liability. Efficiency is essentially the same on either type, but a Type I has better efficiency by definition. A Type II hypervisor must make resource calls to the host operating system. When there is an array of hardware devices, having a host operating system to provide a device interface can provide a better installation over a Type I implementation. Liability, in terms of a cloud service provider, can be an issue with potential security exposures of a host operating system, which may favor a Type I hypervisor.

Client Hypervisor

A *client hypervisor* is just that—a hypervisor installed on a client device, such as a notebook, desktop PC, or the like. Like a server hypervisor, a client hypervisor is either a Type I or a Type II. Client hypervisors isolate the operating system from the hardware, allowing two (or more) operating systems to run on the computer. For instance, a Windows 8 computer could also run a virtualized version of Windows XP and a legacy version of Internet Explorer.

Chapter Summary

> A virtual network is a computer network that doesn't use physical media to create connections between two or more virtual devices. A virtual network can be one of two forms: protocol based or virtual device based.

> Virtual device-based virtual networks are those that interconnect VMs and the VMM or hypervisor.

> A VLAN is a logical LAN set up in a physical network switch or Layer 2-capable router by partitioning the physical LAN into two or more logical LANs.

> A VPN consists of a physical or logical VPN controller at one endpoint and a VPN client at the other endpoint. VPNs fall into one of the following two categories: remote access and site-to-site.

> The major characteristics of a VPN are data confidentiality, data integrity, data origin authentication, data tunneling, and AAA.

> VPN uses one of four protocols to encrypt data: IPsec, PPTP, L2TP/IPsec, and SSL/TLS.

> A tunneling protocol protects the private communication stream between the two endpoints. Tunneling requires three types of protocols: originating protocol, encapsulating protocol, and transport protocol.

> Digital signatures identify the originator of a transmitted message. The DSA, defined by the DSS, generates and verifies the digital signature of a message at either end of its transmission.

> A vNIC is a software program that creates a network interface that the host operating system sees as a pNIC installed on the physical server. A vNIC connects to a VM in one of two standard ways: virtual machine connection or VMKernel connection.

> A vswitch is a software program through which VMs communicate.

> An HBA connects a physical host server to a storage device or other devices in a network. A virtual HBA limits virtual servers and VMs to assigned virtual data storage.

> Virtual HBA incorporates NPIV, which permits each virtual server to have a unique WWN. NPIV allows several virtual servers to share a single physical Fibre Channel port identifier. Multiple WWPNs and NPIV identifiers can be associated with a single virtual HBA or interface in a storage array or Fibre Channel loop. Each virtual server can then use its unique WWN to access the physical or virtual storage area network (SAN) and see only its own storage space.

> A virtual router is a software program that provides its host with the capability to route network traffic over a LAN in the same way as a hardware router. VRRP can implement one or more vrouters on a network to improve its reliability.

> A vCPU is a component of a CPU with SMP, multithreaded, and multicore design.

> In a virtualized environment, shared memory can support multiple VMs, especially when two or more VMs are running on the same guest operating system and have the same application, components, or data loaded into memory.

> A hypervisor is software that manages a virtual environment made up of several VMs on one server/computer.

> Hypervisors are one of two types: Type I "bare metal" hypervisors and Type II "hosted" hypervisors.

> Type I hypervisors install on a server's bare metal in place of an operating system. Type I hypervisors communicate directly with the physical server hardware through their device drivers or adapters. The hypervisor para-virtualizes each device and makes the device available to the VMs under its control.

> Type II hypervisors operate on top of the host operating system and must interact with the host operating system for CPU, memory, disk, network, and any other resource requirements.

> A client hypervisor is installed on a client device.

Key Terms

Authentication, authorization, and accounting (AAA)

Bare metal hypervisor

Client hypervisor

Data origin authentication

Digital signature

Encapsulating protocol

Hashing

Host bus adapter (HBA)

Hosted hypervisor

Internet Protocol Security Protocol (IPsec)

Inter-process communication (IPC)

Layer 2 Tunneling Protocol (L2TP)/IPsec

Message authentication code (MAC)

N_Port_ID Virtualization (NPIV)

One-way hashing

Originating protocol

Point-to-Point Tunneling Protocol (PPTP)

Remote-access VPN

Secure Sockets Layer/Transport Layer Security (SSL/TLS)

Shared memory

Site-to-site VPN

Symmetric multiprocessing (SMP)

Transport encryption

Transport protocol

Tunnel encryption

Tunneling protocol

Type I hypervisor

Type II hypervisor

Virtual bridge (vbridge)

Virtual central processing unit (vCPU)

Virtual HBA

Virtual local area network (VLAN)

Virtual machine connection

Virtual machine manager (VMM)

Virtual network

Virtual network interface card (vNIC)

Virtual private LAN service (VPLS)

Virtual private network (VPN)

Virtual router (vrouter)

Virtual Router Redundancy Protocol (VRRP)

Virtual switch (vswitch)

VMKernel connection

World Wide Name (WWN)

World Wide Node Name (WWNN)

World Wide Port Name (WWPN)

Review Questions

1. A computer network that uses logical media to create connections between virtual machines is a[n] _____.

    a. private network

    b. public network

    c. physical network

    d. virtual network

2. A VLAN is a _____ LAN created on a physical network switch.

3. True or False? The two types of VPNs are remote-access and point-to-point.

4. A[n] _____ protocol protects a private communication stream between two endpoints.

5. True of False? Digital signatures identify the originator of a transmitted message.

6. A virtual HBA incorporates what feature that permits each virtual server to have a unique WWN?

    a. IPsec

    b. NPIV

    c. SAN

    d. VMK

7. The encryption protocol that applies two encryption methods, tunnel or transport, is _____.

    a. PPTP

    b. L2TP

    c. IPsec

    d. SSL

8. A _____ encryption protocol encodes only the payload in a data packet.

9. True or False? A vswitch is a physical device.

10. What virtual network device is seen by the host operating system as a physical device installed on the host server?

    a. vrouter

    b. vswitch

    c. vNIC

    d. pNIC

11. True or False? One of the ways a vNIC connects to a VM is a VMKernel connection.

12. A[n] _____ hypervisor is installed "bare metal."

13. A[n] _____ virtual network interconnects VMs and the VMM.

14. True or False? A Type I hypervisor is installed on top of a server's operating system.

15. Which virtual network device allows physical and virtual machines to communicate within a virtual network?

    a. vrouter

    b. vNIC

    c. vswitch

    d. vbridge

Answers to Review Questions

1. d
2. logical
3. False
4. tunneling
5. True
6. b
7. c
8. transport
9. False
10. c

11. True

12. Type I

13. virtual device based

14. False

15. c

CHAPTER 6

Management of a Virtual Environment

After reading this chapter and completing the exercises, you will be able to:

- Explain the process for creating, importing, and exporting template and virtual machines
- Describe the reasons for and the procedures of snapshots and cloning
- Differentiate image backups and file backups
- Discuss the management processes of virtual devices

Virtualization is a technology that can improve a computing environment regardless of whether it is a local network or a cloud environment. The basic concept of using a single physical computer to host several virtual servers has an effect on operational costs, operational efficiencies, and the services available to others.

Within the virtualized environment, you have a host server, several virtual servers and machines, and an array of virtual devices that the various services, applications, and users share to accomplish their tasks. In this chapter, you learn about the creation, management, and use of virtual devices, including servers, machines, and virtual peripheral devices.

Creating a Virtual Environment

Creating a virtualized environment involves more than pushing a button or running a wizard. If only it were that simple. On the other hand, for someone with a good working knowledge of networking, resource sharing, and data communications, it shouldn't be that difficult.

Like nearly all things computing, there are three steps to the creation and implementation of a virtualized system: planning, deploying, and managing. In the following sections, you learn about these steps.

Preparing for a Virtual Environment

The first phase in deploying a virtualized computing environment is planning. Without proper planning, you may implement a virtual environment, but not necessarily one that meets your computing needs or employs the system resources effectively and efficiently. Without planning for this major change to your computing approach, you could end up with something that isn't much better than what you started with—even after the expense of the change.

The plan for implementing a virtualized environment should address each of the phases of the installation, configuration, security, monitoring, maintaining, and ongoing activities that include backing up the system and potentially restoring the service. The following sections discuss the recommended phases of a virtualization project.

TECHNICAL PLANNING

Under the assumption that you have a complete analysis of the existing (previrtual) organizational and information technology (IT) environments and understand the impact that virtualization will make on the organization operationally, you should be able to develop the technical architecture to meet the identified needs. The technology plan for a virtual environment must identify the appropriate base for computing, memory, and storage capacities. This base amount of resources must consider the number of virtual machines (VMs) along with the workload profiles of any applications, clients, and monitoring or management agents the virtualized servers may need to support. This step involves capacity planning.

In addition to computing resource requirements of the future system configuration, technical planning includes physical planning that considers space requirements, power and other utility needs, environmental requirements, and housing.

OPERATIONAL PLANNING

Vendor materials, white papers, guides, and product documentation identify from 3 to 12 separate planning steps that, according to each vendor, are extremely vital to the success of your virtualized environment deployment. In fact, every one of them is correct. It isn't the number of steps performed that guarantee a successful deployment of a virtualized environment; it's that you perform the planning (and design) process methodically and completely.

Assess the Current Environment

Although the plan is to replace the current computing environment with a virtualized environment, thoroughly assessing the current operations is a critical step in the process. Before you can create a detailed plan for the computing and organizational resources that the virtual environment will use, you should understand the computing and organizational resources that are currently available. Not only should you know what you have, but you should know the processing capabilities of the current equipment.

It's better to use a performance-monitoring tool to quantify the average, low, and peak demands for storage, memory, processing (central processing units, or CPUs), and network resources on the computers and servers that will be in the new environment. The performance metrics should also reflect resource demands during key periods of the organization, such as month end, peak order-entry times, and other high-usage times. The measured performance should reflect at least an average week of system use; longer is always better.

The assessment should also look at the applications planned to run in the virtualized environment. A software publisher's licensing agreement may have special provisions concerning virtualization or technical support in that environment. If the licensing or support agreements don't mention virtualization, ask.

Virtualization can also affect support processes and procedures. Processes such as backups, system monitoring, security measures, patch management, and general system administration may need alternations for compatibility with the virtualized environment.

Build the Virtual Environment

The major decision when starting to build a virtual environment is which of the various virtualization systems to use. There are numerous virtualization software or platform vendors with products for virtualizing small in-house LANs to enterprise-level environments, and myriad capabilities in between. The size of the organization, its growth plans, and its budget, along with the capabilities of the system, are the considerations.

The hardware considerations for implementing a virtualized environment lie essentially in the right-sizing and plan-based system objectives. If plans call for new computers for servers, make sure they include the features that support virtualization, such as Intel's Virtualization Technology (VT) or AMD's AMD-Virtualization (AMD=V). The sizing of the computers should support multiple VMs on each server.

The chosen storage systems must support not only the performance desired, but also the technology you want to use in the near- or mid-future. Shared storage systems, such as Fibre Channel, Internet Small Computer System Interface (iSCSI), and Network File System (NFS), provide better performance in a virtualized environment over direct-attached storage (DAS). Depending on the criticality of the system, high-availability or live-migration systems may also be a requirement.

Virtual Network

The primary difference between a physical network, one in a nonvirtualized environment, and a virtual network is that the connections in a virtual network consist of virtual devices, especially *virtual network interface cards (vNICs), virtual switches (vswitches),* and possibly *virtual routers (vrouters)* and *virtual firewalls (vfirewalls).* The connections between virtual devices occur under the control of the *virtual machine manager (VMM)* or the virtual system's *hypervisor.*

Virtual networks also implement virtual (protocol based) subnetworks like *virtual local area networks (VLANs), virtual private networks (VPNs),* or *virtual private LAN services (VPLS).* A VLAN is a logical organization of physically or logically separated nodes or VMs that creates a logical broadcast domain. A VPN is an extension of a private network (LAN) to the public network (Internet). A computer connecting to a VPN is able to transmit and receive data via the public network in a way that it appears the computer has a link on the private network directly. VPLS, which is a multipoint VPN, creates many-to-many communications on an Internet Protocol (IP) network or a *Multiprotocol Label Switching (MPLS)* network. Figure 6-1 illustrates the relationship of the components of a virtualized network.

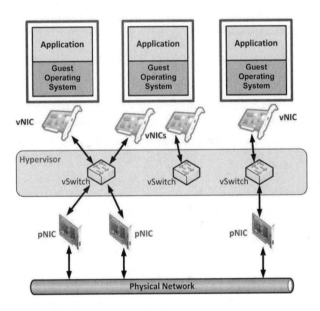

Figure 6-1 A virtualized network environment incorporates VNICs and virtual switches that logically connect through the hypervisor to the physical network.

© 2015 Cengage Learning®.

Virtual NICs

A virtual NIC (vNIC) is a software-based network interface created and managed within a virtual system's hypervisor. A vNIC operates essentially like a physical NIC (pNIC), but in a virtual environment, a pNIC can link to several vNICs. To the network, a vNIC appears to be a pNIC. Hypervisors create a set of virtual input/output (I/O) ports and associate a virtual interrupt request (IRQ) to the vNIC. A vNIC can connect to a network in two ways: bridged to a pNIC or connected to a virtual network.

Because communications between network interfaces occur on Layer 2 (Data Link layer), vNICs are assigned *Media Access Control (MAC)* addresses similar to, but individually unique to, the MAC address of the pNIC. A vNIC that connects to a pNIC creates an Ethernet bridge allowing the vNIC's packets to carry a unique MAC address. To the network, these MAC addresses appear to come from an "actual" network adapter, and any intermediary devices see the vNIC as an "actual" device.

When a vNIC connects to a vswitch or vrouter, the host server and the hypervisor contain it within a private network including any VMs linked to it. To connect to external network resources, the host operating system must switch or route its traffic using an address translation protocol.

A vNIC's IP configuration can be set through the *Dynamic Host Configuration Protocol (DHCP)* running on the host server or set manually through the hypervisor or VMM. If the vNIC is manually configured, its IP address, default gateway, and subnet mask (netmask) are set to static addresses.

VIRTUAL SWITCHES

As shown in Figure 6-1, vswitches are software devices that provide logical connections for vNICs to the virtual network through other vNICs and vswitches, as well as the physical network's pNICs. A virtual network can include a large number of vswitches (along with an even higher number of vNICs). For example, VMware's ESX Server 3 is able to support up to 248 vswitches.

A vswitch provides a number of switching and forwarding functions to the virtual network, including these:

> ➤ *Layer 2 forwarding*: Using only the Layer 2 Ethernet headers of message frames, this function forwards frames to their MAC address destinations.

> ➤ **VLAN tagging, stripping, and filtering**: This function supports the VLAN tag add and strip functions of Ethernet frames and filtering on all Layer 2 frames.

> ➤ **Layer 2 segmentation offloading**: *Large segment offloading (LSO)*, also called *TCP segmentation offload (TSO)* and *generic segmentation offload (GSO)*, queues up large outbound message buffers and allows the network adapter to divide them into separate Layer 2 frames. This not only reduces CPU processing, but increases throughput on the network media. The same function for inbound frames is *large receive offload (LRO)*.

> ➤ **Layer 2 security**: This function supports Layer 2 checksums and frame security.

VLAN Forwarding

Like a physical switch, a vswitch creates and maintains a MAC address/port forwarding table. When a frame arrives at the vswitch, the vswitch examines its forwarding table for the frame's destination address and forwards the frame to the port for the destination. The configuration for a vswitch port can enable it as an access port, which implements VLAN tagging for a single VLAN. If the environment supports multiple VLANs, the vswitch can support virtual guest tagging as well.

For frames transmitted by a VM to another VM on the same VLAN (same vswitch), no tagging takes place. For virtual network traffic to remain internal, the VMs involved must be on the same vswitch. If the two VMs involved are on different vswitches, the frame must navigate to a physical switch and be forwarded back into the virtual network.

VLAN Tagging

VLAN tagging identifies frames transmitted on a trunk line, which is a link that is able to carry multiple frames at the same time and interconnects switches on a network. A trunk typically has several cables or wires to provide increased bandwidth. Because a trunk carries frame traffic from more than one switch, the VLAN tag identifies the VLAN to which the frame belongs. A frame transmitted on a trunk line has a VLAN tag added to it. Figure 6-2 illustrates the difference of the Ethernet frame before and after the insertion of a VLAN tag. When the frame reaches the end of the trunk, the switch removes the VLAN tag and forwards the frame to the port associated with its MAC address in the switch's forwarding table.

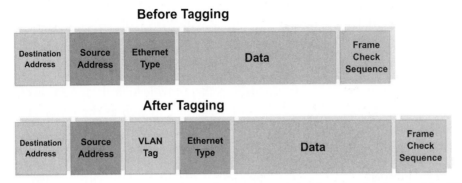

Figure 6-2 The contents of an Ethernet frame without VLAN tagging (top) and with a VLAN tag inserted (below).
© 2015 Cengage Learning®.

VMware and Cisco Systems devices, real and virtual, apply three types of VLAN tags:

> ➤ ***External switch tagging (EST)***: A physical switch performs this type of VLAN tagging.

> ➤ ***Virtual switch tagging (VST)***: A vswitch performs this type of VLAN tagging before the frame leaves the hypervisor.

> ➤ ***Virtual guest tagging (VGT)***: A vswitch performs this type of VLAN tagging under the Institute for Electrical and Electronics Engineers' (IEEE) 802.1Q standard inside a VM.

Virtual Machines

A *virtual machine (VM)* is a software-created computer emulation that takes on the characteristics of the computer it runs on, with its configuration controlled by the hypervisor of the VMM that creates it. The two types of VMs are system VMs and process VMs. A *system VM* provides an operating platform that supports the system elements of a physical machine, including an operating system and device drivers. A *process VM* supports a single process in support of program portability. A system VM has access to the hardware device emulations (virtual hardware) configured on its host system. A process VM is limited to the resources configured within the VM itself.

System VMs

A system VM can operate completely separately from any other VMs on a physical computer. Each VM can run a different operating system (guest operating system) and have a slightly different hardware configuration (virtual hardware) than the physical computer on which it's running. The downside to a VM is that with multiple VMs running on a physical computer, the performance of each VM will be less than the performance of its same applications running on the physical computer alone. Examples of system VMs are the VMs created under VMware and other virtualization software.

PROCESS VMS

A process VM, also called an application virtual machine or a managed runtime environment (MRE), is more like a shell running on the host operating system with a single application. The primary benefit of a process VM is that, because it runs independently of the hardware configuration of the host computer, it can run on any platform in the same way. Examples of process VMs are the Java VM for running routines written in the Java programming language and the .NET Framework that runs on the Common Language Runtime (CLR) VM.

CREATING A VM

In most of the more popular virtualization systems, such as VMware's VM Workstation and Microsoft's Hyper-V, a virtual machine wizard guides you through the creation of a new VM. Figures 6-3 and 6-4 show screen captures of these two VM wizards.

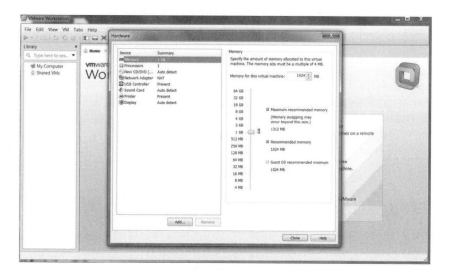

Figure 6-3 The hardware settings of the VMware Workstation New VM wizard.

Source: VMware, Inc.

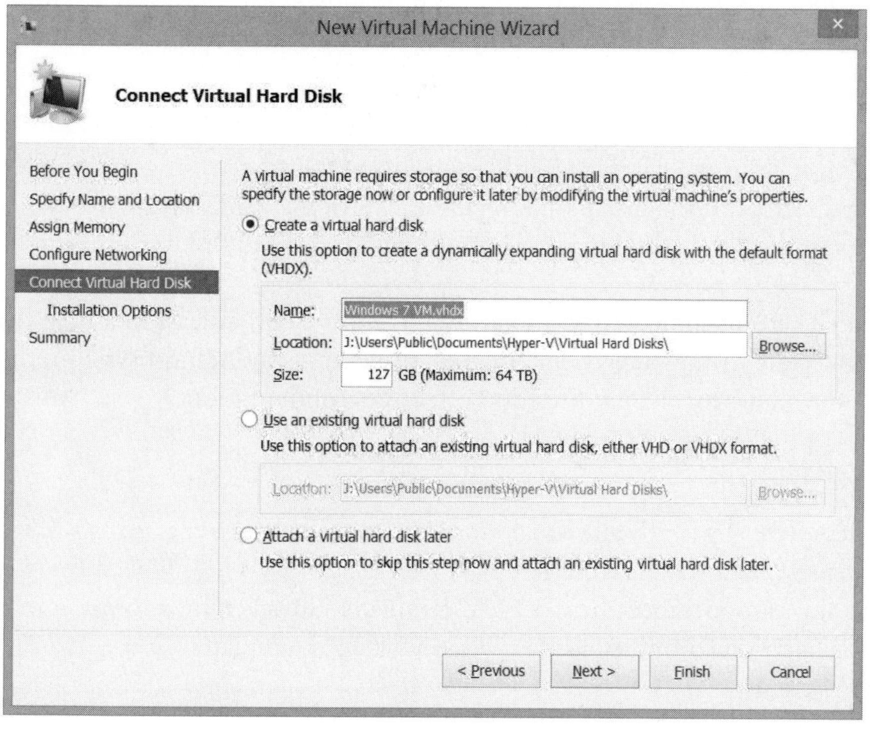

Figure 6-4 The virtual hard disk dialog box on a Windows Hyper-V New VM Wizard.

Used with permission from Microsoft.

The steps used to create a new VM are essentially the same regardless of the virtualization system in use. In general, these steps are as follows:

1. Select the operating system that will run in the new VM. This choice usually includes selecting the operating system and its version. This information sets the default values for the VM, including the amount of memory required, the filename formatting, and the optimum performance settings.

2. Enter a name and a folder/directory where the files associated with the new VM are to reside. Each VM should have its own folder. Understand that if the folder/directory for a VM is on a network hard disk or storage area network (SAN), its performance will be slower than if it is on direct attached storage (DAS) for the local computer.

3. Indicate the number of processors assigned to the VM. The default value is typically two. However, this is true only for computers with two logical processors, including a single-processor computer with hyperthreading active, a dual-core processor, or a multiprocessor computer with two non-dual-core CPUs with no hyperthreading enabled.

Note

Hyperthreading, officially Hyperthreading Technology (HTT), is Intel's implementation of simultaneous multithreading (SMT) that allows a processor to do multiple tasks at the same time. Under hyperthreading, a computer's operating system, if it supports SMT, can create two virtual (logical) cores for each processor core. This reduces the number of instructions waiting in the processor queue and allows the operating system to push two instructions to the processor at a time.

4. Custom installations ("Custom" chosen on the installation type screen) can configure additional options, such as memory settings, or accept the default values provided. However, VMs generally are limited to 2 GB of memory.

5. Set the network configuration for the VM. If the IP address for the VM will come from DHCP or an assigned IP address, select the bridged networking option. Otherwise, select the *network address translation (NAT)* option.

6. If the configuration is a "Typical" installation, this is often the end of the wizard. When you exit ("Finish") the wizard, the wizard creates the appropriate configuration files in the VM's folder/directory. If the installation type was "Custom," additional hardware configuration questions display, including device adapters and the hard disk type for the VM.

Other configuration setting choices may display, but in most cases, at least in a new virtualized environment, the default settings are generally a good place to start. On most systems, the wizard or a companion tool allows for the modification of a VM's configuration.

VM TEMPLATES

One of the features offered by nearly all virtualization software systems is the use of VM templates. A *VM template* represents a standard configuration for a new VM. Many of the virtualization packages provide at least one standard-model VM template. However, the more common use of this feature is to convert one or more locally created VMs into templates for use in creating new VMs on the local system.

The configuration of a VM template can range from only a guest operating system and a single application to all the applications and configurations used by a single department (VLAN). Any template must include an operating system at a minimum. The use of VM templates helps to ensure that the VMs created from a template are set up and configured correctly and consistently. Figure 6-5 illustrates the process of creating a new VM from a template: 1) select the template to create the new VM from the VM library; 2) add the new VM to the virtualized environment; and 3) manage the environment, including the new VM, through the hypervisor.

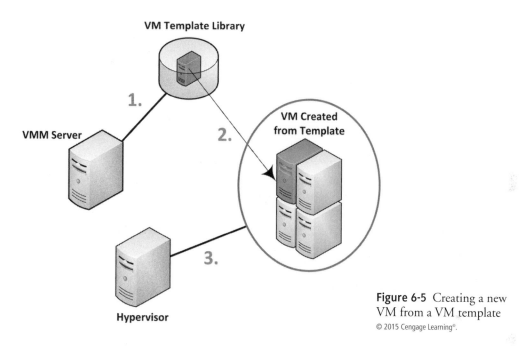

Figure 6-5 Creating a new VM from a VM template
© 2015 Cengage Learning®.

Specifically, a VM template may include configurations for a guest operating system and its associated fields (computer ID, passwords, workgroup or domain ID, and so on), virtual hard disk, CPU, memory, Integrated Drive Electronics (IDE) or Small Computer System Interface (SCSI) devices, network adapters, and more.

An existing VM can be the model for new VM templates, or an edited clone of an existing template can be the basis of a new template. Most VMM systems include the capability to create new VMs from a template; clone an existing VM to a template, which leaves the existing VM intact; or convert an existing VM into a template, removing the VM and creating a template. The last option is perhaps the most efficient in that a standard VM model can serve as the template for multiple VM duplicates.

VIRTUAL DISKS

A *virtual disk (vdisk)* is a logical disk storage device that provides data I/O support for systems or applications running in a VM or in native mode on a host computer. In most cases, a vdisk is a feature of storage virtualization of a disk array, SAN, or network attached storage (NAS). A vdisk implements a mapping table that translates I/O requests for the storage media (virtual disk identifiers) to an associated physical disk identifier. Virtualizing a physical disk medium breaks the physical disk into blocks of data, called extents, which can span two or more physical disk drives.

The file format on most vdisks is *virtual hard disk (VHD)*. The use of the VHD file format creates a platform-independent environment. This allows multiple operating systems to run on a single computer through the implementation of VMs. VHD provides many benefits to a virtualized environment, including the transparent movement of files between the VHD and a host file system, disk drive conversion (from virtual to physical), and data integrity and security features.

VHD files reside on a host file server in a variety of supported formats, including the following:

> *Differencing hard disk*: Each file has a parent and a child image. The parent image contains the original data content of the file, and the child image contains the changes made to the file. The use of the child image allows any changes to the file to be undone or merged into the parent at the end of a process. Some differencing hard disks create multiple child images to support a cloning of the file. Each of the clones has a globally unique identifier (GUID). Figure 6-6 illustrates the use of the differencing disk format.

> *Dynamic hard disk*: Files are dynamically sized to the data they contain at any one time, plus a VHD header and footer.

> *Fixed hard disk*: One or more files with an allocated space equal to the configured size of the vdisk. A fixed hard disk VHD contains raw data and a VHD footer.

> *Linked hard disk*: A file that contains a logical link to a physical drive.

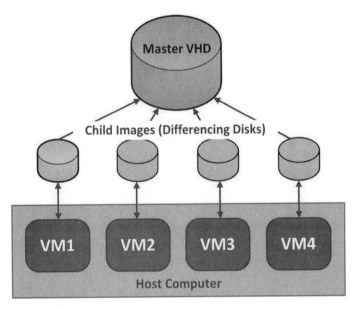

Figure 6-6 Each VM running with a VHD in differencing disk format applies its changes to a child disk.
© 2015 Cengage Learning®.

In a virtualized environment, if each VM had access to a single copy of a file, any changes made to the file by multiple users could overwrite or negate each other. The use of a vdisk, especially one using the differencing hard disk format, allows each user to change the file independently of any other users accessing the file. However, at the end of the processing period, a time-stamp priority or role-based process must consolidate the data to the physical file.

Differencing and dynamic hard disk formats have a limitation of 2,040 GB (around 2 terabytes), which is limited by the 32-bit addressing capability of VHD systems. Several virtualization systems support VHD, including Oracle VirtualBox, VMware ESX Server and Workstation, and Citrix XenSource.

VIRTUAL STORAGE AREA NETWORKS

Two approaches are used to create a *virtual storage area network (VSAN)*. A VSAN can be part of the SAN system itself or in a virtualized environment as a software-created entity controlled by the hypervisor.

SAN-Based VSAN

Like other virtual storage structures, a VSAN can be a logical partition created in a physical SAN. A VSAN partitions and allocates all or part of an entire SAN into one or more VSANs accessible by internal or external users. VSANs are most common in cloud and virtualized environments, and primarily by VMs and virtual servers.

A VSAN provides users with the capability to create a logical SAN using storage virtualization technology. VSANs essentially sit on top of the physical SAN and give the service provider the capability to add or remove subscribers to a service without restructuring the entire physical disk arrangement. VSANs also offer the flexibility of adding or removing storage capacity when needed.

The creation of a VSAN isolates a portion of a physical SAN that virtual devices need for processing and I/O operations. If multiple VSANs are in use, a problem in one VSAN typically doesn't disrupt operations in another. Another benefit of the use of VSANs is that, because each VSAN is independent of any others, there is a reduction in the attack surface of the SAN, increasing its overall security. VSANs also support data redundancy, which further reduces the risk of lost or corrupted data in a catastrophic event.

It's easiest to think of a VSAN as a little virtual disk drive that operates in conjunction with the physical SAN. However, in actual implementation, a VSAN is a collection of specific ports on the Fibre Channel (FC) switches of an SAN. This group of ports is a virtual fabric. Partitioning the ports on an individual FC switch may create several VSANs, even though the ports actually share hardware resources. FC switches and a VSAN port can also combine to create a larger VSAN.

VMware VSAN

VMware recently announced the release of a VSAN capability in its vSphere software. Originally named "vCloud Distributed Storage," this product is now simply virtual SAN, or VSAN. In this context, a VSAN is a software-based virtual distributed storage device maintained within the hypervisor. With a VSAN included in the virtual environment, a single virtual data source is available to any VM enabled for it.

In the virtualized environment, each host provides disk space as partial or whole disk drives to the shared data pool. Each of the hosts contributing disk space must provide at least one *solid state drive (SSD)* and one magnetic drive (standard hard disk drive). Up to eight hosts can participate in a VSAN, but there must be a minimum of three. The VSAN can add host disk drives automatically, in which case the VSAN controller identifies all the disk drives in the environment, or manually, adding only selected drives.

However, each host must have a disk controller that is a *Serial Attached SCSI (SAS)*, a *Serial Advanced Technology Attachment (SATA) host bus adapter (HBA)*, or a *Redundant Array of Independent Disks (RAID)* controller. A RAID controller must operate in either pass-through mode or RAID 0. (See Chapter 9 for more information on RAID and other disk formats.) *Pass-through mode* in RAID, or "Just a Bunch of Disks" (JBOD) or HBAs, is the preferred disk controller mode.

The two operational benefits of a VSAN are performance (SSD) and capacity (HDD). All data I/O operations initially go to SSD, but they eventually go to the HDD. The VMware VSAN allows levels of fault tolerance in its configuration. This setting sets the failure level that the VSAN is to tolerate. For example, if a VSAN is set for a 1 host failure fault-tolerant level, meaning the system sets up recovery resources at this level, the VSAN creates two identical data objects and a third object called a *witness* that provides information relating to recovery and restoring control.

ZONING

A related method to the use of VSANs is zoning. *Zoning* divides a physical SAN into a number of separate subnets, which create a storage environment similar to a VLAN. The purpose of zoning an SAN is to enable load balancing and to limit access to the data resource to only selected users. Like permissions and privileges on a user account, zoning allows administrators to control who has access and what they can see in the SAN. One way to think of zoning is the hierarchical structure of a file system.

Zoning minimizes the risk of data loss, corruption, or theft. It also protects data from attacks and limits the impact of a virus or malware. Zoning does have its limitations, though. Should the number of users (VMs) increase significantly in a short period, the SAN may need restructuring or reconfiguration.

Soft and Hard Zoning

There are two types of zoning: *hard zoning* and *soft zoning*. Under soft zoning, requests to the SAN can query all the storage devices or partitions. However, only the permissioned subset of the SAN is viewable. For example, if a VM scans the content of the SAN, the only storage devices it sees are those allowed under the zoning configuration. A server addressing a device in the SAN directly by its address can defeat soft zoning. The hope is that if users can't see something, they won't know about it. Naïve administrators call this concept "security through obscurity," which isn't actually secure at all.

On the other hand, hard zoning blocks communications across the SAN. To accomplish this, the switches in the SAN must perform frame filtering to restrict requests from flowing to restricted zones. In more recent implementations of SAN, however, the two zoning types have essentially merged to the point that hard zoning is in most SAN switches.

Port and WWN Zoning

Zoning, whether hard or soft, can also apply to particular switch ports (connections to individual storage devices) or World Wide Names (WWNs) of the connected computers. *Port zoning* limits access to data to only designated authorized ports. *Name zoning*, the use of WWNs, restricts access by a device WWN.

Note

A WWN is a unique identifier applied in SANs to identify the devices in the storage network. Part of this identification number is an industry-standard company ID, called an OUI, which strangely enough stands for "company ID." The remainder of the "name" is a serial number that the manufacturer assigns. A WWN is similar in concept to a MAC address. An example of a WWN is 10:00:00:60:69:00:23:74, in which the "006069" is the OUI for Brocade Communications.

In a zoning implementation, a *zoneset* (or zoning configuration file) contains the configuration of each separate zone. The zoneset can contain any type of zone employed, including name zones, port zones, or zones that combine names and ports called *hybrid zones*. Only one zoneset can be active in the SAN at a time.

Snapshots, Clones, and Backups

In a virtual environment, snapshots and clones are completely different objects, despite the fact that they sound similar. A *snapshot* is essentially a backup of a VM that saves a particular configuration or VM state. On the other hand, a *clone* is a working copy of a VM that is ready immediately for use separately from its original.

Snapshots

Although often equated to a backup of a disk volume, virtual disk, or data object, a snapshot captures only the state of a data set or a system at a specific point in time, much like a camera captures only the image of a person or thing at one moment. The purpose of a snapshot isn't to replace a full backup. However, on a running system that may have a high number of modifications to the data, periodic snapshots continuously create recovery points for the system if restoration becomes necessary. A full backup can take quite a bit of time to complete and, if the system is running, miss capturing changes to some data before it completes.

Backups and the time they take may not be an issue on low-availability systems or systems with regular operating periods that include blocks of downtime. However, on high-availability systems that operate 24/7 with little scheduled downtime, unless the data storage is disabled for write actions, a backup may not be the best solution during the processing day.

Snapshots are read-only copies of a data set captured for a short period. Because they capture data in a read-only operation, running applications are able to continue to read, write, or remove data from the data set. There are basically three types of snapshots: pointer-snapshots, read-only snapshots, and read-write snapshots.

Pointer-snapshots start with a full copy of the data set and then capture only changes to the data after that, using pointers to reference the data changes to the initial snapshot. *Read-only snapshots* use an exception table to track changed data blocks. A *read-write snapshot*, also called a *branching snapshot*, is the snapshot type used in most virtualized environments. Read/write snapshots work much like read-only snapshots, except that when a snapshot includes a data block, it's noted in the exception table, and unless the data block changes, it isn't included in future snapshots.

Cloning

A clone is just what it sounds like: a copy of an existing VM. When a copy is made of a VM, the copy is the clone, and the original is the parent of the clone. Although this relationship exists after cloning, the clone is a distinctly separate VM. However, the clone and its parent may share some resources, such as virtual disks. The relationship between the clone and the parent is in name and initial configuration only. Changes made to the parent after cloning do not affect the clone and vice versa, and the logical and physical addresses of the parent and the clone are different.

Creating a VM clone can save the time it would take to install and configure a guest operating system and its applications. A clone of a working VM may have all but a few slight changes to quickly launch a new VM.

There are two basic types of clones: full clone and linked clone. A *full clone* is a complete and independent copy of a VM that shares nothing with its parent after its creation. Another distinction between a full clone and a linked clone is that full clones do not have access to any snapshots of the parent created before the cloning. A *linked clone* is a copy of a VM parent that shares virtual disks with the parent, which allows several VMs to use the same software configuration.

Backups

A backup of a system is essentially a copy of the system created for archival and recovery purposes. Computer systems are electrical appliances, and on occasion they fail or their power source fails. In addition, Mother Nature has a way to render electrical devices useless quite often. For these reasons and several others, creating a backup of a computer system is a best practice, but it is also downright insane not to do so. In general, there are two types of backups: image based and file based.

IMAGE-BASED BACKUPS

An *image-based backup* captures the entirety of a computer or VM, including its operating system, applications, and all associated data. Image-based backups consist of one large file (image). An image-based backup is a form of snapshot, which means that it captures everything, including deleted files and unused disk blocks. Newer versions of image-based backup software provide data reduction techniques and encryption.

FILE-BASED BACKUPS

A file backup copies all or some of a data store to create insurance against data loss or corruption. File backups can be a copy of a single data block or an image of the entire data store. There are four basic types of file backups:

> **Full backup:** A full backup is essentially the same as an image-based backup in that it captures the entire data store. This type of backup provides the capability for a complete restore (called bare metal restore) back to the time of the full backup. In this regard, a full backup establishes a baseline for the other forms of backups. However, as you may guess, a full backup can take a long time to create.

> ➤ **Differential backup:** A differential backup captures the data that changed since the last full backup. As its name implies, this type of backup uses the last full backup as a reference point and captures only data that changed since the reference point. Differential backups can be fast to create, but as the time since the last full backup grows, so will the time required to create a differential backup.

> ➤ **Incremental backup:** An incremental backup captures only data that changed since the last backup of any kind. In most uses, an incremental backup is taken at least daily, and often more frequently. A full backup establishes a set reference point, and an incremental backup taken periodically provides the capability to restore a system to its image as of the last incremental backup. Because it captures only the data that changed, an incremental backup is much faster to create than a full backup.

> ➤ **Reverse delta backup:** A reverse delta backup combines the techniques of other backup types to maintain an up-to-date mirror image of data and the necessary differences to move back to a previous state. A reverse delta backup starts with a full backup. It then continuously synchronizes the full backup with the live data and records the data needed to restore the data to a previous version. This type of backup is best suited for large data stores that change slowly.

Chapter Summary

> ➤ The three steps to the creation and implementation of a virtualized system are planning, deploying, and managing.

> ➤ The implementation plan for a virtualized environment should address the installation phases: configuration, security, monitoring, maintaining, and ongoing activities like backup and restore.

> ➤ The technology plan must identify the appropriate base for computing, memory, and storage capacities. Technical planning includes physical planning.

> ➤ Thoroughly assessing current operations is a critical step. Performance metrics should reflect resource demands during key periods. The assessment should look at the applications planned to run in the virtualized environment.

> ➤ The difference between a physical network and a virtual network is that a virtual network consists of virtual devices, including vNICs, vswitches, vrouters, and virtual firewalls. Virtual networks implement VLANs, VPNs, or VPLS.

> ➤ vNICs are assigned MAC addresses. A vNIC connection to a pNIC creates an Ethernet bridge.

> ➤ vswitches are software devices that provide logical connections for vNICs. Vswitches provide switching and forwarding for a virtual network, including Layer 2 forwarding, VLAN tagging, segmentation offloading, and security.

> ➤ A VM is a computer emulation under the control of the hypervisor or VMM. VMs are system VMs or process VMs.

➤ A VM template represents a standard configuration model for new VMs.

➤ A vdisk is a logical disk storage device that provides data I/O support for systems or applications running in a VM or in native mode on a host computer.

➤ The use of the VHD file format creates a platform-independent environment. VHD files use the following file formats: differencing hard disk, dynamic hard disk, fixed hard disk, and linked hard disk.

➤ A VSAN is a logical partition in a physical SAN. VSANs are most common in cloud and virtualized environments.

➤ Zoning divides a physical SAN into a number of separate subnets. Zoning limits access to data resources to specific users or applications. There are two types of zoning: hard zoning and soft zoning. Port zoning limits access to authorized ports. Name zoning restricts access by device WWN.

➤ An image-based backup captures the entirety of a computer or VM, including its operating system, applications, and all associated data. There are four basic types of file backups: full, differential, incremental, and reverse delta.

Key Terms

Branching snapshot

Clone

Differencing hard disk

Differential backup

Dynamic hard disk

Dynamic Host Configuration Protocol (DHCP)

External switch tagging (EST)

Fixed hard disk

Full backup

Full clone

Generic segmentation offloads (GSO)

Hard zoning

Host bus adapter (HBA)

Hybrid zones

Hypervisor

Image-based backup

Incremental backup

Large receive offload (LRO)

Large segment offloading (LSO)

Layer 2 forwarding

Linked clone

Linked hard disk

Media Access Control (MAC)

Multiprotocol Label Switching (MPLS)

Name zoning

Network address translation (NAT)

Pass-through mode

Pointer-snapshot

Port zoning

Process VM

Read-only snapshot

Read-write snapshot

Redundant Array of Independent Disks (RAID)

Reverse delta backup

Serial Advanced Technology Attachment (SATA)

Serial Attached SCSI (SAS)

Snapshot

Soft zoning

Solid state drive (SSD)

System VM

TCP segmentation offloading (TSO)

Virtual disk (vdisk)

Virtual firewalls

Virtual guest tagging (VGT)

Virtual hard disk (VHD)

Virtual local area networks (VLANs)

Virtual machine (VM)

Virtual machine manager (VMM)

Virtual network interface cards (vNICs)

Virtual private LAN services (VPLS)

Virtual private networks (VPNs)

> Virtual routers (vrouters)
>
> Virtual storage area network (VSAN)
>
> Virtual switch tagging (VST)
>
> Virtual switches (vswitches)
>
> VLAN tagging
>
> VM template
>
> Witness
>
> Zoneset
>
> Zoning

Review Questions

1. True or False? When assessing the performance of an existing system, the metrics developed should reflect resource demands during key processing periods of the organization.

2. A(n) _____ consists of virtual devices.

3. What network-level address is assigned to a vNIC?

    a. WWN

    b. MAC

    c. IP

    d. pNIC

4. True or False? A clone and a snapshot are essentially the same thing.

5. _____ are software devices that provide logical connections for vNICs to the virtual network.

6. A trunk line carries traffic from more than one virtual network element. What is added to frames to identify the source VLAN of the frame?

    a. VM tagging

    b. VLAN tagging

    c. vswitch ID

    d. WWN

7. True or False? A process VM is limited to only the resources defined in its configuration.

8. A(n) _____ is a preconfigured baseline that contains a standard model configuration with which you can create new VMs.

9. What is the file format associated with vdisks?

    a. NTFS

    b. NFS

    c. VHS

    d. VHD

10. True or False? Virtualizing a physical disk breaks it into extents, which can span two or more physical disk drives.

11. Which vdisk file format method uses a parent image for original data content and a child image for any changes made to the data?

    a. Differencing hard disk

    b. Dynamic hard disk

    c. Fixed hard disk

    d. Linked hard disk

12. A(n) _____ is a logical partition created within a physical storage area network.

13. True or False? A VSAN is a collection of specific ports on SAN switches.

14. The purpose of _____ an SAN is to limit access to data resources to only selected authorized users.

15. What type of data backup captures only the data that has changed since the last full backup?

    a. Differential

    b. Incremental

    c. Reverse delta

    d. Periodic

Answers to Review Questions

1. True

2. virtual network

3. b

4. False

5. Vswitches or virtual switches

6. b

7. True

8. VM template

9. d

10. True

11. a

12. vdisk or virtual disk

13. True

14. zoning

15. a

CHAPTER 7

Virtual Resource Migration

After reading this chapter and completing the exercises, you will be able to:

- Describe the general requirements for physical to virtual resource migration
- Discuss the processes and tools used to migrate physical and virtual systems
- List the steps performed in a variety of resource migration scenarios
- Explain the use of maintenance mode in a virtual environment

As virtualized environments continue to justify themselves to organizations and especially their data center managers, at some point nearly all need to migrate their physical environments to a virtual one (physical to virtual, or P2V). This chapter introduces you to the steps involved with this migration and the best practices you should incorporate. In addition, you learn about the justifications for making the migration. Finally, you learn about migrations from virtual to virtual (V2V) and virtual to physical (V2P).

Establish System Requirements

In Chapter 11, you learn about the planning needed for moving to a virtualized environment and the various systems you should include in that planning. However, a plan alone is typically not enough to sell the organization's decision-makers on the need for virtualizing your data center, your service center, and their systems.

Benefits of Virtualization

In a recent study by Forrester Research, Inc. for VMware, data center managers of companies that have fewer than 1,000 employees, who either have migrated from a physical computing environment to a virtualized computing environment or are planning to make this migration in the near term, identified areas of benefit they expect to result from the migration. The study identified six benefit areas:

> **Server utilization**: 72 percent expect to improve their server utilization.

> **Servers**: 52 percent expect to reduce the number of servers in use or be able to avoid or reduce future server acquisitions.

> **Security**: 48 percent expect increased data and system security.

> **System availability**: 42 percent expect to increase their system availability and uptime.

> **Data backup**: 40 percent expect to realize more efficient and effective data backup and data integrity.

> **Management**: 40 percent expect to improve their server and application management.

However, migrating to virtualization just because it's the latest thing isn't a real justification. Moving from a physical environment to a virtualized environment must promise actual savings in costs, efficiencies, effectiveness, and lost time. For some companies, the decision to make the migration to virtualization may come at a "buy point," at which hardware or software is at end-of-life. It may be time for a major operating system upgrade, or the existing environment may not be providing the service levels the organization or its customers expect.

Whatever is forcing the decision to migrate to a virtualized environment, the new system must adequately satisfy the requirements established by the shortcomings of the old system. The new environment must also provide for growth, flexibility, and any other future organizational plans.

Remember that the objective of a migration to a virtualized environment has many benefits, not just the benefit depicted in Figure 7-1. Although the reduction of physical servers in use is perhaps the baseline objective, there are other business reasons. (See "Organizational Justification" later in this chapter.)

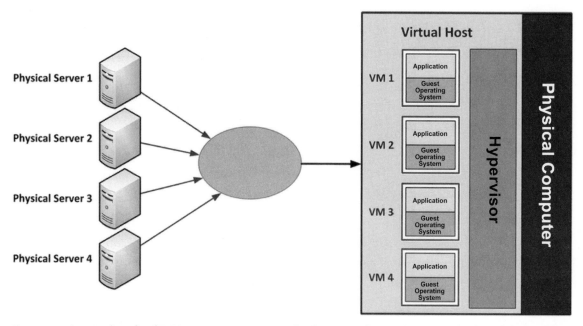

Figure 7-1 A major benefit of P2V migration is a potential reduction in the number of physical servers in the system.
© 2015 Cengage Learning®.

Virtualization Disadvantages

In spite of all of its hype, there can be disadvantages to migrating to a virtualized environment. Organizations can overlook the disadvantages of virtualization due to misconceptions that marketing does nothing to dispel. The single biggest misconception is that applications that run in a physical environment require fewer resources in the virtualized environment. In fact, virtualization typically adds overhead to the computing environment.

Applications that run in the physical environment use more resources and don't run more efficiently in a virtualized environment. Unless the virtualization migration also includes the installation of newer and faster computers, existing applications may run slower. Installing virtualization on existing hardware may negate some of the benefit expected from the migration. Even on new hardware, assigning too many resources to mission-critical applications may affect other applications and services negatively.

Resource Planning

The key to a successful migration of *physical-to-virtual (P2V)* systems has three major steps: plan, plan, and plan. Before the migration begins, it's best to have a solid inventory of the equipment, software, and capacities of the existing environment. With that knowledge, planning for the resource requirements of the virtual system shouldn't result in any surprises when you turn on the virtualized environment.

ORGANIZATIONAL JUSTIFICATION

Information technology professionals have a much clearer vision of the benefits of migrating from P2V. However, senior management and key decision-makers may not. To justify the expense of the migration, it's important to address how the migration benefits the organization.

Before any serious resource planning, in terms of hardware and software needed to accomplish the migration, there are three specific areas to identify:

> **Key business drivers**: In the past, the business drivers for computing systems focused on the ability to retrieve data, print data, and analyze data. As companies move to virtualized environments, the emerging key business drivers are resiliency, high availability, data integrity, disaster recovery, and security.

> **Risk reduction**: The virtualized environment must reduce the overall risk in business operations. Most of this reduction comes from data virtualization and the high availability of data and information.

> **Return on investment (ROI)**: At what point will the investment in the P2V migration show payback? ROI usually comes from savings and cost avoidance, but this could also include operational savings in the organization as well as savings from the information technology (IT) function.

ESTIMATE RESOURCE REQUIREMENTS

After completing a resource and equipment inventory, the next step is to estimate the resources (hardware and software) you need in the virtual environment. Estimating the resources required in the virtualized environment requires a number of related considerations. Some of the most important considerations follow:

> **Application requirements**: Identify for each of the applications that are to run in the virtualized environment the amount of central processing unit (CPU), memory, and storage utilization or space, and apply this to the virtual resources planned.

> **Load scheduling**: Analyze historical data for CPU, memory, network, storage utilization, and demand during peak load periods. This information can help in the scheduling of virtual machines (VMs) between host servers.

> **Resource oversubscription**: Resources in a virtualized environment can be oversubscribed, carefully. Consider the allocations, reservations, and limits for all applications, with mission-critical applications having access to all the resources they require. Also, avoid granting all of a resource to a single VM.

> **Disk I/O**: Resource sharing is a hallmark of virtualized systems. Ensure that sufficient disk input/output (I/O) capacity is available.

The bottom line on the planning of resources for a virtualized environment is that resources must be available when required. Some applications, such as management and monitoring software, often require little memory and disk space, but they have high network interactions. Similarly, an application may require a large memory allocation but little in the way of disk I/O.

AUTOMATED RESOURCE PLANNING TOOLS

A variety of semiautomated and fully automated software tools are available to assist in the *capacity planning* or performing of actual P2V migrations. Many of these tools are vendor specific, meaning they work with one or more of the specific virtualization software systems.

P2V Capacity Planners

The following systems perform P2V capacity and systems planning to assist in the planning of a P2V migration (listed alphabetically with no preference implied):

> **P2V Planner, by 5nine Software, Inc.:** A free version of this tool is available for download (www.5nine.com/p2vhyper-v-vmware-free.aspx), but it excludes the workload and cost optimization features of the full version.

> **SysTrack Virtual Machine Planner, by Lakeside Software, Inc.:** This tool covers the full spectrum of planning needs involved in adoption of desktop virtualization. Information on this tool is available at www.lakesidesoftware.com/systrack_vmp.aspx.

> **Microsoft Assessment and Planning (MAP) Toolkit, by Microsoft Corporation:** This free tool performs a pre-P2V assessment of a physical system in preparation for a migration to a virtual environment. It is available at http://technet.microsoft.com/en-us/solutionaccelerators/dd537566.aspx. Figure 7-2 shows its main page.

> **VMTurbo Operations Manager 3.1, by VMTurbo, Inc.:** This tool provides for the generation of what-if scenarios that project system requirements, allocate resources, and simulate the impact of adding or removing resources. Information about this tool is available at www.vmturbo.com/p2v-planning-no-crystal-ball-required/.

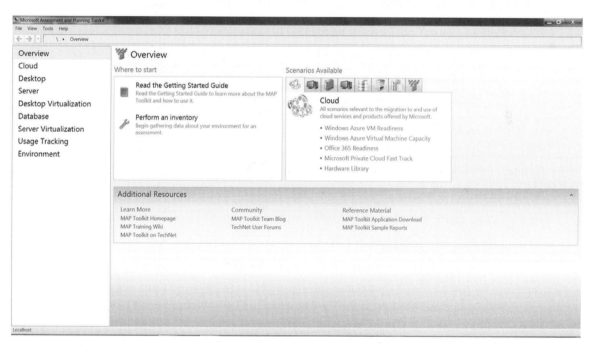

Figure 7-2 The start-up page of the Microsoft Assessment and Planning Tool.
Used with permission from Microsoft.

Physical and Virtual Migration

Migrations from P2V are becoming quite common for legacy systems moving to virtualized environments as data centers and service providers shift to virtualization for cost, flexibility, scalability, and security reasons. However, sometimes a data or service center may move from one virtualization system to another using a *virtual-to-virtual (V2V)* system, and, although rare, move back from a virtualized environment to a physical one using a *virtual-to-physical (V2P)* tool. The following sections discuss the software, tools, and utilities available to perform any of these three migrations.

Note

Migration of a physical environment to a virtual environment or the reverse is typically specific to the actual systems you are migrating. In the sections that follow, the descriptions and action steps are generic and include suggested methods to go about the migration, even to the point of mentioning specific tools you can use. However, there are likely more steps necessary to accomplish a complete migration and realize the successful result you're looking for.

P2V Migration Systems

After you have developed a clear plan of exactly what you want to migrate from its existing, physical environment into the new virtual environment, you can use various software tools to accomplish the conversion. The tool you use depends on the particular characteristics of both the existing and future systems. Carefully study the tools before choosing one, and ensure that it will accomplish the migration in the most error-free, immediately usable way.

The following tools perform all or part of a P2V migration:

> **System Center Virtual Machine Manager (SCVMM), by Microsoft Corporation**: This tool facilitates P2V migrations to Hyper-V. Information on this tool is available at www.microsoft.com/en-us/download/details.aspx?id=10712.

> **PlateSpin Migrate, by NetIQ Corporation**: This tool is a physical/virtual conversion tool that claims to be the "most efficient P2V" tool. Information on this system is available at www.netiq.com/products/migrate/.

> **Ultimate P2V, by Qui Hong, Chris Huss, and Mike Laverick**: This open source tool is among the few that really support P2V migrations on Linux equipment. For information on this tool, visit http://searchvmware.techtarget.com/tip/Ultimate-P2V.

> **Cloud & VM Optimized Edition, by SanXfer**: This tool allows for the upgrade of server hardware, the migration of existing local booting systems into a storage area network (SAN), and the conversion between physical and virtual servers. More information is available on this tool at http://sanxfer.com/sanxfer-cloud-and-vm-optimized-edition/.

> **Double-Take MOVE, by Vision Solutions, Inc.**: This tool provides for the migration of physical, virtual, and cloud server workloads with real-time replication. Information on this tool is available at www.visionsolutions.com/Products/DT-Move.aspx.

> **VMware vCenter Converter Standalone, by VMware, Inc.**: This tool is limited to converting P2V in a VMware environment. To read more about and download this tool, visit https://my.vmware.com/web/vmware/evalcenter?p=converter.

You can perform a P2V migration (or any other form of migration) either online or offline. Although either accomplishes the migration objectives, some migration software limits the conversion to offline only. Should it be necessary, during an online migration, the server(s) is still available for use. Table 7-1 lists the advantages and disadvantages of both online and offline migrations.

Table 7-1 Online and Offline P2V Migrations

Characteristic	Online P2V	Offline P2V
Source computer availability	The source computer is available for normal operations during the migration.	The source computer is offline and unavailable for normal operations during the migration.
Process	The virtual machine manager (VMM) copies local file system volumes and data and consistently creates a read-only snapshot while the server continues to service user requests. The VMM uses the snapshot to create a VHD.	The VMM clones the volume to a VHD and restarts the source computer on its original operating system.
Compatibility	Online P2V is the default for the operating systems on most physical computers.	Offline P2V is the only option for Windows Server migrations and the recommended method for converting domain controllers and Active Directory services.
Advantages	The source computer is available throughout the conversion.	Offline P2V can be more reliable, especially for ensuring data consistency. It is the only option for some P2V migration tools.

© 2015 Cengage Learning®.

WINDOWS P2V MIGRATION

Data centers running Windows Server versions 2008 Release 2 (R2) and later have use of the *System Center Virtual Machine Manager (SCVMM)*, which is part of the Microsoft System Center package of reporting and management tools. SCVMM, in conjunction with other Microsoft utilities, like the Microsoft Operations Manager (MOM) and the Microsoft System Management Server (MSMS), provides for fast P2V migration and balancing of workloads across a virtual system. The balancing of applications and services in the virtual environment uses historical performance data for each application along with the business rules defined to the system.

SCVMM performs P2V migration in either online or offline modes. In the online P2V mode, SCVMM first creates a *volume shadow service (VSS)* snapshot of the connected storage devices, a process that is similar to most backup systems for Windows systems. However, running in the online mode can also have its drawbacks. Several of Microsoft's services and applications, such as SQL Server, Exchange Service, and its domain controllers, perform high-speed disk I/O, which can mean that by the time a snapshot of the storage areas completes, some of the data may have changed. Although the promise of an online migration is that the systems remain available, it's a better idea to stop these applications to maintain data integrity.

Volume Shadow Service (VSS)

VSS, which can also refer to *volume snapshot service (VSS)*, is part of the Windows operating systems and requires NTFS file systems. VSS performs manual or automatic *snapshots* (backups) at the block level of specific data volumes based on set time points over specified interval-defined data storage. VSS writes snapshots to remote (removable or network-attached) storage or on a local device.

VSS performs a read-only copy of the data on a particular data volume, which avoids two common backup problems: file locks and data changing during the copy function. Because VSS opens data volumes and entities in read-only mode, it bypasses any locks on the entities. Data snapshots create restoration points and provide consistent backups taken on equal intervals.

Domain Controller P2V Issues

Microsoft systems include the technology of domain controllers that need special handling compared to most applications, services, and data structures in a P2V migration. The worst that can happen is that the domain controllers end up useless, not to mention the possible disruption to production processing they may cause.

A key concept in Windows networking is the domain. Essentially, a *domain* is like a super-group, which consists of a set of user accounts and host accounts grouped so that administrators can manage them as a single entity. The *domain controller (DC)* facilitates the central management of the domains (and operates the Active Directory). The DC is a server that processes authentication requests (such as login and permissions, privileges, and rights checking) from Windows clients. However, the DC doesn't provide for authorization checking; the Windows Server Authorization Manager (AzMan) manages authorization. The DC concept allows users to access connected network resources through a single set of login credentials.

Perhaps the biggest single issue with migrating DCs is that if the migration clones or copies a DC, the other DCs will know that it has and will not communicate with it to keep it up to date with any changes to the domain accounts. As DCs update one another with account changes, the *update sequence number (USN)*, which is a sequential count that indicates how up to date the DC is, increments for each updated DC. A DC that detects a problem with its USN, compared to other DCs, isolates itself to avoid replicating bad information to other DCs, causing it to become uncoordinated with the system. Another danger is that if too many of the network DCs become uncoordinated, the system may perform a *USN rollback* and really clobber the system.

The key to a successful P2V migration that includes existing DCs is to remember that Microsoft systems don't support DC cloning. VMware doesn't either, for that matter. Using SCVMM, the safest way to migrate a DC in a P2V is to run the migration on the physical server on which a DC is running. The DC converts to a *virtual DC (VDC)*. Then power off the migrated physical server and connect the VDC to the network. The network clients shouldn't see any difference in the authentication function.

LINUX/UNIX P2V MIGRATION

Some of the migration tools listed earlier (see "P2V Migration Systems") can work for P2V migrations on Linux and UNIX servers. However, some may perform only parts of the migration, with other tools required to complete the entire conversion. Linux and UNIX systems typically have an embedded or add-in utility you can use for P2V migrations. For example, Red Hat Linux uses the virt-v2v utility and VMTurbo, VMware's vCenter Converter, or you can use tools like the Linux *disk-to-disk (dd)* command or the Windows command *VHDTool* to convert data volumes to a virtual environment.

Using the virt-v2v tool as an example, the first step in migrating a physical machine to a virtual machine is to install virt-v2v and create boot media to boot up the P2V client and begin the migration of the physical machine. Unfortunately, if the conversion includes large physical disks, the conversion process using this tool may take a long time to complete. Figure 7-3 shows the status display of the virt-v2v performing a P2V migration.

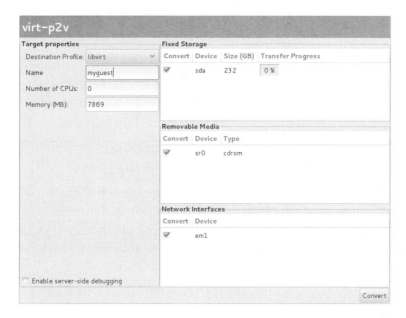

Figure 7-3 The Red Hat virt-v2v during a P2V migration.
Source: Red Hat®, Inc.

V2V Migration

An organization may have any number of reasons for migrating an existing virtual environment to another virtual environment. It may want to move from VMware (or another virtualization software) to Hyper-V (or another virtualization software). The organization may want to move from one version of virtualization software to another, slightly incompatible version on the same system. Or, the organization may want to upgrade its physical hardware significantly. Any of these reasons and several others can lead to a V2V migration.

V2V is the migration of the operating system, application software, and data storage of one VM, vdisk, or disk volume to another VM, vdisk, or disk volume. A V2V target can be a single computer, or it may be several computers. For the most part, V2V copies and restores files, programs, and operating system elements. In fact, a common use of V2V tools is to perform system backup and restore. The majority of V2V tools are part of the VMM or hypervisor of a virtualization system.

Typically, to move a VM to another computer, you only have to move its .VMDK (VMware) or ..VHD (Hyper-V) files to a computer running the virtual server software. In deference to other forms of online migrations, you must shut down a migrating VM before copying it. V2V copies the complete image of a VM and transfers it to another VM (or physical computer).

Similar to the other migration methods, software tools are available to facilitate a V2V migration. The two more popular V2V packages (both of which are free downloads) follow:

> **V2V Easy Converter, by 5nine Software, Inc.:** This tool performs conversion of selected VMware VMs to Windows Hyper-V VMs. More information is available on this tool at www.5nine.com/vmware-hyper-v-v2v-conversion-free.aspx.

> **StarWind V2V Converter, by Starwind Software, Inc.:** This tool converts VMDK to VHD files and converts VHD to VMDK and IMG files. For more information on this tool, visit www.starwindsoftware.com/converter.

V2P Migration

For whatever reason, if a decision has been made to migrate a virtual environment to a physical (nonvirtual) environment, it may not be as "easy" as a P2V migration. In fact, the easiest way to migrate from a virtual system to a physical system is to create the physical servers using "bare metal" installation or configuration. A *bare metal* installation is one in which you create a server by installing a server image (restore) on a blank computer or build it up with its operating system, networking, and major applications.

Your choice of V2P method depends on a few things, such as the virtual system, the host operating system, the file formats in use, and the effort you want to put into this project. In the sections that follow, you learn the basic steps involved for a V2P migration on Windows and Linux systems. You should notice that in terms of the process steps, there isn't that much difference.

Windows V2P Migration

For the most part, V2P migrations use common disk imaging and backup and restore tools and processes that you may use even on your virtualized system. On a Windows system, such as a Hyper-V environment running on Windows Server 2012, a V2P migration consists of only two major steps: creating images of the VMs and system disk, and restoring the captured images onto a physical disk. Another not-so-major step that is still important, if needed, is to configure hardware drivers should the physical environment need them.

V2P Software

Although the two major steps mentioned in the preceding section sound simple enough, they are not. Trying to convert a virtual system to a physical system and sizing the storage correctly, managing application licenses, and avoiding the bottlenecks you were hoping to eliminate by going virtual can be tedious and frustrating. Fortunately, there are software packages available to ease the difficulty and complexity of this task.

The software most often cited as the one to use for not only V2P, but also backup, restoration, disk management, and other system management and monitoring functions, is the Acronis Backup and Recovery Virtual Edition. Figure 7-4 shows its home screen. This system provides the capabilities, among its many others, to capture VM images and restore them securely on physical machines—even bare metal restores. The Acronis tool works equally well in either virtual or physical environments. Another imaging tool used in V2P migrations is Symantec Corporation's System Recovery Virtual Edition.

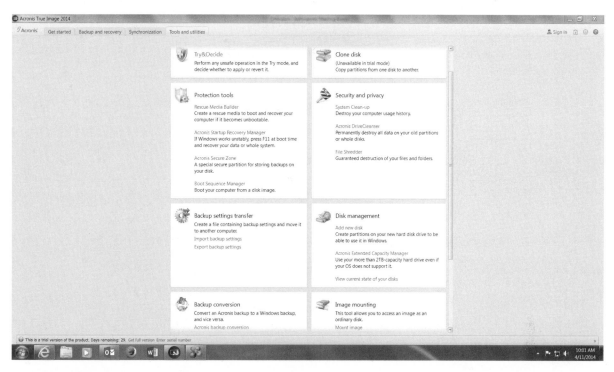

Figure 7-4 The start-up screen of the Acronis Backup and Recovery system.
Source: Acronis International GmbH.

Windows V2P Processes

A V2P migration on a Windows system, regardless of the virtualization software in use, involves several third-party software tools and utilities. These tools can help to prepare and transfer the source VM to a physical hard disk drive. In a Windows environment, the use of the Windows utility *sysprep* prepares an image for transfer to the physical machine. Once the image is ready for transfer, a disk storage tool like Symantec Ghost, Acronis True Image, or Paragon Hard Disk Manager can then transfer the disk image to the physical machine.

The recommended steps in a V2P process for a Windows system follow:

1. Locate the sysprep command in the `\Windows\System32\Sysprep` folder.

2. Run `sysprep.exe` from a command prompt, such as `sysprep.exe /oobe /generalize /shutdown`. Alternatively, choose from its start-up dialog box (see Figure 7-5) the option of Enter System Out-of-Box Experience (OOBE) in the System Cleanup Action pull-down list. Then check the Generalize check box, and choose the action you want to take after sysprep completes, choosing from Shutdown, Restart, and Quit. Click the OK button to start the image preparation.

3. Run the image transfer program you've chosen, and transfer the image file to the physical machine. Figure 7-6 shows the File Transfer Wizard of the Paragon Hard Disk Manager software.

4. Install or ensure that the device drivers are in place on the physical computer.

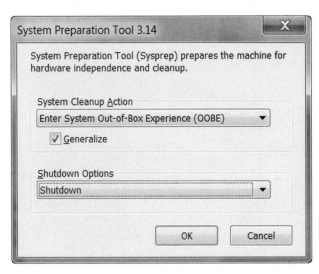

Figure 7-5 The start-up dialog box of the sysprep command.
Used with permission from Microsoft.

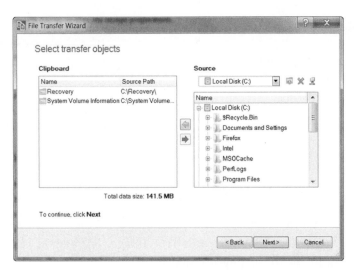

Figure 7-6 The File Transfer Wizard of the Paragon Hard Disk Manager.
Source: Paragon Technologie GmbH.

LINUX V2P MIGRATION

There are fewer options available to migrate a virtualized environment that is running Linux as its host server operating system. Chances are that, unless you are running the host operating system in a Windows environment, you are using virtualization software like VirtualBox, Red Hat Enterprise Virtualization (RHEV), or the like.

The first step in a Linux V2P is the creation of a removable disk boot media (USB device, CD-ROM, or DVD). This allows you to boot up the source machine without activating its operating system, services, and applications. One handy tool you can use to create a boot disk is *UNetbootin* from SourceForge. This tool is free and available for download. UNetbootin runs on most Linux releases, as well as on the Mac operating system and Windows. Figure 7-7 shows a screen capture of the UNetbootin start-up screen.

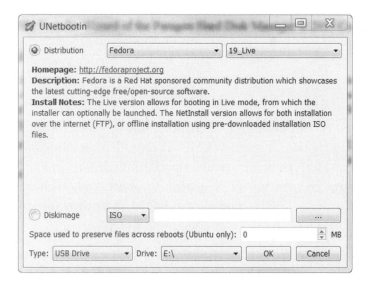

Figure 7-7 The start-up screen of the UNetbootin utility for creating boot media.
Source: Dice Holdings, Inc.

The next step in a Linux V2P migration is to convert the VM images to a raw image using a backup/restore package, like Symantec Backup Exec, and copy the raw image to the physical system using the Linux dd command. Then mount the copied image to the root file system using the *bind*, *mount*, and chroot commands, and make the necessary modifications to the initrd file.

Virtual Environment Maintenance Mode

At a variety of levels, virtual components in a virtualized environment can be idled for maintenance purposes. This includes adding or removing elements, such as VMs, virtual disks, networking devices (vswitch, vNIC), or, depending on the level of the modifications, updating or changing the host operating system. Perhaps the most common use of *maintenance mode* is when administrators place a host computer in that mode to perform hardware service, such as to add more memory, change a physical NIC, or install or replace SCSI or IDE controllers.

Maintenance Mode

Both VMware and Hyper-V provide the capability to place virtualized environment components in maintenance mode. Maintenance mode is not an automatic feature; a system administrator must invoke it. Perhaps the most common use of maintenance mode is host maintenance. When a host computer, which is a part of a virtualized environment, goes into maintenance mode, its VMs either migrate to another active host or go into a saved or idled state, for the duration of the host's maintenance mode suspension.

Migrating (*evacuating*) the VMs to another active host keeps the virtual environment running without a disruption, although it may run somewhat slower because of the reduction in computing resources. Depending on a variety of factors, not all host computers have the capability for evacuation and go into a saved (idle) state. New VMs cannot be opened on a host in a saved state.

Not all VMM or hypervisors automatically migrate evacuated VMs back to their original host. In these cases, the restoration of the virtual environment must be a manual process.

Host Migration

When a host computer is powered off or put into maintenance mode (both preferably), storage area network (SAN) and virtual storage area network (VSAN) controllers remain connected to the VMs evacuated to other hosts. This can be especially important if the host in maintenance mode is in a computer cluster connected to a VSAN. When administrators take a clustered host out of the cluster, they can configure the VSAN controller in one of three ways, depending on the duration of the host's downtime. Here are the three configuration types:

> **Ensure Accessibility**: This option, the default typically, keeps all VMs on the host accessible. This option is best when a host will be out of a cluster only temporarily.

> **Full Data Evacuation**: This option evacuates (migrates) all data to the other hosts in the cluster. However, this option is not appropriate for a host permanently removed from a cluster.

> **No Data Evacuation**: Under this option, the VSAN doesn't evacuate data from the removed host, which could mean that some VMs are inaccessible.

VM Migration

Occasionally, it can be necessary to move a running VM from one host to another. Both VMware and Microsoft have tools to facilitate this action. Microsoft's SCVMM and *Live Migration* and VMware's vSphere *vMotion* tools allow administrators to move files between hosts without scheduling downtime.

The VMware vMotion tool facilitates moving a complete running VM from one physical host to another, without the need to place either host in maintenance mode. In fact, vMotion allows the VM to retain its network addressing, identity, and links and moves the VM's active memory from one VMware vSphere host to another without interruption.

The comparable Microsoft tool, SCVMM (or just VMM), also lets you move active VMs between virtual hosts—even two hosts within the same cluster. During the transfer, VMM puts a VM in saved mode.

VMWARE VMOTION

VMware vMotion is part of the VMware vSphere hypervisor system that migrates active VMs between hosts, but the two hosts must have the same processors. This means that both the source and the receiving hosts must have processors from the same manufacturer (Intel, AMD, and so on). VMotion can migrate eight VMs at a time on an infrastructure with 10 Gbps network media.

VMware vMotion relies on three foundation methods to accomplish VM migration. The first is the ability to encapsulate the entire state of a VM into a single set of files and store them on a shared storage resource, such as Fibre Channel or Internet Small Computer System Interface (iSCSI) SAN or network attached storage (NAS). The second of the foundation technologies is the transfer of active memory and the execution state of the VM transfer on the high-speed network so that the VM can instantaneously begin running on the target machine. Finally, because the network in use by the VM is a virtual network, the VM's network ID, virtual Media Access Control (MAC) address, and links remain the same, allowing the VM to reconnect instantly to the network.

The migration of a VM under vMotion keeps the execution state, network identity, and active network connections; the result of the migration is zero downtime and no disruption to users.

MICROSOFT LIVE MIGRATION

Both the VMware vMotion discussed in the preceding section and Microsoft's Live Migration are *shared nothing (SN)* migration tools. An SN architecture in which each network, whether virtual or actual, node is completely independent. SN nodes don't "share nothing," meaning they don't share memory or disk storage.

Live Migration is a Microsoft Hyper-V feature that allows for the transparent movement of running VMs from one host to another, typically within a cluster, without losing service availability. Live Migration moves a VM over a specified network to achieve load balancing or to establish a failover node in a cluster.

Some see both vMotion and Live Migration as high-availability tools, which neither is actually. The use of these tools is proactive and doesn't require all or part of a system to go offline. *High availability*, on the other hand, is typically reactive and requires some form of downtime, even for a short time.

STORAGE MIGRATION

In general, *storage migration* refers to moving virtual data storage from one storage device or volume to another in the same file format or into a new file format on the target device. Virtual storage migration can occur online or offline. Storage migration is commonly mistaken to be the same as data migration. However, data migration is a bit more generic and includes the migration of data in nonvirtual environments.

Moving data around a virtual network can be tricky, especially if some of the data on a host computer, which belongs to one or more VMs, is in use. To this end, both VMware and Microsoft provide versions of their migration software for moving stored data. These tools are, respectively, Storage vMotion (a component of the vSphere hypervisor) and Storage Live Migration (a component of the Hyper-V VMM). These tools let you move a running VM's file system from one storage system to another without incurring downtime or service interruptions for end users.

Chapter Summary

> ➤ The single biggest misconception of virtualization is that applications require fewer resources in the virtualized environment.

> ➤ Before beginning a migration, have an inventory of the equipment, software, and capacities of the existing environment.

> ➤ Three specific areas to identify are key business drivers, risk reduction opportunities, and the desired ROI.

> ➤ Estimating resources requires considerations of application requirements, load scheduling, resource oversubscription, and disk I/O.

> ➤ Various automated software tools are available to assist in P2V migrations. A P2V migration can be either online or offline.

> ➤ Moving from one virtualization system to another uses a V2V migration.

> ➤ Moving from a virtualized environment to a physical environment uses V2P migration.

> ➤ Windows systems can use SCVMM, which provides for P2V migration and load balancing.

> ➤ VSS performs manual or automatic read-only snapshots at the block level of specific data volumes.

> ➤ Snapshots create restoration points and provide consistent backups taken on equal intervals.

> ➤ A Windows domain consists of user accounts and host accounts grouped for common administration. A DC facilitates the central management of the domains.

> ➤ V2V is the migration of the operating system, application software, and data storage of one VM to another.

> ➤ The most common use of maintenance mode is host maintenance.

> ➤ When administrators remove a clustered host from a cluster, you can place a VSAN controller in one of three configurations: Ensure Accessibility, Full Data Evacuation, or No Data Evacuation.

> ➤ Storage migration involves moving virtual data from one storage device to another using the same file format or a new file format. Virtual storage migration can occur online or offline.

Key Terms

Bare metal

Bind

Capacity planning

Disk-to-disk (dd)

Domain

Domain controller (DC)

Evacuating

High availability

Live Migration

Maintenance mode

Mount

Physical-to-virtual (P2V)

Shared nothing (SN)

Snapshot

Storage migration

Sysprep

System Center Virtual Machine Manager (SCVMM)

UNetbootin

Update sequence number (USN)

USN rollback

VHDTool

Virtual DC (VDC)

Virtual-to-physical (V2P)

Virtual-to-virtual (V2V)

Vmotion

Volume shadow service (VSS)

Volume snapshot service (VSS)

Review Questions

1. Which of the following is not a consideration when planning a migration to a virtual environment?

    a. Key business drivers

    b. Risk reduction

    c. ROI

    d. Desktop hardware replacement

2. True or False? Applications migrated to a virtual environment always require fewer resources.

3. Moving systems and data from one virtual environment to another is a _____ migration.

4. What type of migration moves a virtual environment to a physical environment?

    a. V2V

    b. P2V

    c. V2P

    d. P2P

5. True or False? A P2V migration can be performed only offline.

6. A(n) _____ creates consistent backups of data and restoration points.

7. True or False? Maintenance mode on a VM is exclusively for hardware maintenance.

8. Which of the following is not a configuration for a VSAN controller in a clustered environment?

    a. Ensure Accessibility

    b. Nothing Shared

    c. Full Data Evacuation

    d. No Data Evacuation

9. Moving virtual data from one storage device to another is _____.

10. True or False? The Windows tool sysprep creates an image for a P2V migration.

11. What type of installation creates a server by installing a system image on a clean storage device?

    a. Cold metal

    b. Bare metal

    c. Hard metal

    d. Warm swap

12. What Linux utility can perform a P2V migration?

    a. Hyper-V Live Migration

    b. virt-v2v

    c. UNetbootin

    d. Mount

13. In a Windows environment, a(n) _____ facilitates the management of Active Directory and the system domains.

14. True or False? RHEV is a Linux virtual environment system.

15. .VMDK files are associated with _____ virtualization software.

Answers to Review Questions

1. d
2. False
3. V2V
4. c
5. False
6. snapshot
7. False
8. b
9. storage migration
10. False
11. b
12. b
13. domain controller
14. True
15. VMware

CHAPTER 8

Storage Technologies

After reading this chapter and completing the exercises, you will be able to:

- Describe the architecture and functions of NAS, DAS, and SAN

- Explain the different topologies and communication techniques used in storage technologies

Firt, don't confuse the use of the phrase "data storage technology" with the 1990s digital video tape system by the same name. What you'll learn in this chapter, which is an extension of what you learned in Chapter 3, is about the three major data storage technologies that attach to networks.

In the context of cloud computing, storage networking can provide a centrally located repository for data that is available to multiple users over high-speed network connections. Storage networks, whether for an enterprise, a number of service subscribers, or a private individual backing up her home computer, provide reliability, availability, and accessibility at all levels. Network attached storage is often what people are referring to when they say storage networking. However, as you will learn in this chapter, there's more to storage networking than that.

Network Storage

As stated earlier, the three primary technologies for attaching independent data storage to a network are network attached storage (NAS), direct attached storage (DAS), and storage area networks (SANs). Each of these storage technologies is distinct in its architecture and operation. The sections that follow explain their differences.

Network Attached Storage (NAS)

Network attached storage (NAS) (pronounced as "nazz") is essentially a dedicated file server that provides file sharing services. Figure 8-1 shows the basic makeup of a NAS system.

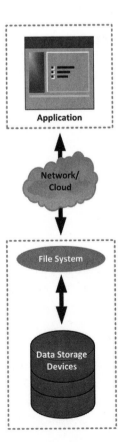

Figure 8-1 In a NAS structure, the application or process runs independent of the storage system.
© 2015 Cengage Learning®.

As Figure 8-1 depicts, when an application or process, one entity, needs data from the data and file storage system, a second entity, it makes its request via the network. The NAS server accesses the storage device and responds with the requested data. NAS is actually just an expanded version of a computer with an external storage device. However, instead of accessing the device through a universal serial bus (USB) port, data access is over the network. A NAS system attached to a LAN allows multiple nodes to share a single data storage entity.

NAS DEVICES

A NAS device, which is usually a network file server combined with hot swappable data storage units (see Figure 8-2), can be a standard computer with an array of disk drives attached. The storage devices are separate from the NAS server, so adding or swapping out the disk storage units doesn't require taking down the network or, in most cases, the NAS server. The NAS server performs all the processing to retrieve the requested data, which the requesting application receives via the network. A NAS system benefits the network by relieving the other servers from data storage management and providing the network nodes with faster data transfer rates and generally higher availability.

The QNAP, Inc. NAS system shown in Figure 8-2 is an example of a NAS network appliance. Typically, the hard drive units in a system like this are in a form of redundant storage, such as a Redundant Array of Independent Disks (RAID) system (more on RAID in Chapter 9). Over a network, data transfers between a node and the NAS system commonly use network file sharing protocols like the Network File System (NFS), the Server Message Block/Common Internet File System (SMB/CIFS), and, on Apple gear, the Apple Filing Protocol (AFP).

Figure 8-2 A self-contained NAS unit with disk storage inserts.
© 2014 QNAP Systems, Inc.

NAS FILE ACCESS

Of the file sharing protocols listed in the preceding section, NFS and CIFS are the two that are most commonly used.

Network File System (NFS)

Originally developed to provide file sharing services for thin clients and diskless workstations, NFS provides access to shared file systems over a network. If a network includes an NAS system, a network node can mount a particular file system using NFS. Although the NAS and the file system are remote, NFS creates the illusion that the disk storage is local.

NFS runs on UNIX and Linux operating systems as a client/server application. It provides users with the capability of viewing, modifying, and writing data files on remote devices or a local hard disk drive completely transparent to the user. The user or application only needs to "mount" the applicable disk partition before it becomes accessible. On a UNIX/Linux system, the term *mount* refers to associating the disk partition with a directory name for addressability and navigation purposes.

Common Internet File System (CIFS)

Windows systems most commonly use CIFS for accessing data from NAS. Like NFS, CIFS is a client/server application that requests data services from a NAS server. CIFS is an enhanced open source version of the SMB protocol, but it is the native file-sharing protocol in Windows systems.

Computers (nodes and servers) running CIFS communicate using a set of message codes, which are in three primary groups:

- ➤ **Connection**: These message codes start or end a connection to a shared resource controlled by a server.

- ➤ **Namespace and file manipulation**: These message codes request access to data files at the server and to view, modify, and write files to the storage media.

- ➤ **Printer**: These message codes add data to a network print queue on a server or to request printer or print queue status information.

CIFS also provides a number of processing features, including these:

- ➤ **Data integrity**: Multiple nodes can access or update files without worry of conflicts because of CIFS's file sharing and file locking features. If one node is updating a file, CIFS blocks all other requests until the update action completes.

- ➤ **Speed optimization**: Optimized to run over dial-up connections as well as high-speed media, such as fiber optics and category copper wire, CIFS also performs well over the Internet.

- ➤ **Security**: Data transfers from or to a CIFS server can be either anonymous or an authenticated and secure access to a named data file or a directory.

- ➤ **Flexible file names:** A file name can use any character set (Unicode), meaning not just English. CIFS also supports Uniform Naming Convention (UNC) file names.

Direct Attached Storage (DAS)

It is highly probable that you have been using direct attached storage (DAS) for at least a few years. DAS is one or more unshared storage devices attached to a single computer, such as the hard disk inside your PC system unit. That's right. The hard disk inside your computer is an example of DAS.

However, in a network, the hard disks inside each network node, while locally DAS, are not an example of network DAS. DAS on a network connects directly to a server, such as a database or file server (server attached storage). Figure 8-3 illustrates this relationship. DAS provides users with a higher level of performance over NAS. A DAS file server reads and writes to and from directly attached storage devices using Small Computer System Interface (SCSI), Serial Advanced Technology Attachment (SATA), or Serial Attached SCSI (SAS) interfaces, as opposed to interacting with remote storage devices via a network.

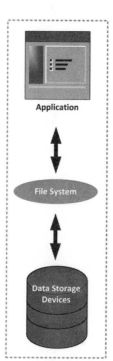

Figure 8-3 A DAS system forms a single data storage entity with a host computer.
© 2015 Cengage Learning®.

The downside to DAS is that it is a directly attached system, meaning that two or more clients or servers cannot directly access it and must interact with an intermediary service. And, unlike NAS and, as you'll see in the next section, SAN, DAS doesn't support a failover function to activate should the file server, to which it's attached, fail. In spite of its limitations, DAS is common in virtualized environments.

Storage Area Network (SAN)

The purpose of a storage area network (SAN) is to transfer block data between computers and shared storage devices. In a DAS environment, there is a cable or other connector between the storage devices and a server or host to create the direct connection. An SAN replaces that cable or connector with a network structure dedicated to data storage and retrieval shared among network storage devices (or *network shares*).

SAN NETWORKING

As shown in Figure 8-4, an SAN provides data access and retrieval support to virtually any client on a network. Although pictured otherwise, the network clients could interact directly with the SAN and not pass through specialized servers. Because of its capability to connect and interact with a network using switches, an SAN creates an any-to-any (meaning no-limit to no-limit) network connection. Because of its network capabilities, you can disperse an SAN's storage elements geographically. The storage devices could be remote, local, or in a LAN, WAN, or the cloud.

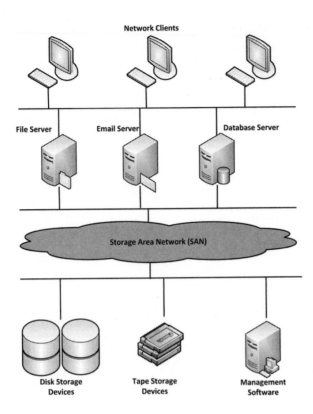

Figure 8-4 Each host connected to SAN believes it has dedicated access.
© 2015 Cengage Learning®.

SAN Standards

The primary standards implemented by SAN are the interconnection standards SCSI and Fibre Channel (FC). (See Chapter 10 for more information on these standards.) SCSI, which is a parallel interface, provides through its various versions and flavors data speeds of up to 160 MBps for up to 16 devices on a SCSI chain.

FC, a serial interface deployed on fiber-optic media, is a more frequent choice for the architecture of an SAN.

SAN Topologies

An SAN consists of servers connected to high-speed input/output (I/O) channels. You should focus on the connection method because the connection method used in an SAN dictates its overall design and capability. There are two connection methods used on SANs: SCSI and FC.

SCSI Connection Method The SCSI connection methodology implements a bus topology, which means it daisy-chains one device linearly in a serial line to another, creating a network of sorts. SCSI is an easy method to use because most modern server-level computers include a host bus adapter (HBA) for SCSI devices to connect.

SCSI identifies connected devices with a *logical unit number (LUN)*. System administrators assign a LUN number (0 to 7 or 0 to 15) using hardware or software settings when adding a device to a chain. Older SCSI standards limited the number of devices to 8, and later versions allow for 16 devices on a chain.

Fibre Channel Connection Method In spite of its name, FC runs just as well on copper wire as on fiber optic lines, just not as fast or as far. Fiber optic cabling in an SAN increases its overall length from 25 meters to around 10 kilometers. FC provides several advantages for its use on an SAN over SCSI. Here are just a few:

> Accepts and connects to multiple physical interface connections

> Separates the physical interface from the transported protocol

> Transports multiple protocols on a common physical interface

FC provides an infrastructure specifically designed to provide communications between data storage devices. An FC SAN incorporates FC switches to direct traffic, but it may also include FC routers to expand the capabilities of the SAN outside of its own network.

Zoning and Masking

On an SAN, whether SCSI or Fibre Channel, a LUN identifies a single hard disk drive or a group or cluster of the storage devices. To enhance the security of the data, you can arrange LUNs into zones. *Zoning* allocates resources for load balancing and selectively restricts access to certain data or devices to certain initiators. On an SAN, the hosts that request services are *initiators*, and the servicing devices are the *targets*.

Zoning is a hardware-level configuration, such as in an FC switch. The zoning on an SAN defines specific initiator/target pairings, although the initiator's designation can represent a group of requesting devices. Zoning applied at the port or HBA level uses device LUNs or World Wide Names (WWNs) and creates *hard zoning*. Every FC device has a WWN hard-coded into it by its manufacturer, much like a Media Access Control (MAC) address. If the device has several ports or interfaces, each of these has a unique WWN as well. Using WWNs for zoning creates *soft zoning*.

Figure 8-5 illustrates zoning in a general way. The file server is a member of the red zone and the green zone. This means that the file server is only able to request services from the storage devices in those zones. Likewise, the email server is only able to request service from the storage devices in the yellow zone.

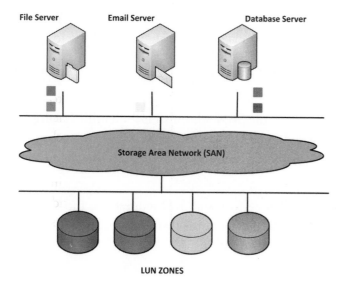

Figure 8-5 A server can only see and request service from devices in a zone to which it is a member.

© 2015 Cengage Learning®.

Soft Zoning Soft zoning is a software thing. It is more of a filtering process than a strong-armed gateway monitor. In intermediary devices, like FC switches, ports have LUNs and WWNs. The configuration of the switch can indicate which WWNs have access to a particular port's WWN. This operates similarly to an access control list (ACL) on an Ethernet switch. A soft zone isn't invincible, though.

If you have an unlisted telephone number with your local voice service provider, anyone requesting your number is unable to get it and therefore can't call you. However, you do share your phone number with good friends and relatives. This select group, which you designate as Zone BFF, includes the only ones who can reach you by telephone. Or so you think. The downside to a soft zone is that any initiator that has the physical address of a target can bypass the soft zone restrictions to access the device. In the same way, if a random dialer happens to generate your phone number, your phone will ring.

Hard Zoning Hard zoning, or port zoning, exists on a hardware level using physical port numbers or WWNs. Hard zoning sets up a port-to-port mapping that defines which ports have access to which other ports. With its definitions at the specific port-to-port level, it is difficult to bypass at the switch. An example of a hard zone is a VLAN, which exists at the switch port level. Only a request coming from a port in the zone of the destination port is valid, and vice versa. To use the telephone example from the previous section, if your phone is set up in a hard zone, only those incoming telephone numbers that you've preapproved would cause your phone to ring.

LUN Masking Zoning is often confused with masking. Zoning allows certain hosts to either have access to or be barred from specific storage devices or groups of devices. *LUN masking* attempts to restrict access to SAN devices by hiding certain LUNs from the view of certain initiators. LUN masking hides a device from some hosts, while allowing others to see it.

When implemented at the HBA level, LUN masking provides some security, but a host with a device's WWN, MAC address, or Internet Protocol (IP) address can defeat it. Implementing LUN masking at the controller level, the controller can filter requests for access and deny access to the blocked hosts. LUN masking is common on zoned SANs as well.

MULTIPATHING

Multipathing software is a failover protection technique that helps to ensure that the SAN stays up and functioning. In any networking environment, it is of major importance that the servers are able to interact with the storage devices. So, if the ability to communicate fails and the servers can't see the disk drives, the network failed.

When implementing multipathing software, the SAN administrator identifies multiple network routes between a server and its authorized (zoned) LUNs. The SAN administration must identify every HBA and port on all appropriate switches and routers through which the server can reach the data storage LUN.

Once set up, the multipathing software then performs all I/O requests on the SAN and routes them to the best available path. Should a path become unusable for some reason, the multipathing software notes this condition and considers other paths.

Storage Provisioning

The process of *storage provisioning* involves a step-by-step sequence of configuration and specification activities for the administrator with this responsibility, typically the SAN administrator. The purpose of storage provisioning is to optimize the overall performance of the SAN and to set up the security and restrictions to keep the data stored in the SAN safe and available.

Storage Provisioning Steps

There are essentially four general steps to the storage provisioning process that should be done in this order: assign identity to LUNs and volumes, verify the network path between storage devices and HBAs, identify and map devices to switch or director ports, and implement zoning and masking. Of course, the final step in storage provisioning is testing.

Each of the provisioning steps includes a number of smaller steps, considerations, and actions to complete a functioning, appropriately provisioned SAN, NAS, or DAS. Manual provisioning of a storage network has been a tedious, time-consuming, and at times, frustrating activity. In the past, server and storage provisioning occurred almost simultaneously and took about the same time to complete. With virtualization now available, server provisioning is an automated, relatively quick activity. However, the process of provisioning storage and the virtualization of storage is a step one/step two activity.

Because the major reason behind just about any network is the access to, retrieval from, and manipulation of data stored on the network, the storage element of a network must be reliable, available, secure, and fast. The importance of the provisioning of the storage devices on a system cannot be overstated.

IDENTIFY DEVICES

Before you get into storage provisioning too deeply, you should have a better understanding of LUNs. In about the same way that formatting and partitioning a hard disk drive in your personal computer creates logical drive letter assignments to specific parts of the hard disk drive, a LUN identifies a specific block of disk storage space on a particular device. Just as you boot your PC from logical drive "C:" and access data on logical drive "D:," the LUN assigned to a block of disk storage marks its start point. For this reason, the LUN is included in the address that the initiator uses.

The assignment of LUNs to storage devices is not a one-to-one thing, although it can be. Typically, large disk storage devices host several smaller LUNs. For example, a 1 TB drive may host five 200 MB LUNs. To the host server, the LUNs appear to be five separate disk drives. Administrators may also combine multiple LUNs into a logical volume group for higher-level administration. A LUN is a volume, and a volume is one of a volume group.

Also included in this step of the provisioning process is the creation of zones and masks. This matching process creates the pairings for which servers can see which LUNs.

Verify the Path and Map Routes

The network connections and addressing must work so that all of the SAN is available to all authorized users when needed. The zoning must be set appropriately to allow each server to access each of its authorized LUNs. In addition, backup and recovery routes must be available and functioning properly. Any alternative path intended to keep the SAN at least partially functioning should there be a failure needs testing to ensure it is zoned and masked appropriately.

At this point in the provisioning, it's a good idea to consider any future expansion forecasted for the SAN and ensure that the SAN will be able to accommodate this growth. It's also a best practice to test the SAN completely before loading live data to it.

Thin and Fat Provisioning

The two approaches to storage provisioning—thin provisioning and fat provisioning—differ primarily in the efficiency of disk use, not technology. Each is a descriptor of the actions of the provisioning performed by the SAN administrator, who could be implementing company policy.

Thin provisioning is more efficient when the resources used are much smaller than allocated so that the benefit of providing only the resources needed exceeds the cost of the virtualization technology used.

Fat Provisioning

The common practice or conventional method for storage provisioning is *fat provisioning*. "Fat" or "thick" provisioning allocates storage space well beyond the current needs of the system. Fat provisioning results in low disk utilization because large amounts of disk storage space are idle.

The temptation to provision a fat system comes from users requesting more capacity than is actually needed. A high-growth application didn't meet expectations, and disk storage is relatively inexpensive, according to the storage vendors. Allocating everything available may seem only natural, but it's really money spent that isn't being used.

Thin Provisioning

Naturally, the antithesis to fat provisioning is *thin provisioning*. Thin provisioning allocates only the "exact" amount of storage space based on system requirements. You can append additional LUNs and volumes as the need for more storage space rises. Thin provisioning is more applicable to larger centralized enterprise-level storage, SANs, and virtualized storage systems, where it optimizes the utilization of available storage.

Where conventional or fat provisioning allocates space beyond the actual need of the system, thin provisioning allocates only the amount of space needed at the time and allocates additional space on-demand. In most thin provisioning environments, the provisioning adds more storage space when requested without downtime. It also avoids over-allocating space by reclaiming unused space from existing allocations.

Chapter Summary

> The three primary technologies for attaching independent data storage to a network are network attached storage (NAS), direct attached storage (DAS), and storage area networks (SANs).

> NAS is a dedicated file server that provides file sharing services. NFS and CIFS are the two most common file sharing protocols.

> DAS is one or more unshared storage devices attached to a single computer.

> An SAN transfers block data between computers and shared storage devices (network shares).

> An SAN creates an any-to-any network connection, which can be geographically dispersed.

> SANs use one of two primary connection methods: SCSI and Fibre Channel.

> The SCSI connection method implements a bus topology on which hosts and devices are daisy-chained one to another.

> Fiber optic cabling in an SAN increases its overall length from 25 meters to 10 kilometers.

> A LUN identifies a specific block of disk storage space on a particular device.

> Zoning allocates resources for load balancing and selectively restricts access to certain data or devices to certain initiators. Zoning is a hardware-level configuration, such as in an FC switch. Zoning applied at the port or HBA level uses device LUNs or WWNs and creates hard zoning. Using WWNs for zoning creates soft zoning.

> On an SAN, the hosts that request services are initiators, and the servicing devices are the targets.

> Every FC device has a WWN hard-coded into it by its manufacturer. If a device has several ports or interfaces, each of the ports has a unique WWN as well.

> LUN masking attempts to restrict access to SAN devices by hiding certain LUNs from the view of certain initiators.

> Multipathing software is a failover protection technique that helps to ensure that the SAN stays up and functioning.

> The process of storage provisioning is a step-by-step sequence of configuration and specification activities.

> There are essentially four general steps to the storage provisioning process that should be done in this order: assign identity to LUNs and volumes, verify the network path between storage devices and HBAs, identify and map devices to switch or director ports, and implement zoning and masking.

> The two approaches to storage provisioning—thin provisioning and fat provisioning—differ in their efficiency of disk use.

> The common practice or conventional method for storage provisioning is fat provisioning, which allocates storage space well beyond the current needs of the system.

> Thin provisioning allocates only the amount of storage space needed for current requirements.

Key Terms

Any-to-any network connection

Apple Filing Protocol (AFP)

Common Internet File System (CIFS)

Direct attached storage (DAS)

Fat provisioning

Fibre Channel (FC)

Hard zoning

Host bus adapter (HBA)

Hot swappable

Initiator

Logical unit number (LUN)

LUN masking

Mount

Multipathing

Network attached storage (NAS)

Network File System (NFS)

Network share

Serial Advanced Technology Attachment (SATA)

Serial Attached SCSI (SAS)

Server Message Block (SMB)

Small Computer System Interface (SCSI)

Soft zoning

Storage area network (SAN)

Storage provisioning

Target

Thin provisioning

Uniform Naming Convention (UNC)

World Wide Name (WWN)

Zoning

Review Questions

1. Which of the following is NOT a technology for attaching data storage to a network?

    a. DAS

    b. NAS

    c. RAS

    d. SAN

2. _____ typically consists of a dedicated file server that provides file sharing services over NFS or CIFS.

3. True or False? DAS supports remote devices independently attached to a network.

4. What identity code is hard-coded into FC devices by their manufacturers?

    a. MAC address

    b. LUN

    c. WWN

    d. Port number

5. An SAN uses two primary connection methods: _____ and _____.

6. True or False? An SAN transfers blocks of data instead of individual files.

7. What is the assigned code that identifies a specific block of data storage or a group of blocks on a disk drive?

    a. MAC address

    b. LUN

    c. WWN

    d.   Port number

8. Soft zoning uses _____ to designate zones.

9. True or False? The hosts that request access to SAN devices are initiators.

10.   What is the term for the zoning applied at the port or HBA level using device LUNs?

      a. Soft zoning

      b. Partitioning

      c. Hard zoning

      d. Fat provisioning

11.   _____ restricts access to SAN devices by hiding the LUN of storage devices.

12.   True or False? Storage provisioning is limited to formatting disk drives and assigning logical drive identifiers.

13.   What type of software provides failover protection to help ensure an SAN remains available to users?

      a. Multipathing

      b. Auto-provisioning

      c. Authentication

      d. Backup/Restore

14.   Conventional provisioning is also known as _____ provisioning.

15.   True or False? Thin provisioning allocates only the storage needed by current requirements.

Answers to Review Questions

1.   c

2.   NAS

3.   False

4.   c

5.   SCSI, Fibre Channel

6.   True

7.   b

8.   WWNs

9.   True

10. c

11. LUN masking

12. False

13. a

14. fat

15. True

CHAPTER 9

Storage Configuration

After reading this chapter and completing the exercises, you will be able to:

- Differentiate between SSD and HDD storage devices
- Explain the different RAID levels
- Identify the common file system types

In cloud computing, data storage is both the reason for a company to move into the cloud and the source of its biggest fears. As a future cloud computing professional, you must have a deep understanding of the physical storage methods available, but also the technologies that ensure that data stored in the cloud is safe and available and that the access, retrieval, and storage of data is consistent, fast, and error-free. To this end, this chapter adds to your knowledge base of data storage by introducing or refreshing your knowledge of storage devices and different storage methodologies and technologies.

Hard Disk Types

Two primary types of hard disk drives dominate the market: standard and legacy *hard disk drives (HDDs)* and the newer *solid state drives (SSDs)*. For the Cloud+ exam, you need to understand the operation and application of each.

Hard Disk Drive (HDD)

Introduced in the mid-1950s, the hard disk drive (HDD) has been the standard for permanent secondary storage in virtually all personal computers since then. Although there have been several variations, its basic design—essentially one or more ferrous oxide coated electromagnetic disk platters mounted to a center spindle, with data stored for later use inside or attached to a computer—has remained relatively stable.

HDD CONSTRUCTION

Figure 9-1 shows the internal construction of an HDD for a mobile device. Although much smaller and compact compared to larger disk drives for desktop PCs, the components and their relationships remain the same.

Figure 9-1 An HDD designed for use in mobile devices.
© 2014 Seagate Technology LLC.

As shown in Figure 9-1, an HDD consists of a disk platter mounted on a center spindle and a read/write head. Figure 9-2 illustrates the placement of these components.

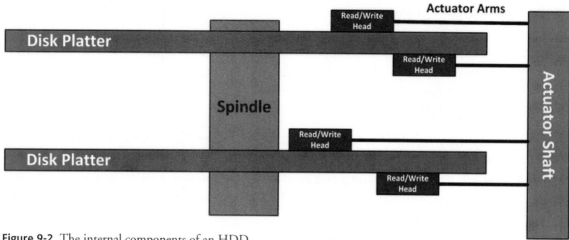

Figure 9-2 The internal components of an HDD.
© 2015 Cengage Learning®.

HDD OPERATION

When an HDD controller (inside the HDD housing) receives a request to store (write) data on the disk drive, a three-step process begins:

1. The drive assigns one or more spaces on the disk, perhaps even on different platters, to receive the data, typically to specific disk heads, *cylinders* (a virtual vertical alignment of the same track number on all platters), and disk blocks.

2. The actuator moves the applicable read/write heads over the designated track on each platter.

3. The read/write head places the data on the disk surface after the applicable block (address) rotates under it.

The faster the platters spin inside an HDD, the faster the drive is able to retrieve or store data. The platters rotate commonly at 5400 revolutions per minute (RPM) or 7200 RPM. Larger disk storage capacity usually means higher rotation rates. Contemporary HDD capacities are more than 1 terabyte (1TB).

Solid State Drive (SSD)

You should already be familiar with flash drives, thumb drives, memory sticks, and the like. These devices connect to your computer through its universal serial bus (USB) ports. Like these devices, an SSD-consists of a set of microchips and has no moving parts, unlike the mechanical complexity and rotation of an HDD. An SSD doesn't move at all, unless you count the electrical signal that moves over its circuitry.

SSD CONSTRUCTION

As shown in Figure 9-3, an SSD is a collection of electronic components that provide for the *non-volatile* (holds its data without a power source) storage of digital data. The integrated circuits of an SSD store blocks of data on flash memory. Because of its lack of physical, moving parts, an SSD is much faster than an HDD. In terms of physical size, an SSD has essentially the same form factor as an HDD.

The key component of an SSD is its controller. The *SSD controller* performs the operations required to read or write data to the flash memory components of the drive. As illustrated in Figure 9-3, the controller consists of an embedded processor, a buffer manager, and a multiplexer/demultiplexer (Mux/Demux) that combines or divides the data stream to and from the flash memory, respectively.

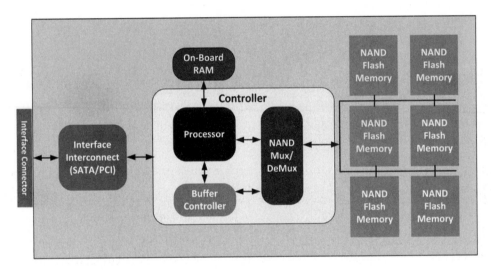

Figure 9-3 The internal circuits of an SSD disk drive.
© 2015 Cengage Learning®.

As shown in Figure 9-3, other components on the SSD include the following:

> **Interface connector and controller**: These components allow the drive to interface through the appropriate connector to the PC bus, commonly Serial Advanced Technology Attachment (SATA) or Peripheral Component Interconnect (PCI).

> **Random access memory (RAM)**: This component supports the processor's operations.

> **Not And (*NAND*) flash memory chips**: The programmable (write), read, and erasable (delete) permanent storage components of the SSD.

Flash-Based and RAM-Based SSD

Although flash-based SSD is more common, *RAM-based SSD* has faster throughput and a more predictable lifetime. Flash-based SSD has a finite number of program/erase (P/E) cycles before it begins to degrade. The flash memory circuits can support only a limited number of erasures and programming (writes) before their storage properties begin to deteriorate.

RAM-based SSD stores data electronically, as opposed to using the magnetic storage of flash-based SSD, on Dynamic RAM or Static RAM integrated circuits (ICs). However, whereas flash-based storage is nonvolatile, RAM-based SSD is volatile and must have continuous power to retain its stored contents. To prevent losing its data, RAM-based SSD must include nonvolatile storage backup, to which its contents transfer when the power is off. Another and more popular way to retain the data on RAM-based SSD is to include battery backup.

SSD Usage

SSD, in general, has a much higher price per stored byte than HDD, but in larger installations, such as enterprise systems or cloud-based subscriber systems, its performance over HDD can be worth it. Because flash-based SSD has an unpredictable lifetime, RAM-based SSD is common when availability and low latency are highly important. Flash-based SSD can be successful in applications where the read/write (P/E) activity is relatively low.

NAND and NOR Flash Memory

Flash memory, whether in a flash drive, in SSD storage, or for machine-level instruction store, is one of two types of circuitry: NAND (not and) or NOR (not or). Flash memory is an evolution of electrically erasable programmable read-only memory (EEPROM) technology.

The difference between these two types of memory is that NAND memory is written in blocks (called pages), and NOR memory reads and writes data in single bytes. NAND is flash memory used for main memory (RAM), memory cards, USB flash drives, and SSD. NOR flash memory is a common replacement for ROM to store system configuration or start-up instructions.

Tiered Storage

The basic concept of *tiered storage* is "first, fast, or last," meaning data storage should be separated into categories of descending need and stored on storage devices of descending speed and capabilities. The data most accessed, most critical, and with the highest need for security in a business or organization should be on the fastest and most available systems. The data least accessed or least needed can be stored on less expensive and possibly portable systems. Data categorized between these two extremes falls to systems appropriate to its need and frequency of use.

Storage Tiers

The scope of each category considers several characteristics of the data, including its level of security, performance requirements, frequency of access, and criticality in day-to-day operations. Although some tiered storage models define from 3–5 tiers (as used in the military classified data model), the most common models define three basic tiers:

> **Tier 1: Restricted**: Mission-critical, frequently accessed, or highly sensitive data

> **Tier 2: Private**: Financial, infrequently accessed, or confidential data

> **Tier 3: Public or transactional**: Event-driven, rarely accessed, unclassified data

The data categorized onto Tier 1 in this model requires reliable, high-performance, and high-availability storage devices, such as SSD. Tier 2 data is essential to operations and, when needed, must be available. HDD is appropriate for Tier 2 data. Tier 3 can include archival data that remains accessible when needed but is not necessarily backup data.

Tiered Storage Operations

The objectives of a tiered storage implementation are to organize, manage, and make available an organization's data store based on its value, access levels, retention, and required capacity. The effective use of tiered storage can reduce data storage costs and make efficient use of storage technologies. An effective tiered storage approach manages costs, the data life cycle, and the installation of the appropriate data storage technologies to support data priorities and their associated access speeds.

DATA CLASSIFICATION

The military classifies data in accordance with the security and protection that certain data requires. However, in the context of data storage in the cloud, *data classification*, while including the consideration of data security, is more about data usage, availability, reliability, and storage structures.

Different organizations use myriad classification schemes, concentrating on the needs of each organization, but ultimately, the result provides essentially the same outcome: a designation of the security, restrictions, access speed, availability, and retention for each level of data defined. Regardless of the simplicity or complexity of the scheme used, the resulting classifications typically are restricted, private, and public, as shown earlier in this section.

STORAGE APPROACHES FOR TIERED DATA

The storage approach for each of the different data tiers should be consistent with the characteristics and requirements of data defined on each, based on their classifications. Tier 1 data, the most sensitive, frequently accessed, and critical data, most likely requires more expensive, reliable, available, and higher-quality storage media. As shown in Table 9-1, Tier 1 data may be on high-level Redundant Array of Independent Disks (RAID) based on SSD or a Fibre Channel SAN. (You'll find more information on RAID in the next section.)

Tier	Classification	Storage Requirements
Table 9-1 Tiered Data		
1	Restricted	High-performance; high-availability
2	Private	Conventional, reliable
3	Public	Removable, portable

© 2015 Cengage Learning®.

Tier 2 data may be on more conventional disk storage systems, such as a network attached storage (NAS) or storage area network (SAN). Tier 3 data, which may include daily or other more frequent backups, can be on removable media, such as tape or recordable discs (CD-R or DVD).

Several vendors provide automated tiered storage systems to manage classified data in a data center or as a Software as a Service (SaaS) or Platform as a Service (PaaS), including EMC Corporation, Hitachi Data Systems, IBM, NetApp, and Sun Microsystems.

RAID

A *redundant array of independent disks (RAID)* allows for storing data in multiple locations (redundant) on a logical disk unit (array) made up of otherwise independent disk storage devices. To an operating system, this logical disk unit appears to be a single storage device. The term RAID in general refers to a variety of methodologies that divide and copy data to multiple storage locations within a clustered disk system. In many ways, RAID is a form of storage virtualization.

RAID stores copies of the same data in separate and distinct locations, which allows for balancing input/output (I/O) actions to and from the disk storage. This improves the performance or the redundancy, or both, of the storage system.

Disk Striping

RAID uses *disk striping* to divide data into smaller blocks that it stores on different partitions on multiple hard disks. The size of the stripes is equal to the size of the smallest partition available. At its simplest level, RAID 0, striping divides a body of data into several stripes and writes each stripe to a different hard disk, as illustrated in Figure 9-4.

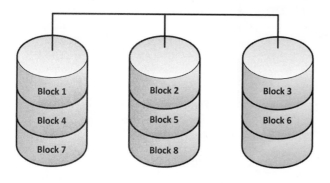

Figure 9-4 Disk striping divides data into blocks that are stored in separate disk stripes.
© 2015 Cengage Learning®.

In the example shown in Figure 9-4, if a data block of 40 MB is to be written to a RAID 0 array and the smallest partition available is 5 MB, then 8 stripes of 5 MB are stored across the available disk drives. Data striping can operate across as many as 32 disk drives.

Disk striping implementations are either single-user or multiuser. Single-user disk striping allows multiple I/O operations from a single user to be serviced over multiple hard disks. Multiuser disk striping expands the number of requests so that multiple requests from multiple users can access multiple disk drives. In single-user disk striping, one hard disk can be servicing one request from the user while another hard disk is taking care of another of the user's requests. In multiuser disk striping, while one hard disk is servicing one user's request, another hard disk can service another user's request.

Another variant of disk striping is parity. One version of disk striping works with parity, and another works without parity. *Disk striping with parity* creates parity files along with a data stripe using error correction and detection algorithms. Should the data become corrupted on a disk drive, a fault tolerance function moves the affected partition offline and attempts to use the parity file to reconstruct the data. Disk striping without parity has no fault-tolerant provisions.

> **Note**
>
> Parity is a binary code function that helps the data recovery process rebuild corrupted data. Parity works on a two-bit pattern where 1-0 has a parity of 1; 0-0 has a parity of 0; and 0-1 has a parity of 1.

Disk Mirroring

Several RAID levels include *disk mirroring* as a key component of their methodologies. Disk mirroring involves the replication of logical disk volumes to another physical hard disk drive. In RAID systems, mirroring occurs in real time to make sure that the data, in the original or the mirror, is always available. Figure 9-5 illustrates mirroring, with each of the data blocks mirrored to a separate hard disk.

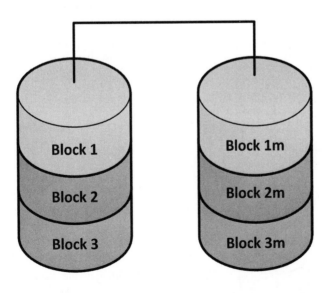

Figure 9-5 Disk mirroring replicates data onto another physical hard disk.
© 2015 Cengage Learning®.

Disk mirroring addresses the issue of disk drives being unreliable computer system components. Mirroring automatically creates or maintains two or more copies of data to ensure that, in the event of a disk failure, the data on the failing device remains available. In a local data center, mirroring provides a fail-safe against hardware failures, but mirroring on a remote access system can also provide for quick recovery of data as part of a disaster recovery plan.

RAID Levels

Over the years since it was introduced in the late 1980s, multiple versions of RAID, called levels, have emerged. Table 9-2 lists the RAID levels you should know for the Cloud+ exam.

Table 9-2 RAID Levels

Level	Name	Description
0	Disk striping	Offers striping with no redundancy. Excellent performance.
1	Disk mirroring	Data is duplicated (mirrored) on two disk drives. No striping.
0+1	Striping with mirrors	Data is striped and stripes are mirrored.
1+0	Mirrored with striping	Data is mirrored and mirrors are striped.
5	Striping with parity	Uses 3–5 disk drives for array. Stores parity information on dedicated disk.
6	Striping with dual parity	Stores redundant parity blocks.

© 2015 Cengage Learning®.

There are many other RAID levels, but most are variations on the six listed in Table 9-2.

RAID 0

RAID 0 applies disk striping only. Although it does spread the data onto two or more hard disk drives, it provides no redundancy or fault tolerance. Compared to conventional hard disk storage techniques, RAID 0 does improve I/O performance by paralleling read and write operations across hard disks. Because RAID 0 doesn't include error detection or correction, a failure of one hard disk results in the loss of all data. Figure 9-4 illustrates a RAID 0 implementation.

RAID 1

RAID 1 applies disk mirroring only. Mirroring provides for data redundancy and a level of fault tolerance. RAID 1 can improve the performance of read operations because the data can be read from any available copy. However, because all copies of a data block must be updated to maintain the mirror, write operations are able to perform only as fast as the slowest drive. Figure 9-5 illustrates the concepts of RAID 1.

RAID 0+1

RAID 0+1 is a hybrid combination of RAID 0 and RAID 1. This RAID level implements disk striping (RAID 0) and then disk mirroring (RAID 1) of the data stripes. The striped data sets are mirrored to create copies of the striped sets. RAID 0+1 requires a minimum of four hard disk drives, and if more drives are used, they must be added in pairs to support the mirroring.

RAID 1+0

RAID 1+0, also RAID 10, is a hybrid combination, but with RAID 1 (the top array) combined with RAID 0. The primary difference between RAID 0+1 and RAID 1+0 is that the data is mirrored and then the mirrored sets are striped across additional disks. This RAID level provides increased fault tolerance because, not only do you have mirrored data, but both the original and the mirror are striped across several drives. As long as all the drives holding a mirror set are functioning as they should, the data remains available.

RAID 5

RAID 5 implements parity blocks and then stripes them across at least three hard disk drives along with the data. Should one hard disk drive fail, the system can reconstruct (recalculate) any missing data using the data's associated parity data. RAID 5 requires at least three drives but is commonly implemented with five drives. However, RAID 5 is able to continue operations with the failure of one drive.

RAID 6

RAID 6 enhances RAID 5 by adding duplicated distributed parity blocks. This RAID level, through double parity, provides for the fault tolerance of two hard disk drives failing. This approach is especially good for large data storage systems that must maintain high availability. Although drive failures do slow the overall performance of the system until the failed drive(s) is dealt with, the data storage system is able to continue supporting data requests. Figure 9-6 illustrates the addition of two parity blocks in a RAID 6 implementation.

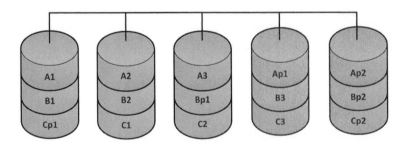

Figure 9-6 RAID 6 adds additional fault tolerance through duplicated parity blocks.
© 2015 Cengage Learning®.

File Systems

In general, a *file system* provides a definition for the naming convention for data files and the logical file and directory/folder organization on the physical hard disk. File systems have a structure of organization and the metadata (data about the data) that describes the location and other logistical characteristics of stored data. Each of the different operating systems (Windows and Linux/UNIX primarily) support a variety of file systems, but typically one specific file system by default.

In the context of cloud computing, the file systems in use must support the mission of the service, the vendor's committed service levels, and the type and size of the data being stored. This section includes a brief overview of six operating systems, the ones you may encounter on the Cloud+ exam.

Disk Allocation

Before a hard disk drive can store data under any file system, it must be ready to accept data in accordance with the requirements of that file system. This involves the creation of the disk allocation units, specifically partitions, cylinders, tracks, and sectors. Each hard disk drive has a designated number of these elements it can support, although the number of partitions (volumes) is really up to the user.

PARTITIONS

Although a hard disk drive is usable in its entirety as one large storage area, it can also support several partitions. Each *partition* is a logical disk drive. Partitioning a disk into multiple partitions allows one physical hard disk drive to appear to be two or more logical disk drives. The logical drives can vary in size to support different uses. In fact, separate partitions can support different file systems. You have most likely used a computer with multiple partitions, with each partition assigned a different logical drive identifier (C:, D:, and so on). Figure 9-7 illustrates a physical hard disk drive divided into four partitions, each of a different size and supporting a different purpose.

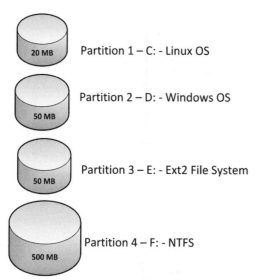

Partition 1 – C: - Linux OS
20 MB

Partition 2 – D: - Windows OS
50 MB

Partition 3 – E: - Ext2 File System
50 MB

Partition 4 – F: - NTFS
500 MB

Figure 9-7 Partitioning a hard disk drive can create multiple logical disk drives.
© 2015 Cengage Learning®.

A partition actually defines a range of disk cylinders in a logical entity. A cylinder is a virtual construction that includes all the same numbered tracks on each of the platters of a hard disk drive. As shown in Figure 9-8, cylinder 79 consists of all the track 79s on each of the disk's platters.

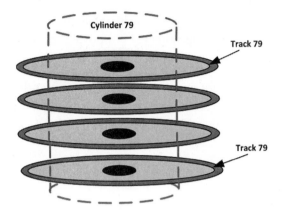

Figure 9-8 A disk cylinder incorporates all the same numbered tracks on a disk drive's platters.
© 2015 Cengage Learning®.

Sectors and Clusters

The surface of a hard disk platter consists of *tracks* (concentric circles of equal size) and *sectors* (segments of a track). Essentially, a hard disk consists of a finite number of sectors, depending on the number of tracks on the disk. Figure 9-9 illustrates the relationship of tracks and sectors. Sectors have an identity consisting of the track number and a sequential number (starting from zero) for each of the sectors on a given track.

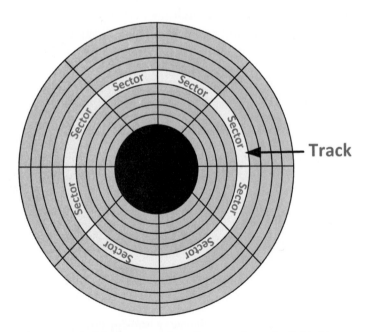

Figure 9-9 A disk platter consists of concentric tracks divided into sectors.
© 2015 Cengage Learning®.

Sectors

A disk sector is the smallest addressable unit that a hard disk drive can read or write in a single operation. An application program can affect a single bit or byte, but it must read in an entire section, change the data, and then write the entire section back to the disk.

Until 2011, disk sectors were uniformly 512 bytes in size. In 2011, manufacturers changed to sectors of 4,096 bytes because advances in error detection and correction technologies made that size more efficient. To an operating system, a hard disk drive appears to be a collection of number-identified sectors, which means that users would need to remember the logical address of each file. To avoid this, file systems came to be.

> **Note**
>
> Sector size has actually increased over the years from 128 bytes to the current standard of 4,096 bytes (4 KB). When hard disks became more common, their section size was equal to that of high-density floppy disk drives at 512 bytes. Other media may have their own standard section sizes, such as a CD that uses a 2,048 (2 KB) sector size.

Clusters

File systems manage a hard disk through disk clusters. A *cluster* is the smallest allocation unit managed by a file system for storing files, directories, and folders. Depending on the hard disk drive and the file system in use, a cluster can be a single sector or, more commonly, a set of consecutive sectors along a track. The size of a cluster is typically a number that represents a power of two. For example, a cluster size of 2^0 contains one sector. The more common cluster size is 2^3, or 8 sectors. A cluster would not contain 5 sectors, nor would it contain 10. These clusters would have to contain either 8 sectors or 16 sectors, respectively.

Although, by definition, a cluster contains contiguous sectors, a cluster can extend beyond a single track. A cluster represents the space allocated to hold a file. Small files stored on a hard disk with larger clusters create slack space (wasted space) on the disk. Large files on a disk allocated in small clusters also create slack space. One thing you should note is that cluster size is not necessarily a function of sector size.

FORMATTING

Before they are usable by a particular file system, virtually all hard disks require formatting for a specific file system. *Formatting* adds the logical data elements required by the file system to allocate and manage the disk. The elements added to the disk vary by file system (discussed later in this chapter). In any case, formatting a disk identifies the cylinders, tracks, and sectors/volumes and establishes the control and management mechanisms of the file system.

Windows File Systems

The primary Windows file systems are the *File Allocation Table (FAT)* and its variations the *New Technology File System (NTFS)* and Microsoft's *Resilient File System (ReFS)*. The first two of these file systems are legacy systems, but because they have proven to be reliable over the years, they are still in use. ReFS is a recent release.

FILE ALLOCATION TABLE (FAT)

The patented Microsoft File Allocation Table (FAT) that originated with the MS-DOS operating system has been available, in one form or another, in the Windows operating systems ever since. As its name implies, FAT constructs and maintains a table containing a map of the location and allocation of files on a disk. FAT has three basic variations—FAT12, FAT16, and FAT32—which differ primarily in the layout of the file allocation table.

The title of the FAT file system comes from the way it organizes files through the FAT it places at the beginning of each volume along with a duplicate copy of the table for redundancy purposes. The FAT and the FAT root directory are set at fixed locations so that system start-up can dependably find them. Like nearly all file systems, FAT allocates the disk volume (partition) in clusters sized relative to the volume size. Figure 9-10 illustrates the allocations made by an FAT file system at the beginning of a disk volume.

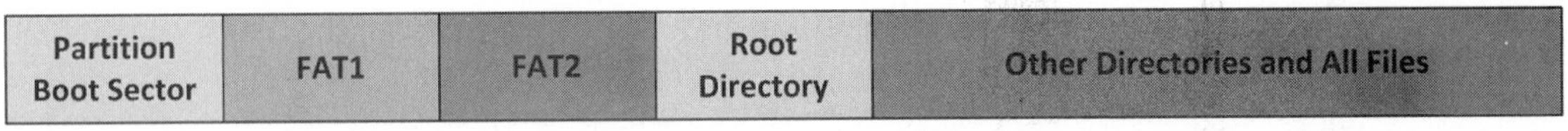

Partition Boot Sector	FAT1	FAT2	Root Directory	Other Directories and All Files

Figure 9-10 The elements added and the allocations made on a disk volume by an FAT file system.
© 2015 Cengage Learning®.

Because of its simple file mapping, an operating system is able to easily locate and track all the pieces of a file. Although FAT is not a commonly used file system, it is the most common method for tracking media between two communicating computers. FAT is also the file system format for moving data between digital devices, such as with flash drives and SSD and a computer.

NEW TECHNOLOGY FILE SYSTEM (NTFS)

The functionality of NTFS is similar to that of FAT. However, NTFS adds one important feature that helps to make it more fault tolerant than FAT. NTFS is a journaling file system, which means it logs all transactions performed against individual files, such as reads, writes, and deletes. This log information can then allow NTFS to recover parts or all of a file system. The primary repair tool is the *CHKDSK* (check disk) command.

NTFS is commonly the file system offered by remote data storage vendors. Because NTFS is a common file system in many organizational data centers, providing this file system on a remote storage service allows users to retain their file permissions, encryption, and compression, among other features.

EXTENDED FAT (EXFAT)

Microsoft also has a file system for flash drives: the *Extended FAT (exFAT)*. Nearly all versions of the Windows operating system since Windows XP support exFAT, as do most Mac OS versions. exFAT is usable when NTFS is not appropriate (usually because of NTFS's data structure overhead requirements) or when the file size limit of the standard FAT32 file system is too small.

MICROSOFT **CHKDSK** COMMAND

CHKDSK is a Windows operating system command-line utility that checks an NTFS (or FAT) hard disk volume for errors. As shown in the following screen capture, the CHKDSK command displays data relating to the integrity of a file system. CHKDSK first checks the integrity of the files, their indexes, and finally their security. It then reports on the allocations made in the file system, including sectors the file system has set aside as unusable.

```
C:\Documents and Settings\Administrator>cd\

C:\>d:

D:\>chkdsk
The type of the file system is NTFS.

WARNING! F parameter not specified.
Running CHKDSK in read-only mode.

CHKDSK is verifying files (stage 1 of 3)...
File verification completed.
CHKDSK is verifying indexes (stage 2 of 3)...
Index verification completed.
CHKDSK is verifying security descriptors (stage 3 of 3)...
Security descriptor verification completed.

  64115383 KB total disk space.
  13268648 KB in 28188 files.
     19396 KB in 3320 indexes.
         0 KB in bad sectors.
    112399 KB in use by the system.
     65536 KB occupied by the log file.
  50714940 KB available on disk.
```

Used with permission from Microsoft.

CHKDSK can repair any disk errors found by reapplying the entries in the transaction log to the affected file(s). However, you do need to have Administrator-level permissions to run CHKDSK.

ExFAT is included here only for completeness. It is not typically a shared resource file system. It is much more common on media devices, such as flat panel televisions, multifunction media centers, and portable media devices.

RESILIENT FILE SYSTEM (REFS)

ReFS isn't necessarily a replacement for NTFS, although it appears similar in many ways. ReFS is a good choice for large amounts of data that need reliability and high availability. When it writes new data to disk, ReFS writes it to a new clean location, rather than over the top of a previously used area. In the background, ReFS then cleans out the used area for its next disk write. ReFS also supports data clustering, the Hyper-V hypervisors, and file shares.

One difference between NTFS and ReFS is that ReFS doesn't use CHKDSK, because ReFS doesn't need it. Any file system repair, if needed, happens as ReFS detects the need for the repair. ReFS uses checksums to detect when data changes and is able to detect corrupted data and recover it quickly.

The UNIX File System

Although UNIX and Linux are similar in terms of their structure and commands, when it comes to file systems, the *UNIX file system (UFS)* offers the foundation for many Linux-specific file systems. UFS is a *hierarchical file system (HFS)*, in which directories and files are in a directory tree structure with its root (starting point) at the top. Figure 9-11 illustrates this structure.

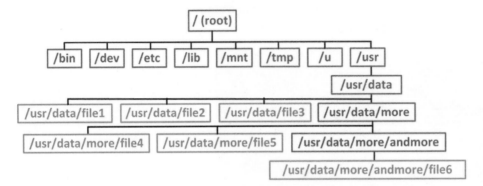

Figure 9-11 The UNIX file system is a hierarchical directory and file tree structure.
© 2015 Cengage Learning®.

Physical Versus Logical File System

UFS defines two seemingly conflicting entities: a hierarchical directory tree and the physical arrangement of data files on a disk partition. However, the directory tree creates a logical file system, and the physical location of files sets up a physical file system. Like all file systems, the physical file system consists of disk partitions, with the physical disk partitions determining the number of files that can be stored and the size of the space available for files.

Each partition has a superblock, data files, and *inodes* (*eye-nodes*) associated with each file. The *superblock* (NTFS and several other file system types use superblocks) contains control information for the operating system regarding a disk partition. Inodes contain essentially the same information as a superblock, but for an individual file.

The hierarchical directory tree, the logical file system, maps the directories and data files into an inverted tree structure, in which all the files in a file system technically belong in or are "descendants" of the root directory via its branches.

UNIX File Types

You should know the various file types defined by UFS, especially the files that define system attachments and devices. UNIX defines four primary file types:

> *Ordinary files*: These files contain data, strings of executable scripts in text form, audio, video, or other forms of text or binary data. Users manipulate these files.

> *Directory files*: These files mark the branches of the root directory in the hierarchical tree structure. Directory files can contain any file of any type for purposes of organizing the files.

> *Special files*: These files link to physical devices, like printers, external storage devices, or any other I/O device attached to the computer. UNIX treats I/O devices as files from which it reads or writes data.

> *Pipe files*: A pipe file is a temporary file that links commands so that the data produced by one command is available for another command.

Linux File Systems

The basic Linux file system is similar to the UNIX file system. The difference is that UNIX development was relatively controlled and standardized by only a few developers. Linux, because it is an open source product, has been essentially developed by committee. In addition to new commands, command versions, and other supplements to the operating system, new file system managers, most of which extend storage limits and add other performance improvements, have been added.

There have been dozens of variations (63 and counting) on the Linux file system since its introduction in 1991. The variations and improvements of the extended file systems (ext2, ext3, and ext4) have been the primary file systems in use. Table 9-3 lists the more common file systems on Linux systems.

Table 9-3 Linux File Systems

File System	Max File Size	Max Volume Size
ext3	2 TB	32 TB
ext4	16 TB	1 Exabyte (EB)
XFS	8 EB	16 EB

© 2015 Cengage Learning®.

Note

Table 9-3 introduced a size abbreviation (EB) with which you may not be familiar. EB represents Exabyte, and to put that into perspective for you, you need to understand GB, TB, and PB as well.

1 Gigabyte (GB) = 1,024 Megabytes (MB)

1 Terabyte (TB) = 1,024 GB

1 Petabyte (PB) = 1,024 TB

1 Exabyte (EB) = 1,024 PB

1 Zettabyte (ZB) = 1,024 EB

In other words, one EB equals approximately one trillion megabytes.

One key concept in both UNIX and Linux file systems is the mount point. Before you can access a file system (volume), you must *mount* it to the system. This terminology comes from the mainframe computer days when computer operators would insert spindle-based hard disks into the disk cabinet/reader and place it online. The operator would then logically connect the disk with a mount command.

In the modern version of the mount action, you logically add a file system to the directory tree to make it available. If you think of the root directory as the trunk of a tree that has a number of hooks on its circumference at the top, mounting a file system involves hooking the file system on one of these hooks. During system start-up, the Linux kernel automatically mounts the file systems (partitions) listed in a file called the fstab (file system table).

EXTENDED FILE SYSTEM (EXT)

The *extended file system (ext)* was the first developed specifically for the Linux kernel. It was the first in a series of extended file systems that evolved into ext4, the version in use today. Based on UFS, it extended the physical disk size for partitions and files and added the Virtual File System (VFS).

Ext2

The *second extended file system (ext2)* replaced the original ext file system. ext2 is still in use as the file system for flash storage media, such as SD cards and USB drives. This is because ext2 does not include journaling, and flash devices have a limited number of write cycles. For a while, ext2 was the default file system in many Linux releases, but ext3 has largely replaced it.

Ext3

The *third extended file system (ext3)* added journaling to the ext2 file system. *Journaling* increases the reliability of a file system and reduces the amount of maintenance and checking required on a file system during start-up and in the event of a system crash.

The Linux operating system supports three levels of journaling:

> ➤ *Basic journaling*: This method writes both the file metadata and the file contents to the journal before writing them to the file system. This involves writing the data twice: once to the journal and once to the partition.

> ➤ *Ordered journaling*: This method only journals the file metadata and is the default journaling method for most Linux versions. Although the data file is written to the disk before the journal data is "committed," interruptions, such as a power failure, during the journaling process can cause some data problems.

> ➤ *Writeback journaling*: This method updates the journal before or after writing data to the disk, depending on its configuration. Only the metadata writes to the journal in this method. Power failures occurring at the beginning of the journaling cycle can create corrupt files.

Regardless of the journaling mode applied, the file system will be consistently correct after a crash. Only the data in a data file may be correct if the file was active at the time of failure.

The fourth extended file system is meant to be the successor to ext3, to which it has backward compatibility. Many of the newer releases of Linux now include ext4 as the default file system, although ext3 is still in use in many versions.

Zettabyte File System (ZFS) on Linux

Zettabyte File System (ZFS) is well suited for large enterprise data storage or subscriber-based data storage in the cloud because of its capability to manage a virtually endless amount of data (a zettabyte [ZB], or a billion terabytes). In addition, ZFS offers a number of other disk management features, including these:

> ➤ **Data integrity**: ZFS uses a checksum algorithm to continuously check and repair data corruption in the background.

> ➤ **Disk pooling**: ZFS organizes disk storage into one large disk pool. ZFS works with data storage devices in much the same way your computer works with RAM. When you need more storage space, you simply add it without the need to partition or format the added drive.

> ➤ **RAID**: ZFS supports most RAID levels through software RAID, which means it doesn't need a RAID controller. ZFS provides a robust set of data integrity functions, including protection against silent corruption (bit rot or degradation), power spikes, parity errors, and device performance errors (phantom writes, driver errors, and accidental overwrites). Default ZFS RAID (RAID-Z) is a mirroring scheme, but there are also RAID-Z modes that are similar to RAID 5, and RAID 6.

Virtual File Systems

A *virtual file system*, or virtual file system switch, allows applications to access various formal file systems in a consistent manner. This allows an application running in a virtual client to access local or networked storage devices supported by different operating systems, such as Windows, UNIX, or Linux, transparently. The VFS allows the application to access data uniformly without regard to the formats of the actual underlying file systems.

A VFS creates a contract (logical link) between an operating system kernel and its file system. This allows for the addition of new native file systems simply by creating a contract with the new system. Should the operating system or its file system change through revision or replacement, it may require adjustments to the VFS contract, but this is a relatively minor step compared to the flexibility VFS provides.

Some clustered file systems give the appearance of a VFS. These forms of file sharing can offer applications access to file systems through a standardized request to a specific operating system and file system. On the other hand, nearly all the more popular VFSs are also clustered file systems.

Clustered File Systems

In larger data centers or service providers in the cloud, clustering computers is a common practice toward providing for redundancy, throughput performance, and availability. In this configuration, the data stored in support of these servers must be able to share the data without too much contention. A *clustered file system* allows an individual file system to mount to multiple servers at the same time. This enables the servers to see that the file system is solely mounted to it when, in fact, it is sharing the file system with other servers. Many clustered file system approaches are simply direct attached storage (DAS) for each server or computer, which is not really a clustered file approach. Some so-called clustered file systems are just a parallel file system that spreads data across multiple storage devices for the purposes of redundancy and reduced latency.

There are two general approaches to a clustered file system: a cluster of servers with access to a specific file system and a replicated file system to which several servers have concurrent access. In a shared-disk configuration, access to a shared file system is inherent in its design. However, without a system to monitor access and write activities, it could prove chaotic for frequently accessed data. This is the role of the clustered file system: to ensure the integrity of the shared data when multiple requests are for the same file, not to mention the single point of failure in this approach.

However, with *shared disk* systems like SAN and NAS, the underlying approach is actually "shared nothing." The managing file system replicates the underlying file system in real time to another storage device and maintains enough copies to provide multiple accesses to a file, although each request goes against a different copy of the data. In reality, the file system shares nothing in this shared disk approach.

The primary issue with attempting to manage these approaches to data management is concurrency. Clustered file systems take concurrency seriously. Many store metadata on the shared partition, and others store the metadata on a separate metadata server. Either way, clients see the same and consistent view of the file system.

A clustered file system also aggressively protects the data from corruption. When a client attempts to write bad data or fails during an update activity, the other active clients initiate fencing, meant to fence out the offending client. There are several approaches to fencing, with the common one being "Shoot the Other Node in the Head," meaning to block its access.

A few of the clustered file systems, all of which are also virtual file systems, are the Global File System (GFS) for Linux, the Oracle Clustered File System (OCFS) available for Linux, and the Virtual Machine File System (VMFS) on VMware systems.

GLOBAL FILE SYSTEM (GFS)

Although it is essentially a shared disk file system implemented in Linux computer clusters, the *Global File System (GFS)* (and its later release GFS2) differs from other shared disk systems because of its access methods. GFS treats all nodes of a cluster as peers, regardless of their actual roles as servers or clients. All nodes have direct and concurrent access to shared block storage.

GFS requires that the cluster hardware allow access to all nodes of the shared storage devices and applies a lock manager to control this access. The lock manager blocks access to other nodes for a data file retrieved for an update or remove action by a node. GFS doesn't include a lock manager and must use the Distributed Lock Manager (DLM) on Linux systems.

ORACLE CLUSTERED FILE SYSTEM (OCFS)

The *Oracle Clustered File System (OCFS)*, or its latest version OCFS2, is a file-sharing system that allows the nodes of a computer cluster to share data files. Although Oracle does provide its Real Application Clusters (RAC) clustering software, OCFS is also compatible with Linux clusters.

Initially, the intent of OCFS was to work with Oracle file systems, but that limitation no longer exists. OCFS is available as open source for Linux implementation.

VMWARE VIRTUAL MACHINE FILE SYSTEM (VMFS)

The *Virtual Machine File System (VMFS)* is the clustering file system for VMware's server virtualization software ESX and vSphere. Virtual servers and machines are able to access the same file system simultaneously. Under VMFS, the creation of new VMs is independent from the storage administration. Changing volume sizes or configuration does not disrupt the operations of the virtual network.

VMFS deploys on virtually any network storage device, including Small Computer System Interface (SCSI), Internet SCSI (iSCSI), Fibre Channel, or Fibre Channel over Ethernet (FCoE) SAN. VMFS is the default storage management for virtualized block-based disk storage.

Chapter Summary

> An SSD consists of a collection of electronic components that provide for the nonvolatile storage of digital data. The SSD controller performs read or write operations to the flash memory components. The internal components of an SSD are interface connector and controller, RAM, and NAND flash memory chips.

> Tiered storage separates data into categories of descending need and stores each category on storage devices of descending speed and capabilities. The primary tiers of data are restricted, private, and public.

> Data classification classifies data by usage, availability, reliability, and storage structures.

> RAID stores data in multiple locations on a logical disk array made up of independent disk storage devices.

> Disk striping divides data into smaller blocks that it stores on different partitions on multiple hard disks. Disk striping is either single-user or multiuser. Disk striping with parity creates parity files using error correction and detection algorithms.

> Disk mirroring replicates logical disk volumes to another physical hard disk drive in real time.

> RAID 0 applies disk striping only.

> RAID 1 applies disk mirroring only.

> RAID 0+1 is a hybrid combination of RAID 0 and RAID 1 that applies disk striping and then disk mirroring on the data stripes.

> RAID 1+0 is a hybrid combination with RAID 1 combined with RAID 0. RAID 1+0 mirrors the data and then stripes the mirrored data.

> RAID 5 implements parity blocks and then stripes them across at least three hard disk drives along with the data.

> RAID 6 enhances RAID 5 by adding duplicated distributed parity blocks.

> A file system provides a definition for the naming convention for data files and the logical file and directory/folder organization on the physical hard disk.

➤ FAT and NTFS are the primary Windows file systems. FAT organizes files through its file allocation table and root directory that are set at fixed locations for system start-up. NTFS is a journaling file system that logs all transactions against individual files.

➤ UFS is a hierarchical file system in which directories and files are in a directory tree structure with its root at the top. Each UFS partition has a superblock, data files, and inodes associated with each file.

➤ The ext file system, based on UFS, extends the physical disk size limit and adds the Virtual File System (VFS). ext3 adds journaling to the ext file system.

➤ ZFS is well suited for large enterprise data storage or subscriber-based data storage in the cloud because of its capability to manage a virtually endless amount of data.

➤ VFS allows applications to access various formal file systems in a consistent manner.

➤ A clustered file system allows an individual file system to mount to multiple servers at the same time.

➤ VMFS is the clustering file system for VMware's server virtualization software ESX and vSphere.

Key Terms

Basic journaling

CHKDSK

Cluster

Clustered file system

Cylinder

Data classification

Directory files

Disk mirroring

Disk striping

Disk striping with parity

Extended FAT (exFAT)

Extended file system (ext)

File Allocation Table (FAT)

File system

Formatting

Global File System (GFS)

Hard disk drive (HDD)

Hierarchical file system (HFS)

Inodes

Journaling

Mount

NAND flash memory

New Technology File System (NTFS)

Nonvolatile

Oracle Clustered File System (OCFS)

Ordered journaling

Ordinary files

Partition

Pipe files

RAID 0

RAID 0+1

RAID 1

RAID 1+0

RAID 5

RAID 6

RAM-based SSD

Redundant Array of Independent Disks (RAID)

Resilient File System (ReFS)

Second extended file system (ext2)

Sector

Shared disk

Solid state drive (SSD)

Special files

SSD controller

Superblock

Third extended file system (ext3)

Tiered storage

Track

UNIX file system (UFS)

Virtual File System (VFS)

Virtual Machine File System (VMFS)

Writeback journaling

Zettabyte file system (ZFS)

Review Questions

1. What is the storage medium of an SSD?

    a. Disk platters

    b. Integrated circuits

    c. Optic drives

    d. Radio frequency magnetic disk

2. The storage approach that classifies and stores data according to its usage, availability, and reliability is _____ storage.

3. True or False? The primary tiers of data are confidential, private, and personal.

4. RAID stands for _____.

    a. Random Arrays of Independent Disks

    b. Reliable Arrays of Inexpensive Disks

    c. Redundant Array of Independent Disks

    d. Real-time Authorization of Integrated Data

5. Disk _____ separates data into smaller blocks that are stored on separate physical disks.

6. True or False? RAID 0 applies disk mirroring only.

7. Which level of RAID applies disk striping and then mirroring of the disk stripes?

    a. RAID 0

    b. RAID 1

    c. RAID 0+1

    d. RAID 1+0

    e. RAID 6

8. RAID 1 applies disk _____ only.

9. True or False? A file system manages only the physical disk hardware.

10. Which of the following RAID levels does NOT implement disk mirroring?

    a. RAID 1+0

    b. RAID 0+1

    c. RAID 1

    d. RAID 5

11. ____ is the file system best suited for large enterprise data storage because of its capability to manage a virtually endless amount of data.

12. True or False? The FAT file system implements journaling.

13. Which disk access methodology allows multiple servers to mount simultaneously an individual file system?

    a. FAT

    b. Clustering

    c. Hierarchical

    d. Virtual

14. The clustering file system for VMware is _____.

15. True or False? RAID 6 enhances RAID 5 by adding duplicated distributed parity blocks.

Answers to Review Questions

1. b
2. tiered
3. False
4. c
5. striping
6. False
7. c
8. mirroring
9. False

10. d

11. ZFS

12. False

13. b

14. VMFS

15. True

CHAPTER 10

Protocols

After reading this chapter and completing the exercises, you will be able to:

- Describe the purpose and application of access and common protocols in the cloud computing environment

- Describe the management differences of certain protocols

- Identify the common ports used in cloud computing

A s is true in virtually all networking, various protocols provide the rules, guidelines, and formats to the cloud computing environment. These protocols come from the work of a number of technology initiatives, standards organizations, and private vendors. Some of these protocols are legacy, such as Transmission Control Protocol (TCP), Internet Protocol (IP), and the Ethernet (802.x) protocols, others are enhanced versions of existing protocols like Hypertext Transfer Protocol (HTTP) and Small Computer System Interface (SCSI), and some are relatively new or just emerging, including Fibre Channel over Ethernet (FCoE), Internet Small Computer System Interface (iSCSI), and Convergence Enhanced Ethernet (CEE).

Cloud computing protocols fall into one or more of four categories: platform protocols, access protocols, common protocols, and data center management protocols. Chapter 3 introduced you to platform protocols, such as Representational State Transfer (REST) and Simple Object Access Protocol (SOAP). This chapter serves as a refresher or an introduction to the protocols in use in cloud computing, depending on your experience and knowledge. You will likely encounter the information in this chapter on the Cloud+ exam.

Access Protocols

In general, *access protocols*, or network access protocols, are the standardized rules for conducting communication sessions over a network. These protocols fall on Layers 2 (Data Link) and 3 (Networking) of the Open Systems Interconnection (OSI) network model to manage and share control of data frames and packets. Network access protocols provide various functions, including allotting network addresses, creating point-to-point connections, establishing links between nodes, identifying the shortest path between nodes, and managing and discovering nodes.

Any protocol that operates on the Data Link and Network layers of the OSI model are network access protocols. The more common protocols in this category are Address Resolution Protocol (ARP), Neighbor Discovery Protocol (NDP), the Point-to-Point Protocol (PPP), most tunneling protocols, such as the Point-to-Point Tunneling Protocol (PPTP) and Layer 2 Tunneling Protocol (L2TP), and the Open Shortest Path First (OSPF) protocol.

You are likely to find questions that ask about or reference more contemporary access protocols than those mentioned in the preceding paragraphs. In fact, the access protocols that you should know are the Fibre Channel Protocol (FCP), FCoE, and iSCSI. You should also have a solid understanding of Ethernet networking.

Fibre Channel Protocol (FCP)

Fibre Channel (FC) is the generic name for a high-speed networking technology common for interconnecting networks to data storage devices. It is an international standard from both the International Committee for Information Technology Standards (INCITS) and the *American National Standards Institute (ANSI)*. FC's origins lay with supercomputers, but it is now common in *storage area networks (SANs)* on enterprise networks. In spite of its name, FC is compatible with electromagnetic (radio frequency) interfaces, as well as fiber optic media. In the same way, "Channel" in its name doesn't mean that it can only support channel communications; FC is also a network protocol.

In its most common usage, FCP transports SCSI signals on FC networks. However, under its standard, an FC network can include and will interconnect multiple physical media types. It also provides a high-speed transfer rate for large amounts of data from multiple protocols over a common physical medium by separating the logical protocol (data formatting) from the physical media.

CHANNELS VERSUS NETWORKS

Although the difference is largely semantics, you should understand the difference between a channel and a network transmission medium, which are the basis of the two types of peripheral device communications. Channel refers to a peripheral input/output (I/O) interface with a host computer that is capable of transporting large data between the two devices. A channel minimizes overhead by processing the movement of the data on the physical media with little or no software involvement.

On the other hand, a network uses host-to-host communications largely under software (driver) control.

FIBRE CHANNEL TOPOLOGIES

Fibre Channel nodes (devices) interconnect in one of three topologies: *point-to-point (FC-P2P)*, *arbitrated loop (FC-AL)*, and *cross-point switched (FC-SW)* or *fabric*. An *FC fabric* is at least one switch that connects to multiple nodes, each of which contains one or more ports or I/O adapters through which they communicate over an FCP channel. Table 10-1 lists the operational characteristics of these FC topologies.

Table 10-1 Fibre Channel Topologies

Topology	Maximum Ports	Address Length	Medium Access
FC-P2P	2	N/A	Dedicated
FC-AL	127	8-bit (ALPA)	Arbitrated
FC-SW	16,777,216 (2^{24})	24-bit (port ID)	Dedicated

© 2015 Cengage Learning®.

As shown in Table 10-1, addressing in Fibre Channel varies with the topology in use. Because P2P is essentially peer-to-peer, addressing isn't an issue. The 8-bit address in the FC-AL topology is the Arbitrated Loop Physical Address (ALPA) of an NL_port (or FL_port), much like a Media Access Control (MAC) address in Ethernet. On a fabric (FC-SW) topology, addressing consists of a 24-bit port identification code assigned to the port by the fabric when the port logs in or initiates on the fabric.

A general node is an *N_port* in FC terminology, and the connections between the ports of nodes are links. As you'll see in the sections that follow, FC designates its node ports by type, usage, and function. Table 10-2 lists a few of the more common node port types in the FC technology.

Table 10-2 Fibre Channel Node Ports

Port	Name	Location	Usage
N_port	Node port	Node	FC-P2P or FC-SW
NL_port	Node Loop port	Node	FC-AL
F_port	Fabric port	Switch	Connects to N_port
FL_port	Fabric Loop port	Switch	Connects to NL_port
E_port	Expansion port	Switch	Creates inter-switch link (ISL)
EX_port	Expansion port	Router	Connects to E_port

© 2015 Cengage Learning®.

FC Point-to-Point (FC-P2P) Topology

Two devices directly connected over an FC link form a basic FC-P2P topology. Figure 10-1 illustrates a direct channel link between the N_port on each of two devices—in this case a server and a data storage device. This connection is commonly between a processor device (such as a computer) and the hardware device controller on the peripheral device. The point-to-point topology is the default topology for FC.

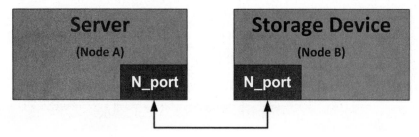

Figure 10-1 A Fibre Channel point-to-point channel link is between two N_ports.
© 2015 Cengage Learning®.

FC Arbitrated Loop Topology

The second FC topology is the FC arbitrated loop, or FC-AL. FC-AL is capable of interconnecting from 2 devices to 126 devices using connection points called *L_ports*. An FC arbitrated loop configures L_ports, which may be input/output (I/O) devices or processor-based systems, in a loop (or ring) topology.

One advantage that an FC-AL configuration can have over other ring or loop topology-based systems is that it doesn't require a hub or switches. Each device needs only an FC-compatible I/O adapter. FC-AL is the most common implementation of FC technology at a local level. Figure 10-2 illustrates a basic FC-AL implementation commonly called a *private loop* because it consists of only local nodes or NL_ports. An NL_port is an N_port included in an FC-AL loop, thereby becoming an NL_port.

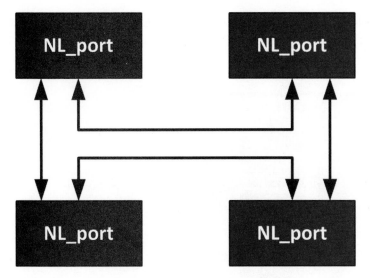

Figure 10-2 An FC-AL private loop topology used for a local network.
© 2015 Cengage Learning®.

In an FC-AL topology, all the devices linked into the loop equally share the available bandwidth and the management of the entire loop. A designated loop master or control node doesn't exist in the loop's initial configuration. Each time the loop initiates, the nodes negotiate for which node performs the loop master activities. The nodes also arbitrate for control of the loop so they can communicate with another node. Only one link (node-to-node connection) can be active at a time, and a node must wait until all other nodes have had a chance to communicate before they can have another turn. This may sound overly complicated, but remember that all this happens at extremely high speeds. Table 10-3 lists the various line and throughput speeds of FC protocols.

Table 10-3 Fibre Channel Speeds			
Protocol	**Line Rate**	**Data Speed**	**Year Introduced**
1GFC	1.063 Gbps	200 MBps	1997
2GFC	2.125 Gbps	400 MBps	2001
4GFC	4.250 Gbps	800 MBps	2004
8GFC	8.500 Gbps	1,600 MBps	2005
10GFC	10.52 Gbps	2,550 MBps	2008
16GFC	14.025 Gbps	3,200 MBps	2011
32GFC	28.05 Gbps	6,400 MBps	2015 (forecasted)
128GFCp	4x28.05 Gbps	25,600 MBps	2015 (forecasted)

© 2015 Cengage Learning®.

In Table 10-3, the protocols, or protocol flavors, as some call them, designate the approximate line speed in gigabits for the technology. The letters "GFC" stand for *Gigabit Fibre Channel*. The line rate given for each protocol is the transfer speed of the protocol on the FC links. The data speed represents the megabyte transfer rate or throughput on a fully duplexed line.

The nodes in an FC-AL topology can be storage devices configured into a disk loop, which is a common use of this topology. As illustrated in Figure 10-3, each storage element with an FC I/O interface can be included in the FC-AL loop.

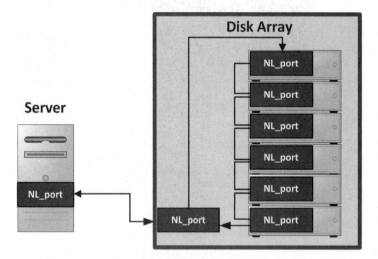

Figure 10-3 An FC-AL private disk loop is a common implementation of the FC technology.
© 2015 Cengage Learning®.

FC Cross-Point Switched/Fabric Topology

Cross-point switched, commonly referred to as fabric, is the third FC topology. At the lowest level, an FC-AL topology can link to a fabric topology, as shown in Figure 10-4. As Figure 10-4 illustrates, an FL_port can replace one or more of the NL_ports to link an FC-AL node to a fabric.

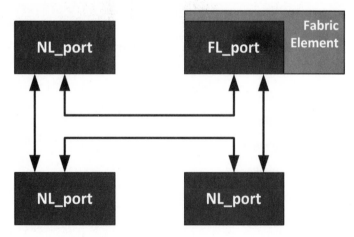

Figure 10-4 An FC-AL topology adapted to link into an FC fabric.
© 2015 Cengage Learning®.

However, to deploy FC to a larger network, even the cloud, a fabric topology, takes on the configuration of the simple fabric implementation shown in Figure 10-5. Note that each of the attached nodes sees the fabric as a single structure. The fabric sits on a mesh networking topology, as illustrated in Figure 10-6.

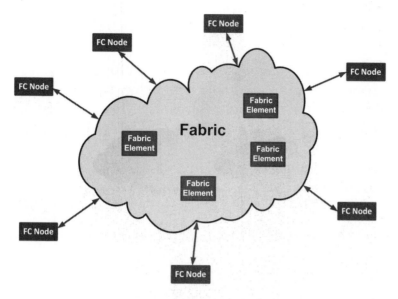

Figure 10-5 An FC fabric provides linkage and switching to a variety of node types.
© 2015 Cengage Learning®.

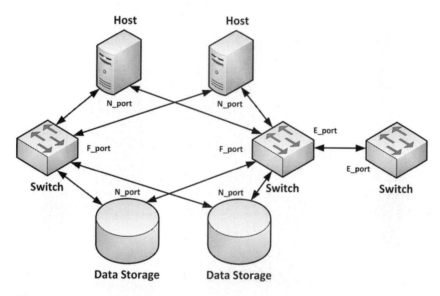

Figure 10-6 An FC fabric links together various devices into a mesh structure.
© 2015 Cengage Learning®.

There is no practical limit to the number of devices interconnected to a fabric. However, the addressing space limits the number of nodes to 16,777,216 or 2^{24}. The makeup of the fabric and its structure are transparent to the nodes linked to it through F_ports. Each node/port only manages its point-to-point link to the fabric.

PROTOCOL SUPPORT

FC consists of a set of hierarchical functions that are compatible with and support a variety of existing protocols, separated into channel protocols and network protocols. FC supports several channel protocols, including SCSI, *Intelligent/Integrated Drive Electronics (IDE)*, the *Intelligent*

Peripheral Interface (IPI-3), the *High-Performance Parallel Interface (HIPPI)* protocol, and the *Single Byte Command Code Set (SBCCS)*.

The network protocols supported by FC include Ethernet, Token Ring, and Fiber Distributed Data Interface (FDDI), among others. In comparison to these legacy protocols, the newer FC protocols provide the following characteristics, either in common with or in contrast to them:

➤ Asynchronous signaling, which allows for maximum throughput even under heavy traffic loads

➤ Ability to operate over serial media and smaller connectors, reducing the cost to install and support

➤ Scalability, in that FC can carry multiple protocols simultaneously, including both channel and network

➤ Switching, which eliminates shared media and shared bandwidth

➤ Transmitted data, which is independent of the medium in use

Fibre Channel over Ethernet (FCoE)

Fibre Channel over Ethernet (FCoE) is an adaptation of the FC technology that enables FC data frames for transmission on *10 Gigabit Ethernet* or faster networks. FCoE develops an independent mapping of the Ethernet networking and incorporates the Ethernet physical and link layers, retaining all other FC constructs to provide interfacing to other FC channels and networks.

FCoE is common in large data centers that use Ethernet for their TCP/IP network and FC for I/O operations to their SAN or network attached storage (NAS). In this configuration, FC is a second protocol running on the network media along with the IP traffic. However, because FCoE runs above Ethernet on the network, it is not IP-compatible, which means it cannot be routed across IP-routed networks.

Internet Small Computer System Interface (iSCSI)

In Chapter 3, you learned about object-based storage, including storage in the cloud. The primary protocol that facilitates storing and retrieving of data from location-independent data storage facilities is the *Internet Small Computer System Interface* (*iSCSI*, pronounced as *eye-scuzzy*). The iSCSI protocol supports transmission of data over virtually any network, from local area networks (LANs) to the full Internetwork and everything in between.

The iSCSI protocol is an SAN protocol that allows an organization to consolidate its data storage in a central location—even a remote location—and gives users the impression that the data is stored on local devices. Under this protocol, a client (an *initiator*) requesting data sends a *Command Descriptor Block (CDB)* containing a SCSI command to a SCSI storage device (a *target*) on a remote server. The target then becomes the initiator to return the requested data to the original initiator, now the target. Table 10-4 lists a sampling of SCSI command codes.

Table 10-4 SCSI Command Codes

Hexadecimal Code	Command
0B	Seek
A5	Play Audio
A8	Read
AA	Write
01	Rewind
2C	Erase
2E	Write and Verify
56	Release
92	Locate

© 2015 Cengage Learning®.

Each of the devices attached to a SCSI loop has a unique identification code. In a typical SCSI implementation, the SCSI controller polls the loop to find the devices that are connected and then assigns each one a 7-bit sequence number or hop count. On an FC-AL loop, the controller queries each port for its World Wide Name (WWN). The iSCSI protocol uses a complex device identification process because of the unlimited number of devices or ports it can support. All these device discovery and identification processes run each time a loop initializes or whenever you add or remove a device from the loop.

Note

See Chapter 5 for more information on WWN.

Operationally, iSCSI facilitates two hosts to exchange SCSI CDBs containing commands (see Table 10-4) over an IP network, including intranets, LANs, wide area networks (WANs), and the Internet. This protocol provides a lower-cost alternative to the dedicated infrastructure of Fibre Channel, with the exception of FCoE.

Common Internet Protocols

In the context of computing, networking, and the cloud, a *network protocol* defines a convention or a standard set of formats and rules to use in establishing a connection, communicating, and moving data between linked endpoints. This definition may also define the syntax, connection type and layout, and synchronization method of the communication link. Protocols don't actually do anything; they are merely standards, definitions, formats, rules, procedures, and so on. When people speak of protocols, they take on functionality, but that isn't real. On virtually every network, some combination of hardware and software implements protocol configurations for use.

Protocols differ in purpose and function from one standard to another. Some are universal; some are national; and a great many are vendor specific. However, for the most part, all protocols perform one or more of a specific set of functions:

> ➤ Detecting the medium of the physical connection (wired or wireless)

> ➤ Detecting the presence of the endpoints

> ➤ Establishing the parameters of the communication channel (hand-shaking)

> ➤ Formatting the data set (segment, packet, frame, datagram, and so on) for transmission

> ➤ Negotiating the characteristics of the communication connection

> ➤ Starting (nail-up) and managing a communication session

> ➤ Performing error detection or correction

> ➤ Recovering a lost connection

> ➤ Terminating (tear-down) a session or connection

On the Internet, some protocols are classified as "common" protocols. What makes them "common" is that they are the *de facto* convention and they are readily available, typically open source, and universally recognized for specific functionality. There are 30 or more different protocols in the general classification of common network protocols. Most of the common protocols, if not all, depending on who makes the list, are in the TCP/IP suite and operate on the various layers of the OSI model. Table 10-5 lists the more common of the common protocols by the layer of the OSI model on which each operates.

Table 10-5 Common Internet Protocols by OSI Model Layer

Layer	Protocol	Function
Data Link	Address Resolution Protocol (ARP)	IP to MAC address resolution
	Point-to-Point Protocol (PPP)	Direct connect communications
	Layer 2 Tunneling Protocol (L2TP)	VPN tunneling
	Ethernet (Media Access)	LAN media access and control
Network	Internet Protocol (IP)	Datagram addressing and forwarding
	IPv4	Version 4 with 32-bit addressing
	IPv6	Version 6 with 128-bit addressing
	Open Shortest-Path First (OSPF)	Link-state routing
	Interior Gateway Protocol (IGP)	Distance vector routing
Transport	Transmission Control Protocol (TCP)	Reliable datagram delivery
	User Datagram Protocol (UDP)	Simple transmission delivery

Application	Dynamic Host Configuration Protocol (DHCP)	Configuration of network clients
	Domain Name System (DNS)	WWN to IP address resolution
	File Transfer Protocol (FTP)	File transfers between hosts
	FTP Secure (FTPS)	TLS/SSL security on FTP
	Hypertext Transfer Protocol (HTTP)	Structure code interpretation
	Hypertext Transfer Protocol Secure (HTTPS)	HTTP on TLS/SSL
	SSH FTP (SFTP)	SSH security on FTP
	Simple Mail Transfer Protocol (SMTP)	Email transmission on IP
	Secure Shell (SSH)	Secure client/server transmission
	Transport Layer Security/Secure Sockets Layer (TLS/SSL)	Certificated secure data transmission

The following sections discuss the common protocols you should know for the Cloud+ exam.

Data Link Protocols

As listed in Table 10-5 in the preceding section, the Data Link (Layer 2) protocols you should know for the Cloud+ exam and for networking in general are ARP, L2TP, PPP, and, although not a protocol as such, Ethernet.

ADDRESS RESOLUTION PROTOCOL (ARP)

Local area networks address each node using its MAC address, which is its Data Link layer address. There is little worry of address conflicts or duplications because MAC addresses become electronically embedded permanently in the interface component of networking devices. This arrangement works great for Ethernet, which is a Data Link layer media access technology. However, should an external device want to communicate directly with an internal network device, the external device most likely has a Network Layer address, such as an IP address, to reference the target node. The external device wants to communicate with 134.168.1.107 (IPv4), but the Ethernet network knows that node only as C0-18-85-5D-35-95.

This is where *Address Resolution Protocol (ARP)* comes in. ARP converts IP addresses (like 134.168.1.107) into the physical or MAC address (C0-18-85-5D-35-95) of a device on a Link layer network. The most common use of ARP is with IPv4 on an Ethernet (IEEE 802.3 [wired] or IEEE 802.11 [wireless]) network, although it is common with FDDI, Frame Relay, and *Asynchronous Transfer Mode (ATM)* as well. IPv6 uses the NDP for local network address resolution. Figure 10-7 shows the network connection details of a Windows computer. Notice that it has both a physical (MAC) address and an IPv4 address. ARP uses these addresses.

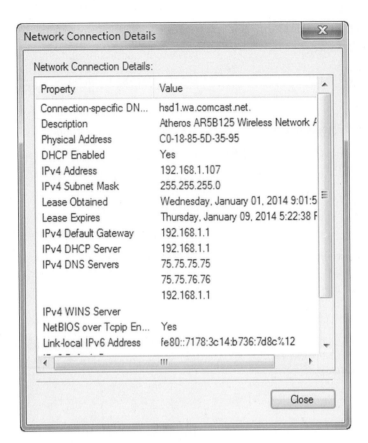

Figure 10-7 Each networked device has a physical address and an IP address.

Used with permission from Microsoft.

Here is how ARP works:

1. Computer A and Computer B are on the same network with no switches, bridges, or routers intervening.

2. Computer A wants to communicate with Computer B; it obtains Computer B's IP address using DNS—192.168.1.107.

3. To get a message to Computer B, Computer A needs Computer B's MAC address—C0-18-85-5D-35-95.

4. Computer A looks in its cached ARP table, which it built from previous searches or received messages. If Computer B's MAC address is under its IP address, Computer A uses the MAC address and sends the message.

5. If Computer A cannot find the address in its ARP table, it must send a broadcast ARP message to the MAC address FF-FF-FF-FF-FF-FF, which all the nodes on the network accept, requesting the MAC address for the station with the IP address of 192.168.1.107.

6. Computer B recognizes its IP address and responds with its MAC address (and its IP address, so Computer A can put both addresses in its ARP cache). Computer B also updates its own ARP cache with Computer A's information.

The mirror image of ARP is Inverse ARP (InARP). This protocol sets up the opposite (the inverse) actions of ARP. Instead of converting an IP address to a MAC address, InARP converts a MAC address into an IP address. In InARP, the requesting node requests the Network Layer address of a node from its neighbors, hoping that either the node in question or a node with the requested information responds.

POINT-TO-POINT PROTOCOL (PPP)

The *Point-to-Point Protocol (PPP)* is an encapsulating protocol that operates on the Data Link layer of the OSI model to set up direct connections between two network nodes. It is popular because it can provide authentication, encryption, and compression. PPP is common in serial communications and telephony, including cellular phones, and some fiber optic transmissions. Internet communications, now broadband communications, also use PPP. It is also the protocol of choice for dial-up access to Internet service providers (ISPs). Digital Subscriber Line services use PPP variants, including PPP over Ethernet (PPPoE) and PPP over ATM (PPPoA).

PPP is compatible with both synchronous and asynchronous circuits, as long as the circuit is full duplex (bidirectional). PPP supports the transmission of IP, Internetwork Packet Exchange (IPX), and AppleTalk. However, its ability to carry other protocols has made it popular for tunneling.

Like the PPP setup, a tunnel has only two endpoints, which makes PPP a good option on the Data Link layer to establish a connection between two virtual interfaces. PPP assigns IP addresses to the virtual endpoints, which then provide destination addresses for the two ends of a tunnel. In fact, when L2TP/IPsec (discussed in the section that follows) is the tunneling protocol in use, PPP provides IP addresses for the tunnel endpoints.

LAYER TWO TUNNELING PROTOCOL (L2TP)

Layer Two Tunneling Protocol (L2TP) is most common on virtual private networks (VPNs) in general usage, but ISPs also use it to deliver content to users. L2TP is a common protocol, but how it works and what it provides is often confused or mistaken. In the sections that follow, you'll learn about the concepts and elements that make up this protocol.

Tunneling

In the context of network communications, a *tunneling protocol* encapsulates the data payload from the frame or packet of another network protocol. The encapsulating protocol becomes the delivery protocol. Tunneling, in this context, is like the payload encapsulated inside a space shuttle that is journeying up to the International Space Station. If the payload fires out into space, there is a good chance of damage, destruction, or becoming lost in space.

On a network or an internetwork, the packets of a protocol may not be compatible with the active protocols on a particular delivery network, or they may need a secure path through an untrusted network. To continue the analogy, the delivery protocol becomes the space shuttle, and the data payload of the protocol needing protection is the payload carried in the protocol's transport bay.

L2TP Tunneling

Like all tunneling protocols, L2TP encapsulates another protocol's frame into a protective packet. L2TP creates a UDP datagram to which it adds a header. Although L2TP is by definition and name a Layer 2 (Data Link) protocol, it actually runs on Layer 3 (Network) through UDP.

PPP is perhaps the most common protocol encapsulated by L2TP. This protocol doesn't have an encryption capability of its own and depends on other protocols, but primarily Internet Protocol Security (IPsec), to secure packets. It also must depend on other secure protocols for authentication and data integrity. When L2TP combines with IPsec, it becomes, logically, *L2TP/IPsec*.

> **Note**
>
> L2TP/IPsec transmits over both a secure channel and a tunnel. A secure channel guarantees the security of all traffic. A tunnel is a channel, but one on which packets travel untouched. In L2TP/IPsec, IPsec establishes a secure channel, and L2TP provides a tunnel.

L2TP works on a client/server methodology. The client end, the *L2TP Access Concentrator (LAC)*, initiates the tunnel and negotiates with the server end, the *L2TP Network Server (LNS)*, to create the tunnel session—the "call." Either end can initiate the call and create the tunnel. Traffic between the LAC and the LNS is bidirectional.

The packets in a call are either control packets or data packets. A control packet contains reliability features, but data packets do not. Any delivery reliability for a data packet is the responsibility of the protocol nested inside the L2TP packet. Figure 10-8 illustrates the session or call dialog between the LAC and the LNS. The initial request, sent by either end, is a request for a tunnel ID. The responding end acknowledges the requested ID (with an ACK message) and requests a tunnel ID of its own, which the originating end acknowledges with an ACK message as well, as shown in Figure 10-8. At this point, the tunnel exists.

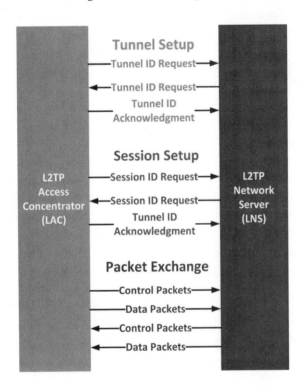

Figure 10-8 This is a simplified illustration of the setup, control, and communication on an L2TP call.
© 2015 Cengage Learning®.

The next step is to nail up the call. Essentially, the same process of request and acknowledgment creates the session and its identity. At this point, with both the tunnel and the call established, the LAC and the LNS may begin exchanging control and data packets.

ETHERNET

Ethernet has been in use for so long that it's difficult to decide where to begin a discussion on this Data Link layer networking technology. Assuming that you are new to networking and are trying to learn about cloud computing toward taking (and passing) the CompTIA Cloud+ certification exam, you should study this section carefully. If you have been in networking for three or more years, this section should be a good refresher for you. Fully expect to encounter at least one question that references or is specific to Ethernet on the certification exam.

Ethernet History

A project by the University of Hawaii in the 1970s to link the islands of Hawaii via a network yielded *Ethernet*. Its namesake is "luminiferous ether," which at one time was thought to carry light throughout the universe. In February 1980, the Institute of Electrical and Electronics Engineers (IEEE) established the 802 committee to develop networking standards. This resulted in the IEEE 802.3 Ethernet standard that defines Physical and Data Link layer network specifications and is still the definitive standard today for both wired and wireless LANs.

Ethernet has evolved with improvements in media and network device technologies, growing from its original 2 Mbps, 5 Mbps, and 10 Mbps configurations to *Fast Ethernet* (100 Mbps), *Gigabit Ethernet* (1000 Mbps or 1 Gbps), and *10-Gigabit Ethernet* (10 Gbps).

Ethernet is not a protocol, *per se*. It is a Physical and Data Link layer transmission and media access technology. Ethernet is actually a family of networking technologies that control who or what can connect to the network media to share the bandwidth, control the transmission of frames on the media and avoid and detect collisions of transmitted frames, and provide unique and unduplicated device addressing. Network protocols like IP rely on Ethernet for its MAC and transmission technologies.

Media Access Control (MAC)

In one form or another, the network topologies of an Ethernet network involve a network node connected to a network medium to which other network nodes are also connected. Figure 10-9 illustrates the bus topology of an Ethernet network. Each of the computers, including a server, directly connects to the network cable or backbone. The computers, including the server, all share the available bandwidth of the network. The characteristics of the network medium and the network devices installed on the computers determine the available bandwidth. If the network adapters in the computers and the cabling support Gigabit Ethernet, all the computers on the network share the nominal 1-gigabit bandwidth.

The transmission technology on a wired network is actually simple. A computer transmits a message to another computer on the network by placing an electromagnetic charge on the network cable. This electrical signal contains binary value representations of the message's data. A wired cable can hold only one electrical charge at a time, so every station connected to the cable sees the message. Information in the message indicates the intended recipient node of the message, and the nodes (network interface controllers [NICs]) ignore the message if it's for another node. The downside to this method is that if two nodes transmit at the same time, their transmissions clobber each other and render both unintelligible. This condition is a collision.

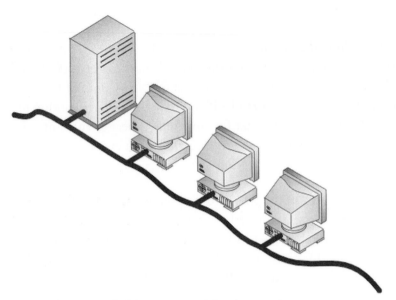

Figure 10-9 A simple Ethernet network in a bus topology.
© 2015 Cengage Learning®.

On a network similar to the one shown in Figure 10-9, the Ethernet standards provide a mechanism to detect collisions. On a full-duplex LAN, *Carrier Sense Multiple Access with Collision Detection (CSMA/CD)* allows a node to detect if another node is occupying the carrier (medium) and waits until the carrier is available to send its message.

On newer or larger networks, a segment of nodes or a single station connects to a switching device (hub, switch, or router) that largely eliminates the threat of a collision. Figure 10-10 shows an Ethernet network using this arrangement. The switching device forwards the message toward its destination. In this arrangement, a collision can only occur when a node and the switch both transmit to each other simultaneously.

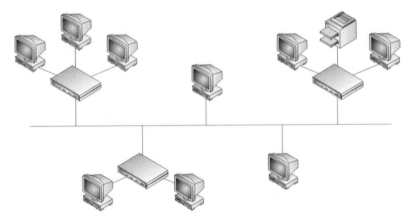

Figure 10-10 A switched Ethernet network virtually eliminates collisions.
© 2015 Cengage Learning®.

Media

The original cable medium for Ethernet was coaxial cable, which is still a viable option. However, the Ethernet physical layer specifies the use of twisted-pair copper cabling, fiber optics, and wireless signaling. Ethernet cable standards specify compatible media using mnemonics that indicate the speed, signaling, and media type. For example, the Ethernet standard assigns a 10 Mbps Ethernet medium that transmits using baseband signaling over twisted-pair copper cabling the mnemonic of *10BASE-T* (10 for the speed, BASE for baseband, and T for twisted-pair). Table 10-6 lists the more commonly used media specifications for Ethernet.

Table 10-6 Ethernet Media Standards

Designation	Media	Speed	Distance
10BASE2	50-Ohm Coaxial	10 Mbps	200 meters
10BASE-T	Twisted-pair (TP) copper	10 Mbps	100 meters
10BASE-F	Fiber-optic	10 Mbps	2,000 meters
100BASE-T	TP copper	100 Mbps	100 meters
1000BASE-T	TP copper	1 Gbps	100 meters
1000BASE-SX	Multimode fiber optic	1 Gbps	550 meters
1000BASE-LX10	Single-mode fiber optic	1 Gbps	10 kilometers
10BASE-LX4	Single-mode fiber optic	10 Gbps	10 kilometers
40GBASE-CR	TP copper	40 Gbps	7 meters
100GBASE-CR	TP copper	100 Gbps	7 meters
100GBASE-SR	Multimode fiber optic	100 Gbps	100 meters

© 2015 Cengage Learning®.

Note

The IEEE and several cabling and switching vendors are developing terabit (1 trillion) standards and media systems that they plan to introduce in 2015.

Carrier Ethernet

Carrier Ethernet refers to telecommunications technologies deployed by network service providers (NSPs) (common carriers) to extend Ethernet services beyond LANs. Organizations are increasingly connecting their local networks to WANs over Ethernet transmitting on both wired and wireless connections. In many of these situations, Ethernet networks are supporting geographically dispersed multiple site networks. In addition, Ethernet networks are now carrying big data, backup services, and video.

NSPs have had to provide Ethernet services beyond the local network, offer sufficient bandwidth to service the growing data and media transmission needs of their customers, and maintain robust Quality of Service (QoS). To meet these demands, carriers had to include access to a wide range of media, including fiber optics and wireless; provide scalability and fast implementation; and offer the low cost and simplicity of Ethernet.

Metro Ethernet Services Building on the standards for the *metropolitan area networks (MANs)*, the telecommunications industry formed the Metro Ethernet Forum (MEF) to define services to meet the needs described in the preceding section. The MEF defined three levels of service (see Figure 10-11):

> ➤ **E-Line**: A point-to-point communication link that connects two Ethernet ports/interfaces over a WAN service.

> ➤ **E-LAN**: A multipoint-to-multipoint communication service that connects two or more customer interfaces to provide the functionality of an Ethernet network to all endpoints.

> ➤ **E-Tree**: A multipoint communication service that connects a host root endpoint to a subscriber's endpoint.

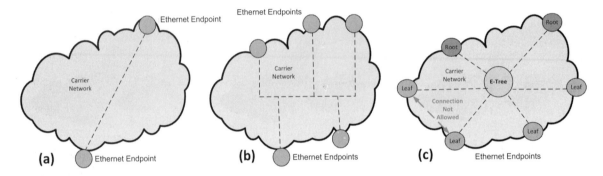

Figure 10-11 The MEF defines three levels of expanded Ethernet services: (a) E-Line, (b) E-LAN, and (c) E-Tree.
© 2015 Cengage Learning®.

As illustrated in Figure 10-11, the MEF E-Line and E-LAN, while providing an extension of their respective networks through the cloud, are just extensions of existing networks. However, an E-Tree includes support for SaaS and PaaS vendors. The root of the E-Tree could be an application server, a streaming video server, or just about any hosted service, providing content delivery over Ethernet. The leaves of the E-Tree would then be the subscribers of the root service. On an E-Tree, a leaf cannot connect directly to another leaf; it could be bad for business.

Several high-speed communications technologies are in use to support carrier Ethernet, including Synchronous Optical Networking (SONET), Multiprotocol Label Switching (MPLS), and Carrier Ethernet Transport (CET). It's not important for you to know these technologies for the Cloud+ exam, but you may encounter them in your future as a certified cloud computing professional. In fact, the MEF has developed a certification for Carrier Ethernet technicians.

Network Protocols

On the OSI model's Network layer, the most active protocol, in terms of use, is the *Internet Protocol (IP)*. IP is the primary communication protocol on the Internet and the World Wide Web (WWW). IP defines the fundamentals of moving data across an internetwork (networks interconnected).

IP defines the logical-level addressing of the nodes and devices on a network. It defines the routing function that enables data to move from gateway to gateway in the same room; in the same building; in the same town, state, or country; or around the world.

Perhaps the best place to start a review of IP is with IP addressing. So much depends on the validity and accuracy of the Internet address of a website, document, service, or any addressable entity on the Internet and web. IP addresses are assigned to virtually every device attached to a TCP/IP network anywhere in the world. An IP address is a logical address, which means that a human, protocol software, or application assigns it to a physical, logical, or virtual entity. The IP addressing schemes serve two purposes: identifying host devices, and providing a logical device location function.

> **Note**
>
> Remember that physical network devices carry a permanent and unique MAC address embedded in it during manufacturing. The association between an entity's physical and logical addresses is temporary.

There are two active versions of IP: IPv4 and IPv6.

IPv4

The primary protocol still in use on the Internet is *IP version 4 (IPv4)*. In addition to the standards for forwarding IP packets across the internetwork, IPv4 defines a 32-bit, 4-*octet* (a set of 8 bits) address, like the one shown in Figure 10-12. The combination of values of all four octets provides the whole of an IPv4 address. As shown in Figure 10-12, the IPv4 address assigned to a particular networked device is 192.168.1.255. The integer values in an IPv4 address convert to binary (see Figure 10-12) for storage and transmission.

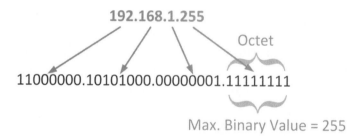

Figure 10-12   An IPv4 address is composed of four 8-bit octets.
© 2015 Cengage Learning®.

IPv4 Datagram

The foundation of IP is the format of its datagram, which is the primary element defined in this protocol. Table 10-7 details the fields in an IP datagram.

> **Note**
>
> Understand that the formatted data set defined by IP is either a datagram or a packet. It depends on whether the transport protocol is a UDP (datagram) or a TCP (packet). Officially, the most common is datagram.

Table 10-7 IPv4 Datagram Format

Field	Size (Bits)	Description
Version #	4	IPv4 = 4; IPv6 = 6
Internet Header Length (IHL)	4	Length of header in the number of 32-bit words
Type of Service (TOS)	8	Defines QoS features and differentiated services
Total Length (TL)	16	The total length of the datagram in bytes
Identification	16	Fragment identification number
Flags:		
Reserved	1	Not used
Don't Fragment	1	1 (don't fragment) or 0 (okay to fragment)
More Fragments	1	1 (more fragments follow) or 0 (last fragment)
Fragment Offset	13	Number of 64-bit fragments for offset
Time to Live (TTL)	8	Number of router hops before discarded
Protocol	8	The higher-layer protocol encapsulated
Header Checksum	16	A checksum value of the datagram header
Source Address	32	The IP address of the originating host
Destination Address	32	The IP address of the intended recipient host
Options	Variable	Values and flags for various datagram options
Padding	Variable	Depending on length of Options
Data/Payload	Variable	A higher-layer packet or a fragment of one

© 2015 Cengage Learning®.

Visualize that you've requested information from a website. The Application, Session, and Transport layers do their stuff and hand a packet to the Network layer and IP. The first decision IP must make is whether, depending on the size of the data in your request, to fragment your message. IP bases this decision on the *Maximum Transmission Unit (MTU)* of the next downstream pathway recipient, which is not necessarily the ultimate, intended recipient. The MTU gives the maximum datagram length that the interface is able to accommodate.

By design, IP works with all types of devices, ports, and interfaces. As a result, it must be flexible to accommodate the data throughput capabilities of the different devices. So, when IP (at some point between its originator and destination) encounters a lower MTU than was used for the incoming data, it must break up the data into fragments that are equal to or smaller than the MTU of the restricting device.

Table 10-7 identifies 32 bits of identification, flags, and offset values that communicate the fragmentation of the datagram. The Identification field carries a sequence number, in relationship to the other related fragments of the original message, which enables the recipient to reassemble the message in order. The two flags—Don't Fragment and More Fragment—indicate to upstream devices whether a datagram can be fragmented (again perhaps) and whether a specific datagram is or isn't the last fragment in a set, respectively. The Fragment Offset field contains the number of 64-bit blocks to skip over to place this fragment into its rightful position in the original message.

IPv4 Addressing Modes

In the context of networking communications, the method used to transfer a message from one node to one or more destination addresses is *broadcasting*. Network standards categorize broadcasting on the Network and Data Link layers using three addressing modes: *unicast*, *broadcast*, and *multicast*.

Unicast Addressing Mode "Uni" means one, as in unicycle, so it should be no surprise that unicast refers to a message transferred to a single destination. Unicast is the primary addressing mode on Ethernet and IPv4 networks, especially when a specific client requests resources or data from another node on the network (that is, client/server systems). Both IPv4 and IPv6 support unicast addressing.

However, unicast addressing does have a weakness. If an IPv4 message arrives at a network switch with a MAC address unknown to the switch, the switch broadcasts the message to all its ports and the devices connected to each.

There are several unicast protocols, including HTTP, SMTP, and FTP, all of which use TCP on the Transport layer. A datagram containing a single specific destination address is a unicast message.

Broadcast Addressing Mode The broadcast address mode transmits a specific block of data to all possible destinations on a network. In this mode, a single sender sends a message to all connected recipients. Like unicast, IPv4 and Ethernet networks support the broadcast addressing mode. ARP (see "Address Resolution Protocol (ARP)" earlier in this chapter) uses this mode to send address resolution inquiries to all the nodes on a network. An IPv4 datagram with a destination address of 255.255.255.255 indicates to the network that the message is a broadcast. IPv6 replaces broadcast addressing with a variation of the multicast addressing mode.

Multicast Addressing Mode Multicast addressing mode facilitates sending a specific data block from one or more originators to multiple destinations. In IPv4, the destination address is a multicast group address from the range 224.0.0.0 to (and including) 239.255.255.255. The sender transmits the datagram with a multicast address, and multiple receivers watch for messages from that multicast group address.

Because of its many-to-many capabilities, multicast datagrams move on the network via a multicast distribution tree. Each time a datagram reaches a branch point on a network (a fork of the tree), the network must copy and forward the datagram to all the branches. This method ensures that only one copy of the datagram travels on any network link.

Multicast uses two types of distribution trees: source trees and shared trees. A source tree branches from the root of the tree, with the possible recipients connected to the branches, something like leaves. Routers and Layer 3 switches perform this action using a multicast forwarding table. Figure 10-13 illustrates a multicast source tree. In this illustration, the sender broadcasts a multicast message. The source or root router (connected directly to the sender) uses the destination addresses to determine the branch of the routing map the message is to be forwarded.

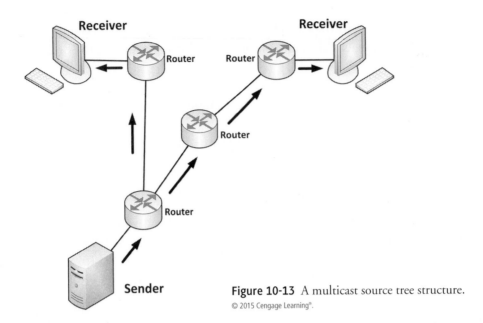

Figure 10-13 A multicast source tree structure.
© 2015 Cengage Learning®.

A shared tree differs from a source tree with the designation of a central point within the network. Multicast sources (senders) transmit multicast datagrams to this central point, officially the rendezvous point (RP). The receiving network nodes join the multicast at the RP. The RP forwards incoming multicast traffic to the branches (the RP is always the root) on which the multicast group members are located. Figure 10-14 illustrates the insertion of an RP into a network to form a multicast shared tree.

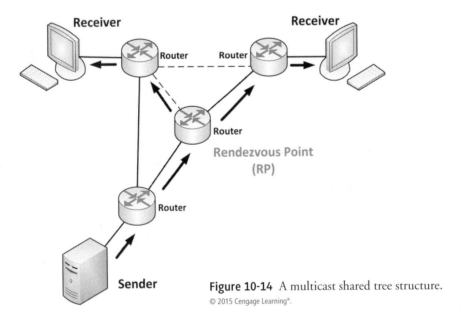

Figure 10-14 A multicast shared tree structure.
© 2015 Cengage Learning®.

There are numerous examples of multicasting on the web. When you subscribe to watch any live video content over the Internet, the sender adds your destination address to the multicast forwarding table, and you begin to receive the multicast video stream. For events that attract a larger number of viewers, such as the NCAA Final Four, multiple senders may share the forwarding table to ensure video quality and fast transfers.

IPv6

IP version 6 (IPv6) is the successor to IPv4. (No, there was no IPv5.) The impetus to develop IPv6 came from the concern that the Internet and the web were quickly using up all the IPv4 addresses available. Short-term addressing solutions helped to ease the crisis, but with the exponential growth of the Internet, the demand for IP addresses kept increasing. IPv6 is slowly taking hold, but some enterprises, service providers, and ISPs prefer to remain on the IPv4 system and not purchase upgrades or new equipment compatible with IPv6.

Although IPv6 does add several new features and protections, its most important feature is its expanded addressing scheme, which expands the number of directly addressable entities on the Internet from just under 4.3 billion (IPv4) to somewhere around 340,282,366,920,938,463,463,374,607,431,770,000,000, or 2^{128}. The IPv6 address string includes 128 bits divided into 16-octets. An IPv6 address, which is typically expressed in hexadecimal (for space considerations), can be something along the lines of 2011:db7:0:1243:0:765:9:1. Notice the use of colons (:) as separators in an IPv6 address.

Like IPv4, IPv6 implements three network and routing addressing classes. However, one of the IPv4 addressing modes is gone from IPv6: broadcast. Here are the three IPv6 addressing modes:

> **Unicast addressing**: Unicast addressing under IPv6 is essentially the same as that defined under IPv4. A single source addresses a datagram to a single destination.

> *Anycast* **addressing**: Like the broadcast and multicast addressing modes, anycast creates a one-to-many routing configuration. The main difference is that messages don't go to all possible receivers. The RP forwards the data stream to only the receiver branch that is logically nearest to it. About the best example of the use of anycast is distributed DNS systems and caching services that anycast for load balancing between geographically separated data centers.

> **Multicast addressing**: Multicast addressing is the same under IPv6 as it is under IPv4 (see "Multicast Addressing Mode" earlier in the chapter).

Higher-Layer Protocols

Above the Network layer of the OSI model are groups of protocols that combine into the higher-layer or higher-level layers that define the higher-layer protocols. Figure 10-15 shows two of the higher layers—Transport and Application—on which the remaining protocols you should know for the Cloud+ exam operate. Yes, the Session and Presentation layers are missing from Figure 10-15, but the protocols you need to know aren't dependent on character conversions and session control, other than that provided by TCP and UDP (discussed later in this section).

The higher-level protocols you learn about in this section are *Transmission Control Protocol (TCP)*, *User Datagram Protocol (UDP)*, *Dynamic Host Configuration Protocol (DHCP)*, *Domain Name System (DNS)*, *File Transfer Protocol (FTP)* and its secure versions SFTP and FTPS, *Hypertext Transfer Protocol (HTTP) and HTTP Secure (HTTPS)*, *Simple Mail Transfer Protocol (SMTP)*, and *Secure Shell (SSH)*.

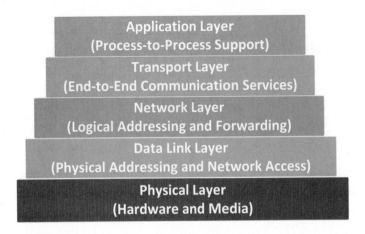

Figure 10-15 The hierarchy of OSI model layers.
The Transport and Application layers are higher-layer protocols.
© 2015 Cengage Learning®.

Transport Layer Protocols

The two primary protocols that operate on the Transport layer are TCP and UDP. These protocols provide transmission services to the Application layer to work in conjunction with lower-level protocols, primarily IP, to move streams of data between nodes on a network. Transport layer protocols ensure the reliable transmission and receipt of messages and may provide error-checking and data-flow controls.

Transport layer protocols operate with either connection-mode or connectionless-mode of transmission. TCP is a connection-mode protocol, and UDP is a connectionless-mode protocol.

Transmission Control Protocol (TCP)

The IP actually manages the delivery of data across a network, but TCP tracks the individual packets and fragments to ensure their integrity and arrival at their destination. Because TCP is a connection-mode protocol, it manages and ensures the existence of a connection (link) throughout the exchange of messages between two endpoints.

TCP is essentially the communications link between the Application layer and the Network layer. When an Application layer protocol sends a request or response message to a web server, TCP relieves that protocol (or the originating program) of dividing the message into IP-size fragments and then works with IP for their transmission. At the receiving end, TCP reassembles the IP fragments back into the original message.

Occasionally, network problems cause one or more fragments of a message to duplicate, become lost, or arrive out of sequence. When this happens, TCP is capable of detecting these issues and can request the originator to resend the lost fragments; it can put out-of-order fragments into the proper sequence and help to reduce network congestion to avoid these problems.

TCP's overhead functions—error detection and delivery guarantee—do add a small amount of latency to its transmissions compared to UDP (see the next section). However, TCP is all about accuracy, not timeliness. Although TCP does work with most of the more common Application layer protocols and services, such as HTTP, SMTP, FTP, and SSH (all discussed later in the chapter), it is not well suited to real-time applications like Voice over IP (VoIP).

User Datagram Protocol (UDP)

The User Datagram Protocol (UDP), like TCP, is a Transport layer protocol. However, their similarities end with the fact that they both work with IP to move data (in the form of datagrams) across a network. UPD is a connectionless-mode transmission protocol. This means that UDP provides no guarantees for messages arriving error-free, in sequence, or without duplication.

UDP is best suited for instances in which error detection and transmission management is either not needed or performed by the application program. Without this overhead, UDP is a faster, if not more unreliable, choice over TCP.

Application Layer Protocols

There is some difference between how the OSI and the TCP/IP network models define the *Application layer*. The OSI model defines it as the user interface that displays data, images, video, and audio in formats compatible with human senses, such as sight and sound. The TCP/IP model broadens the Application layer to become an abstraction layer in which a program converts user-provided data into encoded messages for transmission across a network. Application layer protocols and programs work directly with TCP or UDP to set up process-to-process or application-to-application communications on a network.

Dynamic Host Configuration Protocol (DHCP)

The Dynamic Host Configuration Protocol (DHCP) automates the network configuration of network nodes without the intervention of a network administrator (other than to initially set up DHCP). When a DHCP server receives a broadcast DHCP request from a network node (DHCP client), typically at start-up, the DHCP server sends a unicast message to the requestor node that includes the following:

> ➤ **IP address**: The DHCP server has a pool of IP addresses assigned by the network administrator.

> ➤ **Lease:** This is the length of time until the configuration assigned to the node expires.

> ➤ **Routing parameters**: The configuration also includes the node's subnet mask (on subnetted networks) and the default gateway (Internet/WAN gateway) for the network.

When a node disconnects, shuts down, restarts, or powers off, the IP address assigned to the node returns to the address pool for reassignment. When the lease time expires, the node requests the DHCP server to renew its configuration.

Domain Name System (DNS)

The Domain Name System (DNS) is not a protocol, but a hierarchically arranged system of databases and data caches that associate IP addresses with easily remembered and human-readable names: *Uniform Resource Locators (URLs)*. Perhaps the best example of how DNS works is the telephone book.

Much like a person's name is easier for most people to remember than a phone number or street address, a website's URL is typically easier to remember than the site's IP address. Nothing prevents you from just using an IP address; all browsers accept an IP address and will navigate to its site. However, it's likely easier for you to remember www.tonyspizza.com than 174.142.90.219, right?

Unlike the phone book, though, DNS is not an alphabetically organized list. It's a hierarchical network of distributed servers. The elements of the URL determine the path through the network to locate the reference entry for a particular website or Internet location and obtain its IP address. Figure 10-16 illustrates how this works.

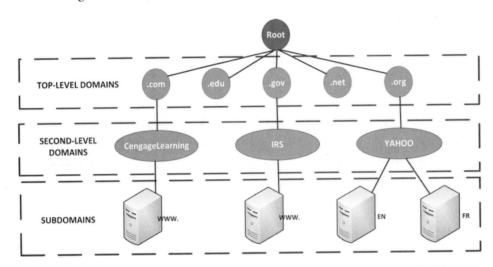

Figure 10-16 DNS is a hierarchical network of servers that translate URLs into IP addresses.
© 2015 Cengage Learning®.

A URL consists of three major sections, back to front: a *top-level domain (TLD)*, a second-level domain, and a subdomain. A TLD is the last element in a URL, such as the .com in Tony's URL. Other examples are .edu, .gov, .info, .net, and .org. There are 22 TLDs in use in the United States, not including the more than 250 country-specific TLDs. Each TLD has one or more servers that map the TLD to its second-level domains. As shown in Figure 10-16, cengagelearning, irs, and yahoo are all second-level domains. A second-level domain can have several subdomains or none, but the most common subdomain is still www.

Using the DNS to navigate to the Internal Revenue Service, you enter its URL as www.irs.gov. Your browser sends out a DNS request for its IP address, which it needs for its datagram request. DNS navigates to the .gov name server and looks up irs to get the address of its subdomain www.

FILE TRANSFER PROTOCOL (FTP)

FTP is one of the common Internet protocols that transfer files from one network host to another using TCP. FTP establishes separate control and data links on different ports of the hosts. The service requestor must authenticate with an assigned username and password or choose to authenticate as an anonymous user if the FTP server allows it. Dozens of FTP user clients are available, such as WS_FTP, SmartFTP, and FileZilla. FTP Secure (FTPS) and SSH FTP (SFTP) are secure versions of FTP.

FTP Secure (FTPS)

FTP Secure (FTPS) applies Transport Layer Security/Secure Socket Layer (TLS/SSL) security at the client through an explicit method. Using the explicit security method, which is known as FTP-ES, the FTPS client requests security services from the FTPS server, which then invokes a mutually agreed encryption algorithm. However, if the client doesn't request security, the server can terminate the session, continue with an unsecure session, or limit the requests of the client.

SSH FTP (SFTP)

SSH FTP, also *Secure FTP* or *SFTP*, is an FTP extension of the Secure Shell (SSH) protocol that provides secure file transfer capabilities. SFTP transmits over an SSH secure channel, which is an encrypted channel that cannot be compromised. In addition, the SFTP server authenticates the client and makes this identity known to the protocol.

HYPERTEXT TRANSFER PROTOCOL (HTTP)

The *Hypertext Transfer Protocol (HTTP)* is a data transfer protocol that operates with a standard client/server request and response methodology. The data moving between a client, typically a web browser, and the server, generally a web server, is composed of HTTP request messages from the client to the server. The client is requesting resources, most commonly *Hypertext Markup Language (HTML)* files, which the server provides in a response message. The response message may contain only status information, or it may contain the requested web page content.

The HTTP client sets up a TCP connection to port 80 (more on ports later in the chapter) on the server, which polls that port for client request messages. The server must either send back a status ("OK") message or respond with the requested content. The server can also send back an error message, like the dreaded Error 404 status.

HTTP Secure (HTTPS) is not exactly a protocol. It is actually HTTP layered on top of TLS/SSL, which provides the security of TLS/SSL to the communications capabilities of HTTP.

SIMPLE MAIL TRANSFER PROTOCOL

The Simple Mail Transfer Protocol (SMTP) is a legacy protocol for transmitting electronic mail across a network. In today's networking environment, mail servers use SMTP to send and receive mail messages, while email clients use SMTP only to send messages to mail servers for forwarding. Email clients commonly use the Post Office Protocol (POP3), the Internet Message Access Protocol (IMAP), or a proprietary mail system, like Microsoft Exchange.

SMTPS is the secure version of SMTP, which again is not really a protocol because it lays itself on top of TLS/SSL to connect over a secure channel.

Ports and Binding

It's common for networking professionals to associate a port with an interface on a networking device. However, as logical as that may sound, a port really isn't hardware. A port is a software-created communications endpoint that is specific to a particular application, process, or most commonly, a protocol. A port actually resides inside the host operating system.

Common Ports

The use of ports is inherent to the function of Transport layer protocols, especially TCP and UDP. The purpose of a *port* is twofold: 1) it allows outbound and inbound traffic to share a single IP address (the gateway address); and 2) it allows for the identification of an arriving service request or response. For example, if a packet comes in for port 80, the host knows immediately that the message is HTTP formatted and exactly where it goes. When a packet transmits, the port number associated with its protocol or application and the destination's IP address combine to create the full destination address of the intended recipient. The destination IP address directs the routing used to get the message to the host server of the recipient. Once there, the host uses the port number to identify the specific process associated with the port number.

The use of ports is so standard that the Internet Assigned Numbers Authority (IANA) maintains an official list of port numbers. Table 10-8 lists the common (well-known) ports you should be familiar with for the Cloud+ exam.

Table 10-8 Common Port Numbers

Port Number	Protocol/Application
20	FTP Data
21	FTP Commands
22	SSH
25	SMTP
53	DNS
68	DHCP
80	HTTP
443	HTTPS
1293	IPsec

© 2015 Cengage Learning®.

Trunk Ports

Like a tree has many branches attached to its trunk, a process associated with a trunk port is able to receive and process two or more signals at the same time. A *trunk port* can also connect switching centers or multiple nodes (originators or destinations) in a communication system, such as the telephone system, video distribution, or the like. Trunks interconnect switches and routers to create networks; they connect LANs into virtual LANs (VLANs) and WANs.

Trunking is the use and management of trunks in a communication network. It is most common in support of VLANs. Trunking assigned to a single port makes that port capable of servicing all traffic of a VLAN on a particular switch. So configured, the port becomes a trunk port.

Port Binding

Computers (nodes or servers) associate their I/O channels through Internet sockets. A *socket* is a combination of the Transport layer protocol in use, the port number associated with a particular process or application, and its IP address. This association, a binding, allows the computer to send and receive data to and from the network.

The computer's operating system transmits outgoing data from the process and application ports and forwards incoming network traffic to the process matching the arriving packet's IP address and port number. Bindings are limited to just one per IP address and port combination. Port conflicts can occur when two or more applications attempt to bind a particular port to the same IP address and protocol. Figure 10-17 shows a list of active bindings on a Windows computer.

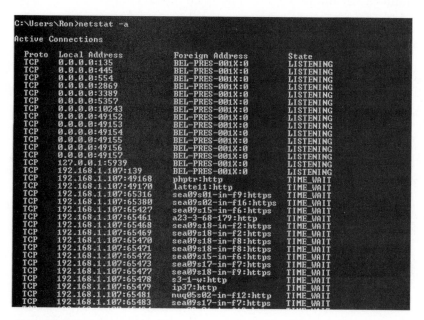

Figure 10-17 The results of a netstat –a command on a Windows computer showing the active bindings and their status.
Used with permission from Microsoft.

In Figure 10-17, the Proto column shows the bound protocol, and the Local Address column lists the local IP address (the first four numbers) followed by the bound port number (after the : character). The State column indicates that the operating system is "listening" to the port, which means the socket is being monitored for incoming traffic.

Chapter Summary

> Access protocols are standardized rules for conducting communication sessions over a network. Their functions include allotting network addresses, creating point-to-point connections, establishing links between nodes, identifying the shortest path between nodes, and managing and discovering nodes.

> Fibre Channel (FC) is the generic name for a high-speed networking technology common for interconnecting networks to data storage devices. FC is compatible with electromagnetic interfaces, as well as fiber optic media.

> Fibre Channel over Ethernet (FCoE) enables FC data frames to travel on 10 Gigabit or faster Ethernet networks.

> Internet Small Computer System Interface (iSCSI) facilitates storing and retrieving data from location-independent data storage facilities. iSCSI supports transmission of data over virtually any network.

> A network protocol defines a standard set of formats and rules to use in establishing a connection, communicating, and moving data between linked endpoints.

> The Data Link (Layer 2) protocols you should know for the Cloud+ exam and for networking in general are ARP, L2TP, PPP, and Ethernet. ARP converts IP addresses to physical or MAC addresses. The most common use of ARP is with IPv4 on an Ethernet network. L2TP is most common to VPNs. PPP is an encapsulating protocol that sets up direct connections between two network nodes. Ethernet is a Physical and Data Link layer transmission and media access technology.

> A tunneling protocol encapsulates the data payload from the frame or packet of another network protocol. The encapsulating protocol becomes the delivery protocol.

> The Ethernet Physical layer specifies the use of twisted-pair copper cabling, fiber optics, and wireless signaling.

> Carrier Ethernet refers to telecommunications technologies deployed by NSPs to extend Ethernet services beyond LANs.

> IP defines the fundamentals of moving data across an internetwork and the logical-level addressing of the nodes and devices on a network. It also defines the routing function that enables data to move from gateway to gateway.

> IPv4 defines a 32-bit, 4-octet address. The three broadcasting types of IPv4 are unicast, broadcast, and multicast.

> IPv6 has an expanded addressing scheme that includes 128 bits divided into 16 octets, which are separated by colons (:). IPv6 implements three addressing modes: unicast addressing, anycast addressing, and multicast addressing.

> The two primary protocols on the Transport layer are TCP and UDP. Transport layer protocols operate with either connection-mode or connectionless-mode. TCP is a connection-mode protocol, and UDP is a connectionless-mode protocol. TCP includes error detection and delivery guarantee. UDP provides no guarantees for messages arriving error-free.

> DHCP automates the network configuration of network nodes by supplying nodes with IP address, lease, and routing parameters.

> DNS is a hierarchically arranged system of databases and data caches that associate IP addresses with URLs.

➤ FTP transfers files from one network host to another using TCP. FTPS applies TLS/SSL security at the client end. SFTP provides secure file transfer capabilities over an SSH secure channel.

➤ HTTP is an HTML data transfer protocol that operates with a standard client/server request and response methodology.

➤ SMTP transmits electronic mail across a network. SMTPS is the secure version of SMTP that runs on top of TLS/SSL to connect over a secure channel.

➤ A port is a software-created communications endpoint specific to a particular application, process, or a protocol. A port resides inside the host operating system. The ports you should be familiar with for the Cloud+ exam are ports 20, 21, 22, 25, 53, 68, 80, 443, and 1293.

➤ A trunk port is able to receive and process two or more signals at the same time. Trunking is the use and management of trunks in a communication network.

➤ A socket is a combination of the protocol in use, the port number associated with a particular process or application, and its IP address.

Key Terms

10BASE-T

10 Gigabit Ethernet

Access protocols

Address Resolution Protocol (ARP)

American National Standards Institute (ANSI)

Anycast

Application layer

Arbitrated loop (FC-AL) topology

Asynchronous Transfer Mode (ATM)

Broadcast

Broadcasting

Carrier Ethernet

Carrier Sense Multiple Access with Collision Detection (CSMA/CD)

Command Descriptor Block (CDB)

Cross-point switched (FC-SW) topology

Datagram

Domain Name System (DNS)

Dynamic Host Configuration Protocol (DHCP)

E-LAN

E-Line

Ethernet

E-Tree

Fast Ethernet

FC fabric

Fibre Channel (FC)

Fibre Channel over Ethernet (FCoE)

File Transfer Protocol (FTP)

FTP Secure (FTPS)

Gigabit Ethernet

Gigabit Fibre Channel

High-Performance Parallel Interface (HIPPI)

HTTP Secure (HTTPS)

Hypertext Markup Language (HTML)

Hypertext Transfer Protocol (HTTP)

Initiator

Integrated Drive Electronics (IDE)

Intelligent Peripheral Interface (IPI-3)

Internet Protocol (IP)

Internet Small Computer System Interface (iSCSI)

IP version 4 (IPv4)

IP version 6 (IPv6)

L_port

L2TP Access Concentrator (LAC)

L2TP Network Server (LNS)

L2TP/IPsec

Layer Two Tunneling Protocol (L2TP)

Maximum Transmission Unit (MTU)

Metropolitan area networks (MANs)

Multicast

N_port

Network protocol

Octet

Point-to-point (FC-P2P) topology

Point-to-Point Protocol (PPP)

Port

Private loop

Secure FTP (SFTP)

Secure Shell (SSH)

Simple Mail Transfer Protocol (SMTP)

Single Byte Command Code Set (SBCCS)

Socket

Storage area networks (SANs)

Target

Top-level domain (TLD)

Transmission Control Protocol (TCP)

Trunk port

Tunneling protocol

Unicast

Uniform Resource Locator (URL)

User Datagram Protocol (UDP)

Review Questions

1. Which of the following allows FC data frames to travel over a 10-gigabit Ethernet network?

    a. FCoA

    b. FCoE

    c. iSCSI

    d. None of the above

2. ARP is a(n) _____ layer protocol.

3. True or False? In a tunneling protocol, the encapsulating protocol becomes the delivery protocol.

4. What type of protocol defines a standard set of formats and rules to use in establishing a connection, communicating, and moving data between linked endpoints?

   a. Application

   b. Transport

   c. Network

   d. Data Link

5. The _____ Physical layer specifies the use of twisted-pair copper cabling, fiber optics, and wireless signaling.

6. True or False? IPv4 defines a 128-bit, 4-octet address.

7. TCP and UDP operate on what OSI model layer?

   a. Application

   b. Transport

   c. Network

   d. Data Link

8. A _____ is a software-created communications endpoint specific to a particular application, process, or a protocol.

9. True or False? A socket is a combination of the protocol in use, the port number associated with a particular process or application, and its MAC address.

10. An IPv6 address separates its octets using what character?

    a. Asterisk (*)

    b. Period (.)

    c. Semicolon (;)

    d. Colon (:)

11. _____ automates the network configuration of network nodes by supplying nodes with IP address, lease, and routing parameters.

12. True or False? The two primary protocols that operate on the Transport layer are TCP and IP.

13. FTPS applies what security technology to secure file transfers?

    a. SSH

    b. IPsec

    c. TLS/SSL

    d. None of the above

14. HTTP is associated with port _____.

15. True or False? DNS is a locally hosted logical to physical address resolution protocol.

Answers to Review Questions

1. b

2. Data Link or Layer 2

3. True

4. b

5. IEEE 802.3

6. False

7. b

8. port

9. False

10. d

11. DHCP

12. False

13. c

14. 80

15. False

CHAPTER 11

Virtual Environment Planning

After reading this chapter and completing the exercises, you will be able to:

- Explain the process of capacity planning for a virtualized environment
- Describe the hardware, technology, and software considerations of virtualized environment planning

A virtual computing or networking environment isn't something you can just jump into without knowing your business model and policies and planning how the virtual environment is to support them. To effectively plan for a virtualized environment for a single organization or a multitiered enterprise, you must complete the same steps. The same issues, although on differing scales, are inherent regardless of the size of the computing environment and the organization it supports.

This chapter covers the more important considerations in the planning for a virtual environment, some large (at the organizational level) and some seemingly small (such as *Basic Input/Output System [BIOS]* settings). Regardless of their seeming importance, addressing each of them can help to ensure a successful implementation of a virtualized computing environment.

Capacity Planning for a Virtual Environment

Information Technology (IT) departments commonly are more reactionary than proactive. Any planning performed typically focuses on how to correct the frequently reported performance problems or the installation of new technology as a means to eliminate commonly occurring issues in the short term. Ideally, IT management should be looking to implement systems, technology, and policies that both improve the customer experience and avoid future problems altogether—before they happen. The goal of this planning should be the development of a forward-looking plan to configure IT services so that they provide sufficient computing power for the future needs of the organization. This process is *capacity planning*.

Capacity planning for a virtual environment doesn't mean projecting the amount of disk storage needed in the future, nor is this a one-time event. Capacity planning is more about ensuring that the virtual environment you want to create will be able to accommodate your current and future computing needs. Your planning should address the computing needs of your current applications and the applications or services you want to add. It must also consider how you will distribute the computing load in a virtual environment.

You can use one of several approaches to produce an effective capacity plan for a new (or improved) virtualized computing environment. However, regardless of the approach you use, whether it is at a management level or a detailed data center resource level, many of the steps are the same and involve gaining commitments from senior management.

ITIL Capacity Planning

The *Information Technology Infrastructure Library (ITIL)* defines an approach to capacity planning that provides for the alignment of an organization's business needs with its IT services. The goal of the ITIL approach to capacity planning is to develop an "optimum and cost-effective" plan for IT services that are matched to an organization's business policies and demands. The ITIL approach also links to its definitions of capacity management (more on this later in this section).

The ITIL capacity planning approach involves five major planning activities:

> ➤ Aligning IT services with customer requirements

> ➤ Matching IT services to the organization objectives and policies

> ➤ Reducing the impact of service changes and transitions

> ➤ Ensuring that quality, reliability, and efficiency are of sufficient levels to support organizational objectives and policies

> ➤ Providing continuous service improvements

MEETING CUSTOMER REQUIREMENTS

Customer requirements or customer needs can be difficult to nail down. There is an old saying in capacity planning that if you ask a ditch digger what he needs to do a better job, the answer will likely be that he wants a bigger shovel. All too frequently, the organization gives him just that—a bigger shovel—without regard to how to make the task more efficient for the good of both the employee and the organization. In this instance, a backhoe may have been a better choice.

When an IT department looks to ensure its resources are in line with customer needs, it must consider the future of the customer's task and provide resources that are more efficient to use, to support, and to change as needs change. If management says that it wants to reduce the staffing in a particular cost area even though the workload is likely to increase, IT must consider future solutions that require fewer employees to accomplish more transactions.

MATCHING IT SERVICES TO ORGANIZATION OBJECTIVES

All functions within an organization should be structured, staffed, and focused on achieving the objectives of the organization. Of course, this includes the IT services unit. The services provided by IT through a virtualized environment or through the services it contracts for a cloud services provider must justify its cost against how it supports and meets the goals of the organization.

Any change in the capacity and capabilities of IT services must align with the current and future needs of the organization. The more closely these present and future service changes match where the organization on the whole is going, the easier it will be when it becomes time for major changes in IT, such as moving into the cloud or implementing virtualization.

REDUCING THE IMPACT OF CHANGES

Your planning should also include the steps you will take when you introduce changes to make the transition from existing to future as transparent as possible to end users. All the technology in the world cannot overcome confusion or resistance from the people who actually use it. Inclusion, orientation, training, and live testing can be strong tools to minimize the resistance to change naturally found in an organization.

The planning should also address any future bottlenecks or points of lesser performance. It should address any foreseeable overload, slow performance, or the cause of low-level or disaster recovery. In a virtualized environment, remember that all the virtual machines (VMs) essentially use the same central processing units (CPUs), storage, and memory on the physical servers. You must also consider whether cloud service providers have the scalability to grow with your business.

ENSURING THAT SERVICE LEVELS SUPPORT ORGANIZATIONAL OBJECTIVES

This phase of the capacity planning process relates directly to the outcomes of the previous step. In this phase, you must consider whether the hardware, software, staffing, and contracted services under consideration, along with the skill requirements of the entire organization, will uphold the service-level expectations of the organization. Consider that major changes in IT services usually spawn the expectation of increased services and performance.

PROVIDING CONTINUOUS SERVICE IMPROVEMENTS

Whether on a managerial or administrative level or at the detailed IT services level, any capacity planning must address how current and future systems will deliver continuing improvements in the services provided. Senior management may not see the value of investments that fail to improve on the overall performance of IT services. This is not always easy to do, because many of the technologies that should offer the most improvement in service are likely only conceptual or not a reality at the time of your planning.

IT Services Capacity Planning

A management-level capacity planning process is necessary before the development of a truly effective IT services capacity plan. IT planning must address the vision, objectives, and expectations of the organization for IT services. With this guidance, IT administrators can then develop a forward-looking plan that has the most efficient and effective IT services plan, including its capacities, to match its services to the demands and needs of the organization.

In the context of capacity planning for IT services, the focus is on determining the amount of physical hardware required to support the virtual machines and servers the organization needs to meet its objectives. The capacity planning for a cloud service provider is more complex. Its business plan, its goals, the number of planned subscribers, and the company's *Service Level Agreements (SLA)* further complicate this planning.

There are three primary considerations to include in the capacity planning at the IT services level:

> ➤ Identify service level requirements

> ➤ Inventory current capacity

> ➤ Plan

IDENTIFY SERVICE LEVEL REQUIREMENTS

For the most part, IT services provide service for user workloads. The first step in this phase of capacity planning is to categorize the workloads supported by IT services and identify the service level expectations for each. *Workload categorization* should consider the customer (department or user), the type of workload (financial, inventory, order processing, and so on), and the processes involved in the workload (online interactive, batch processes, as required processing, and so on).

For each of the workloads identified in the organization, you should determine its measureable unit of work. Is it a sales transaction at a fast food counter? If so, what are the IT resources utilized in accomplishing this unit of work. Is it on the scale of closing the accounting books at the end of a period? What IT resources (and possibly departmental resources) are required for its completion? Should this work unit be broken down into smaller ones?

In addition, for each work unit identified, the end user's expectation of service must be quantified, as well as possible. Without this measurement, IT services don't have a target upon which to base their capacity planning. For example, an organization identifies an online order entry as a workload. In its analysis, performed in conjunction with the inside sales department, the organization determined that this involves the sales entry application to be running concurrently for six workstations, with each requiring at least three disk inputs/outputs (I/Os), requiring subsecond response times. From the analysis that also includes the projection of a significant increase in inside sales volume, IT administrators can project the hardware and virtual elements required to supply the desired or compromised service levels.

INVENTORY CURRENT CAPACITY

Four steps are involved with measuring (inventorying) the current capacity of a data center or IT service center:

1. Measure the performance of any items directly stated or referenced in an SLA or business policy. It will be difficult to determine the adequacy of the current capacity without formalized stated performance targets. This information tells you whether the current capacity of the existing environment can meet projected needs.

2. Measure the usage of both hardware and software resources, including CPUs, I/O devices, disk storage, and memory. This measurement can identify those resources that are currently near capacity and may limit future capacity growth.

3. Match the resources used to accomplish each of the workloads identified in the earlier phase and determine which workloads are the primary users of each resource. The purpose behind this step is to identify those workloads that have the heaviest utilization of each resource.

4. For each workload, identify the components of its response time, if applicable, to determine the resources that affect response time the most.

PLAN FOR THE FUTURE

Depending on the planning horizon against which capacity is being planned (6 months, 1 year, or 3 years), the next step is to project the resource capacities IT services must have to support projected business services in that time frame. If the earlier planning phases have adequately defined the future processing requirements, then projecting the appropriate system configuration to meet service level performance should be somewhat easier.

The first step in this phase is to forecast the future requirements of IT services to meet future organizational needs. A part of this planning is to determine how far into the future the existing resources will continue to satisfy projected service levels. This planning should also address all future processing requirements from any source in the organization. The source of future requirements could be from growth (volume, acquisitions, mergers, or divestitures) by the organization, new applications, or foreseen technological advancements.

AUTOMATED CAPACITY PLANNING TOOLS

There are numerous automated capacity planning tools available for use. Typically, these tools are relatively expensive, but depending on the size of the data center or cloud service center, they could be a good investment.

For virtual environments, the VMware Capacity Planner tool is the market leader. HP has the Microsoft Virtual Solution Server Sizer, and NetIQ offers the PlateSpin. PowerRecon includes workload tracking. These tools are good for planning a shift to a virtualized environment.

Virtualization Hardware Considerations

In addition to the planning and designing tasks for the implementation of virtual computing, several setup and configuration steps may be necessary to ensure the success of the environment. This section looks at some additional planning and design considerations along with some hardware settings and configurations you should consider.

Virtualization Design Considerations

When considering the hardware requirements for a virtualized computing environment of any size, here are some important things to keep in mind:

> ➤ Virtual machines can add significant overhead to existing resources, especially CPUs and memory.

> ➤ You shouldn't try to virtualize on the cheap. The use of high-end hardware enhances the reliability, availability, scalability, and needed redundancy of the system.

> ➤ Virtual environments share resources. Make sure that sufficient I/O capabilities are available, especially for storage I/O operations.

> ➤ Carefully consider their need before implementing multiple virtual CPUs (vCPUs) on VMs, because they can introduce latency to application performance through queuing.

ESTIMATING HARDWARE REQUIREMENTS

An important part of planning and designing a new (or expanding) virtual environment is to project the amount and type of hardware resources required to meet the expected service levels of the organization, now and in the future. The major reason for data center virtualization is to save the expense of hardware; it may be difficult to understand that, initially, you may need to add hardware.

To estimate the server requirements for a virtualized environment, you need to establish a *baseline* estimate of the server requirements for existing or new applications that are to be a part of the virtualized environment. Do you have more server capacity than you need at present? Or are you barely scraping by? This analysis also establishes your existing system performance profile.

Next, you should profile each application expected to run on a virtual machine. Study the performance data for each application running in the existing hardware environment to learn how and when the application uses system resources, especially CPU, memory, the network, and data storage. With CPUs and memory, how much of the resource is consumed, and for how long? With network and data storage, know the number of I/O transactions along with the demanded bandwidth and storage, respectively. Longer periods of data analysis result in data that is more reliable, but a month of data for a commonly used application should be sufficient. Although it's unlikely to happen, the sum of the measurements for all applications provides a worst-case look at peak hardware demands should all the applications be running simultaneously.

In addition to the worst-case scenario, you should model the resource demands of restarting the environment or the processing load of periodic or recurring events, such as regularly scheduled online sales or perhaps a holiday rush. To complete the performance profile on the existing system, you should model any events that could launch multiple applications or functions, all running concurrently, such as fault management, service desk troubleshooting tools, or automated root-cause analysis tools that could start up during peak demand.

BIOS FEATURES FOR VIRTUALIZATION

An often-overlooked part of a virtualization implementation is the BIOS settings on the servers. Many IT administrators believe that just installing a computer with processors that have virtualization extensions guarantees high-level performance and system stability. However, without enabling certain BIOS settings, the processor may not perform to the level desired. By enabling certain BIOS settings, the processor can use the virtualization features that support the functionality of virtual machines. On the other hand, disabling certain BIOS settings can provide system stability. In addition to the virtualization extensions for the processor and memory, other virtualization settings can enable virtualization for I/O operations, such as device interrupts and *direct memory access (DMA)* transfers.

You should never assume that a processor's BIOS settings enable virtualization extensions by default, regardless of what the manufacturer's documentation, or hype, might imply. In fact, some motherboards disable virtualization by default to accommodate the use of nonvirtualized processors. With the virtualization extensions disabled, a processor will run in nonvirtualized mode, meaning just one server and one workload.

Two important processor-level security features that protect the BIOS code from corruption or modification are *Trusted Execution Technology (TXT)* and *Trusted Platform Module (TPM)*. In a virtualized environment, TXT and TPM protect the system against "blue pill" virtualization attacks by creating a *chain of trust* that allows virtual machines to start up securely. Hypervisors that support the *Measured Launch Environment (MLE)* feature measure the first executable block of the hypervisor and, if no modification exists, start-up continues, in accordance with the rules of the *Launch Code Policy (LCP)* that the system administrator sets up.

Trusted Execution Technology (TXT)

The Intel TXT provides assurances at start-up (boot) that the computer and its operating system are authentic and that the operating system is trusted. TXT measures the system firmware and BIOS to make its judgment. TXT protects the platform against software attacks aiming to steal sensitive information by corrupting the BIOS code or modifying the configuration of the platform.

Trusted Platform Module (TPM)

TPM provides several security features through a set of *Platform Configuration Registers (PCRs)*, which are special-purpose registers with extensions that store a variety of measurements, encrypted using SHA-1 hashing to create a chain of trust. The measurements performed may include program code, data structures, configuration data, or anything else that can be stored in memory. At start-up, a comparison of the stored measurements and their live equivalents can detect if a discrepancy exists between the store measurement and the live measurement. If it appears that a modification occurred, TPM halts the boot process. Here's the process used for a start-up on a computer with a TXT/TPM-embedded processor:

1. On power-up, TXT verifies system firmware measurements prior to the boot process.

2. TXT verifies the measurements of the hypervisor.

3. If all measurements verify, TPM releases (unseals) the device encryption key.

4. TPM allows the operating system, virtual machines, and applications to start.

5. If any of the measurements is invalid, TPM issues a system lockup and blocks the start-up from proceeding.

Virtualization Technology (VT)

Intel and AMD processors, especially those released after 2011, incorporate *Virtualization Technology (VT)*, which is also known as hardware-based virtualization technology. VT accelerates the primary features of a virtualized platform, including these:

- Acceleration of platform control between the hypervisor and guest operating systems

- Ability of the hypervisor to assign I/O devices to guest operating systems

- Optimized virtualization on a network through adapter acceleration

- Support of porting legacy applications on new platforms

- Improved system security and stability

Under software virtualization, the hypervisor emulates hardware resources to the operating system. Hardware-assisted virtualization allows the operating system to directly interact with network resources without the need for emulation or para-virtualization.

Intel Virtualization Technology (Intel VT) is a set of hardware enhancements to Intel server and client platforms that provide software-based virtualization solutions. Intel VT allows a platform to run multiple operating systems and applications in independent partitions, allowing one computer system to function as multiple virtual systems.

VIRTUAL ENVIRONMENT HARDWARE SIZING

One of the most important planning and design steps you should perform when preparing to install a virtualized computing environment is to determine the number, size, interface, and compatibility of the various physical hardware and virtual hardware components that will make up the environment. Questions like, "How many VMs can run on a server?," "How many vNICs can be interfaced to a NIC?," and "Can you interface vNICs to a NIC?" need answers before you get too far into the implementation planning.

Sizing Host Servers

The physical host servers in a virtualized environment are the packhorses that carry the weight of the infrastructure. It's important not to undersize the servers, but oversizing a bit isn't all bad. There are four basic criteria for sizing a host server computer: memory, processor, network, and storage resources.

Memory There is a simple answer to the question of how much memory a physical host server should have: as much as it will hold. On the other hand, a virtual server should have only as much as its VMs require. Remember that you can overcommit memory for the VMs, but you do run the risk of virtual memory swapping. Having as much physical memory as possible not only provides the flexibility needed for implementation and fine-tuning, but allows for the addition of more virtual machines as they are needed.

Processors The primary consideration for sizing the processor in a host server has to do not only with the performance required, but also with how many VMs the host server is to support. *Multicore processors* have two to ten CPUs (cores), each of which can support as many as four VMs per core.

How many cores a virtualized environment should have is dependent on the native operating system installed and the specific applications supported by the VMs. Another consideration is the number of *virtual CPUs (vCPUs)* configured to each VM. A vCPU is a VM's virtual processor that runs on a physical CPU. Each VM can have four to eight vCPUs, depending on the virtualization software in use and the number of processors and core of the host.

Unfortunately, there is no standard formula to compute the number of vCPUs and VMs required for a standard installation because there really aren't standard installations. The maximums, which shouldn't be confused with reality, for VMware's ESX are 512 vCPUs per host and 25 vCPUs per core, which should indicate the flexibility available to configure the host and VM requirements. A good rule of thumb to start out with is three to five vCPUs per physical CPU. Monitor the system and adjust the ratios up or down as needed to improve performance.

Network Adapters Although not restricted to only the physical or virtual server, one of the main sizing issues for a virtual network is the number of *physical NICs (pNICs)* and *virtual NICs (vNICs)* the virtualized environment will need. The actual number of pNICs relates to whether the physical network includes a network attached storage (NAS) or a storage area network (SAN), has connections to networked peripherals or other networking devices, and extends as desired for redundancy. Figure 11-1 illustrates the relationship of pNICs to vNICs. Although this figure shows only a single VM and one vNIC, the VM and any other VMs could have more than one vNIC.

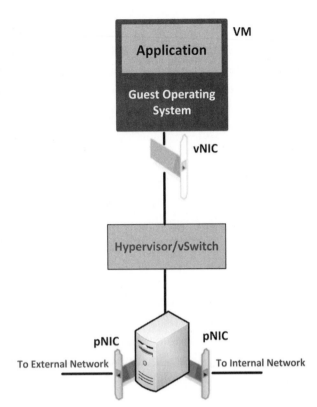

Figure 11-1 A virtual machine's vNIC can be switched to any number of host server pNICs.
© 2015 Cengage Learning®.

Disk Storage Another important consideration when configuring a virtual environment is disk storage. It's not so much how much storage, although that can be just as important, but what kind and technology of storage. On a smaller virtual network, direct attached storage (DAS) may work effectively enough, but the scalability and flexibility of the network should it need to grow is limited. For a more robust virtual network, especially one expected to grow in volume, size, or scope, an SAN may be the best choice, although it is the most expensive option. Another popular option is *storage as a service (SaaS)*, which can provide immediate scalability as well as backup and recovery services.

Regardless of the choice, you should ensure that the storage space available is sufficient for the virtual network components, primarily virtual servers, and VMs. How much you need again depends on the configuration of the virtual network, the frequency of snapshots, plus 10 to 20 percent for unplanned growth.

Virtual Machines per Server The size of the applications that run in the VMs determines the number of VMs a host server is able to support. Conceivably, a host server can support more than 100 VMs, or it may be able to run only 1. The VMs running on a host server should consume around 80 percent of the server's capacity for cost effectiveness. However, the host server, overall, should also provide capacity for unplanned or staged growth.

Memory Virtualization

Memory virtualization is a process that uncouples the primary memory (random access memory [RAM]) on one or more computers to create a memory pool that the processes running on the computers contributing to the pool can share. Memory virtualization in a nonvirtualized environment of clustered servers allows the processors to share a memory pool. However, the two types of memory virtualization discussed in this section are software-based virtualized environment memory sharing and hardware-based virtualized environment memory sharing.

In a virtualized environment, the *hypervisor* or *virtual machine manager* (*VMM*) manages all memory. A part of the management memory is set aside for the hypervisor. The hypervisor then allocates the remaining memory to the VMs. Each VM consumes a certain amount of memory based on its execution size plus any additional memory for virtualization overhead.

Similar to the Windows operating system's virtual memory feature, when memory reaches capacity, the hypervisor stores idle virtual memory pages on disk. Both the virtual and the physical memory is in pages (blocks) that range, depending on the processor in use, from 4 KB to 2 MB.

CONFIGURED, SHARED, AND RESERVED MEMORY

One of the key settings of a VM is its configured memory size. When a VM initiates on a guest operating system, the configured memory is the amount of memory given to the guest operating system for allocation. However, the configured memory size is unrelated to the amount of memory that the hypervisor allocates to the VM. The amount of memory allocated to the VM depends on its resource settings that define its reservation, share, and limit.

> **Note**
>
> Remember that a guest operating system running in a VM believes it is running on a physical machine. The configured memory size is the amount of memory that the guest operating system believes it controls.

Reservation

The *memory reservation* setting for a VM sets the guaranteed minimum amount of physical memory the VM needs to run efficiently. This setting should be at a level that provides enough memory for the VM to run without needing to page memory to disk. With its full reservation of memory, a VM gets to keep this memory, even if it's idle. If the VM's full reservation amount isn't available at start-up, the hypervisor continues to assign it any unused memory until it reaches its reservation amount.

Share

In the general context of computing, *shared memory* is a pool of physical memory that several computers, applications, or services can access simultaneously. However, in a virtualized environment, a share, as it relates to memory, is something quite different. The share setting on a VM indicates the relative priority a VM has when it needs to request additional memory beyond its reservation for overhead. Overhead memory is a reserved memory allocation that holds a VM's frame buffer and data structures.

Limit

The *limit* setting for a VM indicates the maximum amount of physical memory that the guest operating system can allocate it at start-up. However, the VM's configured size can also limit its memory allocation.

MEMORY SHARING

The objective of memory sharing in a virtualized environment is to minimize the number of memory pages a particular workload (such as order entry) requires. Workloads that involve running the same VMs with the same applications accessing the same data lend themselves to higher levels of over-commitment, resulting in as much as 30 percent less virtual memory than would be required on dedicated physical memory.

Memory over-commitment occurs when a hypervisor allocates more memory space than is physically available on its host system. For example, a hypervisor may start four VMs, each with a configured space of 1 GB, on a host with only 2 GB of RAM.

SOFTWARE-BASED MEMORY VIRTUALIZATION

In a cooperative manner, the hypervisor and each VM combine functions to create *software-based memory virtualization*. The hypervisor creates a mapping of each of the guest operating systems' memory pages ("machine pages") to the physical memory pages ("physical pages") of their underlying computers. This allows each VM to visualize the memory on its host as one contiguous addressable memory space. The hypervisor then intercepts all VM memory commands and communicates directly with the host processor's *memory management unit (MMU)*. This approach to memory virtualization eliminates the overhead of address translation. Figure 11-2 illustrates the structure of software-based memory virtualization.

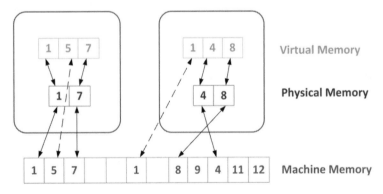

Figure 11-2 The layers of virtualized memory on a virtual server, machine, and software.
© 2015 Cengage Learning®.

HARDWARE-ASSISTED MEMORY VIRTUALIZATION

Some microprocessors have *hardware-assisted memory virtualization* embedded in their firmware. The AMD SVM-V and the Intel Xeon 5500 processors implement hardware-assisted virtualization using two page table layers. Processors use page tables to store the associations between physical memory addresses and virtual memory addresses.

An application running in a virtual memory environment thinks it is running in a large block of contiguous physical memory. In reality, the physical memory actually in use is likely to be smaller, distributed blocks of memory or in a memory page written to the hard disk. The memory page table stores the association of the physical addresses of the memory assigned to an application and their virtual memory equivalents.

In the two-layer page table approach of the AMD and Intel processors, the first layer is essentially the page table maintained by virtually all processors, but the second layer contains the mappings of host physical page addresses to machine page addresses. The processor's *translation look-aside buffer (TLB)*, maintained by the MMU, caches the more active mappings. In a single-layer approach to virtual memory, if the virtual address is not found in the TLB (a miss), the hardware accesses the physical memory to rebuild the address pair. However, in the two-layer approach, the second layer provides a form of backup should a miss occur on the TLB.

Chapter Summary

> Capacity planning for a virtual environment is ensuring that a virtual environment is able to accommodate current and future computing needs.

> The ITIL approach to capacity planning provides for the alignment of an organization's business needs with its IT services.

> The services of a virtualized environment or a cloud service must justify its cost against the goals of the organization.

> Management-level capacity planning is necessary for a truly effective IT services capacity plan.

> Virtual machines can add significant overhead to existing resources, especially CPUs and memory.

> Because virtual environments share resources, sufficient I/O capabilities must be available, especially for storage I/O operations.

> Carefully consider their need before implementing multiple vCPUs on VMs, because they can introduce latency to application performance through queuing.

> To estimate server requirements for a virtualized environment, establish a baseline estimate of server requirements for existing applications to be in the virtual environment.

> Two important processor-level security features are TXT and TPM. TXT and TPM protect against "blue pill" attacks by creating a "chain of trust" that allows virtual machines to start up securely.

> TXT provides assurances at start-up that the computer and its operating system are authentic and that the operating system is a trusted operating system.

> TPM uses PCRs to store measurements and hashing to create a chain of trust. On power-up, TXT verifies system firmware measurements prior to the boot process.

> ➤ VT accelerates the primary functions of a virtualized platform.

> ➤ A virtual server should have at least as much memory as its VMs require.

> ➤ A VM's memory reservation setting sets the guaranteed minimum amount of physical memory the VM needs to run efficiently.

> ➤ A memory share indicates the relative priority a VM has when it needs to request additional memory beyond its reservation for overhead.

> ➤ Memory sharing minimizes the number of memory pages a workload requires.

Key Terms

Baseline

Basic Input/Output System (BIOS)

Capacity planning

Chain of trust

Direct memory access (DMA)

Hardware-assisted memory virtualization

Hypervisor

Information Technology Infrastructure Library (ITIL)

Launch Code Policy (LCP)

Limit

Measured Launch Environment (MLE)

Memory management unit (MMU)

Memory reservation

Memory virtualization

Multicore processors

Physical NICs (pNICs)

Platform Configuration Registers (PCRs)

Service Level Agreement (SLA)

Shared memory

Software-based memory virtualization

Storage as a service (SaaS)

Translation look-aside buffer (TLB)

Trusted Execution Technology (TXT)

Trusted Platform Module (TPM)

Virtual CPUs (vCPUs)

Virtual machine manager (VMM)

Virtual NICs (vNICs)

Virtualization Technology (VT)

Workload categorization

Review Questions

1. _____ ensures that a virtual environment is able to accommodate current and future needs.

2. Which of the following is NOT a planning activity in the ITIL planning approach?

    a. Aligning IT services with customer requirements

    b. Ensuring that only future service levels are met

    c. Matching IT services to the organization objectives and policies

    d. Providing continuous service improvements

3. True or False? Workload categorization considers customer, type of work, and type of process.

4. _____ add overhead to existing resources, especially CPUs and memory.

5. What processor-level technology helps to ensure that a computer and its operating system are authentic in a start-up process?

    a. BIOS

    b. TPM

    c. TXT

    d. MLE

6. True or False? During start-up, if TPM senses a measurement is invalid, it issues a warning but continues the start-up procedure.

7. TPM uses _____ to encrypt the measurements used to create a chain of trust.

8. Virtualization technology (VT) is also known as _____.

   a. Software-based virtualization technology

   b. Hypervisor acceleration

   c. Hardware-based virtualization technology

   d. Legacy porting

9. Under software virtualization, the _____ emulates hardware resources to the guest operating system.

10. True or False? Four important areas to consider when sizing host servers are memory, processors, bandwidth, and storage.

11. What is the upper limit of vCPUs per processor core for VMware ESX?

    a. 4

    b. 8

    c. 10

    d. 25

12. In a virtualized environment, _____ manages all memory.

13. True or False? The memory reservation setting for a VM sets the guaranteed minimum amount of physical memory the VM needs to run efficiently.

14. True or False? In a virtualized environment, a share, as it relates to memory, indicates the amount of memory a VM has available to share with other VMs.

15. What memory virtualization technique uses a two-layer memory page table?

    a. Software-based memory virtualization

    b. Hardware-based memory virtualization

    c. Memory caching

    d. Virtual memory

Answers to Review Questions

1. Capacity planning

2. b

3. True

4. Virtual machines (VMs)

5. c

6. False

7. SHA-1 (hashing)

8. c

9. hypervisor (VMM)

10. False

11. d

12. hypervisor (VMM)

13. True

14. False

15. b

Implementation

After reading this chapter and completing the exercises, you will be able to:

- Explain the use and value of switching and routing to both internal and external networks

- Discuss the various configuration options of network ports

- Identify the application of classful and classless subnetting and supernetting

- Explain the functions of NAT and PAT

- Discuss the use of VLANs and the purpose of VLAN tagging

- Explain the processes of network optimization

- List the various utilities and commands available for connectivity testing

- Identify the elements that should be included in system documentation

Whether they are virtual or not, networks should have an established and documented base configuration. This base works like an "at minimum" configuration and provides the fundamental services, features, and capabilities required by the network and the applications that run on it. In this chapter, you learn about the various configurations that should receive your attention when planning and implementing a network of any kind and, after you implement the network, some tools you can use to monitor and manage the network.

Switching and Routing

Regardless of whether the network you are configuring will support a physical network or a virtual one, the network is sure to involve switching and routing at some level. Although network switching and routing are definitely part of all wide area networks (WANs), for the Cloud+ exam, you should have some knowledge of these functions at the local area network (LAN) and virtual local area network (VLAN) levels. In either a nonvirtualized or a virtualized environment, switching and routing at the local data center level are essentially the same.

Network switches and routers are essential core devices in any network beyond simple office or home networks. Organizations with a dozen or more end user nodes on a network that connects to the Internet will have at least one switch and router. A network switch and a router each serve a function that is vital to the efficient operation and connection of the network in the eyes of its end users. Figure 12-1 illustrates a simplified diagram of a network that incorporates a switch and a router.

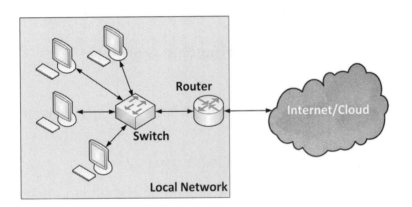

Figure 12-1 A simple network that includes a switch to service network nodes and a router to interface with the Internet.
© 2015 Cengage Learning®.

Network Switching Basics

Network switches connect multiple network nodes (servers, computers, printers, and so on) that are on the same network within a single department, floor, building, or campus. A switch creates access to the shared resources of a network and a communication link between the networked devices. Two types of switches are common to most LANs: *managed switches* and *unmanaged switches*.

MANAGED SWITCH

A managed switch is one that allows a network administrator to access it for purposes of configuration, function, and interface assignment. A managed switch provides greater flexibility for network control, management, and monitoring. A managed switch provides all the functionality of an unmanaged switch (see the next section), plus the capability to configure what data transmits over the network and which users or services have access to it.

UNMANAGED SWITCH

An unmanaged switch is a preconfigured, plug-and-play device that essentially works right out of the box. Typically, an unmanaged switch allows network devices to communicate, but because it has a fixed configuration, there is no provision for reconfiguration by local administrators.

Network Switching

At one time, a network hub provided the interconnectivity among networked devices. However, a hub merely sends all messages it receives to all the devices attached to its ports, as depicted in Figure 12-2. This can cause unnecessary traffic and bandwidth consumption on the network. In contrast, a switch examines every message and forwards each message only to the port and network segment on which its addressee is located, as illustrated in Figure 12-3.

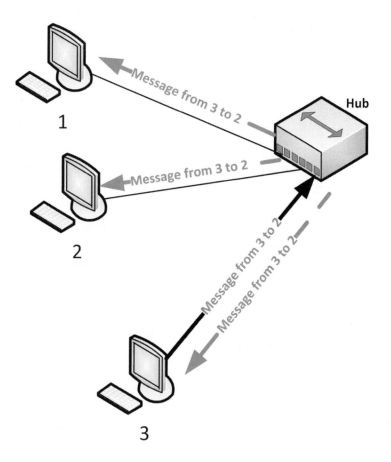

Figure 12-2 A network hub shares all segment traffic with all the nodes connected to it.
© 2015 Cengage Learning®.

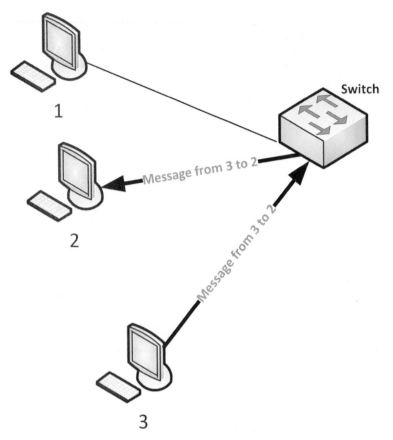

Figure 12-3 A network switch examines network traffic and forwards it only to the segment of the intended destination.
© 2015 Cengage Learning®.

A switch creates a map of the Layer 2 physical addresses (Media Access Control [MAC] addresses) of the nodes located on the network segment attached to each of its interface ports. A switch gets addresses from messages that arrive on a particular port and those it forwards to a specific port. When a message arrives at the switch, the switch compares the sending and destination addresses to the address table. If the addresses reside on different segments, the switch forwards the message to the interface port associated with the destination address. If the two addresses are on the same network segment, the switch drops (filters) the message because the destination node will have already seen the message. A switch also filters out improperly formatted or other bad messages.

In addition, a switch divides a network into multiple collision or broadcast domains. Recall the discussion in Chapter 10 on Ethernet network collisions. Each of the interface ports on a switch connects to a separate network segment, which on a switched network is also a separate *broadcast domain*. Reducing the potential for network collisions and unnecessary broadcast traffic improves the overall performance of the network.

Routing

Network routers link networks. In their most common use, routers connect LANs to a WAN, including the Internet, allowing multiple internal nodes to share a single WAN connection.

Routers also provide a dispatching function by determining the better of the available routes across the network so that data moves the quickest way possible.

Routing moves data across interconnected networks (internetwork) from itself to its counterpart router in front of the destination address. To accomplish this, a router must determine a routing path through the internetwork. Once a router determines the path, it forwards the packet to the next router (hop) in the chosen path. To accomplish this, the IP address of the intended recipient across the network remains in the packet, but the next hop address is that of the next upstream router. An intermediate router (one between the sender and the destination network) performs the path determination process again and forwards the packet on its way to its destination.

PATH DETERMINATION

Different routing protocols use a variety of metrics to determine which of the available next hops represents the better alternative to use. A router applies algorithms to an individual metric or a combination of these metrics, such as path length, available bandwidth, hop count, latency (delay), packet size (expressed as a *Maximum Transmission Unit or MTU*). Using these metrics, a router makes its choice of the best path available on which it can forward a packet.

A router maintains a *routing table* that stores the applicable metrics and other route information, which varies with the protocol and its algorithms. Routers perform routing on all received packets that pass its filtering processes. Like a switch, a router drops packets addressed to its own network and forwards only those that its configuration allows. When a router receives a packet, it uses its routing table to associate the destination address with the best next hop available.

ROUTING INFORMATION

Routers that are directly inline communicating routing information with each other share information back and forth to keep the internetwork up to date on the status and viability of different path choices. The routing information updates can be all or only part of a router's routing table. Using this incoming information, a router can maintain a nearly real-time version of the state of each next hop.

Routing protocols maintain two types of routing information in their routing tables: static routes and dynamic routes. A *static route* is an optional entry that a network administrator adds that fixes the next hop information for a particular destination address. *Dynamic routes* are those that the router uses in routing information to determine the better next hop decision.

Routers use the information in routing tables much like the post office or a package service uses its service network map to forward mail or packages. If for some reason, the Chicago distribution center is unavailable because of weather or some other catastrophic event, mail destined for Seattle from New York may go via Atlanta to get to its destination. The same is true for routed packets. If the normally used next hop for packets going from New York to Seattle is down, the router forwards the packet to the next available router on the path to its destination. The router updates its routing table with the information that the failed hop is not available and shares it with its neighboring routers.

Switching in Virtual Environments

A virtual network consists of the same networking devices as a nonvirtual network with the exception that the networking devices are software-created devices. The nodes of a virtual network are virtual machines (VMs), each of which sends and receives data to and from the network. Like a nonvirtual network, VMs interact with a server, which on the virtual network is a virtual server.

In a virtual environment, a virtual network is not much different from a physical network. Most virtualization software includes a virtual network manager, such as VMware's vSphere or Hyper-V's Virtual Machine Manager (VMM), which coordinates and controls the interactions of the virtual devices much like the networking functions of a nonvirtual operating system, like Microsoft Windows Server. Although it may seem that a virtual network should be more complicated on its functional level, it is about the same as its nonvirtual counterpart.

A *virtual switch (vswitch)* is software that interconnects VMs and allows them to communicate with each other. A vswitch operates much like its physical counterpart. It forwards packets to the appropriate virtual network segment by analyzing incoming packets. In some systems, the virtualization software includes the vswitch capability, but it can also be part of the host computer's firmware.

The term "vswitch" connects VMs to the virtual network and controls how a VM communicates with another VM. A vswitch is associated with a physical NIC (pNIC), or uplink adapter, which gives it a connection to the physical network through the host server. A vswitch connects to only a single host server at a time. However, in a typical installation, virtual NICs (vNICs) provide the interface connection to a vswitch for the VM.

A vswitch provides the bridging connection between the virtual network and the physical network. Once the vswitch establishes this connection, the VMs attached to it can send data to and receive data from the virtual network and any device attached to the physical network, local or remote. To connect to any part of the virtual or physical networks, a VM must associate with a vswitch. However, it's also possible that a vswitch may not be associated with a pNIC, in which case it serves as only an internal vswitch in the virtual network that cannot communicate beyond its virtual server. Figure 12-4 depicts a virtualized network containing vswitches.

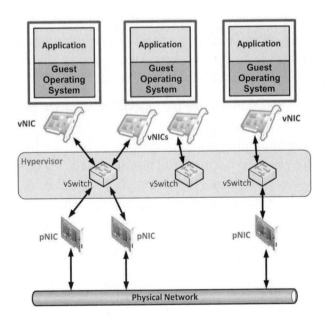

Figure 12-4 Virtual switches provide linkage between the virtual network and the physical network.
© 2015 Cengage Learning®.

Network Port Configuration

You learned about the common network ports in Chapter 10, but you need a deeper understanding of ports and their configuration for the Cloud+ exam. This section refreshes your knowledge of network ports and goes on to expand on what you learned in the earlier chapter.

Ports and Sockets

A *network port*, represented as a unique number identifier, allows specific applications, services, and protocols to share network resources concurrently. In general, network ports associate with Transmission Control Protocol/Internet Protocol (TCP/IP) connections, primarily in conjunction with the use of TCP or User Datagram Protocol (UDP). With a port number combined with an IP address, a network packet self-identifies the protocol in use and the application or service that is to process the payload of the packet.

One way to think of a port number is like an extension number in a company telephone system. Outside callers call the main number of the business, and a receptionist or the system itself transfers the call to the extension of the person to whom they want to speak. In much the same way, the destination IP address of the packet is the "main" address, and the port number is the "extension" to which the packet is directed. Instead of Fred or Judy, though, the packet passes to Internet Explorer on a user's desktop or the company's intranet for additional forwarding.

TCP and UDP ports range in number from 0 (zero) to 65535. The ports from 0 to 1023 are the "well-known" ports. The port numbers from 1024 to 49151 are the "registered" ports. The ports above 49151 (through 65535) are "dynamic" or "private" ports that are temporarily available for use by applications.

> **Note**
>
> The Internet Assigned Numbers Authority (IANA) is the official body that assigns port numbers to specific uses. However, this does not prohibit or block unofficial uses of ports to unofficial and unregistered uses. To see the complete list of current port assignments, visit www.iana.org/.

Figure 12-5 shows a screen capture of a `netstat -o` command list of the active connections on a Windows computer. It also shows the ports in use. (See "Netstat" later in the chapter for more information.) At the end of each foreign IP address, the number following the colon (:) is the port number requested by the sending party. This combination of an IP address and the port number creates a socket.

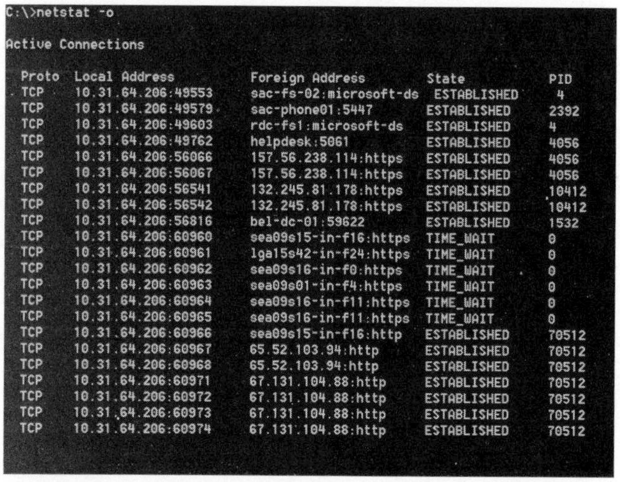

Figure 12-5 A netstat –o display showing the ports in use on a Windows computer.

Used with permission from Microsoft.

Port Configuration

Although in most systems, the process of linking a port or a socket to a process is mostly automatic, network administrators can typically set bindings through the configuration file of the operating system or hypervisor. Network bindings enable network interface controllers (NICs), device drivers, protocols, and services to communicate with each other. Another part of network port configuration is port forwarding. You learn about both of these topics in the sections that follow.

Port Binding

Binding is just what it sounds like: tying two network resources together so that they are able to communicate. After a binding, bound components are able to share services or resources. Any specific network component can be bound to any number of other network components or resources, but only on a one-to-one basis. On a Windows system, you can display the established bindings in the Advanced Settings dialog boxes, such as the one shown in Figure 12-6.

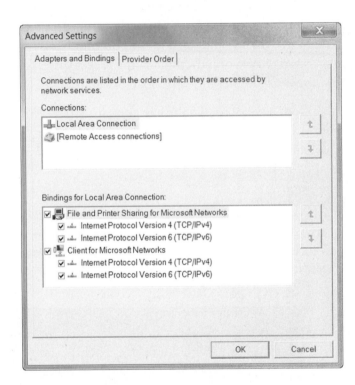

Figure 12-6 The network bindings for a Windows computer.
Used with permission from Microsoft.

Port Forwarding and Port Triggering

Port forwarding is often confused with port triggering. The difference is that port forwarding permits a remote computer to establish a connection to a specific node or service on a private LAN, and *port triggering* listens on one port and creates a connection on a different port.

Port Forwarding

Port forwarding, also called port mapping or tunneling, performs three primary functions:

> ➤ Reroutes the destination address or port number in certain packets to designated addresses

> ➤ Provides a pass for certain packets through a packet filter or firewall

> ➤ Forwards certain packets to a specific application or service

An example may help you understand this. From your network workstation, you send a request for a webpage to 10.0.0.10:8080. At the remote site, the router or an intermediate host intercepts the request's packets and modifies their destination addresses to 10.0.0.20:8080, a web server, which services the request. In this example, the IP address of 10.0.0.10 represents the gateway router for the remote network. When the router receives the request, it searches its routing table and forwards the packet to the internal IP address, 10.0.0.20, and port 8080 to the appropriate service—in this case a web server.

Port forwarding also allows certain traffic, identified by its IP address, its port number, or both, to pass through a firewall or be redirected into a perimeter network (*demilitarized zone*, or *DMZ*). A DMZ can be a physical or logical subnetwork that provides access to an organization's public information, such as an extranet or a web server, removing access to the organization's primary internal network.

Typically, a router performs port forwarding, but web proxy servers and gateway servers can also provide this service. The closer you implement port forwarding to the external network, the better it can keep unwanted traffic out of your network and speed along common requests. In addition, using port forwarding can permit the creation of a tunnel by allowing the requesting site to access a secure service on the servicing host.

Port Triggering

Port triggering allows for an internal application or service to set up temporary port forwarding to itself. For example, an application or service running on a LAN sends an outbound port 50 packet to its router. The router's configuration indicates that for this application or service, port 50 is a trigger that sets up forwarding for all inbound port 80 traffic to the application or service issuing the trigger. Port triggering does expire, depending on the router and its configuration. When the trigger times out, the router stops the forwarding. If the trigger is constant, the triggering application or service must constantly renew it by continually sending packets out on the triggering port. Understand, also, that only one source can activate a particular trigger.

VIRTUAL PORT GROUPS

In a VMware virtualized environment, the capability exists to create port groups. A *port group*, in this context, clusters vswitch ports under a common configuration, such as bandwidth. One way to think of a port group is a virtual hub that connects multiple VM ports to a single vswitch. Port group members see network traffic sent by any of the other members of the same port group; all port group members have the same configuration and attributes, and a port group connects only to a single vswitch. However, a vswitch can connect to more than one port group. Another attribute that the members of a port group share is a common VLAN tag. (See "VLAN Tagging" later in this section.)

Subnetting and Supernetting

Perhaps the primary benefit to IPv6 is that it is not likely to run out of IP addresses any time soon. However, this is not the case with IPv4, which, when it was introduced, was thought to offer IP addresses for everyone. Unfortunately, as networking in general and the Internet have become extraordinarily popular, Internet Protocol version 4 (IPv4) essentially ran out of IP addresses. Before Internet Protocol version 6 (IPv6), and continuing today, network administrators had to devise ways to stretch their allotment of IP addresses to serve their growing networks. This need gave rise to two addressing techniques: subnetting and supernetting.

Subnetting

On a network in which all the nodes attach directly to a single backbone, the nodes share the available bandwidth, may lose productivity through signal collisions, and must sort through network traffic addressed to other nodes to find any messages addressed to them. When you apply *subnetting* to a network, you create two or more small network segments, or subnets. Each subnet is a separate collision domain, reduces the contention for the bandwidth, and sees only its traffic, all of which combine to improve network performance. A bonus is that you are able to extend internal or private IP addressing to the subnet.

IPv4 Addresses

As you learned in Chapter 10, an IPv4 address is a 32-bit field containing four 8-bit octets. Depending on the IPv4 address class (Classes A, B, or C), a specific number designates the network ID, and the remaining bits represent the host ID. Routing and forwarding use the network ID, which is typically the IP address of the router or other gateway device for a network. The host ID then represents the IP address of the host within the network ID. Figure 12-7 illustrates the portions of the IPv4 address used for the network ID and host ID in the three address classes. This type of subnetting is *classful* or class-based subnetting because it considers the address class of the IPv4 address.

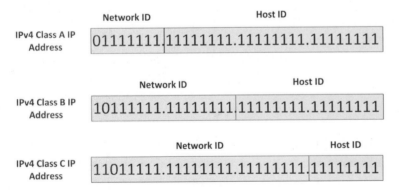

Figure 12-7 Each IPv4 address class uses a differing number of bits to represent the network ID and the host ID portions of the IP address.
© 2015 Cengage Learning®.

For example, in the address 192.168.32.101, which is a Class C IPv4 address, the first three octets (24 bits), 192.168.32, represent the network ID, and the last octet (8 bits) represents the host ID. By definition, each of the address classes can indicate more or less networks and hosts. Table 12-1 shows the addressing potentials of each address class.

Table 12-1 IPv4 Address Classes

Class	IP Address Range	Number of Networks	Number of Hosts[1]
A	0.0.0.0–127.255.255.255	126	16,777,214
B	128.0.0.0–191.255.255.255	16,384	65,534
C	192.0.0.0–223.255.255.255	2,097,152	254

[1] The number of hosts shown is per individual network.

© 2015 Cengage Learning®.

Note

IPv4 also defines two additional address classes: Classes D and E. Class D is reserved for multicasting, and Class E is reserved for experimental use.

SUBNET MASK

One of the more magical things a router or switch performs on a network is to determine the network ID (network IP address) and the host ID (network IP of the host) represented in an IPv4 address. However, although it may seem like magic, it is actually just plain old Boolean algebra at work. Piece of cake, right?

Regardless of whether a host resides on a subnet, routers and switches still need to extract the network ID for forwarding purposes. To this end, every network or subnetwork must have a *subnet mask*. A subnet mask is essentially a binary filter for a network address. The basic rule is simple; in binary form, any subnet mask bit set to 1 indicates that the corresponding bit in the IPv4 address is used, and any subnet mask bit set to 0 indicates that the corresponding bit in the address is not used, and a zero results. Figure 12-8 shows an example for each address class.

Figure 12-8 A subnet mask is applied to extract the network ID from an IPv4 address.
© 2015 Cengage Learning®.

As illustrated in Figure 12-8, only the digits in the subnet mask set to 1 allow the data in the IPv4 address to pass through to the network ID. This allows forwarding outside of the destination network by routers and intermediate switching.

SUBNETTING

In reality, subnetting does not really save IPv4 addresses and does not afford much in the way of added security to a network. So why subnet? It boils down to providing a simple way of dividing network nodes into separate collision domains and different network segments for consistency of configuration, shared bandwidth, and access control.

One of the primary reasons an organization may subnet its network is to separate organizational units onto their own mini-networks so that one unit does not interfere or have to contend with the traffic of another. Although this does not provide much in the way of total security, separating the Accounting department from general office users, it can help prevent inadvertent access. And yes, a VLAN may accomplish the same thing, but nothing says a subnet couldn't also be a VLAN.

Another reason to subnet is that broadcast traffic on the network can affect network performance. In a single network structure (one without subnets), every node receives and processes every broadcast message sent out from a variety of network services and protocols, such as Address Resolution Protocol (ARP), NETBIOS, multicast, and BOOTP. So it is possible that broadcast traffic can flood the network and really slow it down. Subnetting this type of network using Layer 3 switches or routers, which do not forward broadcast messages, keeps local traffic local, improving the performance of the overall network.

Using Figure 12.9 as an example, if, after subnetting, node 192.168.4.1 sends a message to node 192.168.4.20, the message doesn't need to leave that subnet, and the router will drop it. The same holds true for nodes within the 192.168.5.0 subnet.

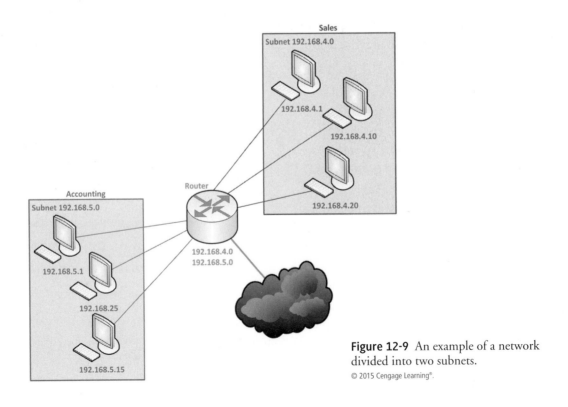

Figure 12-9 An example of a network divided into two subnets.

© 2015 Cengage Learning®.

Classless Subnetting

Subnetting that is based on the address class of IPv4 addresses is classful subnetting. Although classful subnetting is still in use on a significant number of networks, classless subnetting replaced classful subnetting in the mid-1990s as the standard. The formal name of the classless approach to subnetting is *Classless Inter-Domain Routing (CIDR—pronounced as cider)*.

CIDR merely takes the class-based network ID and its associated number of bits and replaces them with a single designation that states how many bits represent the network ID. For example, an IPv4 Class B address uses 16 bits to represent the network ID. (See Figure 12-7 earlier in the chapter.) In a CIDR representation, you would append a suffix of /16 to the IPv4 address. If you wanted to use 17 bits for the network ID, something you could not do in a classful approach, you would add /17 to the end of an IPv4 address. In CIDR notation, an IPv4 address appears as 192.168.4.20/24, with the /24 indicating that 24 bits of the address represent the network ID.

The capability of using a variable number of bits to express the network ID is *variable-length subnet masking (VLSM)*, which allows for the creation of subnets of various sizes. VLSM allows network administrators to size a network and its subnets more appropriately, perhaps, to the specific needs of their organizations. In addition, using a number of bits other than the standard classful standards (8, 16, and 24) opens the capability to aggregate subnets into larger networks or *supernets*.

Figure 12-10 shows an example of the effect of using 23 bits to designate a network ID. The IPv4 address shown in CIDR notation, 192.168.4.0/23, uses 23 bits to represent the network ID of this address. Notice that the range of addresses this notation reveals also includes what would be the Class C network of 192.168.5.0, achieved by turning on the last bit of the network ID.

CIDR Notation 192.168.4.0/23

	Network ID	Host ID
Binary Form	11000000.10101000.0000010	0.00000000

Address Range 192.168.4.0 - 192.168.5.255

Figure 12-10 An IPv4 address expressed in CIDR notation, its representation in binary form, and the IPv4 addresses it addresses.
© 2015 Cengage Learning®.

Note

Fortunately, you don't have to be a binary or Boolean algebra guru to compute CIDR designations. There are several CIDR address calculators on the web you can use to determine the right network IDs and numbers of hosts for your network. For one of the better CIDR calculators, visit www.subnet-calculator.com/cidr.php.

NAT and PAT

Two additional tools initially developed to reduce demand for IPv4 addresses are network address translation (NAT) and port address translation (PAT). Essentially, what NAT and PAT do is translate internal (private) IP addresses into external (public) IP addresses. Using these tools, a local network needs to have only a single (or very few) public IP addresses that are exposed to the networks outside of a LAN.

Network Address Translation (NAT)

Network address translation (NAT) creates a one-to-one mapping between internal IP addresses and an external (or routable) IP address. IPv4 and IPv6 define blocks of IP addresses intended for use on private networks (see Table 12-2), such as a LAN. These networks operate behind a router, which means that for the router to forward any packet with a destination address beyond the local network, NAT must replace the source IP address with an external (global) address.

Table 12-2 IPv4 Private Addresses		
Class	Start	End
A	10.0.0.0	10.255.255.255
B	172.16.0.0	172.31.255.255
C	192.168.0.0	192.168.255.255

© 2015 Cengage Learning®.

NAT supports two types of address translation: static NAT and dynamic NAT. Static NAT is the simpler of the two. Commonly referred to as one-to-one NAT, *static NAT* affects only the source IP address and recalculates any checksums that include the IP address. The remainder of the packet is unchanged. The addresses used for the translation are preloaded to the NAT translation table and remain there until they're removed.

Dynamic NAT includes the functions of static NAT, but instead of a one-to-one mapping in the NAT translation table, a pool of external addresses is available. Dynamic NAT modifies all incoming and outgoing packets to replace internal addresses with external addresses (outgoing) or to replace external addresses with the internal address of the originating node on the internal network (incoming). The translation table for dynamic NAT contains entries only after a packet arrives that requires translation.

Port Address Translation (PAT)

Port address translation (PAT) works much like static NAT, with the addition of using TCP/UDP port numbers to modify a single IP address into multiple unique addresses. If two internal addresses attempt to access the Internet at about the same time, PAT assigns both the same external address but appends a different port number to each, resulting in two unique addresses. This allows for the static translation of several addresses to a single external address, with each assignment made unique by the addition of a port address.

VLAN and VLAN Tagging

One of the challenges for network administrators is maintaining user permissions and rights. In any organization, several groups of workers exist whom, within any particular group, have the need to access the same data and perform the same functions. For example, all the Accounting personnel need to access financial, vendor, and purchasing data. Simple. Just assign them to a particular subnet, right? What if they aren't on the same floor or in the same building? Or perhaps they're not even in the same city? What then?

Virtual LAN (VLAN)

A *virtual local area network (VLAN)* is a logical network of network nodes grouped by software that shares a common configuration, permissions, and access. A node's membership in a VLAN is not controlled, nor is it even relevant, to its physical location. The nodes included in a VLAN can be in the same department, in the same building, or somewhere in the same company. Like a physical subnet, a VLAN creates a separate broadcast domain. Figure 12-11 illustrates the logical concept of a VLAN.

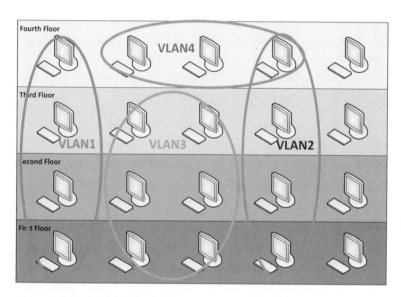

Figure 12-11 A VLAN logically groups network workstations.
© 2015 Cengage Learning®.

VLANs provide network administrators with the flexibility to organize a network without regard to where a node is located or how it connects to the network. Using a VLAN means you avoid moving around equipment and running separate cabling to affect the same result physically. Cloud-based VMs can be included in a VLAN as opposed to connecting them directly to the Internet.

VLAN Tagging

The *802.1Q* standard issued by the Institute of Electrical and Electronics Engineers (IEEE) defines and supports VLANs on Ethernet networks. This standard defines the process of tagging Ethernet frames (Layer 2 message units) and their processing by network bridges, switches, and routers. On an Ethernet network, on the portion of the network that is 802.1Q conforming (in other words a VLAN), frames are tagged. Frames transmitted on the portion of the network that is not 802.1Q conformant do not receive tags.

VLAN tagging inserts a VLAN ID field into each conforming frame that identifies the particular VLAN to which the frame belongs. Network switches use the VLAN ID to determine which port or interface to forward the frame. This includes broadcast frames as well.

Network Optimization

There are as many approaches to optimizing a network, regardless of the network's scope, as there are blog writers and so-called "experts." Several approaches recommend starting with the Physical layer (cabling, fiber optics, or wireless media) and removing any existing or potential bottlenecks. Others point to the applications running on the network as the most important place to start. However, in nearly all approaches, the efficient and effective performance of network devices, including bridges, switches, and routers, is critical to achieving peak performance for any network.

Of course, optimizing a network and identifying problems and opportunities can depend on the size, scope, and service-level commitments of the network. An optimization analysis should also look to the future and consider the impact of integrating new technologies—such as mobile computing, Bring Your Own Device (BYOD), cloud computing, virtualization, and the possible implementation of IPv6—into the network and the organization.

Network optimization includes the processes and activities performed to ensure that a network operates at its highest available level of efficiency. Network optimization is applicable to every level of network operations, including LANs, WANs, metropolitan area networks (MANs), enterprise networks, and even networks in the cloud. Its functions range from resolving data flow bottlenecks, maintaining real-time data in routers and switches, and most any other activity that ensures a network fulfills its Service Level Agreements (SLAs), whether internally or to external subscribers.

Regardless of the level or type of network, the starting step is the creation of a *network baseline*. A network baseline measures and rates the performance of a specific network under real-time situations and loads. A baseline analysis report tests, measures, and records, under both normal and peak situations, the network's connectivity, its utilization, the protocols in use, and the throughput times for a variety of normal transactions. The network baseline identifies any existing or potential problems with the network's bandwidth, throughput, and accessibility, as well as any vulnerabilities or potential exploits uncovered. With the data of the baseline, opportunities for optimization and improvement should be apparent.

WAN Optimization

WAN optimization looks to improve the efficiencies of Layer 3 (Transport) operations of the extended network. Whereas LAN optimization primarily focuses on eliminating media bottlenecks and improving client/server performance, WAN optimization examines and analyzes current and future network performance and needs in key performance areas, including throughput, bandwidth, latency, protocol efficiencies, and areas of congestion, where too many packets are dropped.

The analysis of a WAN should also consider the distance and nature of the network. There are essentially two basic WAN categories (and topologies): *Branch to Headquarters (branch)* and *Data Center to Data Center (DC2DC)*. A branch WAN connects a remote operation with a main or intermediate data center. Typically, a branch WAN involves lower bandwidth and shorter connection times. A branch WAN generally involves a variety of protocols in support of email, transaction-based content, database access, and web content request and display.

A DC2DC WAN tends to cover a longer distance and a greater dependence on routing and switching in the cloud. Communications between data centers require more bandwidth on fewer links, each of which carries more data over a longer time than a branch WAN. A DC2DC WAN is more likely to involve virtualization, replication, and higher levels of data management, security, and backup and recovery processes.

NETWORK OPTIMIZATION TOOLS

Because of the size and scope of most large LANs and the nature of WANs or MANs, it can be advisable to use a network optimization appliance or software system to create a baseline, monitor, measure, analyze performance, and recommend solutions for problem areas on a network. Some of the more popular appliances and systems are available from Blue Coat Systems, Cisco Systems, Exinda Networks, Ipanema Technologies, and Riverbed Technology.

Connectivity Testing

Often a network problem may be something simple, such as a connectivity or device communication issue. Various command-line utilities are available on virtually every networkable operating system that you can use to test a wide range of communication and connectivity areas. In the following sections, you learn about how to use these tools and the best use of each.

Network Ping

The *ping* command, which at one time stood for Packet Internet Gopher, is a standard command-line utility used to test a network connection. It actually performs two test functions and can answer two questions for you: does a clear connection exist between your location and a specific remote network? If so, what is the latency on the connection to and from that location? The ping command is available in nearly all operating systems, as well as on many routers.

The ping utility sends out timed *Internet Control Message Protocol (ICMP)* requests to the network address or domain name and displays the total time elapsed for a response message to arrive. Figure 12-12 shows two examples of the ping command's display on a Windows computer. The upper instance of the ping command shows that a connection does exist between a local computer and the yahoo.com gateway. It also shows the response time for five iterations of the ICMP request/response, which in this example ranges from 91 milliseconds (ms) to 134 ms. Also notice in the upper example that the IPv4 address for this domain was returned.

```
C:\>ping yahoo.com

Pinging yahoo.com [98.139.183.24] with 32 bytes of data:
Reply from 98.139.183.24: bytes=32 time=96ms TTL=48
Reply from 98.139.183.24: bytes=32 time=134ms TTL=48
Reply from 98.139.183.24: bytes=32 time=92ms TTL=48
Reply from 98.139.183.24: bytes=32 time=91ms TTL=46

Ping statistics for 98.139.183.24:
    Packets: Sent = 4, Received = 4, Lost = 0 (0% loss),
Approximate round trip times in milli-seconds:
    Minimum = 91ms, Maximum = 134ms, Average = 103ms

C:\>ping 192.168.0.10

Pinging 192.168.0.10 with 32 bytes of data:
Request timed out.
Request timed out.
Request timed out.
Request timed out.

Ping statistics for 192.168.0.10:
    Packets: Sent = 4, Received = 0, Lost = 4 (100% loss),
```

Figure 12-12 Two examples of the use of the ping command to test the connectivity between two network endpoints.

Note

In Figure 12-12, each line of the ping command's display ends with a line to the effect of $TTL = 48$. TTL stands for Time to Live, and the number indicates how many hops (routers) the command can traverse before timing out. Therefore, in this case, if it takes more than 48 hops to reach the pinged address, the ping command would simply time out.

Traceroute

Traceroute (or *tracert* on Windows computers) is another command-line utility that displays the path (route) between a local node and another IP address or domain name and the transit time of the ICMP request and the remote location's response. Figure 12-13 shows the display produced by the traceroute (tracert) command on a Windows computer.

```
C:\>tracert yahoo.com

Tracing route to yahoo.com [98.139.183.24]
over a maximum of 30 hops:

  1    <1 ms    <1 ms    <1 ms  10.31.64.1
  2    <1 ms    <1 ms    <1 ms  75-147-191-18-Washington.hfc.comcastbusiness.net [75.147.191.18]
  3     *        *        *     Request timed out.
  4     8 ms    11 ms     8 ms  te-0-0-0-2-sur03.ferndale.wa.seattle.comcast.net [68.87.207.137]
  5    10 ms    15 ms     9 ms  ae-41-0-ar03.seattle.wa.seattle.comcast.net [69.139.164.33]
  6    13 ms    11 ms    16 ms  he-1-5-0-0-11-cr01.seattle.wa.ibone.comcast.net [68.86.94.65]
  7    14 ms    11 ms    11 ms  208.178.58.89
  8   136 ms   100 ms    90 ms  64.215.30.22
  9    91 ms    98 ms    93 ms  ae-3.pat2.bfz.yahoo.com [216.115.97.209]
 10    88 ms    99 ms    95 ms  ae-4.msr1.bf1.yahoo.com [216.115.100.25]
 11    88 ms    89 ms    91 ms  UNKNOWN-98-139-129-X.yahoo.com [98.139.129.169]
 12    89 ms    91 ms    90 ms  et-17-1.fab3-1-gdc.bf1.yahoo.com [98.139.128.41]
 13    92 ms    91 ms    93 ms  po-11.bas2-7-prd.bf1.yahoo.com [98.139.129.179]
 14   113 ms   101 ms    95 ms  ir2.fp.vip.bf1.yahoo.com [98.139.183.24]

Trace complete.

C:\>
```

Figure 12-13 An example of the traceroute (tracert) command to display the network path between two network points.

As shown in Figure 12-13, a traceroute was run for the domain name yahoo.com. The next 13 lines of the display show the intermediate hops (routers) the message passed through to reach its destination. Traceroute tests each hop three times and records the response time for each. The display for each hop, numbered in sequence, has four columns: the three tests on each hop and the name and/or IP address of each hop. Notice that hop 3 timed out with no response to any of the three tests and the messages sent to another path (line 4), which was successful. Also note that as the distance from the local node increased, so did the average response time of each test.

Given the result shown in Figure 12-13, the nonresponding router on line 3 or the intermittent latency shown by the hop on line 8 might be the cause of any latency or throughput issues. Traceroute (or ping) is a good tool for determining whether a connectivity problem is internal or out on the Internet.

Netstat

The *netstat* (network status) utility displays the listening (open) ports on a computer as well as any active network connections, both incoming and outgoing. Typically, netstat identifies possible malware or other security issues. Netstat is another command-line utility supported by virtually all operating systems.

Because any open port on a computer can be an entry point for an attack, it may be useful to know exactly what connections are open and which services or protocols are running on each. Netstat provides this information.

Like most command-line utilities, netstat provides numerous command-line options to customize the information displayed. Figure 12-14 shows the various options and the information each option adds to the display.

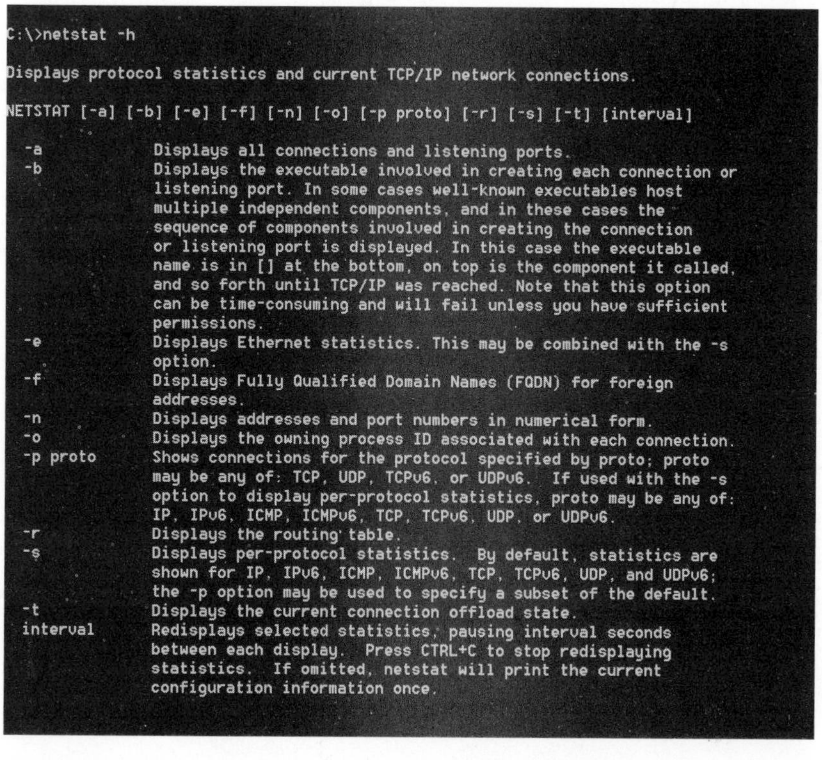

```
C:\>netstat -h

Displays protocol statistics and current TCP/IP network connections.

NETSTAT [-a] [-b] [-e] [-f] [-n] [-o] [-p proto] [-r] [-s] [-t] [interval]

  -a            Displays all connections and listening ports.
  -b            Displays the executable involved in creating each connection or
                listening port. In some cases well-known executables host
                multiple independent components, and in these cases the
                sequence of components involved in creating the connection
                or listening port is displayed. In this case the executable
                name is in [] at the bottom, on top is the component it called,
                and so forth until TCP/IP was reached. Note that this option
                can be time-consuming and will fail unless you have sufficient
                permissions.
  -e            Displays Ethernet statistics. This may be combined with the -s
                option.
  -f            Displays Fully Qualified Domain Names (FQDN) for foreign
                addresses.
  -n            Displays addresses and port numbers in numerical form.
  -o            Displays the owning process ID associated with each connection.
  -p proto      Shows connections for the protocol specified by proto; proto
                may be any of: TCP, UDP, TCPv6, or UDPv6. If used with the -s
                option to display per-protocol statistics, proto may be any of:
                IP, IPv6, ICMP, ICMPv6, TCP, TCPv6, UDP, or UDPv6.
  -r            Displays the routing table.
  -s            Displays per-protocol statistics. By default, statistics are
                shown for IP, IPv6, ICMP, ICMPv6, TCP, TCPv6, UDP, and UDPv6;
                the -p option may be used to specify a subset of the default.
  -t            Displays the current connection offload state.
  interval      Redisplays selected statistics, pausing interval seconds
                between each display. Press CTRL+C to stop redisplaying
                statistics. If omitted, netstat will print the current
                configuration information once.
```

Figure 12-14 The command options for the netstat utility.

As shown earlier in the chapter in Figure 12-5 and now in Figure 12-15, netstat can display information on the listening (active) ports as well as any established connections. This information can be restricted to only active port connections (-a option), a single protocol (-p option), as well as the process ID (PID) of the service or application associated with each port.

```
C:\>netstat -a -o

Active Connections

  Proto  Local Address          Foreign Address        State           PID
  TCP    0.0.0.0:135            BEL-109-001:0          LISTENING       768
  TCP    0.0.0.0:445            BEL-109-001:0          LISTENING       4
  TCP    0.0.0.0:2701           BEL-109-001:0          LISTENING       3168
  TCP    0.0.0.0:3389           BEL-109-001:0          LISTENING       1368
  TCP    0.0.0.0:5357           BEL-109-001:0          LISTENING       4
  TCP    0.0.0.0:49152          BEL-109-001:0          LISTENING       440
  TCP    0.0.0.0:49153          BEL-109-001:0          LISTENING       932
  TCP    0.0.0.0:49154          BEL-109-001:0          LISTENING       1096
  TCP    0.0.0.0:49190          BEL-109-001:0          LISTENING       556
  TCP    0.0.0.0:49191          BEL-109-001:0          LISTENING       540
  TCP    0.0.0.0:49192          BEL-109-001:0          LISTENING       2260
  TCP    0.0.0.0:51516          BEL-109-001:0          LISTENING       1532
  TCP    10.31.64.206:139       BEL-109-001:0          LISTENING       4
  TCP    10.31.64.206:60079     helpdesk:5061          ESTABLISHED     4056
  TCP    10.31.64.206:60092     sac-phone01:5447       ESTABLISHED     2392
  TCP    10.31.64.206:60099     157.56.238.121:https   ESTABLISHED     9228
  TCP    10.31.64.206:60100     157.56.238.121:https   ESTABLISHED     9228
  TCP    10.31.64.206:60164     bel-dc-01:59622        ESTABLISHED     1532
  TCP    10.31.64.206:60166     rdc-fs1:microsoft-ds   ESTABLISHED     4
  TCP    10.31.64.206:60181     132.245.1.121:https    ESTABLISHED     4056
```

Figure 12-15 An example of a netstat display.
Used with permission from Microsoft.

Nslookup and Dig

Nslookup (name server lookup) displays the Domain Name System (DNS) server information for a particular fully qualified domain name (FQDN). As shown in Figure 12-16, the nslookup inquiry for cengagelearning.com yields the display that first gives the information of the requesting station and then displays the requested site and its IP address.

```
C:\>nslookup cengagelearning.com
Server:  bel-dc-01.              .org
Address:  10.31.32.10

Non-authoritative answer:
Name:    cengagelearning.com
Address:  69.32.133.11
```

Figure 12-16 The results from an nslookup command asking for the DNS information for a specific domain name.
Used with permission from Microsoft.

The organization Internet Software Consortium (isc.org), which developed the nslookup utility, has recently deprecated it in favor of a new utility, *dig*. This new command is part of the *Berkeley Internet Name Domain (BIND)* system, which allows for the creation and management of DNS servers. As shown in Figure 12-17, dig provides more information regarding the DNS data available for a particular website.

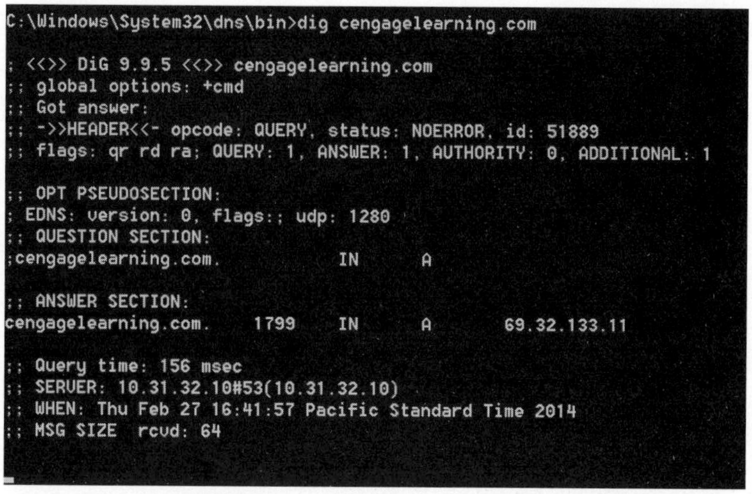

```
C:\Windows\System32\dns\bin>dig cengagelearning.com

; <<>> DiG 9.9.5 <<>> cengagelearning.com
;; global options: +cmd
;; Got answer:
;; ->>HEADER<<- opcode: QUERY, status: NOERROR, id: 51889
;; flags: qr rd ra; QUERY: 1, ANSWER: 1, AUTHORITY: 0, ADDITIONAL: 1

;; OPT PSEUDOSECTION:
; EDNS: version: 0, flags:; udp: 1280
;; QUESTION SECTION:
;cengagelearning.com.            IN      A

;; ANSWER SECTION:
cengagelearning.com.    1799    IN      A       69.32.133.11

;; Query time: 156 msec
;; SERVER: 10.31.32.10#53(10.31.32.10)
;; WHEN: Thu Feb 27 16:41:57 Pacific Standard Time 2014
;; MSG SIZE  rcvd: 64
```

Figure 12-17 The results from a dig command asking for the DNS information for a specific domain name.

Ipconfig/Ifconfig

Ipconfig, which is short for Internet Protocol Configuration, is a command-line utility available on Windows systems that displays the current TCP/IP configuration and allows for the management of a host's Dynamic Host Configuration Protocol (DHCP) or DNS settings. The Linux/UNIX counterpart, *ifconfig* (interface configuration), is similar to the ipconfig command, with a few extras. Figure 12-18 shows the basic display of the ipconfig command.

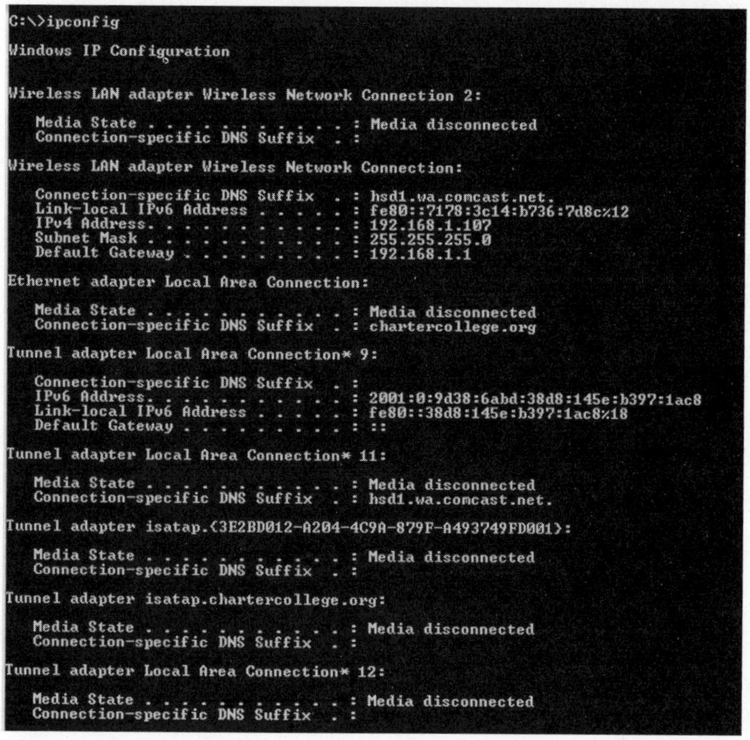

```
C:\>ipconfig

Windows IP Configuration

Wireless LAN adapter Wireless Network Connection 2:

   Media State . . . . . . . . . . . : Media disconnected
   Connection-specific DNS Suffix  . :
Wireless LAN adapter Wireless Network Connection:

   Connection-specific DNS Suffix  . : hsd1.wa.comcast.net.
   Link-local IPv6 Address . . . . . : fe80::7178:3c14:b736:7d8c%12
   IPv4 Address. . . . . . . . . . . : 192.168.1.107
   Subnet Mask . . . . . . . . . . . : 255.255.255.0
   Default Gateway . . . . . . . . . : 192.168.1.1
Ethernet adapter Local Area Connection:

   Media State . . . . . . . . . . . : Media disconnected
   Connection-specific DNS Suffix  . : chartercollege.org
Tunnel adapter Local Area Connection* 9:

   Connection-specific DNS Suffix  . :
   IPv6 Address. . . . . . . . . . . : 2001:0:9d38:6abd:38d8:145e:b397:1ac8
   Link-local IPv6 Address . . . . . : fe80::38d8:145e:b397:1ac8%18
   Default Gateway . . . . . . . . . : ::
Tunnel adapter Local Area Connection* 11:

   Media State . . . . . . . . . . . : Media disconnected
   Connection-specific DNS Suffix  . : hsd1.wa.comcast.net.
Tunnel adapter isatap.{3E2BD012-A204-4C9A-879F-A493749FD001}:

   Media State . . . . . . . . . . . : Media disconnected
   Connection-specific DNS Suffix  . :
Tunnel adapter isatap.chartercollege.org:

   Media State . . . . . . . . . . . : Media disconnected
   Connection-specific DNS Suffix  . :
Tunnel adapter Local Area Connection* 12:

   Media State . . . . . . . . . . . : Media disconnected
   Connection-specific DNS Suffix  . :
```

Figure 12-18 The results from the ipconfig command.

Another common use of the ipconfig or ifconfig utility is the management of the DHCP settings on a host computer. Should you want to change the IP address assigned to a host by DHCP, you'd use a two-step process. The first step is to issue an ipconfig /release (or ifconfig /release) command to cancel the existing lease on the current IP address assigned to the computer. The second step is to issue an ipconfig /renew (or ifconfig /renew) command to request a new IP address and a new lease. Ifconfig can also set the IP address and subnet mask for an interface, as well as enable or disable the interface.

Route

The *route* command displays and allows modifications to the contents of a local IP routing table. As shown in Figure 12-19, the route command displays the contents of the routing tables on the local host, including, as shown, both IPv4 and IPv6 routing tables, if present.

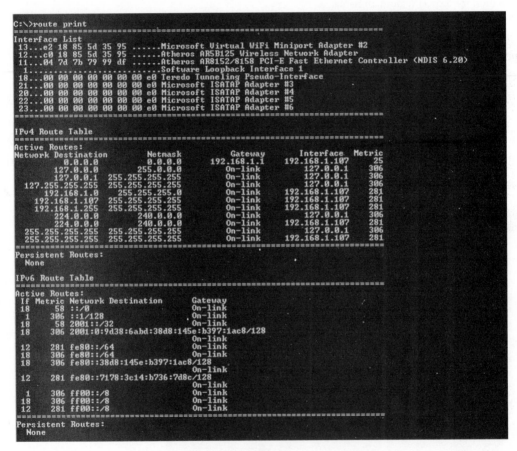

Figure 12-19 An example of the route command display using the print option to list the contents of a local host's routing tables.
Used with permission from Microsoft.

The route command also allows an administrator to add, change, or delete entries in a local routing table, including clearing the entire table of all but host routes (subnet mask of 255.255.255.255), loopback routes (IPv4 address 127.0.0.0), or multicast routes (subnet mask of 240.0.0.0).

Configuration Documentation

Often the Achilles heel of any network administrator is documentation of the network for which she is responsible. In addition to general documentation, network diagrams, system logs on trouble-shooting and repair activities, and manufacturer's documentation on all network devices, the documentation must contain the current configurations of all configurable components. The detail configuration settings of the switches, routers, bridges, firewalls, and so on, should be in the documentation along with any changes made so that the documentation always represents the current configuration.

The format of *network documentation* can vary by organization, network scope, and entity providing technical support (in-house or contracted). Regardless, the information contained in the documentation should be consistent and complete. Network documentation should be a "living" document, in that it represents the configuration of the network as it exists at any given moment. Some of the more important contents that should be included in network documentation follow:

> ➤ **Key community members**: The names, addresses, and contact information for all network administration personnel, along with the contact information of the key individuals from major vendors, contractors, and service providers.

> ➤ **Protective elements**: Detailed information on the protective systems included in the network, such as antivirus software, antimalware software, firewall rules, and intrusion detection/prevention systems.

> ➤ **Backup and recovery**: Information on the software or hardware used for backup and recovery, the location for offsite storage, access information, encryption information, and any media rotation guidelines.

> ➤ **Detail configuration**: A printout, screen capture, or recorded configuration settings for any network device configured outside of vendor defaults.

> ➤ **Data storage**: Detailed information on file system settings and drive mappings.

> ➤ **Internet**: Detailed information on gateway devices, DHCP configuration, IP addresses, network subnet masks, the protocols in use (and how they are used), and current DNS information.

> ➤ **Security**: Security policies, procedures, and investigation processes.

> ➤ **Remote access**: Any remote access to the network via extranet, remote access service (RAS), or virtual private network (VPN), including who, how, and when.

The items in the preceding list are in addition to network diagrams, hardware and media inventories, and system maintenance logs.

Chapter Summary

- ➤ Networks should have an appropriate base configuration that provides fundamental services, features, and capabilities.

- ➤ Network switches and routers are essential core devices in any network beyond simple office or home networks.

- ➤ Network switches connect multiple network nodes on the same network. A switch creates access to shared network resources and communication links between networked devices. There are two types of switches: managed and unmanaged.

- ➤ Routers connect LANs to WANs, including the Internet, and allow multiple internal nodes to share a single WAN connection. Routers also forward packets on the best available path across the network.

- ➤ Routers apply algorithms to metrics, such as path length, available bandwidth, hop count, latency, packet size, and other measurements, to choose the best path through the inter-network to forward a packet.

- ➤ Routers maintain routing tables that store applicable metrics and other route information. When a router receives a packet, it uses its routing table to associate the destination address with the best pathway available.

- ➤ A virtual switch interconnects VMs and allows them to communicate with each other.

- ➤ Network ports are identified by unique numeric identifiers and allow specific applications, services, and protocols to share network resources concurrently.

- ➤ Binding ties two network resources together so that they are able to communicate.

- ➤ Port forwarding permits a remote computer to establish a connection to a specific node or service on a private LAN, and port triggering listens on one port and creates a connection on a different port.

- ➤ A port group clusters vswitch ports under a common configuration.

- ➤ Subnetting a network creates two or more network segments or subnets, each of which is a separate collision domain, reduces the contention for the bandwidth, and sees only its traffic, all of which combine to improve network performance.

- ➤ A subnet mask is a binary filter for a network address.

- ➤ Classless subnetting is CIDR, which states the number of bits that represent the network ID. The variable number of bits to express the network ID is VLSM. CIDR opens the capability to aggregate subnets into supernets.

- ➤ NAT creates a one-to-one mapping between private addresses and public routable addresses, replacing the source address with a public address. PAT works like static NAT but adds TCP/UDP port numbers to convert a single IP address into multiple unique addresses.

➤ A VLAN is a logical network created through software to share a common configuration, permissions, and access. The IEEE 802.1Q standard defines and supports VLANs on Ethernet networks and provides for VLAN tagging.

➤ Network optimization includes the processes and activities performed to ensure that a network operates at its highest available level of efficiency. The initial step is the creation of a network baseline.

➤ WAN optimization looks to improve the efficiencies of Layer 3 (Transport) operations of the extended network. There are two basic WAN categories: branch and DC2DC. A branch WAN connects a remote operation with a main or intermediate data center. A DC2DC WAN covers a longer distance and a greater dependence on routing and switching in the cloud.

➤ Various command-line utilities are available to test communication and connectivity areas, including ping, traceroute (tracert), netstat, nslookup, dig, ipconfig/ifconfig, and route.

➤ In addition to general documentation, network diagrams, system logs on troubleshooting and repair activities, and manufacturer's documentation on all network devices, the documentation must contain the current configurations of all configurable components.

Key Terms

Berkeley Internet Name Domain (BIND)

Binding

Branch to Headquarters (branch) WAN

Broadcast domain

Classful

Classless Inter-Domain Routing (CIDR)

Data Center to Data Center (DC2DC)

Demilitarized zone (DMZ)

Dig

Dynamic NAT

Dynamic route

IEEE 802.1Q

Ifconfig

Internet Control Message Protocol (ICMP)

Ipconfig

Managed switch

Maximum transmission unit (MTU)

Netstat

Network address translation (NAT)

Network baseline

Network documentation

Network optimization

Network port

Network switch

Nslookup

Ping

Port address translation (PAT)

Port forwarding

Port group

Port triggering

Route

Routing

Routing table

Static NAT

Static route

Subnet mask

Subnetting

Supernet

Traceroute

Tracert

Unmanaged switch

Variable-length subnet masking (VLSM)

Virtual local area network (VLAN)

Virtual switch (vswitch)

VLAN tagging

WAN optimization

Review Questions

1. What network device can be inserted into a LAN to create smaller broadcast domains and VLANs?

   a. Bridge

   b. Router

   c. Switch

   d. Hub

2. True or False? An unmanaged switch operates unattended after a network administrator sets its initial configuration.

3. A _____ uses an algorithm to determine the best path on which to forward a packet.

4. _____ associates two network resources so they can communicate with one another.

5. True or False? A virtual switch interconnects VMs and allows them to communicate with each other.

6. Subnetting that ignores the address classes of IPv4 and uses VLSM to indicate the bits identifying the network ID of an address is _____.

   a. Classful subnetting

   b. Classless subnetting

   c. NAT

   d. PAT

7. The address translation protocol that appends port numbers to IP addresses to convert them to unique addresses is _____.

   a. CIDR

   b. VLSM

   c. NAT

   d. PAT

8. True or False? A port group clusters vswitch ports under a common configuration.

9. A _____ is a binary filter used to extract the network ID from an IPv4 address.

10. True or False? Network optimization focuses on resolving network issues that prevent a network from operating at its peak performance.

11. Developing a _____ is the first step of performing network optimization.

12. What command displays the network path taken between two endpoints?

    a. traceroute

    b. ping

    c. netstat

    d. dig

13. What command is used to verify that a connection exists between two endpoints?

    a. traceroute

    b. ping

    c. netstat

    d. ipconfig

14. A _____ WAN topology connects a remote location with a main data center.

15. True or False? You can use the netstat utility to manage the DHCP settings on a host computer.

Answers to Review Questions

1. c
2. False
3. router
4. Binding
5. True
6. b
7. d
8. True
9. subnet mask
10. True
11. baseline
12. a
13. b
14. branch
15. False

CHAPTER 13

Monitoring

After reading this chapter and completing the exercises, you will be able to:

- Explain the concept and purpose of network and system monitoring
- List the TCP/IP system management and monitoring protocols
- Describe the configuration and use of alert notifications
- Discuss resource licensing and pooling in a cloud-computing environment

I n a cloud-computing environment, especially a virtualized environment, the reliable performance of resources at Service Level Agreement (SLA) levels is critical. Only through constant monitoring and configuration management can a service center maintain peak performance of all resources.

In this chapter, you learn about the reasons and purpose of monitoring network and system resource performance and availability, the Transmission Control Protocol/Internet Protocol (TCP/IP) protocols and utilities that provide information on resource performance, how monitoring software can generate alert notifications based on system configuration, and the issues of resource licensing and pooling in a virtualized cloud computing environment.

Effective Network Monitoring

For most organizations, their internal network and its connections to external networks is essential to their business functions and day-to-day operations. Monitoring a network to detect or prevent problems can help to avoid the risk of losing crucial network-accessed resources and business continuity. Effective network monitoring should be proactive and thorough.

Areas to Monitor

An effective *network monitoring* program should extend beyond connectivity, not that it's not also very important. It's just that there are myriad areas and components of a network that may also contribute to its failure to meet its service levels or its downtime.

Here are some recommendations for what should be in an effective network monitoring program:

> **Proactive monitoring**: A proactive monitoring program can detect and avoid future problems.

> **Performance and availability**: A monitoring program should measure the performance, availability, and fault tolerance of each of the potential failure points on a network.

> **Notification methods**: Any monitoring software used should provide a variety of problem notification methods, including email, paging, text messaging, or telephone contact.

> **Business application alerts**: Key line of business applications should include rule-based alerts, logging, and reporting. The monitoring program should also include an event-log review process that's either manual or automated.

> **Hardware alerts**: All key hardware components in the network should issue rule-based alerts that use the available notification methods for immediate attention.

> **Daily performance reports**: A robust utilization and performance reporting system should be in any effective monitoring program along with the process for the review of trends and anomalies.

An effective monitoring program should include the following network components:

> **Servers**: Include the following server components in the monitoring program: central processing unit (CPU) usage, memory usage, available disk storage space, application and system log entries, network connectivity, hardware status, and backup performance.

> **Network connectivity devices**: Routers, switches, firewalls, and other network appliances monitored for connectivity, firmware updates, and rule-based forwarding.

> **Business applications**: Key line of business applications monitored for throughput and application-specific logs monitored for errors or unauthorized access attempts. Storage as a Service (SaaS) and web-based applications monitored for availability and response.

Monitoring Protocols

A variety of network management, monitoring, and maintenance protocols and utilities are available to assist network administrators in monitoring network activity. The primary three, in addition to those discussed in Chapter 12, are Simple Network Management Protocol (SNMP), Windows Management Instrumentation (WMI), and Intelligent Platform Management Interface (IPMI).

SIMPLE NETWORK MANAGEMENT PROTOCOL (SNMP)

The *Simple Network Management Protocol (SNMP)* is a TCP/IP suite protocol that manages and monitors network devices. SNMP consists of four primary components: the SNMP manager, the managed devices, SNMP agents, and a *management information base (MIB)*. *Managed devices* on a network can be just about any device on a network, including routers, switches, servers, workstations, and printers.

The *SNMP manager* communicates with SNMP agents on the managed network devices. The functions of the SNMP manager include sending queries to SNMP agents, processing the responses from the agents, configuring the agents, and interacting with device agents about triggered events. Managed devices commonly have an *SNMP agent* built in or included in their software. The SNMP manager and agents can be a standard utility associated with a network operating system, third-party software, or specific to a particular vendor.

A managed device with its SNMP agent enabled collects a set of variables from the MIB, updates them as needed, and provides this information to the SNMP manager when queried. The device agent alerts the SNMP manager in the case of a prescribed event or should a certain event count exceed or fall below a threshold.

Each SNMP agent maintains an MIB entry with its device parameters and managed metrics. The SNMP manager then uses the database to request specific information from the agent and sends it along to the network's management system, which is a console-based software package, such as HP's OpenView or IBM's NetView. An MIB entry lists the statistical and control values for each managed element on the network. In effect, the MIB contains the questions the SNMP manager can ask the SNMP agent about the attributes and controls identified for it.

SNMP defines four commands that SNMP elements communicate through:

> ➤ **GET**: This command is sent by the SNMP manager to the SNMP agent of a managed device to retrieve values from the agent.

> ➤ **INFORM**: An SNMP manager acknowledges a TRAP message using this command.

> ➤ **SET**: An SNMP manager uses this command to change or assign a value on a managed device.

> ➤ **TRAP**: An SNMP agent sends out this command to notify the SNMP manager of the occurrence of a defined event.

SNMP has two versions commonly implemented: SNMP version 1 (SNMPv1) and SNMP version 2c (SNMPv2c). A more secure version, SNMP version 3 (SNMPv3) is also available. SNMPv1 and SNMPv2c implement community (network) security. Other less common versions, SNMPv2u and SNMPv3, provide user-based security.

WINDOWS MANAGEMENT INSTRUMENTATION (WMI)

Windows Management Instrumentation (WMI) is an *application programming interface (API)* that is part of the Windows operating system that provides for the control and management of network devices and systems, most commonly on enterprise-level networks. A variety of scripting and programming languages, including ActiveX, VBScript, Perl, Visual Basic, C++, and Microsoft PowerShell, can use the WMI API to create device management and control routines.

WMI defines a platform-independent specification that facilitates information sharing with other management systems. WMI management standards interchange with SNMP. WMI is the Microsoft implementation of the *Web-Based Enterprise Management (WBEM)* standard that defines the management of distributed and networked computing environments. WMI uses the *Common Information Model (CIM)*, which is an industry standard for providing data about network devices and software applications that network administrators and management software use to perform management and control actions on network elements.

INTELLIGENT PLATFORM MANAGEMENT INTERFACE (IPMI)

The *Intelligent Platform Management Interface (IPMI)* is a standard computer system interface that allows network administrators to access network devices that may be powered off or unresponsive for other reasons. IPMI provides an alternative for administrators to access network devices other than through an operating system or login.

IPMI operates separately from a device or network operating system. It allows administrators to manage various servers using a message-based hardware interface. This allows it to manage a remote system without an operating system or another system or network management package. IPMI is able to provide services in three different situations: before the operating system starts on a computer; when a remote computer or device is powered off (but connected to power); when an operating system has crashed or there has been a system failure.

The *Data Center Management Interface (DCMI)* is a system management standard based on IPMI for use in data center environments. Although it uses IPMI interfaces, DCMI reduces the number of interfaces and provides for power control and other administrative areas unique to data centers.

Syslog

Syslog is an *Internet Engineering Task Force (IETF)* standard for logging computer system messages supported by a variety of network devices, including printers, switches, routers, and the like, on multiple or diverse platforms. The syslog standard, which runs primarily on Linux/UNIX systems, facilitates the consolidation of different devices and systems into a single central system log file. The flexibility of the syslog standard separates the software that generates system log entries from the software that reports or analyzes the log file entries. Syslog also supports its use for system management and system and network security auditing.

The syslog standard defines three content and operational layers:

> **Syslog content**: This is the information included in a syslog message.

> **Syslog application**: This layer defines message generation, interpretation, routing, and storage activities.

> **Syslog transport**: This layer transmits messages to and receives messages from system components.

A syslog message (packet) has three parts: message priority, message header, and message content. There is no minimum length for a syslog message, but it cannot exceed 1,024 bytes in length.

Syslog Severity Codes

The *message priority code* indicates the severity and the facility (source) of the message. Both the severity and the facility are numerical values stored in an 8-bit field. The *message severity code* occupies the high-order three bits, indicating one of the eight possible severity codes. Table 13-1 lists the eight severity codes and their meanings.

Table 13-1 Syslog Severity Codes

Code Value	Description	Meaning
0	Emergency	System unstable or failing
1	Alert	Immediate action required
2	Critical	Critical conditions detected
3	Error	An error condition detected
4	Warning	A warning or possible failure condition exists
5	Notice	System normal but potential problem detected
6	Information	Informational messages
7	Debug	Debug information

Syslog Facility Codes

The remaining five bits of the syslog priority code represent the source or cause of the syslog message. Using five bits, 24 facility codes are available for use. A specific meaning is assigned to 16 of the available facility codes, with the remaining 8 codes available for local definition. Table 13-2 lists the syslog facility codes and the facility each identifies.

Table 13-2 Syslog Facility Codes

Code Value	Facility
0	Kernel messages
1	User-level messages
2	Mail system messages
3	System daemon messages
4	Security/authorization messages
5	Syslog internal messages
6	Printer messages
7	Network messages
8	System-to-system (Unix-to-Unix Copy, or UUCP) messages
9	Clock daemon messages
10	Security/authorization messages
11	FTP daemon messages
12	Network Time Protocol (NTP) messages
13	Log audit messages
14	Log alert messages
15	Clock daemon messages
16–23	Local use 0–7

© 2015 Cengage Learning®.

Alert Systems

An alert, in the context of system monitoring and management, is a message automatically sent by a device, application, or utility to one or more persons as a notification of a condition, fault, failure, or potential issue. Typically, an alert is a notice of a time-sensitive action required by an administrator.

A notification system, whether in a device operating system, system monitor, or system management system, sends an alert message by one or more supported methods. The more common methods for sending alert messages, such as SNMP messages and syslog messages, are email, *Short Message Service (SMS)*, instant messaging (IM), desktop alerts, and telephone (voice) calls. To differentiate between alert messages and spam (junk messages), the U.S. Federal Communications Commission (FCC) approved an emergency alert text-messaging system in 2008 as an extension of the Rich Site Summary (RSS) system.

> **Note**
>
> SMS is a text messaging service common to cellular telephones, tablet computers, webpages, and other mobile communication devices.

ALERT TRIGGERS

Not all *alert notifications* are necessarily emergencies. The trigger for an alert message, which administrators configure, could be that something is working just fine, something seems fishy, something needs immediate attention, or something has crashed. Administrators can set triggering conditions on a variety of metrics and thresholds from good to very bad in the majority of the available monitoring systems.

> **Note**
>
> A search of the Internet should find more than 60 network monitoring systems, which does not include server monitors, disk storage monitors, and other device or system-specific monitors.

One of the leading information technology (IT) infrastructure monitoring systems, Nagios XI from Nagios Enterprises, provides a robust example of how notification events occur and how to configure alert notifications. Understand that the following paragraph and section reflect this one particular system, but also that these examples are representative of monitoring systems in general.

You can configure alert notifications with several attributes, including a notification interval that defines the time interval between notifications of a particular event. However, notifications do not occur just because the interval has expired. The monitoring system only sees an event that triggers an alert notification when a service check runs on its particular schedule. If an event condition remains in alert status, the time interval on a notification threshold determines when to resend an alert.

ALERT NOTIFICATION FILTERS

Monitoring systems allow notification filters to avoid unnecessary notifications going out at different alert levels. The Nagios system defines the following filters, which are representative of most monitoring systems:

> ➤ **System-wide filter**: You must enable or disable alert notifications in the main configuration files of the monitoring system. Disabling alert notifications blocks all notifications under any conditions.

> ➤ **Downtime filters**: The system doesn't send alert notifications when a service, device, or host is in a period of scheduled downtime.

> ➤ **Flapping filters**: A router that supports dynamic routing can develop a condition known as "flapping." This typically occurs when the configuration of the router is set for load balancing between two specific routes. Under this condition, the router sends out one path as the best route and follows that up by sending out another path as the best route. If flap detection is on, an alert notification goes out; otherwise, it doesn't.

> ➤ **Device/service-specific filters**: The configuration of each monitored element can have alert notifications set for different condition levels, including warning states, critical states, recovery states, and failure or nonresponsive states.

> ➤ **Notification period filters**: Each monitored device can have a specific period configured during which alert notifications may be sent.

> ➤ **Prior notification filters**: If an alert notification occurred in the past, the configured time interval must expire before sending out another notification on the same issue.

> ➤ **Contact filters**: Each contact entered into the system has its own set of filters that are unique to that contact only. Contact filters establish the condition level under which the contact receives an alert notification. Notification period filters and prior notification filters apply to individual contacts.

When installing a monitoring system, you assign a contact person or group to each host, device, or service that is to receive any alert notification triggered from that element. When the monitoring system sends an alert notification from a particular element, each member of the contact group receives the alert. Some systems also permit the assignment of multiple contact groups on an element and remove any duplicated persons from the outgoing alerts.

ALERT NOTIFICATION METHODS

The primary default notification method of monitoring systems is email. However, most also offer support for any number of notification methods or provide an interface for third-party notification systems. Most of the more popular monitoring systems do not incorporate notification messaging in their core elements for the sake of flexibility. The Nagios monitoring system supports, after configuration, email, pagers, SMS (cell phone), WinPopup messages, IM, audio alerts, and more.

A popular choice for email messaging is the *Simple Mail Transport Protocol (SMTP)*. You can use SMTP to email alert notifications by setting TCP/UDP port 25 (SMTP) as the notification port in the monitoring system's configuration.

Baselines and Thresholds

Perhaps the first thing you must do when installing a performance monitoring system is to establish a *performance baseline*. A baseline establishes the normal, acceptable levels of operation for the system, network, devices, or services against which a monitoring system can measure abnormal performance. The baseline should also include consideration for the timeframe in which the monitored system must perform.

On a Windows system, you can use the *Windows Performance Monitor (WPM)* to determine CPU or processor utilization, as shown in Figure 13-1. You can run WPM on a local server or remotely on a host or server. Before this monitor or any other can be of help to establish a baseline, you must know what it is you want to monitor. Typically, if the server is a specialized server, such as an SQL server, a print server, and so on, you should set the baseline to measurements that relate to its function. For instance, on an SQL server, you should monitor SQL performance objects, or on a print server, you might want to monitor the CPU, memory, and perhaps temporary disk storage space.

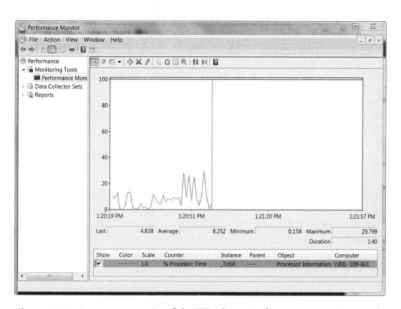

Figure 13-1 A screen capture of the Windows Performance Monitor tracking processor utilization.
Used with permission from Microsoft.

Most monitoring systems work with either performance objects or counters. *Objects* represent whole things, such as a processor, memory, disk space, or network connectivity devices. *Counters* drill down into objects to determine one or more specific performance attributes. Table 13-3 lists performance counters that you might configure in a performance monitor.

With objects identified to the performance monitoring system and counters set for each, the next task is to establish the performance *thresholds* that trigger alert notifications. For example, on a router object, you configure a flapping counter. You set the counter minimum value to 30 seconds and the maximum to 300 seconds. If the monitoring system queries the object/counter and a value greater than 30 returns, it generates a warning message. Should the counter return a value greater than 300, a critical or emergency notification generates.

Configuring the best set of counters on each object and setting their thresholds may take some trial and error. Many vendors, such as Cisco Systems, have threshold recommendations on their websites.

Table 13-3 Performance Counters		
Object	**Counter**	**Measurement**
Memory	Available Memory	Measures the amount of nonallocated memory available at any given point.
Memory	Page Faults	Measures the number of times per second requested that data is not present in memory.
Memory	Page Reads	Measures the number of hard page faults that require data from the hard disk.
Process	% Processor Time	Measures the amount of processor time each active process is using.
Process	Working Set	Measures the total memory a process is using for its code, threads, and data.
Processor	% Processor Time	Measures the amount of time a processor is productively working and not idle.
Processor	% User Time	Measures the amount of time a processor is supporting application or user-initiated processing.
System	Processor Queue	Measures the number of tasks queued awaiting the processor. In multiple core systems, this is the queue length for all processors.
Disk	Disk Reads	Measures the number of disk reads per second a disk storage device is processing.
Network interface	Bytes Total	Measures the total incoming and outgoing bytes per second on a NIC or port.
Network segment	% Broadcasts	Measures the percentage of total bandwidth consumed for broadcast messages.
TCP	Segments	Measures the total incoming and outgoing network segments per second on a network link.

© 2015 Cengage Learning®.

CPU Reservations/Entitlements/Shares

Without any other subscribed service levels than are ordinarily offered to customers by a cloud service, especially a virtualized one, the VM that a subscriber runs on will not have a particular priority for a virtual CPU (vCPU) or physical CPU resource. In some cases, the subscriber can ask for a guaranteed CPU resource *reservation* or an *entitlement*. Every VM has an assigned share of hardware and virtual resource allocation that includes an uncommitted CPU reservation. In reality, the actual amount of CPU resource a VM may realize is a factor of the hypervisor in use, its scheduling algorithms, the number of competing VMs, and several other variables.

In the context of CPU utilization, a CPU *share* is the prorated percentage of CPU resource given to each process. While the common default for a process is eight shares, how much of the available CPU time a process gets can depend on the number of processes the CPU is servicing. On the other hand, a CPU *reservation* allocates a specific percentage of the CPU resource to a process.

The reservation is available to the process should it need it. The amount of CPU resource specified in the reservation is the *soft limit*, from which other processes can borrow time, should the reserved process not use it all. Most CPUs set aside about 20 percent of their available processing time for their system functions, which leaves 80 percent for CPU shares. On a multiple core processor, the number of cores available reduces these percentages. For example, on a dual core processor, only 10 percent is set aside for the system, and 90 percent is available for shares.

In an enterprise environment or a cloud service that hosts multiple subscribers, *hard limits* can be set on resource utilization. In these instances, a subscriber may demand a fixed share of CPU resources and be willing to pay for that share. In this case, a hard limit can be set that allows the subscriber's processes to consume only the subscribed amount of CPU resource. Both soft limits and hard limits can be set for almost any service, including CPU resource utilization. When a subscriber uses more of a service than the soft limit (reservation) for that subscriber for that service, a quota timer starts. A *quota* on a service limits the amount of time a subscriber can exceed the soft limit without going over the hard limit.

An example of how these three metrics combine to control a subscriber's use of a service is the limits and quota on hard disk usage. A subscriber to a SaaS agrees to a soft limit of 12,000 data blocks (input/output [I/O] operations) and a hard limit of 15,000 blocks with a quota time of 7 days. If the subscriber exceeds the soft limit over a seven-day period, the management system blocks the subscriber from disk I/O until usage falls back below the soft limit. The same action results from the subscriber exceeding the hard limit at any time.

Resource Licensing

Whenever you install software on a computer, you must accept the user licensing conditions, typically presented in the form of an *end user licensing agreement (EULA)*, for the software from its publisher. On a single computer, installing the software is routine, and the EULA terms are generally acceptable. However, in a virtualized environment that supports multiple subscribers, licensing of system resources can become complex.

The primary issue with software licensing in a virtualized service, especially one that operates in the cloud, is the changing meaning of the word "machine." In most end user agreements, "machine" referred to a single physical entity. However, in the wonderful world of virtualization, a "machine" is a conceptual or virtual entity. Many licensing agreements still do not differentiate between something real and something virtual, but this is changing quickly.

One of the ways service providers, hardware vendors, and software publishers cooperate to verify resource licensing is through *device fingerprinting*. Using the standard published by the *Cooperative Association for Internet Data Analysis (CAIDA)*, the basis for a hardware device fingerprint is a value produced by an algorithm that uniquely identifies every remote device interacting with a server.

In the past, the configuration information of the requesting web browser was a device fingerprint. The *clock skew* form has largely replaced the browser for fingerprinting incoming requests from remote hosts. This form of device fingerprint allows the servicing host to identify the remote host even without cookies enabled.

Device fingerprinting operates under two primary principles: diversity and stability. Diversity requires that all remote hosts (web clients) have a universally different fingerprint value, and no two remote hosts have the same device fingerprint. Stability requires that the value assigned to each remote host does not change during a computing session. In reality, these are desired goals, but they may not be attainable in that they are somewhat mutually exclusive.

Third-party software systems, such as Sentinel RMS from SafeNet, Inc. and FlexNet Manager from Flexera Software, are available to track and manage software licensing utilization in both enterprise and virtualized cloud service environments. This type of software can block the use of software by a VM or use VM fingerprinting to limit the use of licensed software. It can also act as a meter for charge-back purposes.

Chapter Summary

- Monitoring a network to detect or prevent problems can avert the risk of losing crucial network-accessed resources and business continuity. Effective network monitoring should be proactive and thorough.

- Various utilities are available to assist network administrators in monitoring network activity. The primary network management, monitoring, and maintenance protocols are SNMP, WMI, and IPMI.

- Administrators can use SNMP to manage and monitor network devices.

- WMI is an API that provides for the control and management of network devices and systems.

- IPMI is a standard computer system interface that allows network administrators to access network devices.

- Syslog is a standard for logging computer system messages. A syslog packet has three parts: message priority, message header, and message content.

- An alert notification is a message automatically sent by a device, application, or utility to one or more persons as a notification of a condition, fault, failure, or potential issue. The methods for sending out alert messages are SNMP, syslog, email, SMS, IM, and telephone calls.

- Monitoring systems allow notification filters to avoid unnecessary notifications.

- A performance baseline establishes the normal, acceptable levels of operation for the system, network, devices, or services against which a monitoring system can measure abnormal performance.

- Monitoring systems work with performance objects and counters. Objects represent whole entities, and counters are representative of specific performance attributes.

- A CPU share is the prorated percentage of CPU resource assigned to a process. A CPU reservation allocates a specific percentage of the CPU resource to a process. The amount of CPU resource specified in a reservation is a soft limit. A hard limit is the percentage of use a process cannot exceed. A quota limits the amount of time a process can exceed the soft limit.

> ➤ Service providers, hardware vendors, and software publishers verify resource licensing through device fingerprinting. Device fingerprinting operates under two primary principles: diversity and stability.

Key Terms

Alert notification

Application program interface (API)

Clock skew

Common Information Model (CIM)

Cooperative Association for Internet Data Analysis (CAIDA)

Counters

Data Center Management Interface (DCMI)

Device fingerprinting

End user licensing agreement (EULA)

Entitlement

Hard limit

Intelligent Platform Management Interface (IPMI)

Internet Engineering Task Force (IETF)

Managed devices

Management information base (MIB)

Message priority code

Message severity code

Network monitoring

Object

Performance baseline

Quota

Reservation

Share

Short Message Service (SMS)

Simple Mail Transport Protocol (SMTP)

Simple Network Management Protocol (SNMP)

SNMP agent

SNMP manager

Soft limit

> Syslog
>
> Threshold
>
> Web-Based Enterprise Management (WBEM)
>
> Windows Management Instrumentation (WMI)
>
> Windows Performance Monitor (WPM)

Review Questions

1. System and network administrators should perform _____ to avoid the risk of losing crucial network-accessed resources and business continuity.

2. True or False? Effective network monitoring should be proactive and thorough.

3. Which of the following is NOT a protocol for monitoring network activity?

   a. SNMP

   b. SMTP

   c. WMI

   d. IMPI

4. WMI is a(n) _____ that provides for the control and management of network devices and systems.

5. True or False? IPMI is a standard system interface that allows network administrators to connect to remote operating systems.

6. True or False? The standard utility for logging computer system messages is SMTP.

7. A(n) _____ is automatically sent by a system resource to notify of a fault, failure, or potential issue.

8. What is the percentage of a resource assigned to a process called?

   a. Share

   b. Reservation

   c. Quota

   d. Hard limit

9. What is the specific percentage of a system resource allocated to a process called?

   a. Share

   b. Reservation

   c. Quota

   d. Hard limit

10. A _____ sets an upper limit on the amount of a resource a process can consume.

11. True or False? Monitoring systems use notification filters to avoid unnecessary notifications.

12. What establishes the acceptable levels of system performance against which system monitoring can measure actual performance?

    a. Performance objects

    b. Performance counters

    c. Performance baseline

    d. Performance quota

13. Monitoring systems use performance objects and _____.

14. True or False? A resource quota limits the amount of time a process can exceed the soft limit.

15. What technology or method can cloud service providers use to verify and control resource licensing utilization?

    a. Device fingerprinting

    b. Software fingerprinting

    c. Biometric identification

    d. User authentication

Answers to Review Questions

1. performance monitoring

2. True

3. b

4. application program interface (API)

5. False

6. False

7. alert notification

8. a

9. b

10. hard limit

11. True

12. c

13. counters

14. True

15. a

CHAPTER 14

Physical Resource Allocation

After reading this chapter and completing the exercises, you will be able to:

- Explain the concept and process of allocating physical and virtual resources
- Discuss resource pooling
- Describe physical resource redirection and mapping
- List the various types of remote access tools

T he relationship between physical computing resources and their virtual counterparts is a vital part of establishing a virtualized environment. In this chapter, you learn about the various methods used to associate physical components with virtual components as well as the methods you can use to remote connect to a virtualized system. In addition, you learn about the concept of resource pooling and its importance to virtualized environments.

Allocating Physical Resources

The allocation of physical resources is a key element of establishing a virtual environment. The physical resources available for allocation are the underlying processing components that facilitate the virtual independence of virtual machines (VMs)—namely, processors (CPUs), memory, and storage, which are the same components that an application running in a nonvirtualized environment must have to operate.

Allocating CPU Resources

The allocation of CPU resources can occur in various ways in both virtualized and nonvirtualized environments. In a nonvirtualized environment, allocation of more or fewer resources to a process (application or service) happens through the assignment of priorities. Raising the priority of a process sets a guaranteed minimum level of the available CPU resources. In virtualized environments that are running on *symmetric multiprocessing (SMP)* systems, the multiprocessor contains two or more independent processors. Each processor can process different programs, using different data, and has the capability of sharing common system services through the system bus.

PHYSICAL CPU ALLOCATION

When setting up a virtual environment, you can allocate physical CPU resources, especially CPUs that are multicore SMP, to provide the resources that VMs require. Most of the CPU allocations occur after the installation of a guest operating system or as part of the creation of a VM.

Following are the CPU-related components for which you should have knowledge and understanding for this action:

> **CPU**: The hardware component inside a computer that executes software instructions by carrying out arithmetic, logic, and input/output (I/O) operations. A *multiprocessing computer* has two or more CPUs, and a multicore CPU has two or more cores (processors).

> **Core**: A computing unit that includes level 1 (L1) cache and the operational units required to execute software instructions. *Multicore processors* have two or more cores.

> **CPU socket**: The mounting frame into which a CPU installs on a computer motherboard. A *CPU socket* installs a single microprocessor. Some motherboards have more than one CPU socket. A *processor core* mounts to a *virtual socket*.

> **Thread**: Short for "thread of execution," a *thread* is an ordered stream of instructions. *Multithreaded processors* or cores multiplex two or more streams of instructions, alternatively processing instructions from each thread.

A couple of other concepts you should know are resource sharing and resource allocation. *Resource sharing* creates shares that designate the relative priority of a VM or a particular resource pool. A VM that has more resource shares than any other VM will have priority over the other VM should they compete for a resource.

Resource shares, reservations, and limits specify the *resource allocations* for a particular VM. These allocation thresholds also establish a relative priority for the resources among the VMs competing for available resource capacity.

SMP Multiprocessing

SMP defines a computer multiprocessor that contains the hardware and software to support two or more identical processors to share a single memory pool, as shown in Figure 14-1. In addition, the processors run under a single instance of an operating system and have equal access to I/O devices. On SMP multicore processors, each core functions as a separate processor.

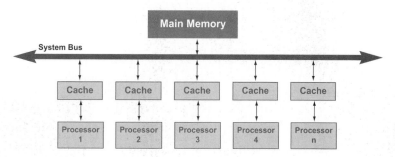

Figure 14-1 The architecture of an SMP multiprocessor.
© 2015 Cengage Learning®.

Virtual CPU Allocations

Virtual CPUs (vCPUs) are part of the SMP multithreaded architecture. Applications running in VMs are dependent on multithreaded and multicore processors. Each of the physical or logical cores of a multicore CPU can have multiple vCPUs assigned through *hyperthreading*, meaning a single physical core supports two logical cores. SMP processors can also divide a thread into multiple physical or logical cores in support of virtualized processes.

The hypervisor of the virtualized environment controls the physical CPU and manages the assignment and allocation of the physical cores and the vCPUs. Essentially, a vCPU is only an allotment of time on a physical or logical core. A physical core can support up to eight vCPUs, but you cannot assign more than four vCPUs to a VM.

There is a catch to the allocation of cores as vCPUs. When you allocate a vCPU (or more than one vCPU) to a VM, the vCPU must be available exclusively to the VM when it starts up, while it's running, and even if the VM is idle or not using all its vCPU allocation. If you allocate a vCPU (and its associated core) to two different VMs, whichever VM starts up first gains exclusivity on the vCPU to the exclusion of any other VM.

The mapping of vCPUs to cores is a dynamic runtime event. The hypervisor assigns vCPUs to physical cores at runtime. Therefore, if there is a shortage of processor cores, a VM cannot execute properly unless a hyperthreaded core is available and can process more than one VM at a time.

CPU Affinity

CPU affinity, also called CPU pinning, ties a process or thread to one or more specific CPUs. Once configured with affinity, a process or thread runs only on the designated processor(s). The purpose of CPU affinity is to bypass the queue scheduling of an SMP environment operating system. The association of a process or thread to a specific CPU labels the CPU as the *kin processor* for that process or thread. When the operating system allocates resources to the process or thread, the allocation is to the kin processor.

However, if Process A and Process B both have affinity to the same processor and another processor is idle, one of the processes is likely to shift to the idle processor and, if all conditions are equal, create an affinity with that processor. Affinity helps when a process thread interrupts with some of its remaining instructions in a processor's cache. Without establishing affinity on the processor on which it was running at the time of the interruption, a delay may occur while another processor loads the remaining instructions. With affinity established, the process stays with the processor with which it started.

Allocating Memory

In a virtualized environment, there is *memory virtualization* and the allocation of memory to a VM. Although they can exist at the same time, there is a difference between the two. Memory virtualization occurs when an operating system combines the main memory of networked servers into a single memory pool that any application running on networked resources can share. Allocating memory to a VM is a virtual environment configuration setting.

MEMORY VIRTUALIZATION

Memory virtualization allows applications running on networked servers to share a much larger pool of memory than they would have access to on a single server. This capability can overcome the possible processing bottleneck of a physical memory limit. At the application level, the memory pool is available through an application programming interface (API) or a memory management system. Because memory virtualization creates what is in effect a large memory cache, system performance improves. Memory virtualization works primarily with dynamic RAM (DRAM).

Memory virtualization is also different from a shared memory system. A shared memory system is available for simultaneous use by multiple applications. The primary purpose of a shared memory implementation is to allow the applications sharing the memory to communicate by passing data to one another. However, shared memory also refers to a single program with multiple threads passing data between themselves.

Memory virtualization improves memory utilization, decreases runtime for I/O-intensive applications, reduces memory needs by sharing a pool, and decreases latency through fewer I/O requests.

VM MEMORY ALLOCATION

A VM's memory allocation is part of its configuration. When you create a VM, you specify the amount of memory it is to have made available by the hypervisor when the VM starts up. The virtual environment software sets the maximum amount of memory you can allocate to a VM.

You can't allocate more memory to a VM than physically exists. During the configuration of a VM, a range of memory options displays, with the high end representing the size of the physical memory.

On a 64-bit host, the memory allocation maximum is 64 GB and on a 32-bit host, the limit is 8 GB. In VMware, for example, if you allocate more than the limit to a VM, the system does not start the VM. Bear in mind that in addition to the memory necessary to run an application in a VM, the virtualization system uses a portion of its memory to control the virtualization. Like other resource allocations in a virtualized environment, memory allocations are in shares, reservations, and limits.

Storage Allocation

One truth that faces all computing is that applications, especially end user applications, must have access to data storage to function. In a nonvirtualized environment, the provisioning of each application includes the assignment of a *logical unit number (LUN)*. The process of creating a LUN sets aside a portion of unused space on the storage system and assigns it to a specific application.

This type of provisioning works fine until the application fills up the allocated space. To enlarge the space provisioned to the LUN, you must stop the application, back up the data, delete the existing LUN, create a new larger provisioning and LUN, restore the data from the original LUN, and restart the application. Because of the time required to complete this process and the disruption caused for users of the application in question, the allocated space in a LUN tends to be much larger than necessary, eating up disk space that may sit empty.

In a virtualized environment, the hypervisor provisions virtual disk space using either thin provisioning or thick provisioning.

THICK PROVISIONING

Thick provisioning, another name for the traditional approach to provisioning, allocates the same amount of resource capacity as a process actually uses. In a virtualized environment, thick provisioning allocates VM disk space to be the same size as the virtual disk.

There are two types of thick provisioning: Lazy Zero or Flat thick provisioning and Eager Zero thick provisioning. In *Lazy Zero thick provisioning*, the hypervisor writes zeroes to the VM disk file (.VMDK) to erase any data from an earlier use before the VM writes to it. The zeroing pads out the file to its fixed size, and the file remains the same size as the virtual disk. A virtual disk provisioned in this manner is "lazy zeroed." The *Eager Zero thick provisioning* is a VMware thick provisioning method that creates a pre-zeroed ("eager zeroed") VM disk in thick format.

THIN PROVISIONING

Thin provisioning, also called *overallocation* or *oversubscription*, avoids the inherent waste of storage resources of the more traditional method. In thin provisioning, a process uses much less of the disk resource than the amount allocated to it. Thin provisioning establishes a LUN from a common pooling of the storage resources, applying oversubscription (overallocation). Typically, a thin provisioned LUN is larger than the storage pool's total size. For example, on a storage resource pool of 10 GB, a LUN may be for 15 GB. Thin provisioning then relies on the operating system or storage system controllers to map the LUNs of running applications and create or resize storage volumes as required, without interrupting applications. Applications interact with LUNs normally without regard to the management of the storage space. Although the application "believes" it has 15 GB of storage space, most likely it is using much less. Figure 14-2 illustrates the difference between the traditional or thick provisioning of a storage space and thin provisioning.

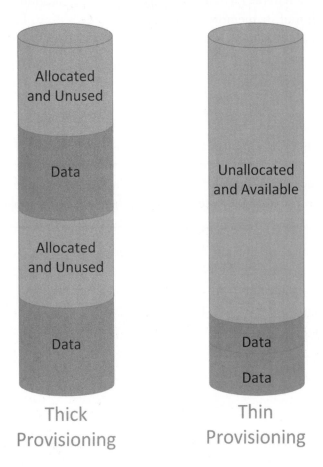

Figure 14-2 Thick provisioning hard-allocates storage space, and thin provisioning allocates space as it is required.
© 2015 Cengage Learning®.

Should the allocated space of a thin provisioned LUN fill up, the operating system or storage system manager recognizes instantly new storage devices or freed up reserved space. Thin provisioning doesn't prevent storage space shortages, and applications running under this form of resource provisioning can suffer the same performance issues they would under thick provisioning. Thin provisioning doesn't replace physical resource management; it just makes it more efficient. The primary benefit of thin provisioning over thick provisioning is that thin provisioning uses only the amount of disk space it requires, whereas thick provisioning allocates fixed blocks of disk space that may or may not be completely used and therefore wasted.

Dynamic Resource Allocation

One of the newer features in virtualization systems is *dynamic resource allocation*, which includes resource pooling and resource clustering. *Resource pooling*, in the context of either virtualization or cloud computing, is the categorization and managing of common resources under a single point of control and allocation. The computing resources in a data center fall into one of three categories:

> ➤ **Computing resources**: This resource pool includes CPU-based components. The computing resource pool includes the processors, memory, cache, firmware, bus, and registers that take part in the execution of instructions and processes. Resource pooling for computing resources relates directly to CPU virtualization.

> ➤ **Network resources**: This resource pool includes the devices, physical or virtual, that format and transmit network messages and the devices that provide network connectivity.

> ➤ **Storage resources**: This resource pool includes the devices, software, firmware, and control systems involved in the storage and retrieval of data from mass storage devices.

Resource pooling has been essentially a cloud-computing concept that is now applicable to virtualized environments as well. In effect, resource pooling allows applications and end users to operate in an environment of virtually infinite and available resources that allows applications to alter their resource commitments on the fly.

Resource pooling applies to data storage, bandwidth, memory, and other processing support resources. The basic objective of resource pooling is to create a computing environment for the cloud service subscriber or the virtual environment user that can flex to meet her processing needs without the requirement to interact with system administrators.

Figure 14-3 illustrates the concepts of resource pooling in a virtual environment. From top to bottom, VMs can share some localized resources and the centralized resource pools as well. The hypervisor manages the resource pools to assign or allocate resources from the pool to individual VMs. The hypervisor also interacts with the physical hardware to add or remove shared resources to and from the resource pools.

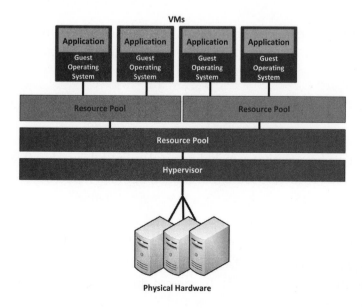

Figure 14-3 The hypervisor manages and controls resource pooling in a virtual environment.

© 2015 Cengage Learning®.

In VMware, a resource pool aggregates the physical hardware into logical resource groups. The hypervisor allocates the pooled components or resource groups to VMs. The VMware *Distributed Resource Scheduler (DRS)* pools resources based on the allocations that the system administrators define. However, dynamic resource assignment is not exclusive to VMware; Microsoft and Citrix also offer this feature in their virtualization software.

Figure 14-4 illustrates the overlaying of the clustering and resource pooling features. As shown, a resource pool can exist inside another resource pool, which can then be inside a cluster. Clustered devices are available as a resource pool to other resource pools and clusters, providing the system with a high level of flexibility.

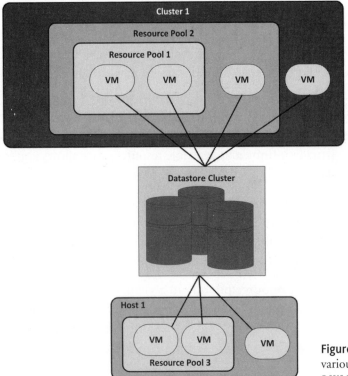

Figure 14-4 Resource pools can exist at various levels of a virtual environment.
© 2015 Cengage Learning®.

Another form of resource pooling occurs in clustered computing infrastructures. In effect, organizing several computers into a cluster automatically pools their resources and creates a single management entity.

Mapping Ports

VMs can map to interface ports on a host computer, including serial, universal serial bus (USB), and parallel ports. The mapping for each of these is somewhat similar, but each has its own particular methods.

SERIAL PORTS

Computers have several types of serial stream interfaces, including Ethernet, FireWire, and USB, that transmit data one bit at a time (see Figure 14-5). In spite of this, a *serial port* is an interface that conforms to the *RS-232C* standard. ("RS" stands for Registered Standard, and "C" is the latest version.) Serial ports have been used throughout the history of microcomputers for modems, data terminals, some printers (in the really early days), and other peripherals, such as industrial controls and some measuring devices.

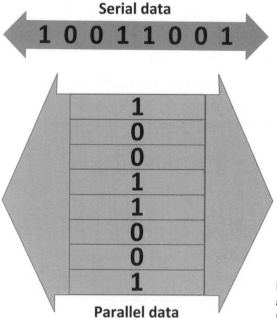

Figure 14-5 Serial data transmits one bit at a time, and parallel data transmits an entire byte at a time.
© 2015 Cengage Learning®.

There are several ways to abstract a serial port into a virtual serial port to a VM. The method used depends largely on what you need the port to do.

> **Physical serial port**: The VM can interface directly with a physical serial port on the VM's host computer. Use this method when you are connecting to an external modem or portable device.

> **File capture**: If you want to capture the data from a virtual serial port sent by an application running in a VM on a host computer, you can redirect the data stream to a file.

> **Named pipe**: In a Linux/UNIX environment, a pipe is a set of commands, processes, or applications lined together in a sort of chain in which the output of one process is the input of the next process in the chain, creating a pipeline between the processes. Whereas an unnamed pipe exists only while the process chain is running, a *named pipe* is a system entity that is available for processes and applications to use whenever they run to pass data. Two VMs can establish a connection between themselves or between a VM and another application on the host computer. A named pipe can also provide for two VMs running on different hosts to communicate via a serial connection.

> **Console server**: Also called a console access server, serial port concentrator, or serial console server, a *console server* provides serial ports that interconnect to the serial ports on other devices, such as servers, routers, or switches. Access to the consoles of connected devices is over a serial link using a modem or terminal emulation software, such as Telnet or SSH. This capability allows a remote user to access a system console via the network.

PARALLEL PORTS

Various peripheral devices connect to a *parallel port* on a host computer, including printers, scanners, device and key dongles, and some external disk drives. A parallel port transmits an entire byte at a time over individual internal wires in the connecting cable, as opposed to a serial port that transmits one bit at a time on a single wire. Figure 14-5 illustrates this difference. While many computer peripherals that once connected through a parallel port now connect through a USB drive, some devices designed to connect to larger high-volume systems may still use a parallel port connection.

The standard for parallel ports is the Institute of Electrical and Electronics Engineers (IEEE) 1284. This standard defines five parallel communication modes through a standard parallel port. Most virtualization software supports up to three directional parallel ports on a VM. The virtual parallel ports are associated with the physical parallel port on the host computer, provided the physical parallel port is of the same parallel format. Most modern host computers with a parallel port use the Extended Capability Port (ECP) port, which is backward compatible with older parallel port formats.

The five parallel communication modes in the *IEEE 1284* standard are (older to newer):

> *Standard Parallel Port (SPP)*: Also called the Centronics standard and compatibility mode, the SPP mode is a one-direction interface designed specifically for printers. Although unidirectional, the printer can communicate some fixed meaning error and status codes to the host computer.

> *Nibble mode*: One-half of a byte (4 bits) is a nibble, which is where this parallel communication mode gets its name. Nibble mode, also called Bitronics mode, communicates only 4 bits at a time and, although originally designed for printers, it is largely obsolete now.

> *Bidirectional mode*: Also called byte mode, this is a half-duplex mode that can transmit in both directions, but like an Ethernet cable, in only one direction at a time. Only the compatibility mode is not bidirectional.

> *Enhanced Parallel Port (EPP)*: The EPP mode for parallel communications was the first of the two "modern" port modes. EPP operates twice as fast as its predecessors. Because of its ability to switch communication direction quickly, it's able to transmit larger amounts of data than the older modes. The latest standard version is EPP 1.7. You may hear about EPP 1.9, but it really doesn't exist.

> *Extended Capability Port (ECP)*: The "extended capability" of the ECP parallel communication mode is the use of *direct memory access (DMA)* to transfer data, removing this burden from the CPU. Nearly all newer parallel printers implement either the EPP or the ECP parallel mode.

A VM can have up to three parallel ports attached to it. Applications running in the VM can send output directly to a parallel port or to a file in a similar manner to a virtual serial port.

PS/2 Ports

In the late 1980s, IBM Corporation introduced a new personal computer, the Personal System/2 or *PS/2*. On the PS/2, 6-pin mini-DIN connectors (DIN stands for Deutsches Institut für Normung) replaced the serial ports—primarily the keyboard and mouse ports. PS/2 color-codes ports with the connector and jack for a keyboard purple, and it color-codes the connector and jack for a wired mouse green. Figure 14-6 shows the keyboard and mouse PS/2 connectors on a PC.

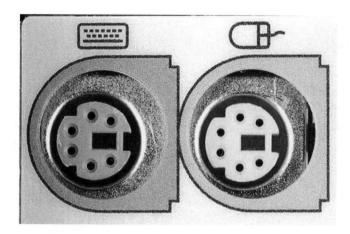

Figure 14-6 The PS/2 keyboard (left) and mouse (right) connectors on a PC.
© 2015 Cengage Learning®.

A VM can connect to a PS/2 for one wired mouse. In fact, if the VM's USB driver does not find a USB mouse on the host computer, it looks for either a virtual mouse (vmouse) or a PS/2 mouse.

Remote Access

In those organizations in which data centers are geographically diverse, administrators must be able to access remote systems for management, configuration, or maintenance. Each of the major virtualization software systems includes methods for connecting to and controlling a remote virtualized environment. The following two sections discuss the remote access tools for Microsoft Hyper-V and VMware, respectively.

Remote Access to Hyper-V

There are three ways to access the Hyper-V hypervisor remotely for management, control, and configuration: Windows PowerShell, Microsoft Server Manager, and Remote Desktop Services.

Windows PowerShell

Windows PowerShell is a command-line shell and configuration management tool built on the .NET Framework. Because it provides access to *Component Object Model (COM)* and *Windows Management Instrumentation (WMI)*, Windows PowerShell gives administrators the capability to perform tasks on local and remote Windows systems. Windows PowerShell also implements *Web-Based Enterprise Management (WBEM)*, *Web Services-Management (WS-Management)*, and *Common Information Model (CIM)* standards from the *Distributed Management Task Force (DMTF)*, which allows administrators to perform management tasks on remote Linux systems and most networking devices. Figure 14-7 shows the command line prompt for Windows PowerShell.

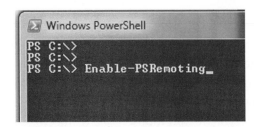

Figure 14-7 The Windows PowerShell window showing the PS command prompt.
Used with permission from Microsoft.

WINDOWS POWERSHELL

To start the Windows PowerShell, run "powershell" from a command prompt. In Windows PowerShell, the command-line actions are actually .NET command-lets (cmdlets), which implement a specific operation or set of operations. Windows PowerShell also provides a scripting language syntax that can create an application from a series of cmdlets saved into an executable file. A Windows PowerShell application has access to data in file systems or system files, such as the Windows Registry, via the PowerShell runtime.

In PowerShell-remoting mode, commands entered on one computer execute on another computer or compatible device. To enable the PowerShell-remoting mode, enter the command `Enable-PSRemoting` on the PowerShell command line, as shown in Figure 14-7.

Server Manager

Server Manager is a management console utility of Windows Server 2012 (and Windows Server 2008) that allows administrators to configure and manage local and remote Windows servers without enabling *Remote Desktop Protocol (RDP)* connections on either computer. You use Windows PowerShell to activate remote management on a local computer through Windows PowerShell.

Remote Desktop Services (RDS)

Windows *Remote Desktop Services (RDS)*, also called Terminal Services in Windows versions 2008 and older, is another Windows service that allows an administrator to control a remote computer or VM via a network connection using RDP. RDS implements a thin client profile in which all input on the client computer transmits to the server for processing.

REMOTE ACCESS TO VMWARE

In a VMware virtual environment, remote users can connect with a shared VM. With somewhat circular logic, VMware calls a shared VM any remotely accessible VM that then becomes a remote VM. In other words, if you can access a VM remotely, it becomes both a shared VM and a remote VM.

VMware Workstation Server

The VMware tools that enable remote access to shared VMs are Remote Workstation and VMware Workstation Server. To connect to a remote VM, a user connects to *Workstation Server*. Access to remote shared VMs is enabled automatically when VMware Workstation Server starts. When a host computer starts Workstation, it automatically connects to the VMware Workstation Server using the identity credentials of the user logged into the host.

Workstation connects to VMware Workstation Server using the *Hypertext Transfer Protocol Secure (HTTPS)* port 443. As many as 100 remote users can connect to one shared VM at any one time. Users on remote Workstation hosts can connect and interact with any host, local or remote, and use or run the shared VMs on it.

Workstation also allows you to connect to a remote server running any of the VMware virtualization system managers (vCenter, ESX, and so on). Depending on your login credentials on the remote host, you can perform any administrative task for which you have authorization. There are VMware Workstation Server versions for both Windows and Linux systems.

SSH Access to VMware

To use *Secure Shell (SSH)* or another terminal emulation utility like *PuTTY* (see Figure 14-8) to access the VMware hypervisor (ESXi) shell, you must first enable it on the shell. Once it's enabled, you are able to run shell commands remotely over the SSH/PuTTY link. The command set you can run is the full set of commands available locally.

Figure 14-8 The PuTTY configuration dialog box supports SSH terminal emulation.

Used with permission from Microsoft.

CONSOLE PORT ACCESS

Many computing devices have a provision for a *console port*. In general, a console port is a connection interface that pipelines, after authentication, an administrator directly to the operating system of a networking device or the hypervisor of a virtual environment. The designation of console port indicates an interface specifically reserved for this function. Connections to a console port require a terminal emulator, like SSH or PuTTY, to drive the communications between the remote device and the local computer.

Most console ports on networking devices are either serial or Ethernet connections dedicated to administrative functions. In a virtualized environment, a console port, while retaining its specific purpose, may be a virtual interface between a software function running a *graphical user interface (GUI* —pronounced as "gooey"). The console port on a VMware system is actually port 902, which "listens" for console/administrator traffic. Responses to the controlling host, local or remote, are on port 443 (SSH).

Microsoft Hyper-V uses a software solution for command and control interfaces. Console access is either local through the VM manager (VMM) and a GUI interface or via RDP and a remote user connecting through a terminal emulator.

Chapter Summary

> The allocation of physical resources is vital to establishing a virtual environment.

> In virtualized environments, SMP multiprocessors with multiple core processors can run different programs, use different data, and share common services through the system bus.

> The CPU-related terms you should know are CPU, core, CPU socket, and thread.

> Resource sharing creates shares on system resources. Resource shares, reservations, and limits specify the resource allocations for a particular VM.

> vCPUs are part of the SMP multithreaded architecture. Each physical core of a multicore CPU can have multiple vCPUs assigned through hyperthreading,

> A virtual system hypervisor controls the physical CPU and manages the assignment and allocation of the physical cores and the vCPUs.

> CPU affinity ties a process or thread to one or more specific CPUs.

> Memory virtualization occurs when an operating system combines the main memory of networked servers into a single memory pool. Allocating memory to a VM is a virtual environment configuration setting.

> Thin provisioning, or overallocation or oversubscription, avoids waste of storage resources.

> Dynamic resource allocation includes resource pooling and resource clustering. Resource pooling manages common resources under a single point of control and allocation. Resource pooling applies to data storage, bandwidth, memory, and other processing support resources.

> Data center resources fall into three categories: computing resources, network resources, and storage resources.

> VMs map to interface ports on a host computer, including serial, universal serial bus (USB), and parallel ports. Computers have several types of serial stream interfaces, including Ethernet, FireWire, and USB, which transmit data one bit at a time. A serial port conforms to the RS-232C standard.

> The ways to abstract a serial port into a virtual serial port to a VM include physical serial port, file capture, named pipe, and console server.

> IEEE 1284 is the standard for parallel port and defines five parallel communication modes: SPP, nibble mode, bidirectional mode, EPP, and ECP.

> There are three ways to access the Hyper-V hypervisor remotely: Windows PowerShell, Microsoft Server Manager, and Remote Desktop Services.

➤ Windows PowerShell is a command-line shell that accesses COM and WMI. Windows PowerShell implements WBEM, WS-Management, and CIM standards from DMTF.

➤ Windows Remote Desktop Services (RDS) is a Windows service that allows control of a remote computer or VM via a network connection using RDP.

➤ The VMware tools that enable remote access to shared VMs are Remote Workstation and VMware Workstation Server. Workstation connects to VMware Workstation Server using HTTPS port 443.

➤ The console port on a VMware system is 902. Responses to the controlling host are on port 443 (SSH).

Key Terms

Bidirectional mode

Common Information Model (CIM)

Component Object Model (COM)

Console port

Console server

CPU affinity

CPU socket

Direct memory access (DMA)

Distributed Management Task Force (DMTF)

Distributed Resource Scheduler (DRS)

Dynamic resource allocation

Eager Zero thick provisioning

Enhanced Parallel Port (EPP)

Extended Capability Port (ECP)

Graphical user interface (GUI)

Hypertext Transfer Protocol Secure (HTTPS)

Hyperthreading

IEEE 1284

Kin processor

Lazy Zero thick provisioning

Logical unit number (LUN)

Memory virtualization

Multicore processors

Multiprocessing computer

Multithreaded processors

Named pipe

Nibble mode

Overallocation

Oversubscription

Parallel port

Processor core

PS/2

PuTTY

Remote Desktop Protocol (RDP)

Remote Desktop Services (RDS)

Resource allocations

Resource pooling

Resource sharing

RS-232C

Secure Shell (SSH)

Serial port

Server Manager

Standard Parallel Port (SPP)

Symmetric multiprocessing (SMP)

Thick provisioning

Thin provisioning

Thread

Virtual CPUs (vCPUs)

Virtual socket

Web-Based Enterprise Management (WBEM)

Web Services-Management (WS-Management)

Windows Management Instrumentation (WMI)

Windows PowerShell

Workstation Server

Review Questions

1. _____ is the processing architecture of a multiprocessor with multiple cores.

2. True or False? Shares, reservations, and limits specify the resource allocations for a VM.

3. What is the standard that defines serial data ports?

    a. ISO 9002

    b. TIA 568b

    c. IEEE 1284

    d. RS-232C

4. A(n) _____ is an ordered stream of instructions.

5. True or False? Through hyperthreading, a physical processor core may have multiple vCPUs assigned.

6. What configuration setting ties a process or thread to one or more specific CPUs?

    a. CPU socket

    b. CPU affinity

    c. CPU mapping

    d. CPU kin

7. _____ occurs when an operating system combines the main memory of networked servers into a single memory pool.

8. True or False? Dynamic resource allocation includes resource pooling and resource clustering.

9. What is the maximum memory allocation for a VM running on a 32-bit host?

    a. 4 GB

    b. 8 GB

    c. 16 GB

    d. 64 GB

10. The provisioning technique under which a process uses less than the total resource allocated to it, allowing for overallocation, is _____.

11. True or False? RDS is a Windows service that allows a user to control a remote computer or VM via PuTTY.

12. A defined system entity on a Linux system that allows two VMs to pass data or instructions is a(n) _____.

    a. Unnamed pipe

    b. Named pipe

    c. Tunnel

    d. Shared memory

13. Resource _____ allows applications to operate with virtually infinite resources, including data storage, bandwidth, and memory.

14. True or False? A VM controls the physical CPU and manages the assignment and allocation of the physical cores and vCPUs.

15. What is the TCP/UDP port for the VMware console port?

    a. Port 80

    b. Port 443

    c. Port 902

    d. Port 1135

Answers to Review Questions

1. SMP

2. True

3. d

4. thread

5. True

6. b

7. Sharing

8. True

9. b

10. thin provisioning

11. False

12. b

13. pooling

14. False

15. c

CHAPTER 15

Security

After reading this chapter and completing the exercises, you will be able to:

- Explain storage security concepts, methods, and best practices
- Identify access control methods
- Compare different encryption technologies and methods
- Describe guest and host hardening techniques

Protecting and securing data and data storage devices goes beyond the methods described in Chapters 8 and 9. Securing a computing environment against internal or external attacks can involve the use of security controls, encryption, and intrusion detection, among other activities.

In this chapter, you learn about the security controls, methods, and activities used to protect the data resources of an organization. You also learn about the various types of encryption methods and host-level security actions that can reduce the vulnerability of the data resource.

Storage Security Concepts

As discussed in Chapter 3, providing the most effective security for data storage systems can be tricky. Data must be secure to prevent corruption or theft, but it also must be accessible to any user with the appropriate credentials and authorization. In addition, the data must be available and as current as possible after a system failure or catastrophic event.

The primary goals of data storage security in a cloud computing environment are the protection of critical data against theft, loss, or corruption and the assurance that data is available when it's needed. These goals must also include securing *data at rest* (data on storage devices) and *data in motion* (transmission of data between two points). What complicates data storage security in a cloud environment, compared to data stored in a local data center, is the distributed nature of data in cloud-based applications.

Another facet of data storage security in cloud services is the service model in use. In Infrastructure-as-a-Service (IaaS) services, the responsibility for data security lies more with the subscriber. In Software-as-a-Service (SaaS) models, the service provider is responsible for data and software storage and protection because these measures aren't visible to the subscriber.

Security can also be an issue regarding data in motion and data at rest. Many organizations believe that data in motion is vulnerable to attack. Data in motion has vulnerabilities, especially for eavesdropping or spoofing. If there is a concern for data in motion security, encryption methods can curb it. Of more concern to most organizations, and rightly so, is the security of data at rest. The best protection for data at rest is redundancy and encryption.

Data Security Controls

An organization must identify and apply certain security controls on its data resource before implementing security procedures and methods to protect it. *Security controls* identify, implement, and monitor the security measures of an organization. Security controls, in any application, fall into one of three primary categories:

> **Preventive controls**: These controls attempt to prevent security breaches or incidents from occurring. For example, door locks, passcodes, biometric systems, and electronic badge readers are all preventive controls.

> **Detective controls**: These controls attempt to detect and identify a security breach while it is happening. Detective controls are associated with intrusion alarms, security alerts, or automatic system shutdown.

> **Corrective controls**: These controls attempt to contain a security breach to minimize any damage the perpetrator has or may cause and quickly restore data resources to their correct or preattack status.

TYPES OF SECURITY CONTROLS

Within each of the security control categories, listed in the preceding section, there are different types and characteristics of security controls. The primary security control types are as follows:

> **Physical controls**: This type of security control includes equipment, building elements, and devices that prevent entry into, access to, or awareness of secured resources. Doors, fences, gates, walls, locks, and fire suppression systems are examples of physical security controls.

> **Procedural controls**: This type of security control includes actions, processes, procedures, management, and training that defines, manages, and monitors the security measures of protected resources. The procedures for an incident response team (IRT), security training, management oversight, and disaster recovery plan are examples of procedural security controls.

> **Technical controls**: This security control type includes technology-based access, authentication, authorization, and prevention processes, hardware, or software. User login (authentication), user identification (authorization), password-protected databases or files, networking devices with preventive capabilities such as firewalls and routers, and antivirus or malware systems are all examples of technical controls.

> **Legal/compliance/regulatory controls**: Outside government authorities, regulatory bodies, trade organizations, and organizational policies often mandate this type of security control. The Health Insurance Portability and Accountability Act (HIPAA) and Federal Information Processing Standards (FIPS) 800-53 are examples of this type of control.

CONTROLS FOR SECURING DATA

The security controls that relate to stored or in-transit data should first classify the data into structured and unstructured data (see Chapter 3) and appropriate data tiers (see Chapter 9). The responsibility for ensuring that the proper security controls are in place falls on service subscribers, although the service provider must implement the controls.

The security controls that should exist for all stored data, regardless of whether it is stored locally or in the cloud, follow:

> **Criticality**: An analysis of all data should classify each data asset as how critical it is to the organization and its operations. As discussed in Chapter 9, critical, operational, and transactional data categories also define the level of security each requires. Any relationships or associations of data in one tier with data from another tier may require a change in the categorization of the data asset.

> **Sensitivity**: All data, including personally identifiable information (PII) and product or service-specific data, must have security controls and measures applied appropriate to the level of confidentiality, sensitivity, or privacy.

> **Data handling**: The appropriate level of data-handling controls and measures should be consistent with the sensitivity of the data. The confidentiality, integrity, and accessibility of the data must be part of any access, storage, and manipulation processes, including its encryption, segmentation, and redundancy.

OBFUSCATION

In the context of data security, *obfuscation* refers to camouflaging certain stored data to protect it. The characters that appear in place of the characters you type when you enter a password are a common example of obfuscation. Obfuscation, also called *data masking*, uses various methods to change out the characters of some or all of the data in a block entity (file, record, database, and so on), in a way that is meaningful to the applications that will access the data.

Figure 15-1 illustrates how the original data, typically stored in production storage, converts to masked or obfuscated data, which is stored in a nonproduction storage space. Although the data in Figure 15-1 is not representative of any particular masking method, it does illustrate the degree of alteration applied to the original data.

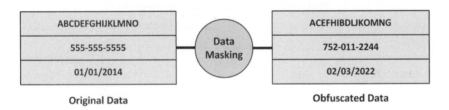

Figure 15-1 Obfuscation or data masking transforms data to make it unusable for anyone attempting to steal it.
© 2015 Cengage Learning®.

Numerous algorithms are applied by data masking software, but here are the more common methods used:

> **Encryption**: This method is perhaps the most effective way to mask data, but when applied, the users who require access to the data must receive the key, which may invalidate the reason for the data masking in the first place.

> **Masking**: Also called masking out, this data obfuscation method scrambles or masks out the data for display purposes. This method masks out a portion of a data field, such as a credit card number, and only a small portion of the whole data value displays. Commonly a masked-out credit card number field results in something like XXXX-XXXX-XXXX-1234.

> **Numeric variance**: This method of data obfuscation raises the numeric value of a data field by a plus or minus amount or percentage. It is popular for dates and monetary amounts because, when applied to an entire dataset, the range of the resulting values is still in a set value range (adjusted for the variance applied).

➤ **Shuffling**: This is a common form of data obfuscation that uses the values of a data field to mask the field. A shuffling algorithm shuffles the characters of a field to generate a new value made up of the original characters, just in a different order.

➤ **Substitution**: This masking approach preserves the look or layout of the data by using a table of substituted values. Substitution masking can be conditional, using a stored value, such as gender, title, department, or any other field that has a limited distribution of values. For example, if gender is the test value for an employee file, any records with an "M" in the gender field could have the first name fields substituted with male names and the data pair (original value and substituted value) stored in a substitution table. Substitution masking is appropriate for PII data, such as telephone numbers, credit card numbers, Social Security numbers, and the like.

Access Control

Controlling who (or what) has access to a network, through access control policies, is the most basic form of data security. Access control can also protect individual resources. Beyond the fundamental use of access control methods for authentication and authorization, applying access control to data storage helps to block unauthorized access to the data resource and, in turn, malicious attacks, data theft, and data corruption.

In general, there are three primary types of access control applied to networks, network resources, and especially data resources: *mandatory access control (MAC)*, *discretionary access control (DAC)*, and *role-based access control (RBAC)*.

Mandatory Access Control (MAC)

Under MAC, only system administrators have control over which users or applications have access to data resources. MAC provides the highest level of access control security for data storage.

MAC applies a security level to data and other network resources by assigning a confidentiality stamp to each asset. The administrators then assign each authorized user a security "clearance" that indicates the highest security level the user can access. A user with a confidential-level clearance could not access top secret or any other security level above confidential.

Discretionary Access Control (DAC)

The owner of a data object controls the access to the object under DAC. This access control method associates an access control list (ACL) with each data object that lists who can access a data object and what they can do with it. The ACL for any given data object lists each authorized user, his access level, and his permissions, which are execute (programs), read, and write.

Virtually all operating systems support ACLs. Windows systems associate an ACL with each data object that contains one or more *access control entries (ACEs)*. An ACE includes the name of each user or user group and a string of bits, and an access mask, which indicates the rights, privileges, and permissions for that name.

ROLE-BASED ACCESS CONTROL (RBAC)

In any organization, logical groupings can differentiate the various roles and access privileges associated with the function they perform. For example, a "sales" group can include the outside salespersons, and the "accounting" group may include all the nonmanagerial accounting clerks. These groups are role based. Because system administrators control access, RBAC is a form of MAC.

Access control is uniform for all members of a role-based group, so it may be necessary in larger organizations to create many role-based groups to accommodate the variances for the similar, but different tasks and access requirements. Any individual assigned to a particular role-based group has only the access and privileges granted to the group. When a user's job duties change, the user moves to a new group that accommodates her new duties and job requirements.

Security Attacks

It has become quite commonplace to read or hear about some form of computer attack in the news. The attack and data theft on Target in late 2013 is perhaps the biggest one in recent history, but it certainly won't be the last. In the context of computers and computer networks, an attack is an attempt to defeat system security measures to gain unauthorized access to a network for the purpose of corruption, theft, or unauthorized use of resources. The data assets stored on a network are the most common target (no pun intended).

Types of Attacks

Literally hundreds of attack types exist, with more coming nearly every day. However, attacks are either active or passive. An active attack attempts to gain access to system resources to alter their contents or change how they operate—and rarely for the better. A passive attack is an attempt to gain access to resources to gain information by observing data or to steal the data for outside use.

Someone on the inside of an organization or someone from outside the organization can perpetrate either an active or a passive attack. Someone with at least partial access to a system typically initiates insider attacks. Insider attacks involve the use of authorized access beyond its authorized limits. Outsider attacks initiate from a person (or a program) who must first gain unauthorized access to system resources. Attackers, who can range from curious hobbyists to organized criminals or terrorists, may just be seeing what they can do, without real harmful intent, or they may want to purposely disrupt, destroy, or steal system resources.

PASSIVE ATTACKS

Passive attacks on a system or network are generally eavesdropping attacks. Common passive attacks listen to network signals looking for unencrypted, clear text passwords and information that can be of use to launch a more aggressive active attack. Some passive attacks may perform network traffic analysis, especially on unsecured wireless networks, to intercept authentication information, lightly encrypted passwords, or user login credentials. The bottom line on a passive attack is that it captures and discloses private information without the sender's permission.

ACTIVE ATTACKS

When an attacker launches an *active attack*, he is purposely attempting to gain unauthorized access to a secured system or network. The underlying objective of an active attack is to bypass or break access control measures, steal or modify data, or insert malware into the system. However, an active attack may also attempt to intercept data in motion or crash a system. Active attackers are evildoers. Only in extremely rare situations do they have anything in mind other than malicious intent.

ATTACK TYPES

Enterprise networks and cloud service-oriented networks are attractive targets for attackers. This doesn't mean that smaller networks or systems aren't targets as well. The security measures and countermeasures of any network should be robust enough to withstand attacks. Of course, a security plan and its policies must consider the levels of risk and loss when deciding the extent of security systems, but protection should be in place for all potential paths of attack. The following sections explain the most common general forms of attacks.

Close-In Attacks

Close-in attacks involve someone physically gaining access to information or data center or network devices, data, and communication media. The purpose of a close-in attack is to modify, steal, or destroy resources. This type of attack requires unauthorized entry into a facility or the observance of a physical activity. A common form of close-in attack is *social engineering*, in which the attacker engages a user through email or by phone to learn security information. The attacker can then use this information to launch an attack on the system.

Other forms of close-in attacks are breaking and entering; using a stolen pass card, badge, or key; using a surreptitiously observed password; or using any illegal or unethical method to gain access to system resources.

Phishing Attacks

A *phishing attack* typically involves an unauthorized replica website presented to be the actual website of a financial or retail company. Victims receive email messages asking them to visit the bogus website, usually from a link in the email message, and enter private information, such as usernames, account numbers, and passwords. The attacker then uses this information to access the company's actual website and steal or purchase whatever she can.

Spoof Attacks

In a *spoof attack*, an attacker intercepts message packets and modifies the source Internet Protocol (IP) address in the packet so the packet appears to have originated from a different location. Spoof attacks are typically an attempt to bypass IP address filters in firewalls and routers.

Denial-of-Service Attacks

A *denial of service (DoS)* attack attempts to consume all the processing capability of a server or network connectivity device so that the server or device is unavailable to its associated network. A DoS attack is typically from a single attacker. However, if two or more attackers collaborate on a single target simultaneously, it becomes a *Distributed DoS (DDoS)* attack. The purpose behind DoS attacks isn't always clear, but the temporary or indefinite suspension of service by the attacked server or device is the general result.

Ping Attacks

The ping command sends Internet Control Message Protocol (ICMP) packets and clocks the response time back from the gateway device at the IP address included in the command line. Two types of attacks use the ping command to crash network-accessible servers or routers.

The first of the two ping attacks is the *ping of death (PoD)*. The PoD attack sends an oversized ping packet to a target computer. Because of its length, the target computer is unable to process it, and the computer crashes. In the past, computers could not process a ping packet longer than the IPv4 Maximum Message Unit (MMU) size of 65,535 bytes. When the target computer attempts to rationalize the packet, it halts or crashes. However, in later TCP/IP implementations, IP fragments this packet, but when the target computer reconstructs the packet from its fragments, a buffer overflow results, and the computer crashes.

The second ping attack is the *ping flood*. This attack is much like a DoS attack in that it sends a high volume of ping ICMP requests, which saturates the target computer, preventing it from processing its normal traffic from its associated network.

Exploit Attacks

If an attacker, inside or outside, learns of a particular vulnerability on a network or application, he can launch an attack that exploits that vulnerability, known as an *exploit attack*. Depending on the nature of the vulnerability, such as weak password controls, a bug in an application, or a gap in the packet filtering of a router or firewall, the attacker can gain access to or crash the targeted device or application.

Overflow Attacks

Overflow attacks, which are primarily *buffer overflow attacks*, *heap overflow attacks*, or *stack overflow attacks*, take advantage of programming weakness in applications or programs written in C or C++. A *buffer* is a fixed size space in memory allocated to a program to accept inputs. A *heap* is a dynamic area of primary memory that a program can request space in to perform data-handling functions under the total control and addressing of the program. A *stack* is another area of memory that a program can use to store variable data values. The value of using a stack in a program over using a heap is that the CPU manages stack memory, and only the program that allocated it manages the heap.

A buffer overfull attack causes a program to write more data to its buffer than it can hold, causing it to write to memory space beyond its allocation. Typically, executable code is included in the overflow, which the program then executes, changing the way the program executes or crashing the program. The preventive measure to prevent buffer overflows is to perform bounds checking within each program. The process of *bounds checking* compares the length of incoming input against the size of the allocated memory and stops the input process should the input exceed the length of the buffer.

Another form of buffer overflow attack is a *host header buffer overflow*, which exploits a flaw in the Apache web server. When an attacker sends a host header to the Apache server, it can overflow the host header buffer and cause the web server to crash.

A head overflow occurs in the heap data area of allocated memory. When a program starts, it allocates heap space dynamically in response to its memory allocation (malloc) command. Should incoming data corrupt the heap and possibly modify internal address and program pointers, it can change the memory allocation or the execution sequence of the program.

A stack overflow attack is similar to the buffer overflow and heap overflow attacks. However, the stack contains data the program has specifically saved in a *pushdown stack* data structure. A pushdown stack works like any of the spring-loaded plate, cup, or grocery store refrigerator shelf features. The last item placed on the stack is the first item available for use, called "first-in, first-out," or FIFO. Whenever a program accepts data from input or moves or copies data using a specified format, the program places the data on the stack. Should the data involved exceed the specific length of the field, a stack error occurs, causing the data to exceed its allocated space and overwrite at least the data in the stack entry below it and possibly others below that. Figure 15-2 illustrates how a stack overflow error may happen.

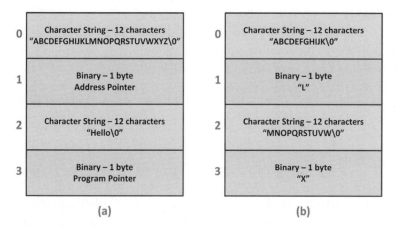

Figure 15-2 The conditions of a program stack after the program accepts data (a) and the effect of accepting data that is too long for the allocated space (b).
© 2015 Cengage Learning®.

As illustrated in Figure 15-2 (a), when a program accepts, moves, or copies data, it passes through the program's stack. When the program accepts what is supposed to be an 11-character string (12 with the termination character) but gets 26 instead, the result is a stack overflow, with a result similar to that shown in Figure 15-2 (b). Notice that the characters in excess of the first stack entry's length overwrite the remaining entries in the stack. When the program retrieves the memory or program pointers to continue processing, it is likely that the program will either crash or operate erratically.

Detection and Prevention

The second best weapon an organization has against attacks on its network and system resources is an *intrusion detection and prevention system (IDPS)*. Of course, the very best weapon is to close all vulnerabilities on the network, but because that's a never-ending task, it's an excellent best practice to install an IDPS on the network. An *intrusion* is any action on the part of an unauthorized network user that violates the security and acceptable use policies or the standard security practices of an organization.

There are two general types of IDPS systems: network based (NIPS) and host based (HIPS). Within the *network-based IDPS*, there are three distinct types of systems: those that concentrate on wired network traffic monitoring, those that operate on wireless media, and those that monitor and analyze network behavior on any or all network types. Network-based IDPSs monitor network traffic on hard-wired network segments and their connectivity devices and analyze the protocol activity on the network to identify suspicious-looking activities.

Wireless IDPSs, like the network-based IDPSs, monitor network traffic on the wireless transmission media looking for suspicious network and wireless protocol activities. The third type of network-based IDPS is *network behavior analysis (NBA)*. In contrast to the network- and wireless-based IDPS, NBA (not the basketball one) watches network traffic on any media looking for unusual flows of traffic, such as repeating transactions, flooding, DDoS attacks, malware, and, if configured appropriately, violations of local security policies. Host-based IDPSs are typically associated with a desktop firewall, antivirus program, or malware monitors.

IDPS is the process applied to a network to detect, identify, and prevent security events and breaches as they are occurring or before they can begin, with the hopes of 1) identifying the intruder; 2) identifying the target vulnerability for remediation; and 3) limiting the damage to network resources and planning for their restoration.

IDPS uses two primary approaches to detecting security incidents: signature-based detection and anomaly-based detection.

SIGNATURE-BASED DETECTION

Signature refers to a constant pattern of characters or data in data objects of any type. The pattern can be in the first so many characters of an executable program, a video, a graphic image, or even a data file. A signature can also be consistently used key words that are associated with a threat, such as an email from a certain sender, the subject of the email, or the name of an email attachment.

The strength of *signature-based detection* is that it is strong against known threats. However, its major weakness is that if a new threat launches, signature-based detection isn't likely to detect it, because it doesn't know of it (at least the first time). A simple change in any of the signatures associated with a threat may allow the threat to elude the detection system. For example, if the file attached to a previously processed email is `openmefirst.doc`, changing the filename to anything else, such as `openmef1rst.doc`, may avoid detection.

ANOMALY-BASED DETECTION

Anomaly-based detection systems attempt to detect unusual changes in the usage or consumption of network resources by users, nodes, connectivity devices, or server-based applications. This type of detection system must build a profile for each of the connected devices on a network. This profile, developed during a "training period," is the basis for "normal" behavior of the network and its nodes. When the detection system detects any deviation from normal activity levels, it notifies the applicable administrators.

One advantage that anomaly-based detection has over signature-based detection is that it can detect new threats and attacks by detecting the change they cause in network operations and activity levels. However, if malware or other malicious software is on the network or system during the creation of the profiles, the detection system could end up virtually useless. An anomaly-based detection system should be part of a network from its beginning to be truly effective.

Another related intrusion detection method is *stateful protocol analysis*. This detection method works much like anomaly-based detection, except that it compares the activity it sees with established profiles provided by device and software vendors.

IDPS IMPLEMENTATION

Although IDPS may be a single system in discussion, many networks implement prevention and detection separately. A common intrusion prevention tool is a network firewall. A firewall attempts to limit access to a network. In doing so, a firewall may deflect an attack on its own network. However, even when they deny access to an attacker, most firewalls don't issue alert notifications regarding the intrusion attempt. Instead, they create a log entry noting the event.

On the other hand, an IDPS provides backup to a firewall (although also placed before the firewall in some cases) by filtering the traffic that the firewall allows to pass. When the IDPS detects potential for an attack or exploitation in this traffic, it sends alert notifications. Remember that detection means the attack may be underway, and prevention attempts to thwart the attack. The detection mode of the IDPS also monitors for close-in or insider attacks on the network.

In general, there are logical places in a network for the parts of the IDPS. Figure 15-3 illustrates the recommended points on a network for IDPS monitoring components.

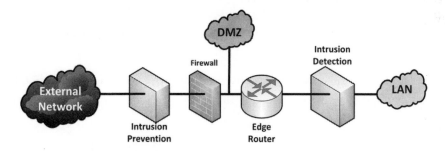

Figure 15-3 The logical placement of intrusion prevention and detection function in a network.
© 2015 Cengage Learning®.

As shown in Figure 15-3, intrusion prevention services can be before the firewall, in parallel to the firewall, or even behind the firewall. In fact, many firewalls include both traditional firewall services, but also IDPS functions. In the same manner, the network's demilitarized zone (DMZ), if it exists, can be after the firewall or before or after the gateway router. Diverting web or unknown traffic into a DMZ eliminates their possibility as attackers to the main network.

Most networks include intrusion detection services behind the router, but before the primary switch, if one is on the network. If a network is without a primary network switch, IDS should be on the network segments after the switch's ports.

Encryption

Encryption is a method of encoding transmitted messages or stored data so that only authorized individuals have access to its original values. Although encryption is a data security tool, it protects the data only from discovery. A hacker or attacker might still be able to access the data, but encrypted data decreases the likelihood of her being able to read or manipulate it.

The process of encryption converts plaintext data into ciphertext by applying an encryption algorithm and an encryption key. The encryption key instructs the encryption algorithm how to convert the plaintext data into ciphertext. The intended recipient of the data via email or other means, or anyone accessing the data with authorization, uses the encryption key to decode (decrypt) the ciphertext back into its original plaintext. Those who lack the encryption key should be unable to convert the ciphertext into plaintext. In most encryption processes, a separate algorithm generates a random key that is associated with the encryption method used to encode the data.

The two general types of encryption methods are symmetric key and public key. These general encryption methods include a variety of algorithms and ciphers applied to encode data. The following sections explain the encryption methods you should know for the Cloud+ exam.

Symmetric Key Encryption

Symmetric key encryption algorithms use the same encryption key for both ends of the encryption process—encoding and decoding—hence the name symmetric. In most applications of symmetric key encryption, the key is the same, but some transformation between the encrypting party and the decrypting party may also occur. The symmetric key encryption method does have its drawbacks. Both parties of the process must have a secret key, which means one has to share it with the other, giving rise to interception. If the key is not kept secret, it defeats the encryption process altogether.

In a symmetric key encryption method, the key used to encrypt the data is the public key, and the key used to decrypt the data is the private key. Table 15-1 provides a quick guide as to which key does what.

Table 15-1 Symmetric Key Use

Action	Symmetric Key Used
Send an encrypted message	Receiver's public key
Send an encrypted signature	Sender's private key
Decrypt an encrypted message	Receiver's private key
Decrypt an encrypted signature	Sender's public key

SYMMETRIC STREAM CIPHERS

A *cipher* is an algorithm that performs encryption or decryption. A stream cipher converts plaintext bits, one at a time, into ciphertext by combining them with a pseudorandom *keystream*. A key algorithm generates the keystream from a random seed number, which becomes the symmetric key for decoding the resulting ciphertext. The stream cipher converts the plaintext by combining the plaintext bits with the key using the Boolean exclusive-or (xor) operation.

The process described in the preceding section was a synchronous stream cipher. Under this type of encryption, a keystream combines with the bits of the plaintext characters to produce ciphertext. Another name for this process is binary additive stream cipher. Synchronous means that the transmitted or stored encoded data and the data being decoded must match exactly. If the data has any extra or missing bits, its synchronization is lost, and the data does not decode. Some methods can overcome this situation, but they are beyond the scope of what you need to know. *Rivest Cipher 4 (RC4)*, also known as ARC4 or ARCFOUR, and Salsa 20 are symmetric stream ciphers.

SYMMETRIC BLOCK CIPHERS

A block cipher works very differently from a stream cipher. A *block cipher* converts a fixed-length number of bits (a block) at a time, typically on large data blocks or bulk data. Block ciphers have been around since 1949 and are still in use in several current encryption methods, like the *Data Encryption Standard (DES)* and the *Advanced Encryption Standard (AES)*.

One limitation of using block cipher for encryption is that it can only encode blocks of data that are equal in length to the encryption key. The encryption process divides variable-length messages into cipher-length blocks, and padding bits are added to any short blocks. This encryption process is the *electronic codebook (ECB)* approach, in which encoding and decoding apply to individual blocks using the symmetric key. Many block ciphers use an iterative approach, meaning encryption occurs in multiple rounds, and a substitution-permutation approach, like AES.

Public Key Encryption

Also called asymmetric encryption, *public key infrastructure (PKI)* encryption requires two distinct encryption keys (hence asymmetric). One of the keys is private (secret), and the other is public. Although these keys are different, the algorithm that creates them links them mathematically. The *public key* encrypts the original data or creates a digital signature. The *private key* (the secret one) then decrypts the data encrypted with the public key. Only the holder of the private key can decrypt the data.

Message authentication applies PKI encryption to create a *digital signature* that allows a recipient to verify the identity of the sender using the sender's public key. Before sending the message, the originator "signs" the message with a digital signature that is an encrypted hash of the message. If a regeneration of the encrypted hash, using the public key, matches that accompanying the message, the recipient has assurance of the message's validity.

PKI encryption algorithms are common in most of the more recently developed encryption methods, including Transport Layer Security (TLS), Pretty Good Privacy (PGP), the Digital Signature Standard (DSS), and Secure Shell (SSH).

Encryption Algorithms and Security Protocols

Numerous encryption and security algorithms and protocols are in use on networks. For the most part, each has its particular use or application. The following sections describe the various encryption algorithms and security protocols you may encounter on the Cloud+ exam.

INTERNET PROTOCOL SECURITY (IPSEC)

The *Internet Protocol Security (IPsec)* protocol, which is a member of the expanded TCP/IP protocol suite, provides security for IP network communication. Its security services include network peer authentication, data origination authentication, and data integrity and confidentiality. IPsec consists of a set of protocols that together provide security at the packet level of a network.

IPsec offers two security service modes: *Authentication Header (AH)* and *Encapsulating Security Payload (ESP)*. The AH mode provides for the authentication of the sender of a message and ESP, which also authenticates senders and supports the encryption of data in transit.

Authentication Header (AH)

Authentication Header (AH) is one of the security protocols under IPsec. Its name describes its primary function: to provide authentication of the contents of a packet or datagram by adding an authentication header that includes a value calculated using the contents of the packet. Depending on the IPsec communication mode in use (tunnel or transport) and the IP version (IPv4 or IPv6), the calculation of the authentication header includes all or only part of the packet contents.

The authentication value calculated by AH is somewhat like a checksum or a cyclic redundancy check (CRC) used with other protocols. However, the calculation of the authentication header value, which is actually the *Integrity Check Value (ICV)*, uses symmetric keys to generate a hash total. If the calculation performed by the data recipient matches the ICV in the AH, the recipient knows that the data arrived unmodified. Otherwise, the packet either is in error or modified in transit. Although AH provides authentication and some integrity, it doesn't ensure privacy, which the IPsec ESP protocols provide.

Encapsulating Security Payload (ESP)

The Encapsulating Security Payload (ESP) protocols of IPsec provide for the same protections afforded by the AH protocol plus data integrity and data confidentiality on two levels. ESP has its own authentication method, similar to AH, but it can also run in conjunction with AH. ESP operates in two modes: transport mode and tunnel mode. The difference between these two modes is the amount of a packet encrypted prior to transmission. Transport mode encrypts only the payload of the packet. Tunnel mode encrypts the entire packet.

An ESP packet uses essentially the same fields in a message format as AH, but because ESP encrypts its data, it must package the packet in a special way. An ESP packet has three parts relating to IPsec security:

> **ESP Header**: This portion of the ESP packet contains two fields: the *Security Parameter Index (SPI)* and the packet sequence number. The SPI is a value that combines with the destination IP address to indicate the *security association (SA)* of the intended recipient. The SA is a set of values that enables the sharing of information between two points.

The sequence number is an integer value that indicates, for fragmented messages, the position of a packet in the fragmented sequence. The ESP header comes before the encrypted data.

> ➤ **ESP Trailer:** This portion of the ESP packet contains two and possibly three entries: any padding required to fill out the encrypted data to the correct length, a Pad Length field, and the Next Header field. As discussed earlier in the chapter (see "Symmetric Block Ciphers"), encrypted data may require padding bits to fill it out to the encryption method's block size. ESP adds any padding required to the end of the encrypted data, and the Pad Length field receives the length of the padding added. The Next Header field contains the IP protocol number of the next header in the series.

> ➤ **ESP Authentication Data:** Like the AH header, this field contains the ICV.

Transport and Tunnel Modes

IPsec operates in two modes: host-to-host transport mode and network-to-network tunnel mode. In *transport mode*, only the data payload of a packet is encrypted or authenticated. Because the IP header remains in plaintext, transport mode packets are open to routing. If AH adds an authentication header, it must not include the source and destination IP addresses because it distorts the ICV and any possible routing in transit or port assignments at its destination.

Tunnel mode encrypts all of a packet, including its payload and headers, and it may add authentication to the packet as well. The encrypted packet then becomes the payload of a new IP packet with a new IP header. Tunnel mode supports virtual private networks (VPNs) on every level, including network-to-network (routers), host-to-network (remote user connections), and host-to-host (instant messaging or chat).

SECURE SOCKETS LAYER/TRANSPORT LEVEL SECURITY

The *Secure Sockets Layer (SSL)* has been a popular protocol for securing (encrypting) message transmissions on networks, including the Internet. Recently replaced by the *Transport Layer Security (TLS)* protocol, SSL is still in use in some installations. SSL is included with virtually all the most popular web browsers.

SSL operates between a web browser and a transport layer protocol, typically *Transmission Control Protocol (TCP)*. Its name derives from its use of sockets (IP address and port number) to pass data between clients and servers. SSL employs both PKI and symmetric key encryption, including the use of digital certificates.

TLS is an enhanced version of SSL, based on Netscape's SSL 3.0, which provides encrypted privacy of data between clients and servers on the Internet. TLS guarantees that no third party can access or tamper with encode messages. TLS has two components: the *TLS Record Protocol* and the *TLS Handshake Protocol*. The TLS Record Protocol provides security on communication links, running on top of a transport protocol like TCP; using an encryption method, such as DES; or omitting encryption, if desired. The TLS Handshake Protocol provides the capability for a client and a server to authenticate each other and agree on an encryption method and its associated keys prior to the transmission of data. TLS runs independently of any application layer protocols. Higher-level protocols (session, presentation, and application layers) can incorporate TLS transparently for secure transmissions.

ENCRYPTION CIPHERS

As has been discussed throughout this chapter, ciphers are available for encrypting data depending on the level of security, privacy, and authentication needed. This section discusses the more commonly used ciphers and their use.

DES/3DES/AES

At one time, DES was the data encryption standard—at least back in the 1970s and 1980s. However, as technology advanced and hackers grew more tenacious, its short 56-bit key length made it susceptible to attacks. It also implemented 64-bit symmetrical block encryption, which became impractical for encrypting several megabits or gigabits of data.

One of DES's successors is *Triple DES (3DES)*. In effect, 3DES applies the DES algorithm three times to encrypt encrypted data and make it secure. However, this process proved to be too slow for software implementation, especially since its design is for hardware implementation, and it is not as widely used as another DES successor, AES.

AES is the current standard for symmetric encryption in U.S. government agencies. It uses several key lengths, ranging from 128 bits to 256 bits, the latter of which provides strong encryption. AES converts data into 128-bit blocks, doubling the size of its DES predecessor.

RSA and DSA

Commonly thought to be closely similar or related in some way, the *Rivest-Shamir-Adleman (RSA)* encryption and authentication system is much different from the *digital signature algorithm (DSA)*.

RSA uses an encryption algorithm that was developed by Ron Rivest, Adi Shamir, and Leonard Adleman in 1977. Despite its age, RSA is still the most frequently used algorithm in web browsers, as well as in many applications, including Intuit's Quicken Pro. RSA is a private entity, RSA Security, which licenses its use to companies wanting to include it in their products. Although its algorithm is proprietary, in general it multiples two large prime numbers and then puts the product through some additional steps that yield a symmetrical private key and its associated public key.

The DSA algorithm converts two large numbers into a value that can confirm the authenticity of the individual sending a message (the signatory), which allows an inference of the integrity of the message itself. DSA both generates digital signatures and verifies them. Signatures are associated with a private key, and a public key verifies the signature. DSA's use was originally for digital signatures, but it can also encrypt data blocks.

These encryption methods provide equally strong encryption. However, their differences lie in their respective strengths and weaknesses. DSA is more efficient at generating keys and signatures and decrypting in general. On the other hand, RSA is more efficient at encryption in general and verification of a digital signature.

RC4 and RC5

Both RC4 and *Rivest Cipher 5 (RC5)* are ciphers developed by Ron Rivest and RSA Data Securities, but they aren't iterations of each other. Although both are variable-key-size encryption algorithms, RC4 is a symmetric stream cipher, and RC5 is a block cipher.

RC4 generates a pseudorandom keystream in bit form and encrypts data using a xor operation, as described earlier. (See "Symmetric Stream Ciphers.") RC5 is a symmetric block cipher that uses variable-length blocks and key sizes. Data blocks can be 32, 64, or 128 bits in length, and key length can vary from 0 to 2,040 bits in length. The standard suggested parameters are a block length of 64 bits and a key length of 128 bits. RC5 is also an iterative algorithm that uses a variable number of passes when converting plaintext to ciphertext, although a user can set the number of passes through a parameter, which can range from 0 to 255, with the standard suggested parameter of 12 passes.

Host Hardening

Hardening, in the context of computer or network security, is the process of increasing the security level of a host or server while lowering its vulnerability to attack. The general vulnerability of a computer is its *attack surface*, and the goal of hardening the computer is to reduce this exposure. Attackers target computers, and especially servers, because they provide easily defeated gateways to valuable data and services.

The vulnerabilities of computers on a network include, among others:

> Software bugs that provide unauthorized access to the computer or its network

> DoS attacks, launched from outside or inside from a host computer, that render a server unavailable to network users

> Exposure of confidential information stored on a server or on the network through an exploited weakness on a network host

> Access to network resources gained through an exploited vulnerability

In its "Guide to General Server Security," National Institute for Standards and Technology (NIST) lists recommendations for hardening servers and hosts on a network. These include the following:

> Configuring the operating system on a computer to enhance its security

> Configuring, installing, and securing application software running on the computer or server

> Applying security and operations patches and upgrades to all hardware and software as required

> Performing security testing, log file auditing, and capturing backups of key data and system files

> Disabling or removing all unnecessary services, ports, applications, and protocols

> Enabling system user authentication at a heightened level

> Disabling or removing unused or default user accounts

> Implementing robust password policy requiring regular password changes

> Installing antivirus and malware detection software

> Installing host and server-based software firewalls

Chapter Summary

> Data must be secure to prevent corruption or theft and provide accessibility to users with appropriate credentials and authorization. Data must be available and current even after system failure or catastrophic events.

> The goal of securing data must include the protection of data at rest and data in motion.

> The best protection for data at rest is redundancy and encryption.

> Security controls are in three primary categories: preventive controls, detective controls, and corrective controls.

> The primary security control types are physical controls, procedural controls, technical controls, and legal/compliance/regulatory controls.

> The security controls for all stored data are criticality, sensitivity, and data handling.

> Obfuscation refers to hiding data to protect it. The common methods used are encryption, masking, numeric variance, shuffling, and substitution.

> Access control limits access to a network and its resources to only authorized users. The three types of access control are MAC, DAC, and RBAC.

> Attacks on a system are active or passive. An active attack attempts to gain access to system resources to alter their contents or change how they operate. A passive attack attempts to gain access to resources to gain information by observing data or to steal the data for outside use.

> Common types of attacks are close-in attacks, phishing attacks, spoof attacks, DoS and DDoS attacks, PoD and ping flood attacks, exploit attacks, and overflow attacks.

> A weapon against attacks is IDPS. An intrusion is action on the part of an unauthorized user that violates the security policies of an organization. The two types of IDPS systems are network based and host based. IDPS uses two approaches: signature-based detection and anomaly-based detection.

> Encryption encodes transmitted messages or stored data so only authorized individuals have access to its original values. Encryption converts plaintext data into ciphertext by applying an encryption algorithm and an encryption key. The two types of encryption are symmetric key and PKI. Symmetric key encryption uses the same key for both ends of the encryption process. PKI encryption requires two distinct encryption keys.

> A stream cipher converts plaintext bits into ciphertext by combining them with a pseudo-random keystream. A block cipher converts a fixed-length block of bits.

> IPsec provides security for IP network communication using AH and ESP protocols. IPsec operates in two modes: host-to-host transport mode and network-to-network tunnel mode.

> SSL and TLS provide encrypted privacy of data between clients and servers on the Internet.

➤ 3DES applies the DES algorithm three times to encrypt data. AES is the standard for symmetric encryption. RSA is the most frequently used encryption algorithm in web browsers. DSA algorithm confirms the authenticity of a message's signatory.

➤ RC4 is a symmetric stream cipher, and RC5 is a block cipher.

➤ Hardening is the process of increasing the security level of a host or server.

Key Terms

Access control entry (ACE)

Active attack

Advanced Encryption Standard (AES)

Anomaly-based detection

Attack surface

Authentication Header (AH)

Block cipher

Bounds checking

Buffer

Buffer overflow attack

Cipher

Close-in attack

Data at rest

Data Encryption Standard (DES)

Data in motion

Data masking

Denial-of-service (DoS) attack

Digital signature

Digital Signature Algorithm (DSA)

Discretionary access control (DAC)

Distributed DoS (DDoS) attack

Electronic codebook (ECB)

Encapsulating Security Payload (ESP)

Encryption

Exploit attack

Hardening

Heap

Heap overflow attack

Host header buffer overflow attack

Integrity Check Value (ICV)

Internet Protocol Security (IPsec)

Intrusion

Intrusion detection and prevention system (IDPS)

Keystream

Mandatory access control (MAC)

Message authentication

Network-based IDPS

Network behavior analysis (NBA)

Obfuscation

Passive attack

Phishing attack

Ping flood attack

Ping of death (PoD) attack

Private key

Public key

Public key infrastructure (PKI) encryption

Pushdown stack

Rivest Cipher 4 (RC4)

Rivest Cipher 5 (RC5)

Rivest-Shamir-Adleman (RSA)

Role-based access control (RBAC)

Secure Sockets Layer (SSL)

Security association (SA)

Security controls

Security Parameter Index (SPI)

Signature-based detection

Social engineering

Spoof attack

Stack

Stack overflow attack

Stateful protocol analysis

Symmetric key encryption

TLS Handshake Protocol

TLS Record Protocol

Transmission Control Protocol (TCP)

Transport Layer Security (TLS)

Transport mode

Triple DES (3DES)

Tunnel mode

Review Questions

1. Securing data resources must include security for _____ and _____.

2. Which of the following is NOT a security control type?

   a. Corrective controls

   b. Detective controls

   c. Stabilizing controls

   d. Preventive controls

3. True or False? A good data program for data at rest includes redundancy and encryption.

4. The term for masking data to hide its values is _____.

5. Which of the following best describes an active attack on a system?

   a. An attempt to gain access to resources to observe data

   b. An attempt to gain access to resources to alter their contents

   c. An attempt to eavesdrop on network media

   d. An attempt to gain a password by observation

6. The access control type that uses a person's position or tasks is _____.

7. True or False? The security services of IPsec include network peer authentication, data origination authentication, and data integrity and confidentiality.

8. A network server is not responding to client requests from within the network. What type of attack may be in progress?

    a. Phishing attack

    b. Overflow attack

    c. DoS

    d. PKI

9. The message encryption and authentication method that uses a secret key is _____.

10. True or False? 3DES is three times faster than DES.

11. The process of reducing the attack surface of a host or server is

    a. Securing

    b. Hardening

    c. Isolating

    d. Bounds checking

12. The security controls that should exist for all stored data are sensitivity, data handling, and _____.

13. True or False? The two types of IDPS approaches are signature based and role based.

14. What type of encryption method converts plaintext bits, one at a time, into ciphertext?

    a. Stream cipher

    b. Asymmetric cipher

    c. Symmetric cipher

    d. Block cipher

15. True or False? PKI encryption uses the same key for the encryption/decryption processes.

Answers to Review Questions

1. data at rest, data in motion
2. c
3. True
4. obfuscation
5. b
6. role-based
7. True
8. c
9. asymmetric or PKI
10. False
11. b
12. criticality
13. False
14. a
15. False

CHAPTER 16

System Management

After reading this chapter and completing the exercises, you will be able to:

- Describe network and IP planning and the associated documentation
- Discuss configuration standardization and its documentation
- Explain system life cycle management
- Explain change management and its related control and accountability activities
- List the actions of capacity management

Managing a computing environment of any size, type, or scope is a complicated affair. Systems and networks require constant monitoring, management, and usually, planning. In this chapter, you learn about some of the most important aspects of managing a computing environment. The topics discussed in this chapter apply equally, although in different degrees, to small information technology (IT) operations, enterprise IT operations, and cloud computing environments. You learn about planning and applying Internet Protocol (IP) addressing, standardizing a system configuration, performing change management, and managing capacity.

Network and IP Planning

Under the general topic of network and logical address (IP addresses) planning, the plans developed in this phase of the overall planning present a network plan from a software perspective. After developing hardware, business requirements, and operational plans, this phase of the planning deals with the functional elements of the proposed or migrated network.

Here are the specific network steps identified in planning:

1. **Identify the network domain(s)**: Identify the domain names you want to register or renew with a domain name registrar. You may want to investigate recently approved top-level domains (TLDs) and the myriad generic TLDs, such as .book, .estate, .community, and .holdings, as well as the more traditional TLDs like .com, .net, .org, and .info. Also, be aware of registered trademarks and trade names to avoid legal hassles.

2. **Obtain an IP network number (network IP address)**: Depending on the size, layout, and scope of the network, you should obtain from your direct-line Internet service provider (ISP) one or more network numbers. A *network number* represents, depending on the classful or classless addressing scheme of the ISP, the network ID portion of the publicly viewed IP address of a network gateway. For example, in the *IP version 4 (IPv4)* address 192.168.32.0/24 (in *Classless Inter-Domain Routing*, or *CIDR*, notation), the first 24 bits (3 octets) represent the network number 192.168.32.

3. **Assign a model IP address**: Create a conceptual layout of the servers, hosts, and devices to which you will assign IP addresses, along with their host names (node names or computer names). This helps you identify subnets and other administrative groupings needed on the network. It also helps you determine if the network requires switching or internal routing.

4. **Choose a name service**: Decide on a name service for the network. For most situations, *Network Information Service (NIS)*, NIS+, *Lightweight Directory Access Protocol (LDAP)*, and *Domain Name System (DNS)* are the choices.

5. **Set the physical design**: Convert the conceptual design into a physical layout that shows the placement, media requirements, addressing, and subnets or groupings (such as virtual local area networks [VLANs]) of the network.

After completing the steps in the preceding numbered list, decide on the monitoring or management system you want to use to manage, monitor, and maintain the network.

IP Addressing Scheme

The size and scope of the planned network directly affects the addressing scheme you choose to use on the network. The size of the network affects the addressing scheme you want to implement. It can influence the IP address class or the number of bits in the network ID, as well as the addressing assigned to subnets, VLANs, and virtual devices. Perhaps the network consists of only a dozen or so independent standalone computers and printers. Or maybe the network must support hundreds of nodes scattered about a single building, a campus, or even in several geographically disperse locations. These situations, along with any planned future growth, determine the capacity of the network ID(s) you request from an ISP.

In a network that implements more than one network ID or encompasses subnets, you should appoint a central authority to administer IP addresses. This central authority retains control over the assignment and use of network IDs and the IP addresses assigned to network devices, subnets, VLANs, and host computers. The central authority also assigns the pools of IP addresses configured for the Dynamic Host Configuration Protocol (DHCP) for the configuration of network devices and hosts.

IPv4 Addressing

An IPv4 addressing scheme can use either a classful or a classless addressing method. In the classful addressing method, the protocol standard preassigns the number of network IDs and hosts per network of the address classes. In contrast, in a classless method, you have more flexibility to determine the number of bits designated as the network ID and, as a result, the host ID.

Classful Addressing

IPv4 *classful IP addressing* was in use before networks grew to the point of needing routing. The use of subnetting, which applies a subnet mask to extract the network ID from an IPv4 address, allows internal network bridging and switching to be efficient, but not so much for routing.

Table 16-1 shows the nominal division of IPv4 addresses in a classful scheme. Each of the address classes shows the length of the network ID, the range of values for the first octet of the network ID, and the number of bits remaining for the host (node) address. Table 16-2 shows the IP address range, the number of networks, and the hosts per network for each IP address class.

Table 16-1 IPv4 Address Classes

Class	Bits/Network ID	1st Octet Range	Bits/Host ID
A	8	0–127	24
B	16	128–191	16
C	24	192–223	8

Table 16-2 IPv4 Address Class Addressing

Class	Network ID Range	Number of Networks	Hosts per Network
A	1.0.0.0–126.0.0.0	126	16,777,214
B	128.0.0.0 – 191.255.0.0	16,384	65,534
C	192.0.0.0 – 223.255.255.0	2,097,152	254

© 2015 Cengage Learning®.

Classless Addressing

Classless IP addressing exists primarily to support routing and less so to facilitate internal network bridging or switching. The CIDR notation, which states the number of bits in the network ID of an IP address and, in turn, determines the network mask applied to extract the network ID, allows routers to group IPv4 addresses into CIDR blocks that a router can store as a single routing table entry. The IP addresses in CIDR have the same binary value in the number of bits indicated by the CIDR suffix. For example, an IPv4 address of 192.168.100.223/16 creates a CIDR block of IPv4 addresses with the value 192.168 in their first 16 bits or first two octets. Each CIDR block identifies a single network, leaving the host ID portion of the address for internal switching or bridging. Table 16-3 lists the CIDR blocks defined by the Internet Assigned Numbers Authority (IANA).

Table 16-3 IANA CIDR Blocks

CIDR Block	Number of Hosts	Network Mask
xxx.xxx.xxx.xxx/32	1	255.255.255.255
xxx.xxx.xxx.xxx/31	2	255.255.255.254
xxx.xxx.xxx.xxx/30	4	255.255.255.252
xxx.xxx.xxx.xxx/29	8	255.255.255.248
xxx.xxx.xxx.xxx/28	16	255.255.255.240
xxx.xxx.xxx.xxx/27	32	255.255.255.224
xxx.xxx.xxx.xxx/26	64	255.255.255.192
xxx.xxx.xxx.xxx/25	128	255.255.255.128
xxx.xxx.xxx.xxx/24	256	255.255.255.0
xxx.xxx.xxx.xxx/23	512	255.255.254.0
xxx.xxx.xxx.xxx/22	1,024	255.255.252.0
xxx.xxx.xxx.xxx/21	2,048	255.255.248.0
xxx.xxx.xxx.xxx/20	4,096	255.255.240.0
xxx.xxx.xxx.xxx/19	8,192	255.255.224.0

xxx.xxx.xxx.xxx/18	16,384	255.255.192.0
xxx.xxx.xxx.xxx/17	32,768	255.255.128.0
xxx.xxx.xxx.xxx/16	65,536	255.255.0.0
xxx.xxx.xxx.xxx/15	131,072	255.254.0.0
xxx.xxx.xxx.xxx/14	262,144	255.252.0.0
xxx.xxx.xxx.xxx/13	524,288	255.248.0.0
xxx.xxx.xxx.xxx/12	1,048,576	255.240.0.0
xxx.xxx.xxx.xxx/11	2,097,152	255.224.0.0
xxx.xxx.xxx.xxx/10	4,194,304	255.192.0.0
xxx.xxx.xxx.xxx/9	8,388,608	255.128.0.0
xxx.xxx.xxx.xxx/8	16,777,216	255.0.0.0
xxx.xxx.xxx.xxx/7	33,554,432	254.0.0.0
xxx.xxx.xxx.xxx/6	67,108,864	252.0.0.0
xxx.xxx.xxx.xxx/5	134,217,728	248.0.0.0
xxx.xxx.xxx.xxx/4	268,435,456	240.0.0.0
xxx.xxx.xxx.xxx/3	536,870,912	224.0.0.0
xxx.xxx.xxx.xxx/2	1,073,741,824	192.0.0.0
xxx.xxx.xxx.xxx/1	2,147,483,648	128.0.0.0
xxx.xxx.xxx.xxx/0	4,294,967,296	0.0.0.0

What the information in Table 16-3 shows is that the more numbers used to designate the network ID in the CIDR block, the fewer the number of host IDs that can be included in the CIDR block. For example, the xxx.xxx.xxx.xxx/22 entry in Table 16-3 indicates that 22 bits of the 32-bit IPv4 address designate the network ID of a CIDR block. As many as 1,024 host ID or addresses can belong to the block. Understand that although IANA defines them, the use of certain CIDR blocks doesn't make good common sense. The /32 and the /0 indicate that there is only one host in a network, the host is the network (/32), and there are 4,294,967,296 hosts that are on par without a network ID (0/0).

IPv6 Addressing

The primary reason for the development of *IP version 6 (IPv6)* was the expectation that the world was fast approaching the complete absorption of IPv4 addresses, which could limit the growth and expansion of the Internet. However, in developing IPv6, its designers also wanted to include methods for address interpretation, assignment, and usage that are more compatible with the evolving direction of internetworking, meaning switching, routing, and cloud services.

IP Version 5

IPv6 is the replacement of IPv4. There was no IP version 5 (IPv5), at least not in the logical addressing scheme of things. The Internet Engineering Task Force (IETF), the folks who decide these things, intentionally skipped over IPv5 as an Internet addressing scheme to avoid confusion with the Internet Stream Protocol version 2, an experimental protocol, called IPv5. IPv5 would have separated certain IP packets for parallel use alongside IPv4. When the IETF abandoned this protocol, it decided that to avoid confusion between a new addressing scheme and what had been IPv5, it would use IPv6 for the new IP addressing scheme.

Although quite different in appearance and substantive structure, IPv6 essentially uses the same addressing concepts of IPv4. Some of the characteristics of IPv4 in use in IPv6 are:

> **Address assignment**: IP addresses are assigned to network interfaces (network adapters, network interface controllers [NICs], or network device interfaces). Typically, a network node (such as a PC with a network adapter attached) has one address assigned, but a router or switch may have several addresses associated with it.

> **Address interpretation**: IPv6 addresses are classless and identify both a network portion (called an *address prefix*) and a host portion in the address. A prefix length number (very much like a CIDR notation) replaces the subnet or network mask of IPv4 and indicates the length of the network portion of the address. The prefix length can be any value between 1 and 128.

> **Logical addressing**: IPv6 addresses operate on the Network layer (Layer 3) of *Transmission Control Protocol/Internet Protocol (TCP/IP)* networks. Network layer addressing is logical addressing, as opposed to Layer 2 addressing or *Media Access Control (MAC)* addresses, which are physical addresses.

> **Network ID**: Identifying the network name/ID in an IP address is a key function of IPv6.

> **Private addresses**: IPv6 does set aside addresses for use as internal addresses, although their use is somewhat different.

> **Routing**: The address structure supports network interface identification and routing.

IPv6 Address Structure

IPv6 addresses are 128 bits in length compared to the 32-bit length of an IPv4 address. This extended length grows the possible addresses from just over four billion IPv4 addresses to more than 340 undecillion (2^{128}, or a number with 11 commas in it). Given that the numbers are so unusual, it's hard to build an understandable case for how large the address space of IPv6 really is. IPv6 has more than 79 septillion times more addresses than IPv4. Compare this to the estimate that there are about 7 quintillion grains of sand on the earth, which means that there are

45 quadrillion times more IPv6 addresses potentially available than there are grains of sand on the earth, or more than 47 septillion IP addresses for every person on earth. In summary, there are, at least for now, plenty of IPv6 addresses.

> **Note**
>
> The actual maximum number of IPv6 addresses is 340 undecillion, 282 decillion, 366 nonillion, 920 octillion, 938 septillion, 463 sextillion, 463 quintillion, 374 quadrillion, 607 trillion, 431 billion, 768 million, 211 thousand, and 456.

IPv6 addresses use *hexadecimal* (Base 16) numbers to represent a network location, which makes the number shorter and easier to convert to decimal. To illustrate the difference between using binary or decimal for an IPv6 address and using hexadecimal (hex), look at Figure 16-1. If you express an IPv6 address in the *dotted decimal notation* of IPv4, it appears as the dotted decimal example at the top of the figure. The next line down, the *full hexadecimal notation*, shows the dotted decimal address expressed in a hexadecimal notation. Notice that the elements of the hexadecimal version combine two of the 8-bit values of the decimal version. For example, the 192.68 octets of the decimal version convert to C044 in the hexadecimal version. The hex C0 represents the decimal 192, the hex 44 represents the decimal 68, and so on, through the rest of the decimal address. The decimal octets combine into a pair of hex values in the hexadecimal conversion. A colon (:) separates each of the paired elements.

Dotted Decimal Notation	192.68.91.45.1.220.0.0.0.0.254.94.193.45.202.28
Full Hexadecimal Notation	C044:5B2D:01DC:0000:0000:FE5E:C12D:CA1C
Leading Zero Suppression	C044:5B2D:1DC:0:0:FE5E:C12D:CA1C
Full Zero Suppression	C044:5B2D:1DC::FE5E:C12D:CA1C
Mixed Mode Notation	C044:5B2D:1DC::FE5E:193.45.202.28

Figure 16-1 The various IPv6 address notations.
© 2015 Cengage Learning®.

In an effort to shorten IPv6 addresses, notation options that suppress zeroes are available: *leading zero suppression* or *full zero suppression*. Leading zero suppression, as shown in Figure 16-1, removes any zeroes found in the first digit of any address element, as shown in the leading zero suppression example, in which the 01DC element is now just 1DC and all zero elements are only a single zero. Full zero suppression adds to the leading zero suppression method by removing the full zero elements and replacing them with a double colon symbol (::).

In the *mixed mode notation* method, the last two elements convert to their decimal equivalents using the dotted decimal notation. This is useful primarily within a local network in which the network prefix is constant or common to a majority of the network traffic.

IPv6 Prefix

IPv6 addresses contain both a network ID and a host ID. The network ID portion of the address is its prefix or network prefix. To extract the prefix from the IPv6 address (remember there is no subnet or network mask in use), the length of the prefix (in bits) is appended to the end of the address in the same manner that IPv4 did using a slash (/) and the integer number of bits in the prefix.

For example, if the prefix in an IPv6 address is 44 bits in length, the notation of the address is C044:5B2D:1DC::FE5E:C12D:CA1C/44. This expresses that the first 44 bits of this address are the prefix or the network ID. This also means that the last 84 bits of the address represent the host ID, also called the *interface*.

IPv6 Address Space Allocation

Although the initial idea with IPv6 was to avoid anything that resembled classful allocation of IP addresses, in reality the first 3 to 10 bits of an IPv6 address have become indicators of various address categories, some of which have more addresses available than others. So far, only a few address categories exist, but the capability to add more in the future exists. The values in the first 3 to 10 bits of an address indicate the address allocation category in which the address belongs. Table 16-4 lists the IPv6 address allocations currently assigned.

Table 16-4   IPv6 Address Space Allocations

Lead Bits	Allocation Category
0000 0000	Unspecified and loopback addresses
0000 0001	Network Service Access Point (NSAP) address allocation
001	Global unicast addresses
1111 1110 10	Link-local unicast addresses
1111 1110 11	Site-local unicast addresses
1111 1111	Multicast addresses

© 2015 Cengage Learning®.

In Table 16-4, a few terms or names may be unfamiliar to you. An *unspecified address* (typically 0:0:0:0:0:0:0:0 or just ::) indicates a message sent from a host to itself in a form of loopback. The actual *loopback address* is ::1 on an IPv6 host. A *Network Service Access Point (NSAP)* is a logical pointer that links the Network layer functions of a network to its Transport layer functions. A *unicast address* is the workhorse of any network because it is the address of a single network node. A *link-local unicast address* indicates a packet intended only for the local network. Routers do not forward link-local addresses. A *site-local unicast address* doesn't include a prefix because any packet with this type of address stays within a local organization or site. Routers forward site-local addresses within a local network but do not forward them externally.

IPv6 EUI-64 Format

IPv6 allows for the use of a network device's MAC address as its interface (host) ID. Network-capable devices have a 48-bit ID code embedded in their circuitry during manufacturing. It really doesn't make sense to make up another name to identify each device on a network. As is the case in TCP/IP networks using IPv4 addressing, a device's MAC address can be associated with its IPv6 address, and the combination of the MAC address and the network ID (prefix) allows the capability to discern either the MAC address or the IP address.

A MAC address consists of two blocks of 24 bits each. The first block contains the *organizationally unique identifier (OUI)*, which is an assigned value that uniquely identifies a device manufacturer. The second block contains a serial number for the specific device. The IPv6 standard includes the definition of a 64-bit *extended unique identifier (EUI-64)*. The EUI-64 code contains the 24-bit OUI and expands the 24-bit serial number to 40 bits, which gives manufacturers more than 60,000 times the number of uniquely identified devices available in the MAC address structure within each OUI.

For example, a network device, perhaps a NIC, has a MAC address of 70-F3-95-08-2F-22. The OUI is 70-F3-95, and the device ID is 08-2F-22. To convert the MAC address into the IPv6 EUI-64 format, follow these steps:

1. Extract the OUI, or the leftmost 24 bits of the MAC address, and move it into the leftmost 24 bits of the EUI-64 format.

2. Extract the device ID, or the rightmost 24 bits of the MAC address, and move it into the rightmost 24 bits of the EUI-64 format.

3. This leaves 16 bits in the center of the 64-bit EUI-64 address, which receives the hex value "FFFE."

4. Place a one (1) in the seventh bit from the left to indicate a local address (as opposed to a value of 0, indicating a universal address).

The EUI-64 address is complete. Figure 16-2 illustrates the process.

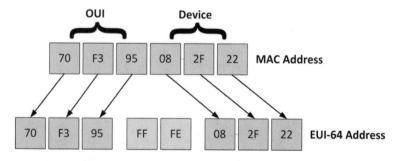

Figure 16-2 The conversion of a MAC address into an EUI-64 address.
© 2015 Cengage Learning®.

IPv4/IPv6 Conversion

The conversion of an IPv4 network to an IPv6 network doesn't have to occur all at once. In fact, converting the addressing on a large network completely could take quite a while. It's been estimated that the conversion of the Internet overall will take several years to complete.

IPv6 is backward compatible with IPv4 for the most part, but some special procedures can make a partial conversion work better. For instance, if you install two new work centers with IPv6 addressing that connect to the main data center by way of IPv4 communications, tunneling and the use of mixed mode IPv6 addressing can provide the compatibility required. Mixed mode IPv6 addresses have IPv4 addresses embedded in them.

Some network devices support both IPv4 and IPv6 addressing but require a special address format known as an *IPv4-compatible IPv6 address*. Figure 16-3 illustrates the relationship between an IPv4 address and an IPv4-compatible IPv6 address. The leading 96 bits of the address contain all zeroes, and the rightmost 32 bits contain the 32-bit IPv4 address. As shown, the resulting IPv6 address has a prefix of :: that indicates leading zero suppression.

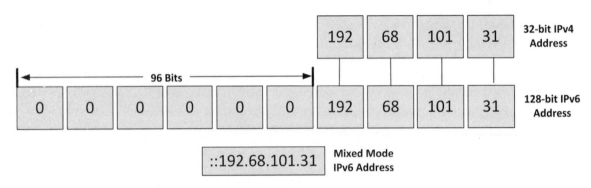

Figure 16-3 An IPv4 address converted into an IPv4-compatible IPv6 address.
© 2015 Cengage Learning®.

Another set of IPv6 addresses, called *IPv4-mapped addresses*, are set aside for IPv4-compatible IPv6 switches and routers. Like the address conversion shown in Figure 16-3, the rightmost 32-bits receive the IPv4 address, but only the first 80 bits contain zeroes. The middle 16 bits receive all ones, resulting in an IPv6 address of ::FFFF:192.68.101.31.

Embedding IPv4 addresses in IPv6 addresses provides a transition bridge between IPv4 and IPv6. IPv4-compatible IPv6 addresses (96 zero bit leader) work with devices that support both IP versions. IPv4-mapped IPv6 addresses are for use with IPv4 devices, not IPv6-compatible, but in an IPv6 network.

IPv6 Multicast and Anycast Addressing

Although unicast addressing is still as dominant on IPv6 networks as it is on IPv4 networks, IPv6 redefines block or bulk message addressing. For one thing, broadcast segments are gone, which should be good news to network administrators in general. In addition, IPv6 redefines *multicast addressing* and adds a new type of bulk messaging, called *anycast*.

IPv6 Multicast Addressing Under the IPv6 standard, multicast addressing is an allocation of the IPv6 address space, which is somewhat similar to IPv4 setting aside Class D addressing for multicast. Under IPv6, all addresses that have the hex value FF in the first 8 bits (all ones) of an address are multicast addresses. This leaves 120 bits (2^{120}) for the addresses of the hosts that are the multicast's recipients. If you want nodes to participate in a multicast, you must put them in the multicast group.

There are two levels of multicast addresses: *globally scoped* and *locally scoped*. A globally scoped multicast address must be unique universally, meaning unique across the entire Internet. A locally scoped multicast address only needs to be unique within its local organization (network). Although global and local are the extremes, there are scope levels in between, such as node, link local, site local, and organizationally scoped.

Multicast messages destined for a specific scope level have special addressing rules. There are two primary IPv6 multicast addresses: fixed scope and variable scope. *Fixed-scope multicast addresses*, also known as *well-known multicast addresses*, are permanently set for the IPv6 address space. Table 16-5 lists the fixed-scope multicast addresses and the set scope limit for each.

Table 16-5 IPv6 Multicast Fixed-Scope Addresses

Address	Scope
FF01::1	All nodes (node local)
FF01::2	All routers (node local)
FF02::1	All nodes (link local)
FF02::2	All routers (link local)
FF02::6	Designated Open Shortest Path First (OSPF)/Interior Gateway Protocol (IGP) routers
FF02::9	All Routing Information Protocol (RIP) routers
FF02::A	All Enhanced Interior Gateway Routing Protocol (EIGRP) routers
FF02::F	All Universal Plug and Play (UPnP) devices
FF05::2	All routers (site local)

© 2015 Cengage Learning®.

In Table 16-5, the value in the second byte indicates the scope of the multicast. As shown, 01 represents node local, 02 represents link local, and 05 represents site local. These same scope values also apply to variable-scope multicast addresses. *Variable-scope multicast addresses* have the same basic format as the fixed-scope multicast, with the exception that variable scope multicast addresses can be registered to and reserved for a specific organization, group, and even a protocol or service. For example, IPv6 reserves the multicast address FF05:0:0:0:0:0:0:FB for messages to *multicast DNS version 6 (mDNSv6)* within a site-local scope.

IPv6 Anycast Addressing *Anycast addressing* is new and unique to IPv6 and is officially a host anycasting service. In effect, anycast is a combination of unicast and multicast. Instead of sending a message directly to a single destination (unicast) or sending a message to a group of recipients (multicast), anycast sends a message to any one member of an addressed group. The one member that receives the message is normally the "closest" member of a group, such as the closest router in a group of routers.

The format for an anycast message address is the same as that used for unicast addressing. Associating more than one interface (host or node) to a single unicast address, such as a server cluster, sets up an anycast group. The purpose behind anycasting is to allow a requestor to send a request to an address and receive the requested service from any servicer at that address. If routing is necessary, an anycast packet goes to the nearest router in a group of routers.

IPv6 Autoconfiguration

IPv6 Stateless Address Autoconfiguration allows some devices to configure their IP configuration settings automatically without the need for a server, such as a DHCP server on an IPv4 network. In addition, this process allows the network to reconfigure all or some of the IPv6 addresses on a network. However, there is a *DHCP version 6 (DHCPv6)* available for use. Using DHCPv6 is a *stateful* process, but the IPv6 autoconfiguration process is stateless because a host configures itself without checking its state or the network's.

The *stateless* autoconfiguration in IPv6 allows a host to generate its interface identifier (EUI-64) address and to create a link-local temporary address, which it can use until it completes a full discovery of the network and its relationship using the *Neighbor Discovery Protocol (NDP)*. At that time, the host creates its permanent network address using the information learned. If the host has more than one network interfaced (multihomed), it configures each interface separately. The specific steps used in the autoconfiguration are as follows:

1. **Generate an EUI-64 link-local address**: A link-local address has a specific value in its first 10 bits, 1111111010. The next 54 bits are zeroes followed by the 64-bit EUI interface identifier derived from the interface's MAC address. After generating this address, the host or node tests this address on the network to ensure that the address isn't somehow already in use, which should almost never happen unless an administrator configured another node manually.

2. **Assign an address**: If the address is unique, the host assigns the link-local interface identifier to the interface. Remember that link-local addresses are not routable.

3. **Identify the network**: Using the IPv6 NDP, the host or node listens for router advertisement messages or sends router solicitation messages in an attempt to identify the closest router, if any. If the node discovers a router, the router directs the node on its autoconfiguration process. The information from the router may provide information to the node used to form its global network address, or it may direct the node to a DHCPv6 server for a stateful configuration.

4. **Configure a global address**: If stateless autoconfiguration is in use, the host uses the network prefix provided by a router and its interface identifier to configure a globally unique IPv6 address.

IPv4 and IPv6 Summary

Table 16-6 shows a side-by-side comparison of the features of IPv4 and IPv6. This isn't to promote one over the other, but rather to give you the features of each comparatively.

Table 16-6 IPv4 and IPv6 Comparison		
Feature/Function	IPv4	IPv6
Address length	32 bits	128 bits
IPsec	Optional	Mandatory
Fragmentation	Routers and hosts	Hosts only
IP-to-MAC resolution	Multicast NDP	Address Resolution Protocol (ARP)
Broadcast messages	Link-level scope	Broadcast addressing
Host configuration	Autoconfiguration	DHCP or manual
Packet size	1280 bytes with no fragmentation	576 bytes with possible fragmentation

© 2015 Cengage Learning®.

Configuration Management and Control

Configuration management ensures that a system maintains its integrity and value to the organization before, during, and after applying changes to it. The management and control of a system involves the issuance and maintenance of the policies, procedures, methods, and tools used to manage, evaluate, and track the existing configuration and any proposed or approved and documented modifications to the system configuration. Configuration management covers all changes to a system, including hardware, software, administrative systems, and changes in administrative personnel. In other words, configuration management is important in all phases of a system's life cycle. In the context of configuration management, a system includes all the resources, assets, and personnel in an organizational computing function.

System Life Cycle Management

A key consideration of configuration management is the life cycle of an entire computing environment, a single software system, specialized hardware devices, or support services. The focus of a *system life cycle management* program should be on the implementation and use of a system because, not only do these life cycle phases incur the most cost, they are also the determinants of the system's utility and how long the system's life will be.

The life cycle of a system, not to be confused with the system development life cycle (SDLC), measures the length of a system's useful life. Systems age in phases. In the introductory phase, the planning for the system determines its need. The second phase is implementation, in which the installation of the system and user training occurs. The third phase, production, is perhaps the longest because it represents the time the system is in production and available for service. The final phase is when the system becomes unneeded or obsolete and is either removed from service or replaced.

Configuration Standardization

Configuration standardization is the part of configuration management that controls the consistency of the configuration of a system in terms of its performance, the compatibility of its components, any planned modifications, and a tracking of modifications made in the past. Configuration standardization involves four action areas, which can sometimes overlap. These action areas are:

> ➤ **Management:** The actions in this area create and maintain formal documentation that organizes all the information, assignments, training, meetings, management procedures, baselining processes, configuration, configuration control procedures, local naming conventions, and any outsourced services or equipment incorporated into the system.

> ➤ **Baselines:** The actions in this configuration control area maintain system baselines, using the procedures specified in the management documentation. The system baselines should identify the service-level policies and a measurement or assessment of the system's performance against these policies at any given time. These baselines become the standards of performance against which you measure all system configuration changes in the future. Following any configuration change on the system, you should reestablish the baselines.

> ➤ **Tracking:** The actions of this area track all requested, planned, or proposed changes to the system configuration and their discussion, approval, planning, or disapproval. This action area maintains a detailed record of any modifications to the system's design, layout, hardware, software, operating policies and objectives, and documentation.

> ➤ **Record keeping and analysis:** The actions of this area measure and record the performance of the system against the current baseline (created after the last system configuration change). This area maintains and analyzes a periodic record of any deviance from the baseline (good or bad). A regular or constant deviation may require a configuration modification.

All organizations, including those with smaller IT operations as well as enterprise-level operations, should define configuration standards that address configuration management, standardization, and performance expectations.

Change Control

Changes, even relatively minor ones, to a computing environment can cause unexpected differences in the performance, stability, or security of the system. For this reason, as well as issues in configuration management, an organization should tightly manage and control any change made to a system, especially unneeded ones. In any computing environment, *change control* is an important component of system management. Change control should be a first priority in cloud services, where numerous customers depend on the stability and availability of its systems.

The IT Infrastructure Library (ITIL) defines change control as "the procedures that ensure that all changes are controlled, including the submission, recording, analysis, decision-making, and approval of the change." Change control is different from change management. *Change management* involves the control and management of changes to any part of the computing environment that can improve the benefit of the computing system to its organization and minimize any potential disruption to the organization. In effect, change management controls the impact of change, and change control oversees the logistics of change. The computing department performs change control, and the overall organization performs change management.

The first step in implementing a change control process is to decide the who, what, when, and how of change control. Who should review requested changes? What changes should the review look at? When should changes be made? How should changes be made, tested, or backed out? A change control process doesn't have to be complicated or elaborate; it just needs to make sure that the change control committee reviews, analyzes, and schedules, if approved, every request for change.

All requested changes should be written with some justification and an explanation of the benefit anticipated. Requests for change can come from users, help desk technicians, system administrators, or perhaps the organization's management. A change committee, consisting of representatives of as many organizational units as appropriate to the scope of the computing environment, reviews the change requests for merit, impact (time and expense), and compatibility with the configuration management scheme.

The applicable technical specialists or department should then review the RFC and develop the details of new components for purchase, who is to affect the change, and when the change will take place. The plan should also address the testing procedure to verify the successful completion of the change and a backout plan in case the change fails to perform as expected.

The final step in the change control process is to gather the documentation for the request, approval (or disapproval), implementation plan, and test results and include them in the change management documentation. Depending on the impact or scope of the change, a new baseline may be necessary as well.

Capacity Management

The main goal of *capacity management* is to make sure that a computing environment has the processing and resource capacity to service existing and defined plans of an organization effectively and efficiently, meaning on time and within budget. In the business environment, capacity exists on three levels: business capacity, service capacity, and component capacity. Because in today's business environment, computing is a fundamental part of the business fabric, capacity management and planning for computing resources must address all three levels.

Business Capacity Planning

The demand for an organization's services, whether they are products or customer service, or both, drives *business capacity planning*, which, in turn, drives all other internal capacity elements. Business capacity also includes the capacity of inventory, staffing, and computing services. Within the scope of the computing services, business capacity derives from service-level commitments, organizational plans, and configuration management.

The demand and utilization rates of a business's systems are an example of business capacity planning in an IT function is. If computing services are in high demand—almost near existing capacities—during the hours of 8:00 a.m. to 7:00 p.m. but in low demand during the 7:00 p.m. to 8:00 a.m. hours, IT has to either plan to add capacity during the heavy usage hours or shift as much of that demand as possible to the low usage hours. On one hand, considerable costs are likely when IT capacity is increased to handle the 8:00 a.m. to 7:00 p.m. period of high demand, not only to provide for some excess capacity to better handle peak usage periods, but to provide additional capacity for growth. The IT function could also work with organizational management to shift the working hours of some employees to move some of the heavy usage demand to the hours of lower demand, saving the expense of an expansion of resources.

Managing demand-generated capacity is a constant activity. Changes to the computing environment may not be able to react quickly enough in a reactive mode. IT should be proactive to known increases in demand before the fact.

Service Capacity Planning

IT services, which can include things often taken for granted by its organization, such as email, Internet, intranet, telephony, instant messaging, teleconferencing, and the like, have capacity limits that are driven by organizational demands. Each IT service has functional and resource requirements that determine how effectively and efficiently it operates. Users just want IT services to work well when they need them, which may be the highest service level commitment that an IT shop can make.

Capacity planning for service elements can involve an analysis of servers, Internet gateways, and maybe even load balancers to ensure that each has the necessary capacity to handle peak service demands along with the desired throughput and availability. Like business capacity planning, *service capacity planning* and actions should be proactive, not reactive. Service capacities directly define component capacities.

Component Capacity Planning

The components of an IT service are the individual hardware and software elements used in providing the service. Components are hard disks, bandwidth, CPUs, workstations, network interfaces, protocols, and security elements. Any service, such as email, depends on the underlying components of the computing environment to provide sufficient capacity for it to carry out its functions as defined by user expectations or a committed Service Level Agreement (SLA).

Component capacity planning analyzes each of the components and resources utilized by an IT service to ensure 1) that the service has sufficient computing capacity to provide its service efficiently, and 2) that all the services that run concurrently have sufficient aggregate capacity to provide their services collectively. Utilization can be a key measurement in the management and planning of current and future capacities. If IT knows the growth (increase in demand) planned for a service, forecasting the addition of capacity in a particular component area can be much easier than exhausting the current capacity and trying to react without service disruptions.

Monitoring and Planning Capacity

Several software systems are available for monitoring and recording the capacities of entire computing environments, including virtual environments, but these systems tend to be quite expensive. Depending on the size and scope of a computing environment, the expense can be well worth the investment. However, an effective capacity planning system can also be a process-driven human-powered procedure.

Service and component capacity management requires the monitoring of start-to-finish capacity against a defined level of service. In combination with a change management procedure, forecasted changes to the system to deal with any exceptions or identified capacity issues have built-in justification. Remember that the key objective is to match capacity requirements with the demand for services.

There are four major steps in a capacity planning process:

1. **Select the monitored resources**: Typically, the resources selected for monitoring are bandwidth, server processors, and data storage devices. However, in larger computing environments, monitoring may also include server memory, peripheral devices, channels, and desktop configurations.

2. **Analyze the results**: Using the information gathered from the monitoring activities, make a comparison against the current system or component baselines and maximum capacity levels of the individual components or resources to identify capacity shortfalls or excesses. This analysis should also include averaged data over extended periods, like weeks or months, to establish trends and peak periods.

3. **Analyze the forecasts**: Estimate the impact of increased or decreased workload forecasts from management, users, and perhaps even developers. You can then analyze this impact against the capacity shortfalls or excesses identified in the previous step.

4. **Establish a timeline**: Develop a forecast or timeline that shows when a given component or resource, or the overall system, will reach capacity. Hopefully, this provides enough lead time for any capacity changes required to meet demand.

The purpose of a capacity planning process is to optimize proactively the performance and efficiencies, not to mention any expenditures necessary, of an organization's computing resources.

Chapter Summary

> Network and IP planning creates a network plan from a software perspective. The specific network elements in this planning include network domain, IP network number, IP address assignment, name service, and physical design.

> The size and scope of the planned network affects the addressing scheme, the IP address class, or the number of bits in the network ID and the addressing assigned to subnets, VLANs, and virtual devices.

➤ IPv4 can use a classful or a classless addressing method. In classful addressing, the number of network IDs and hosts per network of the address classes is predefined. In classless addressing, the number of bits designated as the network ID is open for choice.

➤ Subnetting applies a subnet mask to extract the network ID from an IPv4 address.

➤ Classless IP addressing supports routing. CIDR notation determines the network mask that extracts the network ID.

➤ IPv6 shares many characteristics with IPv4, including address assignment, address interpretation, logical addressing, network ID, private addresses, and routing.

➤ IPv6 addresses are 128 bits in length providing for 2^{128} possible addresses. IPv6 addresses use hexadecimal numbers to represent a network location. IPv6 has several address notations: dotted decimal, full hexadecimal, leading zero suppression or full zero suppression, and mixed mode.

➤ IPv6 appends the length of the prefix to the end of the address using a slash and the number of bits in the prefix. The last 84 bits of an IPv6 address represent the interface.

➤ A unicast address is the address of a single network node. A link-local unicast address addresses only the local network. Routers do not forward link-local addresses. IPv6 provides two multicast addresses: globally scoped and locally scoped, which are either fixed scope or variable scope. Anycast addressing sends a message to the closest member of an addressed group.

➤ The IPv6 standard defines a 64-bit extended unique identifier (EUI-64).

➤ Some network devices support both IPv4 and IPv6 addressing but require a special address format known as an IPv4-compatible IPv6 address. IPv4-mapped addresses are set aside for IPv4-compatible IPv6 switches and routers.

➤ IPv6 Stateless Address Autoconfiguration allows devices to configure their IP configuration settings automatically. Stateless autoconfiguration allows hosts to generate their EUI-64 address and a link-local temporary address.

➤ Configuration management maintains system integrity and value to the organization after applying changes to the system. Configuration management covers all changes to a system, including hardware, software, administrative systems, and changes in administrative personnel.

➤ System life cycle management measures and tracks a system's useful life.

➤ Configuration standardization controls the consistency of a system's configuration in terms of its performance, compatibility of its components, and any planned modifications.

➤ Change control manages the submission, recording, analysis, decision-making, and approval of changes. Change management controls and manages changes to any part of the computing environment that improve the value of the computing system to the organization and minimize potential disruptions to the organization.

➤ Capacity management ensures that a computing environment has the processing and resource capacity to service existing and defined plans. Capacity is on three levels: business capacity, service capacity, and resource capacity.

➤ Service and component capacity management requires the monitoring of start-to-finish capacity against a defined level of service.

Key Terms

Address prefix

Anycast addressing

Business capacity planning

Capacity management

Change control

Change management

Classful IP addressing

Classless Inter-Domain Routing (CIDR)

Classless IP addressing

Component capacity planning

Configuration management

Configuration standardization

DHCP version 6 (DHCPv6)

Domain Name System (DNS)

Dotted decimal notation

Extended unique identifier (EUI-64)

Fixed-scope multicast address

Full hexadecimal notation

Full zero suppression notation

Globally scoped

Hexadecimal (Base 16)

Interface

IP version 4 (IPv4)

IP version 6 (IPv6)

IPv4-compatible IPv6 address

IPv4-mapped addresses

IPv6 Stateless Address Autoconfiguration

Leading zero suppression notation

Lightweight Directory Access Protocol (LDAP)

Link-local unicast address

Locally scoped

Loopback address

Media Access Control (MAC)

Mixed mode notation

Multicast addressing

Multicast DNS version 6 (mDNSv6)

Neighbor Discovery Protocol (NDP)

Network Information Service (NIS)

Network number

Network Service Access Point (NSAP)

Organizationally unique identifier (OUI)

Service capacity planning

Site-local unicast address

Stateful

Stateless

System life cycle management

Transmission Control Protocol/Internet Protocol (TCP/IP)

Unicast address

Unspecified address

Variable-scope multicast address

Well-known multicast address

Review Questions

1. Network and IP planning create a network plan from a _____ perspective.

2. Which of the following are elements of network and IP planning?

   a. Network domain

   b. Network number/name

   c. Name service

   d. All of the above

3. True or False? IPv4 classful addressing limits the number of network IDs and hosts per network by address classes.

4. IPv4 extracts the network ID of an IP address using a(n) _____.

5. What is the length of an IPv6 address in bits?

   a. 32

   b. 64

   c. 128

   d. 256

6. True or False? Using CIDR notation, the /n appended to the address indicates the length of the host ID.

7. A(n) _____ is the address of a single network node in IPv6.

8. Which of the following is not an IPv6 address notation form?

   a. Dotted decimal

   b. Leading zero suppression

   c. Hexadecimal

   d. Hybrid mode

9. True or False? A dash (-) is the symbol used to separate hex pairs in an IPv6 address.

10. The network ID in an IPv6 address is its _____.

11. After applying leading zero compression notation to the IPv6 address shown below, which of the following is the resulting form?

    FE80:0000:0000:0808:87DF:056B:0000:08E5/11

    a. FE80::87DF::08E5/11

    b. FE80::808:87DF:56B::8E5/11

    c. FE8:0:0:0808:87DF:056B::08E5/11

    d. ::56B:8E5/26

12. True or False? Routers forward link-local IPv6 addresses.

13. The IPv6 interface identifier combines the network prefix with the Layer 2 address of the interface. The resulting address is a(n) _____.

14. Which process specifically manages the submission, recording, analysis, decision-making, and approval of changes?

    a. Change control

    b. Configuration management

    c. System life cycle management

    d. Configuration standardization

15. True or False? Capacity management ensures a computing environment has the processing and resource capacity to service existing and defined plans.

Answers to Review Questions

1. software

2. d

3. True

4. subnet mask or network mask

5. c

6. False

7. unicast

8. d

9. False

10. prefix

11. b

12. False

13. EUI-64

14. a

15. True

CHAPTER 17

Optimization

After reading this chapter and completing the exercises, you will be able to:

- Describe the processes of optimizing disk storage devices

- Discuss hypervisor configuration

- Explain various network and system performance concepts and metrics

The goal of an optimization effort is to bring a system as close as possible, if not beyond, its optimal performance levels. Some optimization actions can prevent the addition of new equipment and its cost, and some may not generate discernible savings or performance improvement right away. You must carefully consider, plan, and test each optimization action. After all, even optimization changes are changes.

Optimizing Data Storage

Optimizing disk storage simply means defragmentation to most information technology (IT) people. Although defragmentation can improve the performance of a disk drive, there is really more to it than that on larger systems, including virtualized systems and cloud Storage as a Service (SaaS) service providers. There is a difference, although somewhat subtle, between optimizing a disk and optimizing disk performance.

Disk Optimization

The process of *disk optimization* involves running software that collects fragmented files and rebuilding the file into a single entity. Whenever a data file changes, resulting in the file becoming larger or smaller than its original disk location, the file system stores the newer version of the file or data block in a different available space on the disk.

Operating systems and file systems separate hard disks into blocks into which they store data files sent to the drive for storage. Files written to the disk may require several blocks of storage or perhaps not even a full single block, depending on the size of their content. As applications write or remove data files or blocks from a hard disk drive, the files may not fit back into (or vacate) their original space. In this case, empty blocks can result, leaving fragments of a file scattered about the disk drive. This can lead to large amounts of the disk's storage capacity sitting idle because none of the vacated fragments is large enough (in consecutive blocks) to hold new storage requests. New file storage actions must fragment the file to use the available space on the drive.

When the disk drive receives an input/output request for a fragmented file, instead of reading the data from consecutive blocks, it must seek out the various fragments, slowing down the retrieval process. As a file becomes more fragmented, its retrieval time lengthens. The process of *defragmentation* seeks to remedy this situation.

> **Note**
>
> Fragmentation is a Windows issue. Because of the way Linux and Mac systems store files, fragmentation is not typically an issue on them.

DEFRAGMENTATION

Defragmentation performs one task: reducing the amount of fragmentation on a disk. It accomplishes this task by physically rearranging and organizing the data blocks on a disk drive or other types of mass storage. The goal of defragmentation is to arrange data blocks into the smallest number of contiguous blocks on the storage unit. Defragging a disk drive creates larger areas of free disk space. Many defragmentation utilities also apply compaction as a way to avoid fragmentation in the future.

Fragmentation can increase data retrieval times by causing the drive's read/write heads to seek data in several different parts of the disk. Organizing data in consecutive or contiguous blocks facilitates data retrieval or storage from sequential blocks, eliminating the delay caused by the read/write head moving about the drive.

Windows operating systems include a disk defragmenter utility. Figure 17-1 shows the start-up dialog box for this utility. The Windows Disk Defragmenter in Windows 7 and later allows users to analyze the extent of fragmentation prior to actually defragging the disk. Disk Defragmenter only defrags hard disk drives (HDDs); it does not defrag solid state drives (SSDs).

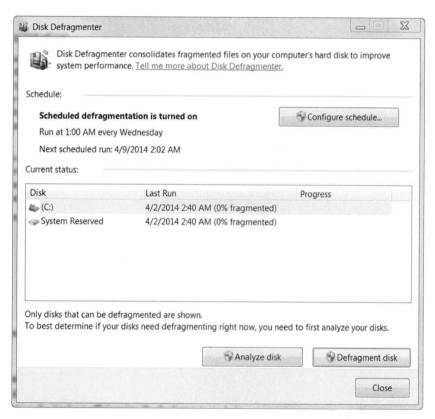

Figure 17-1 The start-up dialog box for the Windows Disk Defragmenter.

On Windows Server systems, the Disk Defragmenter does not defrag blocks or files that are smaller than 64 MB because it assumes that no noticeable improvement in performance results from this action. However, running the Defrag.exe command line utility provides both more control and a full defragmentation regardless of file or block sizes.

Several third-party defragmentation utilities are available, even for Linux and Mac systems. The more popular defragmentation software includes Diskeeper from Condusiv Technologies Corporation, PerfectDisk Pro from Raxco, Inc., and Norton Utilities from Symantec Corporation. There are also freeware and shareware defragmentation utilities available on the web.

DISK PERFORMANCE OPTIMIZATION

On a desktop computer, optimizing the performance of a hard disk drive may provide some noticeable improvement in its response times. However, not optimizing disk storage devices in an enterprise or cloud service environment can result in noticeably slower disk retrieval performance. What's worse is that slower disk input/output (I/O) is something users notice.

Whereas simple actions like defragmentation can resolve performance issues on a host hard disk system, several performance elements must come together to produce the high-level performance and efficiencies required of large (in terms of the number of servers or the number of users accessing the system) data centers. The performance issues involved at this level include mechanical devices, bandwidth, bus loads, the applications in use, and the level of demand on the storage system. Essentially, disk drive performance is a combination of these elements along with the algorithms in use to minimize the amount of mechanical movement in the disk drives.

Larger data centers, such as enterprise and cloud services, typically employ storage arrangement technology, such as storage area network (SAN) or network attached storage (NAS), which are physically organized disk arrays, such as the Seagate rack-mounted NAS device shown in Figure 17-2.

Figure 17-2 An internal look at an 8-bay rack mount NAS storage device.
© 2014 Seagate Technology LLC.

Disk Performance Characteristics

You can optimize the performance of a hard disk. However, there are mechanical limits on any hard disk that restrict the amount of optimization you may realize. Optimizing hard disk performance may require purchasing new disk drives. You should know the various performance measures of HDDs and their importance in the overall performance of the drive. The following sections discuss the disk performance elements you should know before purchasing new disk drives or taking the Cloud+ exam.

Response Rate The amount of time it takes for a disk storage system to process, access, and return requested data or to process, access, and write data from and to a hard disk drive, start to finish, is the *response rate* or response time. Many different drive-specific time factors contribute to the response time of a disk drive. For example, a drive may have a failing actuator arm, or have a lower RPM spindle speed, or its controller transfers data at a slower speed than expected.

Rotational Speed Mechanical disks, those with moving parts, are also rotating disks, such as hard disk drives, optical disk drives, and floppy disk drives. The speed at which the media spins inside these drives can have a lot to do with any latency in an I/O operation. Desktop hard disk drives commonly have *rotational speeds* between 4500 and 7200 RPM. Higher-end disk drives can have rotational speeds of 15000 to 20000 RPM. In any of these drives, the rotational speed is constant. The faster the disk spindle spins the disk platters, the higher its data transfer rate is, but noise and temperature increase as well. Another operational characteristic of hard disk drives is that the read/write heads typically read an entire track (from beginning to end) on one rotation.

Rotational Latency *Rotational latency* is the amount of time it takes for the desired disk sector on a given track of a hard disk drive to rotate to a position under the read/write head. The average rotational latency for any rotating disk drive is one-half the rotational speed of the drive.

Seek Time *Seek time* is the time required for a read/write head to travel to the track and sector where data is to be read or written. Average seek times range from 15 ms on small form factor drives, like a mobile device HDD, to around 9 ms on a typical desktop computer, and to less than 4 ms on higher-end drives in enterprise-level servers.

A drive's track-to-track and stroke times directly affect seek time measurements. *Track-to-track time* is the time needed to move the read/write head to an adjacent track, typically between 0.2 and 1.0 ms. Stroke times are either *full-stroke* or short-stroke. These measures represent the time required to move the read/write head from the outermost track to the innermost track. Full-stroke time is essentially the slowest seek time for the drive. *Short stroking* relates to smaller (physical size) drives used in enterprise or cloud service environments that reduce the stroke size to reduce seek time.

Data Transfer Rate *Data transfer rate (DTR)* is a measurement that is not exclusive to disk drives. DTR relates to any process or device that moves data from one location to another. DTR applies to communication media, network connectivity devices, and hard disk drives, to name only a few.

The DTR of a hard disk drive relates to the time that elapses from when the read/write head begins reading data and transferring it to the disk controller, called the *internal transfer time*, and when the disk controller transfers the data to the host system, called the *external transfer time*. The total transfer time, including both the internal and external times, is obviously much faster on standalone devices with direct access storage (DAS) than it is on network hosts connecting to SAN or NAS via the network.

The DTR of a hard disk drive, also called its *throughput time*, is the slower of the internal transfer time and the external transfer time. Most commonly, a drive's specifications state a disk drive's DTR as *sustained DTR*. A sustained rate is equal to the DTR at its highest peak or burst load.

Input/Output Operations per Second (IOPS) A Windows utility tool is available to monitor or measure the disk performance on a single computer. That tool is *perfmon*. Perfmon (performance monitor), shown in Figure 17-3, can be started from the command line prompt. In addition to other tools available, perfmon provides a link to the Resource Monitor (see Figure 17-4), which you can start from the Accessories/System Tools selection on the Start menu.

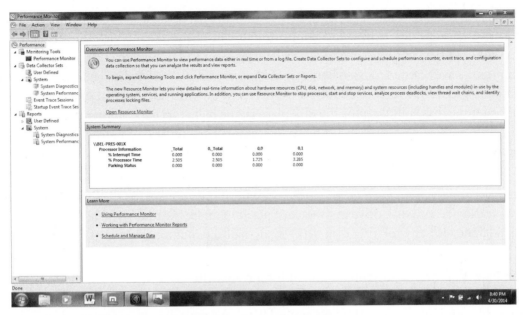

Figure 17-3 The Windows Performance Monitor (perfmon).
Used with permission from Microsoft.

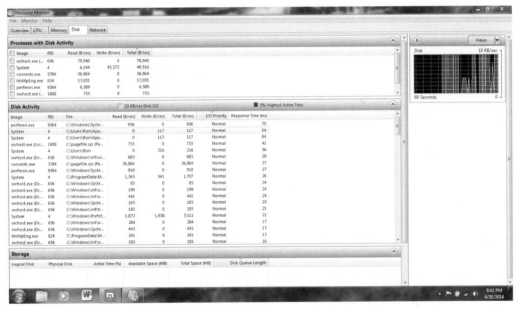

Figure 17-4 The Windows Resource Monitor.
Used with permission from Microsoft.

In the past, when attempting to measure the performance of a storage system, such as NAS or SAN, administrators have been limited to only throughput, which measures the average megabytes (MB) transferred in a given time, typically stated as either read or write bytes per second (B/sec). Figure 17-4 shows throughput metrics on a single computer. Measuring throughput on a large storage system is problematic in that virtual devices and network applications request smaller read/write operations than those on a single computer. Therefore, on larger storage systems and arrays, throughput is less of an indicator of storage performance.

Input/output operations per second (IOPS) measures the number of disk operations (input or output) per second on a storage system. A baseline IOPS metric gives administrators either a maximum performance expectation or a minimum acceptable performance threshold. Regardless of how administrators want to use IOPS, it can indicate current performance levels to the baseline or be used to simulate system performance under an incremental percentage of additional load.

Calculating IOPS involves a formula using rotational speed, disk latency, and seek time. Rotational speed is not specifically included in the formula, but latency and seek time depend heavily on it. Here's the formula to calculate the maximum IOPS for an individual drive:

Average IOPS = one divided by the sum of latency (in seconds) and seek time (in seconds)

In an algebraic statement, the formula looks like this:

$$IOPS = \frac{1}{latency + seek\ time}$$

© 2015 Cengage Learning®.

For example, calculating IOPS on a disk drive with the specifications

➤ **Model**: Seagate Constellation 1000 GB SATA/SAS

➤ **Rotational speed**: 7200 RPM

➤ **Average latency**: 4.06 ms (0.00406 seconds)

➤ **Average seek time**: 9.0 ms (0.009 seconds)

yields an IOPS for this disk of

IOPS = 1/(0.00406 + 0.009) = 1/(0.01306) = 76.6 IOPS

Table 17-1 shows the average IOPS for the predominant HDD rotational speeds in the market. The IOPS calculation yields an approximate 76 IOPS for the example disk drive. Although this drive is at the low end of the average for 7200 RPM disk drives, it is still within the average.

Table 17-1 Average IOPS by Rotational Speed

Rotational Speed	Average IOPS
7200 RPM	75–100
10000 RPM	100–130
15000 RPM	150–190

© 2015 Cengage Learning®.

For the most part, manufacturers publish the average IOPS metric for their hard disk drives. For example, for the Seagate Technologies drive specification given earlier, the manufacturer specifies the IOPS to be approximately 122 IOPS. Remember that manufacturers develop their metrics from drives operating in optimum conditions. Also, remember that the HDD interface type, typically either *Serial ATA (SATA)* or *Serial Attached SCSI (SAS)* (SCSI stands for Small Computer System Interface), doesn't have much to do with disk performance in terms of IOPS.

IOPS is only a predictor of performance and not of reliability, availability, or longevity. Manufacturers also provide these specifications. However, most summarize these characteristics under *mean time between failure (MTBF)*. Keep in mind that rotational speed drives IOPS metrics. An HDD with the same RPM has similar IOPS metrics.

IOPS in Multidisk Systems In an enterprise or cloud service environment, administrators don't install HDDs as standalones. For this reason, the calculations shown in the preceding section, as they are, are essentially invalid for these environments unless they're converted for use with multiple disk sets.

In a RAID 0 disk array in which all the drives are essentially equivalent, having the same rotational speeds and interface standard, IOPS can be calculated for the entire array just by multiplying the IOPS for one of the disk drives by the number of disks in the array. Therefore, if one drive has an IOPS of 77 and there are three drives in the array, you should expect that the array could produce approximately 230 IOPS.

In RAID systems other than RAID 0, calculating an IOPS involves the inclusion of a *RAID write penalty*, which accounts for the fact that a disk write in a RAID system involves several actual writes to disk. For example, a RAID 5 write operation requires four actual writes to the disk array. Table 17-2 shows the RAID write penalty for the more common RAID implementations.

Table 17-2 RAID IOPS Write Penalties

RAID Level	Write Penalty
RAID 0	0
RAID 1	2
RAID 5	4
RAID 6	6
RAID 1+0	2

© 2015 Cengage Learning®.

Because of the write penalty applied to RAID systems, IOPS focuses on write IOPS. Read IOPS, because there is no penalty associated with read operations from RAID, follows the same calculation discussed earlier in the section "Input/Output Operations per Second (IOPS)." To calculate the write IOPS for a multidisk RAID system, you need to know the workload on the array in terms of the percentage of I/Os that are reads and the percentage that are writes. Commonly, 40 percent of the workload are read I/Os and the remaining 60 percent are write I/Os.

The formula to calculate the total IOPS for the disk array looks like this:

Total IOPS = (Workload IOPS * %Read) + ((Workload IOPS * %Write) * RAID Penalty)

Using this formula, a RAID 5 array in a virtual environment that experiences a 1200 workload IOPS in total, with approximately 40 percent of the total IOPS as reads and 60 percent as writes, yields this total IOPS:

IOPS = (1200 * 0.40) + ((1200 * 0.60) * 4) = (480) + ((720) * 4) = 480 + 2880 = 1660

This calculation tells you that on a multidisk set that is running RAID 5, a workload of 1200 IOPS is actually processing 1660 IOPS. If the disk array is capable of processing this level of demand, you're good. Otherwise, you may need to add disks or reconfigure the disk array.

CPU Wait Time   Central processing unit (CPU) wait time is the time a CPU is idle waiting for an I/O operation or some other event to complete. In some systems, this time can be trivial, but in others, a high CPU wait time can indicate there is a problem, most likely caused by resource contention. Wait time is just one of the CPU time indicators. The CPU resource time indicators are typically percentages of the total CPU time for a given process. In a virtualized environment, the different time percentages indicate the activities of a virtual machine (VM).

The primary CPU time indicators for a VM running on a Linux system are:

> **%IDLE**: The percentage of time a virtual CPU (vCPU) is idle with no queued processes

> **%RDY**: The percentage of time a VM application or process is ready to run but must wait to get access to a CPU

> **%RUN**: The percentage of time a VM application or process is executing

> **%WAIT**: The percentage of time a VM application or process is waiting for a queued I/O operation

Storage Tuning

Although most of the bottlenecks in a storage system aren't the fault of the storage system itself, you should have a procedure in place to identify and isolate the problems slowing it down. Typically, the bottlenecks occur in the links that connect storage network services to the disk structures.

The sections that follow discuss some of the actions you can take to ensure your storage network is performing optimally. Some of these actions prepare you for when optimization or tuning becomes necessary. The others discuss action that can identify and remedy storage system issues.

Inventory   Keep a detailed inventory of the equipment, software, and services in the storage network and keep it up to date. This inventory should include every *host bus adapter (HBA)*, switch, and cable in the system with a diagram that shows the connections. Not only will this facilitate troubleshooting, but it should facilitate talking with vendors.

Monitoring It's more important to know the traffic patterns in the storage network than it is to know what any specific device is doing. High-performance storage systems and networks are commonplace in enterprise and cloud service centers. Storage structures like SAN, NAS, and other systems, such as those from EMC Corporation and NetApp, have become critical components of these data centers. Several monitoring tools are available that provide monitoring of the performance and operations of a storage system, including real-time tracking of bandwidth, latency, and other defined thresholds or conditions.

Application Once you have identified the source of a system performance issue, the next step is to enable the SAN or NAS feature, install a new HDD or SSD or storage network switch, or replace the storage network. Regardless of the improvement, upgrades, or replacement components, should unexpected repercussions occur, you need to take immediate action to limit the impact of the change by localizing the changes. For example, dividing an SAN into virtual SANs can localize the server, channel, or application causing the issue.

ISLs One area to watch for performance issues is *inter-switch links (ISLs)* or interconnects between switches. As a storage network grows, ISLs can affect the performance of the storage network. In reality, the latency that an ISL adds is low compared to the latency of the disk drives themselves.

Two ratios that can indicate the possibility of an ISL becoming a bottleneck are the fan-in and the fan-out ratios of the overall storage network. A *fan-in ratio* is essentially how oversubscribed source ports are to target ports and an ISL within the storage network. Fan-in looks at these interchanges from a view external to the storage network (outside looking in). When viewed from the view of the storage network (inside looking out), this ratio becomes the *fan-out ratio*. In an environment in which eight hosts share a single ISL or storage switch port, the fan-in ratio is 8:1 (eight to one). Figure 17-5 illustrates the oversubscription concept with a 1:1 ratio. In this figure, the amount of bandwidth of the demand (requesting) is equal to the amount of bandwidth available on the target (or servicing) side. Should the "in" side increase to 32 hosts at the 8 Gbps rate, the fan-in ratio (and oversubscription) increases to 2:1. The oversubscription at the storage network ports or ISLs should be monitored to ensure that the intended fan-in/fan-out ratios aren't exceeded long term.

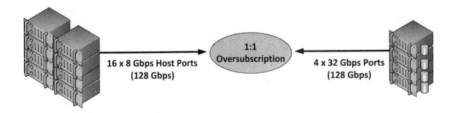

Figure 17-5 An example of a 1:1 fan-in ratio on a storage system.
© 2015 Cengage Learning®.

NPIV In virtualized environments, SAN utilization and performance is a direct function of the VMs demanding the most from the storage infrastructure. Prior to server virtualization, one server ran one application that communicated directly to one HBA and the storage network. Now, several VMs running in the virtualized environment can drive several virtual servers to interface with the storage network though that same single HBA.

The key to balancing the storage network demand of VMs is to identify the VMs that have the highest I/O requests. In the virtual environment, implementing *N_Port ID virtualization (NPIV)* allows an HBA to assign individual VMs a virtual World Wide Name (WWN) that remains with the VM, regardless of its migration from host to host. Under NPIV, switches can track the VMs that are the most active in terms of disk I/O.

Queue Depth The number of pending storage I/Os waiting for processing by the storage system is queue depth. For the most part, on a network storage infrastructure, such as an SAN, this evidences as *HBA queue depth*. The default queue depth on most HBAs is from 32 to 256, which, for most systems, can be too high. In an efficient, responsive storage infrastructure, a queue depth somewhere between 2 and 8 is better. HBA initiators can provide the queue depth of a particular HBA, which allows you to monitor this performance metric and find the balance between too many and not enough.

Multipath I/O In a storage infrastructure with several available paths (multipathing) for storage I/O processing, these requests may be accumulating in one or two particular queues, indicating that the multipathing feature of the storage system may not be working correctly. *Multipath I/O* facilitates fault tolerance and performance improvement by providing more than one link between the server's CPU and the storage system using the system buses, storage device controllers, and storage switches along the connecting links.

An example of multipath I/O is a single SCSI disk connected to two SCSI controllers or a disk drive connected to two Fibre Channel interfaces. Should either of the controllers, channels, ports, or associated switches fail, the host operating system can route storage I/Os to the remaining controller or channel. Except for some minor additional latency, the route change is transparent to the requesting application.

Data Deduplication *Data deduplication* is a software-driven compression technique that eliminates duplicate instances of repeated data from a data store. This technique can reduce the overall size of the data content. Deduplication can also reduce the number of bytes in a data transfer. The deduplication process stores unduplicated or unique data blocks and then compares any subsequent blocks to the stored data. Whenever a match results, the process writes a reference pointer back to the baseline block in place of the duplicated data. Duplicated patterns in data are more frequent than you may imagine, and storing only pointers in place of duplicated data blocks can significantly reduce the overall size of the data content.

Don't mistake deduplication for *data compression*. Although deduplication does reduce the overall size of the stored data, it doesn't go nearly as far as the sophisticated data compression methods embedded into operating systems or available from third-party vendors. Data compression involves the use of encoding algorithms that store data with fewer bits than its original characters or values. Compression algorithms are lossy or lossless. A *lossless compression* algorithm retains the full image of data by removing redundancy, similar to deduplication, but much more sophisticated. *Lossy compression*, as its name implies, may lose some of the data's original image by removing unnecessary information.

Swap Space   A *swap space* is a reserved portion of an HDD that extends a computer's internal memory (random access memory [RAM]) as part of the system's virtual memory function. *Virtual memory* is both a hardware- and a software-based memory management method that effectively increases the memory allocation of a running application.

Virtual memory maps relative memory addresses, or virtual memory addresses, in an application to physical addresses in main memory. If a process or application needs more memory than has been allocated, the operating system may extend the addressable memory to include set-aside portions of a hard disk drive. This capability frees an application from managing its allocation of a shared memory space and allows it to use memory space beyond its allocation. When an application needs more main memory, the operating system identifies any idle portions of the application's memory and swaps it out to the virtual memory space on the HDD. The receiving space is a *swap file*, a *swap space*, or a *pagefile*, depending on the operating system in use. On Windows systems and some larger computing systems, memory blocks are pages, and the swapping process is *paging*.

A swap file is the reserved area of an HDD that has been set aside for the virtual memory extension of a system's main memory. Virtual memory and the use of swap files allow the system to function as if it has more memory than it physically does. When the application needs the swapped-out data again, the swap file transfers back into memory and, if necessary, another memory page swaps out to the swap file.

Windows and Linux/UNIX systems provide a default swap file/pagefile sized to accommodate your applications and services. Administrators can change the size of the swap file using system administration tools, like the one shown in Figure 17-6 for Windows systems.

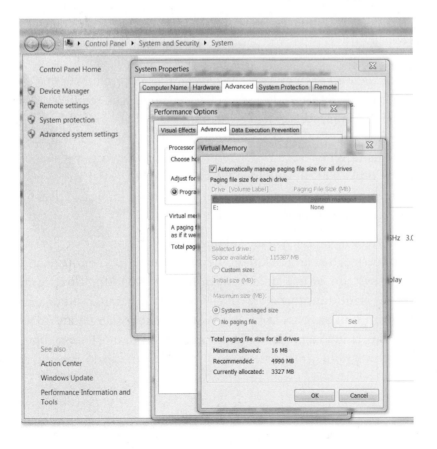

Figure 17-6 The Virtual Memory dialog box for a Windows system facilitates changes to the size of the pagefile and virtual memory.

Used with permission from Microsoft.

Memory Ballooning *Memory ballooning* is a virtual memory management technique that can free any unused memory in one VM and assign it temporarily to resolve memory shortages in another VM. Multiple VMs running on a single host computer must share the physical resources of that machine. The hypervisor only activates ballooning when a host's available memory runs low.

In most virtualization systems, each VM includes a *balloon driver* that the hypervisor can activate to share one VM's unused memory with another VM that needs additional memory. When notified of the memory shortage, the hypervisor sends an alert to the balloon driver of an active VM instructing it to take action (inflate) to parse out any memory not in use. The hypervisor can then assign the ballooned memory to the VM that needs it. Of course, the best situation is not to need ballooning at all, because enough memory is available for all the running VMs.

Another approach to resolve low memory conditions is a variation of the virtual memory techniques discussed in the preceding section ("Swap Space"). Some virtualization-enabled processors free up virtual memory space by creating multiple layers of virtual memory. However, using this approach adds overhead because the hypervisor cannot detect if a VM requires more memory.

I/O Throttling *I/O throttling* is a technique applied to slow down I/O memory requests during low memory conditions. This technique queues up I/O requests from memory and processes them sequentially on a first-in, first-out (FIFO) basis. Throttling the I/O processes slows the system and the demands on memory processing with the objective of preventing the system from crashing.

I/O throttling can set a maximum rate that active VMs are able to request collective I/Os from memory, or any other restrictive device, including storage. However, throttling doesn't apply to I/O requests that the CPU issues. The throttle mechanism is actually a timing mechanism controlled by the CPU that meters out I/O requests with a set time between them. The CPU timing meter holds I/O requests until the delay reaches a preset throttling time minimum.

Throttling can also apply to any of the shared devices, channels, and controllers on an environment with multiple active VMs or systems. In addition, it can apply to situations in which throttling of a certain device or application promotes load balancing, such as if Application A is running in a VM on a high-speed processor. Application B, running on a slower processor, shares a device controller with Application A. Because it can issue I/O requests faster than Application B, Application A can dominate the controller. Throttling Application A's I/O requests allows Application B to request I/Os with less contention for the controller.

Change Control in a Virtual Environment

Change control and management in a virtualized environment is perhaps more important than it is in a nonvirtualized environment. Taking down a single physical server for maintenance shuts down any virtual servers and VMs running on that machine, which can affect processing on the rest of its virtual world. The unfortunate truth in any data center is that the cause of most of its downtime is the result of changes, upgrades, and troubleshooting, but this is especially true in a virtualized environment. Investigating and troubleshooting the impact of changes in a system can account for as much as 80 percent of system downtime.

One of the benefits of a virtualized environment is that VMs can migrate between virtual servers and physical computers automatically. At the same time, these migrations can lead to performance issues on the entire system. The documentation of these movements can be crucial to troubleshooting after you apply software updates, patches, and possibly hardware updates. The new configuration of the receiving host is also important information should issues arise.

Because different servers can apply different security or protections, it is important to restrict the free movement of VMs within a virtual system. At minimum, a mapping of the VMs in the environment to their servers is important to understanding where and which servers are hosting which VMs. Should an outage occur, the response time necessary to get the business-critical applications and services back online may limit the amount of time available to develop this information.

Virtualization Change Management Tools

A variety of software applications and tools can assist in mapping and archiving the current virtual system and network environment. These tools map and track virtual devices, their configurations, their connectivity, and, in some cases, the business processes with which they interact.

An effective virtual environment change management software tool should include the following features:

> **VM monitoring**: This feature monitors designated host servers and the VMs operating on them, including the performance of the server and the applications running on the server itself, as well as those running in the VMs.

> **Enterprise monitoring**: This feature monitors all virtual network devices and servers in the enterprise or cloud service network and computing center.

> **Track changes**: This feature tracks and provides centralized control of all changes to the environment.

> **Compliance tracking**: This feature monitors the system for compliance with internal policies and regulatory requirements, where applicable.

> **Real-time reporting**: This feature provides real-time metrics of performance-critical components, software, and communication.

Change Management Essentials

An effective change management program in a virtualized environment should include visibility, accountability, assessment, and enhancement. Each of these essential elements provides for part of the overall control and management necessary to ensure that a virtualized environment continues to function optimally.

VISIBILITY

Complete visibility of the projected effect that every planned change will have on a virtualized environment can provide for a proactive and preventive view of the potential problems that can arise with the implementation of the changes. Change visibility should also extend to the detection of unauthorized changes. Being able to project the impact and cost of a change or to apply immediate remediation of an unauthorized change can make the difference in a computing environment meeting its service-level commitments continuously without unplanned interruptions. The primary goal of change visibility is the reduction of unauthorized or unplanned changes, which must be the objective of a good change control environment.

ACCOUNTABILITY

While not really intended to place blame when things go wrong, change accountability assigns the responsibility of a planned change so that verification is possible after the fact. As a part of the accountability controls in a change control and management policy, verification ensures that a change resulted in the planned outcomes without unexpected consequences.

Accountability assigns responsibility for a change's effectiveness. To this end, it should include processes that verify that the changes made were restricted to only the planned changes. It must also include verification that any security measures affected by the change are still in place and according to policy.

ASSESSMENT

After the implementation of a planned change or the remediation of an unplanned or unauthorized change, there needs to be an assessment of the key operational and business rule indicators from the measurement of the critical performance metrics and analytics. A change may be operating as it should without apparent issues, but it may be causing a conflict with a security policy or inadvertently corrupting data for a seldom-used application. A holistic assessment of the entire system or environment can provide the assurance that all is as it should be.

ENHANCEMENT

All changes should contribute to a continuous effort to provide an optimal system or environment configuration that meets or exceeds customer or user service-level commitments. The constant use of monitoring software tools can verify that the environment is continuing to improve from one change cycle to the next. Other than replacements to failing components, and perhaps even then, any changes made to the environment should improve or enhance the performance or utility of the system for its users.

Another part of tracking the improvement of a computing environment is the management of the *system life cycle*, especially at the VM level. Third-party and virtualization software vendors offer software tools that provide data for *VM lifecycle management (VMLM)*. VMLM systems allow administrators to monitor and manage the implementation, delivery, operation, and maintenance of VMs throughout their life cycle. VMLM tools are available from Citrix Systems, Inc., VDIworks, and VMware Inc., among others.

System Performance Concepts

Other concepts and entities contribute, detract, or enhance the performance of virtualized environments and cloud computer service centers. This section is less about what and how-to and more about definitions and impacts. Each of the topics covered in the sections that follow is included in the Cloud+ objectives. You should expect to encounter these topics on the exam as components or elements of questions relating to the overall performance of a computing environment.

Metadata Performance

Metadata has three different, although related, meanings in the context of computing systems. Essentially, *metadata* is "data about data," but within metadata, there are three categories: descriptive metadata, structural metadata, and administrative metadata. Descriptive metadata consists of information about the content or context of an object; structural metadata is data about the container of an object; and administrative metadata is data about the management of an object.

Descriptive Metadata

Descriptive metadata is the most commonly recognized form of data about data. For any data object, descriptive metadata can include an object title, the creator's name, dates, subject matter titles and key words (called tags), or a descriptive abstract of the object content. However, descriptive metadata can also include the following items:

> **Collection methods**: A description of the collection of the content, its geographical coverage, and the sampling methods used.

> **Context**: A history of a project or collaboration, the purpose of an object's content, the objectives of the content, and any other descriptive or explanatory information regarding the content of an object.

> **Privacy**: The object's confidentiality, access or use restrictions, or other privacy-related information.

> **Structure**: Information on the structure of data files, the relationships of the files, and other data structure information on the object.

The preceding list is hardly exhaustive; there are as many examples of descriptive metadata as there are types, uses, purposes, and controls on the data content of an object. In summary, descriptive metadata describes the who, what, and when of an object.

Structural Metadata

Structural metadata contains descriptive information about the formatting, processing, and dependencies of an object's data. Some examples may help you to understand this metadata category. The structural metadata for a photographic image may include the camera, aperture, exposure, and file format of the image. Another example is an object that includes the full content of a scanned document, including its structure (document), components (pages), elements (illustrations, graphs, table of contents, and so on), or overall size. Structural metadata describes the structure of the contents of an object.

Administrative Metadata

Administrative metadata includes data on the management, use, and retention of an object. Administrative metadata is generally instructional or regulatory in nature, such as the creation date of an object, its expiration date, the software required to process it, its copyright information, or any file security or integrity data.

Metadata in a Virtual Environment

In a virtualized environment, it is important for the hypervisor to maintain a consistent and accurate view of the virtual system and network at all times. To this end, the hypervisor creates a mapping of the virtual (and physical) components, devices, and services in the virtual environment and stores it as metadata in a *mapping file*. In this particular case, metadata means data about the environment.

The level of detail and the amount of information included in the metadata-mapping file depends on the system's capacity and address space. It's common for administrators to reconcile the space available and the level of detail recorded to the mapping file. However, there are virtualization systems that don't use mapping files, using algorithms to determine system locations when there is a need to access them.

Metadata in Object Storage

Traditionally, file systems store metadata within the object it describes. However, with the explosion of media-rich objects, such as video, image, and audio files, in addition to big data objects, it's better to store metadata external to the object to enhance search or object identification. For this reason, metadata needs to be held either close to its object or centrally and as close to the "surface" as possible.

Centrally stored metadata allows for faster contextual or subject matter searches made to locate a particular object or a set of objects that relate to certain criteria. Once selected through the information in their metadata, the storage system processors can retrieve the selected objects and present them to the requestor.

Metadata Architecture

Storage systems use one of three architectures to store metadata: centralized, distributed, or hybrid. A *centralized metadata architecture* is the more common of the three architectures, but it can also be a single point of failure. All data and object metadata is in one centralized repository that must have constant synchronization with all data I/O activities, which has the capability of becoming a bottleneck as the storage or file system waits for metadata actions to complete. In addition, centralized metadata may have quality issues if data validation processes don't include metadata processing.

A *distributed metadata architecture* collects metadata from the various system metadata stores in real time to provide the most up-to-date information about the content in each system. However, a failure in any of the participating storage systems or a change in the configuration of a source system can lead to the possibility of compromising the distributed metadata. A *hybrid metadata architecture* combines the best of the centralized and distributed approaches by including real-time updates into a centralized repository.

PERFORMANCE ISSUES

Every data I/O request asks to open, close, search, back up, read, save, or replicate a file or object on the storage system, which affects an entry in metadata. Metadata operations include such actions as scans, searches, policy and document management functions, and all individual file or object actions. Every storage operation involves metadata. Because of this, the way a file system handles metadata can have a direct bearing on the overall performance of the storage system. Minimizing metadata operations can improve system performance.

Simply replacing HDD storage devices with SSD devices improves the performance of the storage system, but not necessarily its overall efficiency. At minimum, improve the access and update processes for metadata by keeping the metadata files open, thereby minimizing the overhead of opening and closing the metadata files whenever they require updates. Merging the files, in a small to medium environment, into a centralized architecture may also improve the metadata processing overhead. Implementing metadata management software, such as InfoLibrarian Metadata Repository from InfoLibrarian Corporation, can build efficiency and improve performance in the storage system's metadata. InfoLibrarian Corporation and Quantum Corporation also offer metadata appliances that promise to improve metadata performance by as much as 700 percent.

Cache

Within any computer, there are at least two cache entities: disk cache (also called page cache) and cache memory. The purpose of *disk cache* is to shorten the time required to read from or write to storage. *Memory cache* is also a performance enhancer in that it can forego reading data from storage. Both of these caching methods are attempts to free the much faster processor from having to wait on the much slower hard disk.

DISK CACHE

Disk cache can be either a set-aside area of main memory (RAM) or a segregated portion of a disk drive. The disk cache holds data recently read from or written to storage, in an attempt to prevent the need for a storage I/O to access this same data. Or, the cache may hold data logically adjacent to the last data read, as a predictor of the data likely requested next.

Another form of disk caching is *write caching*. With write caching disabled, every write operation on the disk drives causes a performance and possibly throughput delay while the processor waits for the hard disk drive to complete its processes. Enabling write caching allows the system to transfer data into write cache, which then releases the processor to continue with its next operation without waiting for the write operation to complete. The storage system then writes the contents of the write cache to the disk in the background later. This is *write-back caching*, which is a cycle-saver, provided the power stays on until the data makes it to the disk. In high-volume, high-availability situations, storage administrators may disable write caching to ensure that data always makes it to the disk media.

CACHE MEMORY

Cache memory, also called CPU cache, is memory reserved specifically to reduce the time required to move data from main memory to the CPU. Cache memory is typically smaller, yet faster than main memory and stores instructions and data from commonly used locations in main memory. On some systems, separate caches exist for instructions and data.

When the processor is ready for its next instruction or needs data, it first looks to cache memory for it. If what the processor needs is in cache memory, it retrieves it and continues processing. However, if what the processor needs is not in cache memory, it must wait for the data to move into cache from main memory and then retrieve it. The replenishment processes of cache memory works to out-guess the processor as to what the processor will request next.

There are two, and possibly three, levels of cache memory:

> **L1 (level 1) cache:** *L1 cache* is typically on the same integrated circuit as the processor so it can be extremely close to the processor. It commonly ranges in size from 8 kilobytes (KB) to 64 KB of static RAM (SRAM), which provides high-speed data transfers.

> **L2 (level 2) cache:** *L2 cache*, which is the backup buffer for L1 cache, can range from 64 KB to 4 MB in size. L2 cache is "close" to the processor but uses dynamic RAM (DRAM), which is much slower than SRAM. On multiple-core microprocessors, each core has its own L1 and L2 caches.

> **L3 (level 3) cache:** Not all microprocessors or motherboards implement an *L3 cache*. However, on multiple-core CPUs, all cores share L3 cache. L3 is also DRAM and commonly twice as large as L2 cache on a system.

NIC Bonding and Teaming

NIC bonding and NIC teaming are two different things, although you often hear them used together or interchangeably. *NIC bonding* combines two or more network interface controllers (NICs) or network adapters into a single, and larger, interface. For bonding at the NIC level to work, the switch to which the bonded NICs connect must support *link aggregation*. Bonding is applied at the host or network-level NICs. NIC bonding and port trunking are the same thing.

NIC teaming is a form of link aggregation that implements load balancing and failover. In fact, there are two general methods of NIC teaming: *failover* and *load balancing with failover (LBFO)*. Teaming allows multiple NICS to be associated, which aggregates their bandwidth and prevents the loss of connectivity in the event of a network component failure.

NIC Bonding

Bonding is a software-based structuring of two or more NICS into a single virtual NIC. To implement bonding on a network node, its two (or more) NICS must connect to a switch that has link aggregation enabled and knows that the NICs are bonded. There are different ways to affect bonding. The following sections describe the more commonly used methods.

There are three categories of bonding modes: switch-supported (IEEE 802.3ad), generic, and failover-only.

IEEE 802.3ad Bonding

Within the Institute of Electrical and Electronics Engineers (IEEE) Ethernet standard (IEEE 802.3), the standards for link aggregation on bonded NICs specify the creation of an *EtherChannel* in subsection *IEEE 802.3ad*. Configuring the Ethernet interface ports to which two (or more) NICs connect on a switch for IEEE 802.3ad bonding activates load balancing on the ports. Figure 17-7 illustrates this configuration.

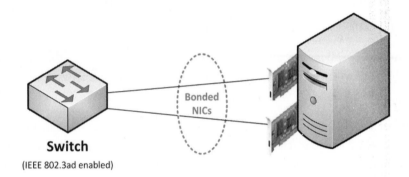

Figure 17-7 Two NICs from a server bonded together with an IEEE 802.3ad switch.
© 2015 Cengage Learning®.

Bonding only provides a benefit if each of the connections is actively sending traffic to the switch. If traffic comes in on one interface, all the traffic goes to the same link all the time. However, if all the interfaces are active, the switch's load balancing algorithm or its round-robin balancing can even out the load on the upstream services.

Generic Bonding

On a Linux system, which has multiple *generic bonding* modes to use, the most commonly used is bonding-alb. The key to this mode working is a network interface that allows its MAC address to be changed. No changes are necessary on a network switch. The bonding-alb option works by using the same MAC address for the bonded NICs. Whichever NIC is transmitting, it does so under the group-assigned MAC address so that the receiving end only sees a single Layer 2 device sending to it and responds on either link without knowing the difference.

Another generic Linux bonding option is "broadcast," which isn't really bonding at all. This option merely sends all outgoing network traffic on all the NICs attached to the host. A third bonding option is balance-tlb, which is a variation on the balance-alb option that receives all incoming traffic on the same interface but load-balances outgoing traffic on its NICs by swapping the MAC address.

Failover Bonding

Failover-only bonding is essentially a hot-swap type of active-backup arrangement. If there are two NICs in a host, one of the NICs is the active NIC and the other is the backup NIC. Should the active NIC fail, the failed NIC is idled and the backup NIC becomes active and takes over.

NIC TEAMING

NIC teaming allows multiple NICs to combine into a team of interfaces that provide backup and failover insurance to each other. A server with multiple teamed NICs can withstand a connectivity loss when one NIC fails. Teaming also aggregates bandwidth so that four 1-GB NICs combine to provide 4 GB of throughput. Teaming does not combine the bandwidth of the NICs; rather, it treats the NIC team as a single large pipe with four individual channels inside of it and uses load balancing across the four interfaces to gain the advantage of their combined bandwidth.

NIC teaming has two modes: failover and load balancing with failover. The NIC team can act in the same way as failover bonding, in which one NIC is active and the other(s) is an active backup. In load balancing with failover, the operating system uses the mode configured to each NIC to distribute different forms of network traffic over the NICs in the team.

Chapter Summary

> The process of defragmentation collects fragmented files and rebuilds them into a single entity.

> Storage performance issues typically involve mechanical devices, bandwidth, the data bus, applications in use, and the level of demand on the storage system.

> Response rate is the time it takes for a disk storage system to process, access, and return requested data or to process, access, and write data from and to a hard disk drive, from start to finish.

> Rotational speed refers to how fast the media spins inside a drive. Rotational latency is the time required for the desired disk sector on a given track of a hard disk drive to rotate to a position under the read/write head. Seek time is the time required for a read/write head to travel to the track and sector where data is to be read or written. DTR relates to any process or device that moves data from one location to another; for an HDD, this is its throughput time.

> IOPS measures disk operations per second on a storage system. A baseline IOPS provides either a maximum performance expectation or a minimum acceptable performance threshold. The formula to calculate maximum IOPS follows: Average IOPS = one divided by the sum of latency and seek time. IOPS is a predictor of performance only. In RAID systems, IOPS includes a RAID write penalty.

> CPU wait time is the time a CPU is idle waiting for an event to complete.

> Bottlenecks occur in the connections between storage network services and disk structures. The actions to take to ensure storage network optimal performance are inventory, monitoring, application, and assessment.

> One area to watch for performance issues are ISLs. Two ratios that indicate a bottleneck are the fan-in and the fan-out ratios.

> In a virtual environment, implementing NPIV allows an HBA to assign virtual WWNs to individual VMs.

> The number of pending storage I/Os for a storage system is queue depth.

> Multipath I/O facilitates fault tolerance and performance improvement by providing more than one link between the server's CPU and the storage system.

> Data deduplication is a compression technique that eliminates duplicate instances of repeated data from a data store. Data compression uses encoding algorithms that store data with fewer bits than its original characters or values.

> A swap space is a reserved space on an HDD used to extend a computer's internal memory (RAM). Virtual memory is both hardware and software memory management that increases the memory allocation of a running application.

> Memory ballooning is a virtual memory management technique that frees unused memory in one VM so it can be temporarily assigned to another VM.

> I/O throttling slows down I/O memory requests during low memory conditions.

> Change control and management is more important in a virtualized environment.

> Effective change management software should include VM monitoring, enterprise monitoring, change tracking, compliance tracking, and real-time reporting. VMLM systems allow administrators to monitor and manage the implementation, delivery, operation, and maintenance of VMs throughout their lifecycle.

> There are three categories of metadata: descriptive metadata, structural metadata, and administrative metadata. Storage systems use three architectures to store metadata: centralized, distributed, and hybrid.

> There are two basic cache types: disk cache and cache memory. Disk cache shortens the time to read from or write to storage. Memory cache attempts to forego reading data from storage. There are three levels of cache memory: L1 cache, L2 cache, and L3 cache.

> NIC bonding combines two or more network adapters into a single interface. NIC teaming is link aggregation that implements load balancing and failover. There are three categories of bonding modes: switch-supported (IEEE 802.3ad), generic, and failover-only.

Key Terms

Administrative metadata

Balloon driver

Centralized metadata architecture

Data compression

Data deduplication

Data transfer rate (DTR)

Defragmentation

Descriptive metadata

Disk cache

Disk optimization

Distributed metadata architecture

EtherChannel

External transfer time

Failover

Fan-in ratio

Fan-out ratio

Full-stroke

Generic bonding

HBA queue depth

Host bus adapter (HBA)

Hybrid metadata architecture

I/O throttling

IEEE 802.3ad

Input/output operations per second (IOPS)

Internal transfer time

Inter-switch link (ISL)

L1 cache

L2 cache

L3 cache

Link aggregation

Load balancing with failover (LBFO)

Lossless compression

Lossy compression

Mapping file

Mean time between failure (MTBF)

Memory ballooning

Memory cache

Metadata

Multipath I/O

N_Port ID virtualization (NPIV)

NIC bonding

NIC teaming

Pagefile

Paging

Perfmon

RAID write penalty

Response rate

Rotational latency

Rotational speeds

Seek time

Serial ATA (SATA)

Serial Attached SCSI (SAS)

Short stroking

Structural metadata

Sustained DTR

Swap file

Swap space

System life cycle

Throughput time

Track-to-track time

Virtual memory

VM lifecycle management (VMLM)

Write-back caching

Write caching

Review Questions

1. The process that collects fragmented files and rebuilds them into a single file is _____.

2. Which of the following is not the source of performance issues with storage systems?

    a. HDD

    b. Bandwidth

    c. Applications

    d. Data content

    e. All of the above

    f. None of the above

3. True or False? Response rate refers to the time after data is written to a disk.

4. The performance metric that measures the number of disk operations a storage system completes in one second is _____.

5. What is the time metric that measures the amount of time a CPU waits for an event to complete?

    a. Ready time

    b. Cycle time

    c. Idle time

    d. Wait time

6. True or False? Memory ballooning frees low-use memory in a VM and assigns it to a VM with a higher priority.

7. When calculating IOPS for a RAID 5 system, a(n) _____ must be added to the calculation.

8. On an ISL, what configuration ratio could inadvertently be causing a communication bottleneck?

    a. Bonding

    b. Fan-in

    c. Teaming

    d. IOPS

9.   True or False? The number of pending storage I/Os for a storage system is its queue depth.

10. A reserved space on an HDD that is used to extend main memory is a(n) _____.

11. Metadata that relates to the formatting, processing, and dependencies of an object is what type of metadata?

     a. Descriptive

     b. Structural

     c. Administrative

     d. Hybrid

12. True or False? I/O throttling slows down or speeds up I/O memory requests depending on the amount of RAM available.

13. The data compression technique that eliminates duplicated instances of data from a storage system is _____.

14. What is the link aggregation technique that provides for both load balancing and failover?

     a. NIC bonding

     b. NIC teaming

     c. Multipath I/O

     d. VMLM

15. True or False? IEEE 802.3ad defines switch-supported NIC bonding.

Answers to Review Questions

1. defragmentation

2. d

3. False

4. IOPS

5. d

6. False

7. write penalty

8. b

9. True

10. swap space

11. b

12. False

13. deduplication

14. b

15. True

CHAPTER 18

Deployment

After reading this chapter and completing the exercises, you will be able to:

- Explain the testing procedures for system deployment
- Discuss the process of a vulnerability assessment
- Describe responsibilities and duties of system testing

I f you are concerned about testing the components of a cloud computing environment, virtualized environment, or both, you have made the decision to migrate some or all of your business applications, development activities, or services to a cloud environment, which likely involves a virtualized environment.

If you are testing a cloud environment, beyond verifying your decision to migrate in-house systems into the cloud, you are testing the new environment for its functionality and efficiencies. Sure, this change was primarily for its cost benefits and its ability to flex with your business needs, but the bottom line is that it must work as good as, if not better than, when the systems were in-house. The same holds true in a virtualized environment, regardless of whether it is in-house or in the cloud. This chapter identifies the test areas and the associated processes you should perform, as applicable, to ensure your new computing environment meets your needs and performs to expectations.

Components of Virtual Systems

Whether you are deploying a virtual system in an enterprise data center or in a cloud service center, it's important to know the various components of the virtual environment and what each does. Throughout this book, you have learned about virtual hardware, virtual machines (VMs), and virtual networking devices. However, you should also know about the various software components of a virtualization system. The sections that follow identify the major software components of VMware and Microsoft Hyper-V virtual environments.

VMware Virtual Systems

As shown in Figure 18-1, the VMware virtual architecture includes the following components:

> *Enterprise/cloud service network*: The consolidated resource that comprises the physical hardware and network resources on which a virtual environment installs.

> *VMware ESX Server*: The virtualization layer that runs on physical servers. It manages the virtualization of processors, memory, storage, and networking resources and their provisioning to VMs. ESX and a smaller version, ESXi, are bare-metal systems that run on physical servers without requiring an underlying operating system. In the VMware environment, ESX and ESXi are the hypervisors.

> *VMware virtual symmetric multiprocessing (SMP)*: Allows a VM to use multiple physical processors (cores) simultaneously.

> *VMware Virtual Machine File System (VMFS)*: A clustered file system for virtual machines.

> *Virtual machine (VM)*: The software abstraction of a computer (machine) that functions like a physical computer. There are two types of VMs: system VMs and process VMs. A *system VM* has the capability of running a complete operating system to create a virtual platform for running applications. A *process VM* runs only a single application using the host computer's operating system for system services. A process VM is limited to the resources allocated within the VM.

> *VMware vCenter management server*: Controls the configuration, provisioning, and management of the virtualized infrastructure. vCenter also controls the assignment of virtualized and physical resources to VMs.

> *VMware Distributed Resource Scheduler (DRS)*: Dynamically allocates and balances the available computing capacity of hardware resources for VMs.

> *VMware high availability (HA)*: Manages applications running in VMs to ensure high availability. If a physical server fails, HA automatically restarts the VMs and applications on other servers with space capacity, commonly with only a slight interruption to the end user.

> *VMware Consolidated Backup*: A centralized fast backup utility for VMs that runs on proxy servers so it doesn't affect the load on the ESX servers.

Not listed are VMware Infrastructure and VMware VSphere. These two products contain some or all of the items of the preceding list. They create and support the total virtualized environment.

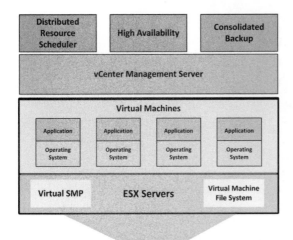
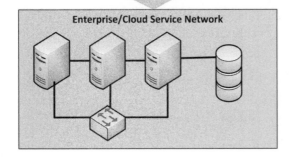

Figure 18-1 A conceptual illustration of the VMware virtualization architecture.
© 2015 Cengage Learning®.

Microsoft Hyper-V

The *Microsoft Hyper-V* architecture exists in two different versions. Hyper-V Server is a standalone system that installs on Windows Server 2012 or 2008. Hyper-V Server is a free, downloadable product. The second version is a configurable part of a Windows Server 2012, 2008, or the 64-bit version of Windows 8 Pro.

HARDWARE-ASSISTED VIRTUALIZATION

Hyper-V requires a 64-bit processor enabled with *hardware-assisted virtualization*, such as the Intel VT or the AMD-V microprocessors. x86 processors define four rings of protection that allow only software with specific privileges to execute on any one of the rings. Figure 18-2 illustrates the rings of protection. As shown, the innermost circle, Ring 0, has the highest protection and requires the highest level of program privilege to run on that ring, such as the operating system kernel. Software executing in Ring 0 is running in *system space*.

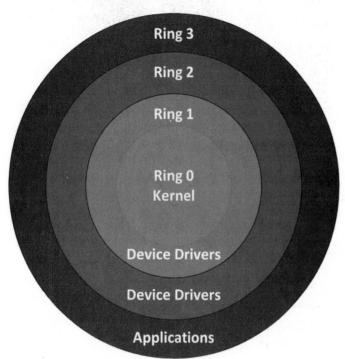

Figure 18-2 x86 microprocessor rings of protection.
© 2015 Cengage Learning®.

As the rings move away from the center, Ring 1 to Ring 3, the level of privilege declines. Ring 1 requires a higher privilege than Ring 2, which in turn requires a higher privilege than Ring 3. As indicated in Figure 18-2, the outer three rings support programs like device drivers on Rings 1 and 2 and applications on Ring 3.

The Intel VT and the AMD-V processors include instructions specifically for a hypervisor running on *Ring 0* that creates a virtual *Ring –1* (minus 1) on which a VM guest operating system can run in system space without affecting any other VMs or the host computer's operating system. Processors with hardware-assisted architecture provide nine machine code instructions that only run on Ring –1 for use by a hypervisor.

Hyper-V runs its hypervisor on Ring 0, which gives it the privileges it needs to process CPU and memory allocations for the VMs, as well as any interface tasks from administration and monitoring tools. Because the hypervisor runs in system space, the guest operating systems of the VMs must run in less privileged space, which creates an issue because operating systems expect to run in Ring 0. To resolve these issues, the hypervisor replaces any privileged functions, normally executed in Ring 0, with hypervisor calls, or *hypercalls*. The hypervisor then performs these tasks for the guest operating system.

HYPER-V ARCHITECTURE

Hyper-V is a hypervisor-centered virtualization technology that supports multiple isolated guest operating systems to share a single computer. Essentially, Hyper-V is the hypervisor and resides on a system between the physical hardware and the host operating system. Figure 18-3 shows a simplistic depiction of the Hyper-V architecture.

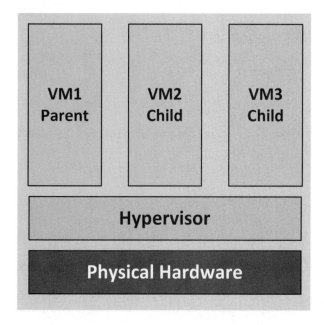

Figure 18-3 A simplified view of the Hyper-V architecture.
© 2015 Cengage Learning®.

> **Note**
>
> If you'd like to get a set of digital posters of the various architectures of Hyper-V, visit www.microsoft.com/en-us/download/details.aspx?id=40732.

Hyper-V VMs

For a guest operating system to run in a Hyper-V VM, you need to install certain services on the guest operating system. The *Hyper-V Enlightened I/O* drivers allow direct access to the Hyper-V *Virtual Machine Bus (VMBus)* virtual network adapter.

Hyper-V creates three different partition types, each of which contains separate functions and activities of the environment. Each partition has its own memory, processor resources, and device interaction policies:

> ➤ **Root partition**: This is the foundation partition of a Hyper-V installation. The *root partition* starts the hypervisor.

> ➤ **Parent partition**: The *parent partition* contains the host operating system and the software services to interact with the hypervisor and the VMs.

> ➤ **Child partition**: A *child partition* contains a VM and its virtualized operating system (guest operating system) and any applications that the VM is running.

Hyper-V has three types of VMs: hypervisor-aware, nonhypervisor-aware, and Xen-enabled Linux kernels. A *hypervisor-aware VM* has the ability to interact directly with the hypervisor for device and control functions. A *nonhypervisor-aware VM* runs older versions of Windows that did not include hypercall capabilities. A Xen-enabled Linux kernel VM runs a Linux kernel that supports virtual storage client (VSC) drivers directly, allowing it to run native and not in emulation.

Child partitions (VMs) run on top of the hypervisor, and with integration components installed, the VM can utilize Hyper-V services fully. The integration components include special Hyper-V Enlightened input/output (I/O) virtual device drivers, called synthetic drivers, and the VSC drivers. These drivers provide the VM with access to the VMBus, which is a memory bus facility that runs completely in Ring 0 mode.

VMware ESX Versus Hyper-V Hypervisor

The primary difference between these two virtualization systems is the design of their hypervisors. The VM ESX hypervisor has a monolithic design, and the Hyper-V hypervisor has a micro-kernelized design.

A *monolithic hypervisor* contains most of its control, management, and interface software on-board. For example, most of the network and disk device drivers are in the coding of the hypervisor. Because of this, the ESX hypervisor runs only on VMware-certified host operating systems that provide approved physical device drivers.

A *micro-kernelized hypervisor* is essentially a thin hypervisor that includes only the bare minimum of coding necessary to perform basic functions. Any device drivers, memory managers, and virtualized services load to the parent partition.

System Deployment Testing

Deployment testing is similar to the acceptance testing for an individual application or hardware system except that the testing is on a whole system of interacting components operating as a single environment. The key deployment testing actions that should be included in your testing procedures include the following:

- ➤ Application servers and delivery
- ➤ Bandwidth
- ➤ Latency
- ➤ Load balancing
- ➤ Replication
- ➤ Storage

Testing Applications

If you were to search the web for "application testing" or "testing applications," you'd likely find a mixture of software development testing how-to articles on testing in the cloud and some about quality testing an application in any environment. Because this book is about cloud computing and the use of virtualization in a computing environment, the application testing described in this section concerns the functional testing of an existing application migrated into a new environment.

TESTING VERSUS QUALITY CONTROL

In many organizations, and among IT professionals themselves, there is some disagreement on why testing occurs. Some say testing focuses on functionality, and others say testing focuses on quality. Testing is essentially about making sure an application, service, or hardware set functions as expected. Quality control, on the other hand, assesses the overall quality of these components, individually or as a system.

Testing is *quality control*, which involves testing the quality of an application or other system component. Therefore, the issue is really, "What is quality?" First, quality is a perception. The quality of an application is the perceived capability of the application to perform its activities to a set level of expected results. The more detailed the expectations are, the better the formed perceptions can be. This is where test strategies and test plans come into play.

Test Strategies

Although it's always better to formalize a test strategy into a written document that is formally approved by key decision-makers, the primary purpose of a *test strategy* is to outline the why, what, and how of the testing approach before actual testing begins. In other words, you need to know the reasons for the testing and its expected outcomes, the features to test, and the methods of performing the testing for each feature. A test strategy provides an overall roadmap for the testing process.

For each of the features or functions, the test strategy should set a level of testing. There are four testing levels (as illustrated in Figure 18-4):

> *Unit testing*: This level of testing focuses on the smallest unit of the tested item to isolate it from the remainder of the system. After all units of a system test successfully, the next levels of testing may proceed.

> *Integration testing*: This level of testing verifies the functional performance and reliability of an integrated set of related system components. The test plan should include simulations of shared data, inter-process communication, and input and output interfaces. After testing each integrated set successfully, tests can move on to include multiple integrated sets.

> *System testing*: As its name implies, system testing measures the capability of an entire system (all the integrated sets)—such as a virtualized system or network, a cloud service data center, or perhaps a localized network—to functionally produce the predefined expectations of its test plan. Although system testing does test the design, its focus is on the functionality and behavior of the system as a whole.

> *Acceptance testing*: This level of testing is more typically associated with software development, but it can also be included in environmental or system tests. Essentially, an acceptance test, also called a user acceptance test (UAT), attempts to replicate the "real-life" use of a product, system, or entire computing environment. Computing migrated to a cloud or virtual environment (or both) typically undergoes acceptance testing as part of system testing.

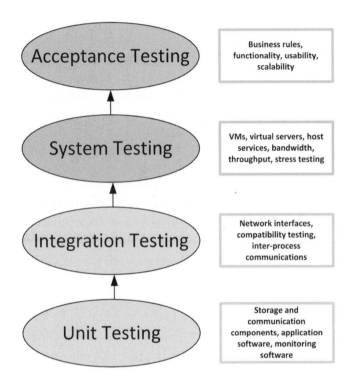

Figure 18-4 The four general levels of product and system testing.
© 2015 Cengage Learning®.

Unit and Integration Testing

It's probably easier to understand just what unit or integration testing tests from a list of the units, subsystems, or integrated sets involved in this level of testing. Some of the areas tested as either units or integrations include the following:

> *Compatibility testing*: This type of testing evaluates whether hardware or software is compatible with other hardware, software, the operating system, a virtual environment, or a network. Compatibility testing can also include tests for the compatibility with a database management system, a browser, or the available bandwidth.

> *Load testing*: This type of testing determines how a system performs under low, average, and high load conditions. The "load" could be user-initiated transactions, several high I/O applications, or peak bandwidth demands. The objective of load testing is to identify any bottlenecks that exist or performance degradations under heavier than normal loads.

> *Failover testing*: Often tied to recovery testing, failover testing tests a system's capability to continue operating if an extreme event occurs. Failover testing can also test a system's ability to add additional resources during a component or system failure or in the event of the system reaching a preset performance threshold.

> *Recovery testing*: This type of testing is often confused with reliability testing, but the two are completely different. Recovery testing measures the capability of a component, integrated set, or system to determine how fast it can recover from some form of failure or catastrophic event.

> *Reliability testing*: This type of testing measures the consistency of an application to perform the same functions repeatedly and produce the same results. Business rules or service-level commitments define the objectives for reliability testing, which can incorporate the results of other tests, such as stress testing, security testing, and network testing.

> *Scalability testing*: Scalability testing is most common when a subscriber tests a cloud service, such as Software as a Service (SaaS) or Platform as a Service (PaaS), to determine the system's capabilities to scale itself to the demands of the subscriber. This testing often combines with load testing or failover testing on local systems and private clouds.

> *Security testing*: Security testing has many levels and objectives. Its overall purpose is to identify security flaws and vulnerabilities in an application or system that may defeat the defined security policies of an organization. Security testing attempts to validate the confidentiality, integrity, authentication, and authorization of an application or a system. Various testing methods are associated with security testing, including vulnerability scans and assessments and penetration tests.

> *Stress testing*: The objective of stress testing is to determine if defined specifications are met, what the safe usage limits are, and what potential failure points of a system or application exist.

> *Volume testing*: This type of testing, although related to stress testing, load testing, and scalability testing, measures the capability of an application or system to function under a set amount of data. The "amount of data" in volume testing may be the size of a database, the limits of a log file or transaction tank, or a measurement of the input/output (I/O) demands.

TEST RISKS

In any testing procedure, there are often unforeseen risks or conditions that can undermine the validity of the test. Nearly all these risks are controllable, but each requires special attention to mitigate its impact on the test results. The four major areas of risk to a testing procedure include the following:

> **Requirements**: If the overall requirements, design, layout, or specifications of a system are not clear, it can be ambiguous as to exactly what a testing procedure verifies. Any misunderstanding between the organization's business rules and the design or execution of computing systems can be fatal and costly.

> **Resources**: If the required levels of human, technical, and internal or external resources aren't available during the testing process, portions of a test may not be possible. If documentation is also involved in the testing, and it should be, not having the resources to interpret, modify, or create the documentation may create confusion or misconceptions down the line.

> **Quality**: The objective of the testing procedure must be to verify the quality of the item under test or identify any defects or flaws that detract from its quality for further development, design, or study. All aspects of a testing procedure must focus on the quality of the testing.

> **Scheduling**: Depending on the scope of the test plan or the item under test, allowing sufficient time to complete the entire test, plus any retests, is a must. Unrealistic testing schedules, which don't address the availability of the components in the test—human, technical, or otherwise—can doom a test before it really gets started.

Cloud Testing

The driving force behind the testing of a cloud service, regardless of whether you are the provider or the subscriber, is the *Service Level Agreement (SLA)*. An SLA is a formal agreement document that spells out in specific terms, metrics, and quantities (and on occasion qualities) what a service delivered to a customer provides. To the provider, the SLA is a commitment of the service that a customer can expect. To the subscriber, the SLA is the quantification of the performance levels expected and purchased. In either perspective, the SLA defines the contractual agreement between the two parties.

The commitments of an SLA must be measurable by either party, but the SLA typically assigns this responsibility to one party or the other. Regardless of who is measuring performance, it's the responsibility of the provider to ensure the delivery of the SLA's performance metrics. To this end, the testing and management of the cloud environment must be a continuous operation for the provider.

SERVICE AVAILABILITY

Cloud service subscribers want high availability, meaning they want anytime, anywhere access to their subscribed services, applications, data, and platforms. To the subscriber, reliability is part and parcel with availability, which means the expectation is for true high availability—services that are available 24/7 and are never (okay, rarely) offline, as indicated in the SLA with lots of nines. Table 18-1 lists the various availability levels expressed in the "nines." The "nines" is a common quantification of the level of availability of a system or service. Understand that availability and "uptime" are not the same. A service can be up but unavailable because of a network failure.

Table 18-1 Percentages of Availability

Availability	Downtime/Year %	Downtime/Year Time
90.0 % (1 nine)	10%	36.5 days, 72 hours
99.0% (2 nines)	1%	3.65 days, 7.2 hours
99.9% (3 nines)	0.1%	8.76 hours
99.99% (4 nines)	0.01%	52.56 minutes
99.999% (5 nines)	0.001%	5.26 minutes
99.9999% (6 nines)	0.0001%	31.5 seconds
99.99999% (7 nines)	0.00001%	3.15 seconds

The number of nines in an availability metric can also designate an *availability class*. For example, a service that commits to "4 nines" is also offering Class 4 availability. Your electrical utility company likely offers Class 3 or 4 service. The service availability level in an SLA must be realistic. Only a service provider who never has to take down a system for maintenance, expansion, or updating and never suffers weather or disaster-related events may be able to offer service availability levels above "4 nines." Customers want more nines, of course, but they must also be realistic in their demands because more nines cost more money.

A major consideration for a service provider is the communication links between its data center and the subscriber and the role they play in service availability. If the service provider is able to assure the availability of its data center systems, its testing focus must then be on the communication links. If the service provider subscribes its communication lines from a long-haul communication company, it too is subject to an SLA, which must factor into the service provider's availability commitment. In addition to periodic testing for service assurance, service monitoring must be a part of the test plan.

CLOUD TESTING LAYERS

To ensure a new service center is functioning at SLA standards or to maintain services at the SLA standards, a cloud service provider needs to run regular periodical tests on four layers of its operation:

> ➤ **Communications**: The data communications services between the service center and subscribers, typically the wide area network (WAN) communications links, are the foundation of service availability and assurance. Redundant paths should be available and regular testing performed on all communication services for bandwidth, availability, and efficiency.

> ➤ **Infrastructure**: Test the servers, the VMs, the shells, and the network connecting to data storage systems regularly to ensure service availability (uptime) and efficiency.

> ➤ **Monitoring**: Cross-check the configuration, metrics, thresholds, and functions of monitoring systems regularly to ensure that reported results are accurate and give a true picture of system performance.

> ➤ **Availability**: Frequently measure system uptime and availability against SLA commitments to ensure the system is performing within established service-level thresholds.

Software tools are available, some free and some for purchase, that combine the functions of performance monitoring, threshold reporting and alerts, and graphical imaging for performance metrics. Figure 18-5 shows a screen capture from the Soasta CloudTest software. This software integrates monitoring, reporting, and testing into a single software tool.

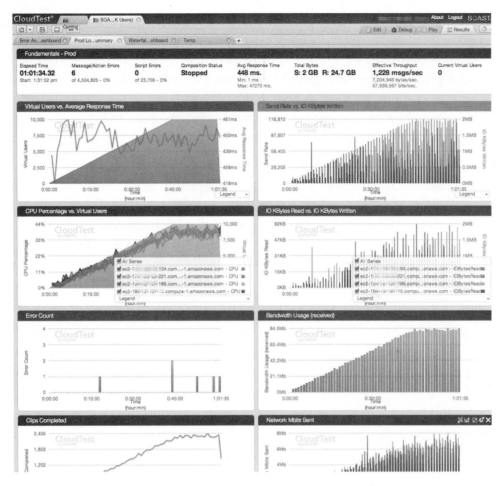

Figure 18-5 The Soasta CloudTest software displays network and system performance metrics.
© 2014 Soasta.

END-TO-END TESTING

Depending on the SLA commitments of a cloud service provider, downtime can be a disaster to the service provider and its subscribers. Availability of the subscribed services must be the highest priority of a cloud service provider. Availability doesn't just mean that subscribers are able to reach the service over a WAN connection; it also means that the actual subscribed computing services are available and functioning properly. Ensuring end-to-end availability of the cloud service regular testing is essential.

End-to-end testing involves connectivity testing, including latency testing, network monitoring, and the monitoring of the key computing services including data storage system performance, and, if virtualization is implemented, the configuration of VMs and virtual network devices.

Latency can be the boon or the bane of a cloud service. Too much latency in the end-to-end performance of a cloud service undermines the perceived "quality" of the service overall. *Latency* is an element of throughput and turnaround time seen by subscribers. The capability for a cloud service to perform as if it were a local service for subscribers is what attracts and retains cloud service customers. Therefore, reducing latency from the end-to-end performance of a cloud service must be a constant goal for the service provider.

Because cloud service providers rarely own the WAN services used to connect subscribers to their data centers, they must take it on themselves to test and measure network performance. Service providers really don't have much influence over the communication lines in the cloud; they do have control over the links that connect their operations to the communication infrastructure. This connection is, in the jargon of the communications world, the "last mile." Using network monitoring and analysis tools in the service center, a cloud service provider can measure WAN performance. This information can determine where the service provider must compensate for the performance of the WAN by lowering its SLA throughput commitments or improving communication performance within the service center.

To ensure *end-to-end availability*, both the cloud service provider and the cloud service subscriber have responsibilities, and the SLA should spell out the responsibilities of each party. Figure 18-6 shows the monitoring and test points that each party should monitor within the areas under each party's control. The "M" symbols in Figure 18-6 show each of the network and system points for monitoring and testing.

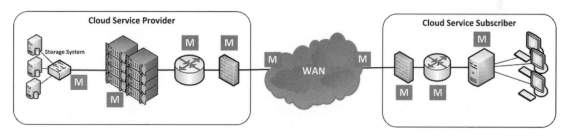

Figure 18-6 The monitoring and testing points, indicated with an "M" symbol, that end-to-end testing should include.

© 2015 Cengage Learning®.

Figure 18-6 shows within the data center of the cloud service provider that there are at least four monitoring and testing points. The first two points are where the internal network connects with the WAN, indicated in the figure at a firewall or a router. The third point is on the physical and virtual servers, if applicable, to measure both in-bound and out-bound traffic, memory usage, and I/O volumes. The final point is on the storage system servers or switches to measure latency and I/O volumes. If possible, network monitoring on the WAN should measure for network latency. For the cloud service subscriber, the measurement points are essentially the same. A storage system isn't in the figure, but, if present, its measurement is also important.

QUALITY OF SERVICE TESTING

Quality of Service (QoS) is a general term that measures the performance of a computing system quantitatively to established performance metrics. Although QoS may sound much like an SLA, it's common that an SLA will quote a QoS level of performance. In other words, the SLA commits to providing a specified QoS. However, the judges of QoS are always the end users. Although QoS is commonly associated with communications, it can include cloud services as well.

In a cloud service environment, QoS is the combined quantitative measurements of many interrelated components of the overall service. The service components typically included as part of QoS include bandwidth, throughput, transmission latency, availability, and transmission error rates.

The testing, monitoring, and measurement of the key throughput and availability elements of a cloud system provide the metrics to determine the QoS. Figure 18-7 shows the start-up screen for the SolarWinds Orion network monitoring application, which is an example of the network performance monitoring systems available.

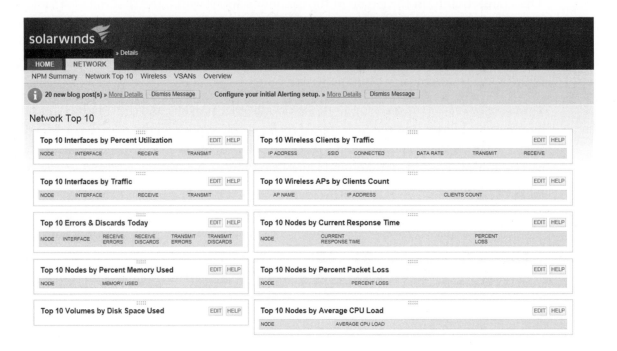

Figure 18-7 The Network Top 10 page of the SolarWinds Orion network monitoring software.
Source: SolarWinds Worldwide, LLC.

Virtual System Monitoring

Most cloud service providers' infrastructures incorporate virtualization, which allows the service center to support multiple SaaS and PaaS services on less physical hardware than would otherwise be necessary. Virtualization provides increased efficiency by lowering the operating costs of equipment, staff, facilities, and utilities.

Cloud service providers must monitor the throughput performance of the physical and virtual networks. Specialized virtual environment performance monitoring software and hardware appliances can measure the QoS and SLA metrics on virtual applications, VMs, virtual servers, and virtual networking devices, as well as their interactions with storage and backup systems.

A variety of virtual server, VM, and network monitoring software is available to allow the tracking of the performance of the components in the virtual system. Figure 18-8 shows the dashboard of the Zabbix 2.2 monitoring system, which is representative of the monitoring tools available.

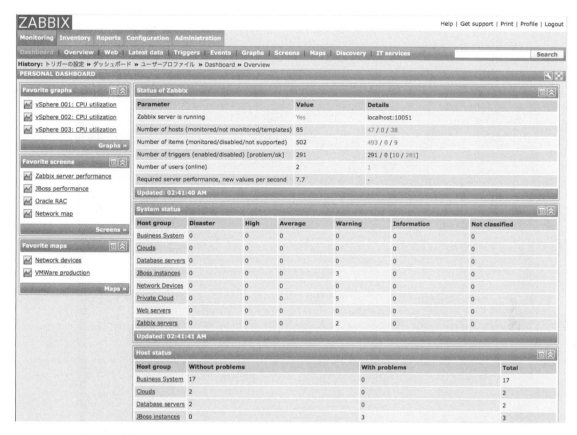

Figure 18-8 The Dashboard window of the Zabbix 2.2 monitoring system.
Source: Zabbix SIA.

PENETRATION TESTING

Even after all the testing, monitoring, and configuration of the internal computing environment, there is still an important system feature that requires constant verification: security. Cloud service providers and large enterprise data centers are prime targets to those individuals who would attempt to penetrate the security of large or data-rich targets. To protect data center operations and either the enterprise's or a customer's data assets, you or a third-party "white hat" service should perform penetration testing on the system on a regular basis.

Penetration testing simulates an attack on a system or network with the purpose of identifying any security weaknesses or vulnerabilities that hackers could exploit to gain access to resources or to corrupt or crash the system. There are two approaches to penetration testing: white box and black box.

White box ("friendly") penetration testing has all the information it needs, including all background and system information, to attempt to penetrate access, authentication, authorization, and manipulation controls. *Black box* ("unfriendly") penetration testing has no information about the organization, except maybe its name, which attempts to simulate a brute-force attack by a hacker. In either case, the testing identifies any vulnerabilities found, the security measures defeated, and the security measures that withstood the attack.

There are several penetration testing software tools available, although they range in capabilities from attempting to bypass passwords to full vulnerability identification testing. An example of a full-service penetration testing software tool is Nessus from Tenable Network Security. Figure 18-9 shows the vulnerability results screen in Nessus.

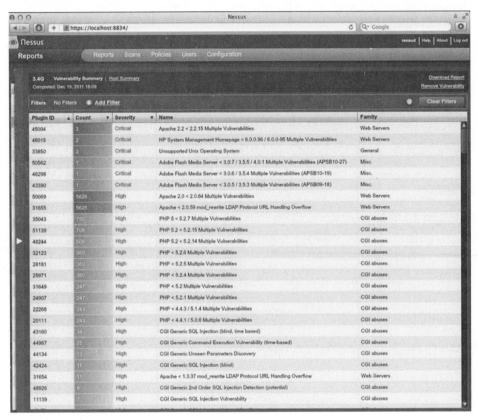

Figure 18-9 The Vulnerability Summary screen of the Nessus penetration testing system.
Source: Tenable Network Security®.

VULNERABILITY ASSESSMENT

A *vulnerability assessment* is similar to penetration testing but goes beyond the penetration test to identify, quantify, and prioritize or rank any vulnerability found in an IT system. In addition, a vulnerability assessment (also vulnerability analysis) evaluates the effectiveness of existing security measures. A full vulnerability assessment goes beyond running a vulnerability scanning software tool and includes human analysis of the identified vulnerabilities and their associated risks.

A vulnerability assessment has three major steps, as illustrated in Figure 18-10, which are to perform a vulnerability assessment, identify where vulnerabilities exist, and mitigate or at least address the identified vulnerabilities. A vulnerability assessment captures only a single point-in-time for a system, so as shown in Figure 18-10, this should be a continuous process. Even the smallest change in the hardware or software of a system can expose new vulnerabilities.

A few of the better penetration testing software tools also perform vulnerability assessments. However, on individual computers or in small to medium data centers, there are free downloadable tools that can be effective enough, such as the Microsoft Baseline Security Analyzer, shown in Figure 18-11.

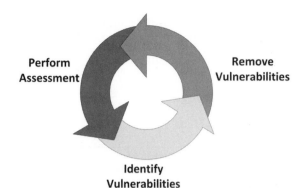

Figure 18-10 The vulnerability assessment process is a continuous activity.
© 2015 Cengage Learning®.

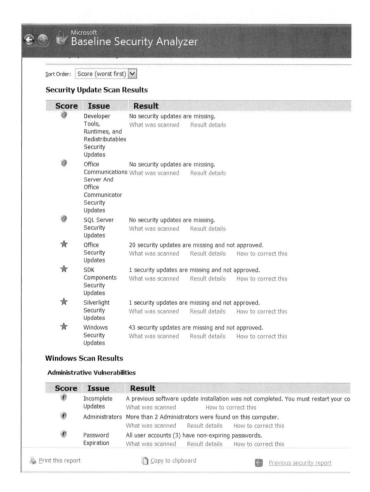

Figure 18-11 The scan results window of the Microsoft Baseline Security Analyzer.
Used with permission from Microsoft.

Separation of Duties

Although considered more of a network security requirement, *separation of duties* in system and network testing can ensure that the decisions made concerning the relative health and stability of a cloud service or data center are facts. A separation of duties is an auditing control that directs an organization to separate the tasks in a process to two or more individuals. For example, the purchasing agent of a company shouldn't also be the person who pays the bills. The opportunity for theft and fraud is too great in that situation. Too many instances at too many companies have led to the requirement that any tasks that affect the monetary flows of a company should be separate and performed by different individuals.

In a large data center or a cloud service provider, the person monitoring the performance of the network, virtual system, or storage system, for example, should not be the person making tactical or strategic decisions regarding the results. In fact, in larger installations, the person monitoring the software should be a different person from time to time.

Chapter Summary

> The VMware virtual architecture includes the following components: ESX Server, Virtual SMP, VMFS, vCenter Management Server, DRS, HA, and Consolidated Backup.

> The Microsoft Hyper-V architecture exists in two versions. Hyper-V Server and a configurable role in Windows Server 2012, 2008, or the 64-bit version of Windows 8 Pro.

> Hyper-V requires a 64-bit processor with hardware-assisted virtualization.

> Software executing in Ring 0 is running in system space. Ring 1 has higher privilege than Ring 2, which has higher privilege than Ring 3. Device drivers run on Rings 1 and 2 and applications on Ring 3.

> Hyper-V runs its hypervisor on Ring 0.

> Hyper-V has three partition types: root partition, parent partition, and child partition.

> Hyper-V has three types of VMs: hypervisor-aware, nonhypervisor-aware, and Xen-enabled Linux kernels.

> The VMware ESX hypervisor is monolithic, and Hyper-V hypervisor is micro-kernelized.

> The deployment testing actions included in procedures include application servers and delivery, bandwidth, latency, load balancing, replication, and storage.

> Quality control assesses the overall quality of these components, individually or as a system.

> The purpose of a test strategy is to provide an overall roadmap for the testing process.

> The four testing levels are unit testing, integration testing, system testing, and acceptance testing. The areas tested include compatibility testing, load testing, failover testing, recovery testing, reliability testing, scalability testing, security testing, stress testing, and volume testing.

> The major risk areas in a testing procedure are requirements, resources, quality, and scheduling.

> An SLA is a formal agreement document that details the metrics, quantities, and qualities that a service will provide.

> Cloud service subscribers expect high availability typically expressed as availability classes in an SLA.

> A cloud service provider should run regular periodical tests on communications, infrastructure, monitoring, and availability.

> End-to-end testing includes connectivity testing, latency testing, network monitoring, and the data storage system.

> QoS measures the performance of a computing system quantitatively to establish performance metrics.

> Penetration testing simulates an attack on a system or network with the purpose of identifying any security weaknesses or vulnerabilities that hackers could exploit. White box penetration testing has all the information it needs to penetrate access, authentication, authorization, and manipulation controls. Black box penetration testing has no information about the organization, except maybe its name.

> A vulnerability assessment identifies, quantifies, and prioritizes any vulnerability found in an IT system.

> Separation of duties is an auditing control that separates the tasks in a process to two or more individuals.

Key Terms

Acceptance testing

Availability class

Black box

Child partition

Compatibility testing

End-to-end availability

End-to-end testing

Enterprise/cloud service network

Failover testing

Hardware-assisted virtualization

Hypercalls

Hyper-V Enlightened I/O

Hypervisor-aware VM

Integration testing

Latency

Load testing

Micro-kernelized hypervisor

Microsoft Hyper-V

Monolithic hypervisor

Nonhypervisor-aware VM

Parent partition

Penetration testing

Process VM

Quality control

Quality of Service (QoS)

Recovery testing

Reliability testing

Ring 0

Ring −1

Root partition

Scalability testing

Security testing

Separation of duties

Service Level Agreement (SLA)

Stress testing

System space

System testing

System VM

Test strategy

Unit testing

Virtual machine (VM)

Virtual Machine Bus (VMBus)

VMware Consolidated Backup

VMware Distributed Resource Scheduler (DRS)

VMware ESX Server

VMware high availability (HA)

VMware vCenter management server

VMware Virtual Machine File System (VMFS)

VMware virtual symmetric multiprocessing (SMP)

Volume testing

Vulnerability assessment

White box

Review Questions

1. Hyper-V requires a _____-bit processor.

2. True or False? The Hyper-V hypervisor runs on Ring 3.

3. Not more than how much downtime is indicated by a "four-nines" availability commitment for a year?

   a. 36.5 days

   b. 8.76 hours

   c. 52.56 minutes

   d. 31.5 seconds

4. The VMware ESX hypervisor is a(n) _____ hypervisor.

5. True or False? QoS measures the performance of a computing system quantitatively and compares it to established or committed performance metrics.

6. When an organization assigns the responsibilities of a test procedure to different individuals, it is practicing

   a. Load balancing

   b. Quality control

   c. Vulnerability assessment

   d. Separation of duties

7. Software running in Ring 0 is running in _____ space.

8. True or False? Xen-enabled Linux kernels are a type of Hyper-V VM.

9. Device drivers on an SMP microprocessor system execute on what processor ring(s)?

   a. Ring 0

   b. Ring –1

   c. Rings 1 and 2

   d. Rings 2 and 3

   e. Ring 3 only

10. A(n) _____ is a formal agreement that details the metrics, quantities, and qualities a service will provide to a customer.

11. True or False? The host operating system runs in a child partition on a Hyper-V system.

12. What is the process an organization performs to identify and secure any possible points of exploitation in its systems?

    a. Vulnerability assessment

    b. Penetration testing

    c. Deployment testing

    d. High availability

13. _____ testing includes connectivity testing, latency testing, and network monitoring.

14. True or False? A test strategy provides an overall roadmap for a testing process.

15. Which of the following is not a general testing level?

    a. Unit testing

    b. Integration testing

    c. Environmental testing

    d. Acceptance testing

Answers to Review Questions

1. 64

2. False

3. c

4. monolithic

5. True

6. d

7. system

8. True

9. c

10. SLA or Service Level Agreement

11. False

12. a

13. End-to-end

14 True

15. c

CHAPTER 19

Availability and Disaster Recovery

After reading this chapter and completing the exercises, you will be able to:

- List the solutions available to meet availability requirements

- Discuss the various methods of fault tolerance

- Explain disaster recovery concepts and terminology

- Describe the disaster recovery methods

The key to success as a cloud service provider is availability, meaning that the systems subscribers have contracted for are available and working, as they should, whenever the subscriber wants to use them. In this chapter, you learn the ways to keep a system available in the face of system or component failures, as well as in the event of both natural and man-made disasters.

Availability

In the general sense, *availability* simply means that a system, service, communications link, or device will work properly when it is required. However, availability isn't typically the concern; it's *downtime*. Users, customers, and system administrators all want the same thing—to have computer systems always available with absolutely no unplanned downtime.

There are myriad causes for downtime. Some are trivial to the information technology (IT) folks but important to a user who enters the wrong Uniform Resource Locator (URL). Others may be incidental, like a short-term power outage. Still other causes can be mysterious, at least until you learn of the "backhoe fade" caused by someone digging up the fiber-optic cable connecting you to the Internet. In addition, some causes can be catastrophic, such as a hurricane or tornado striking the data center directly, which you'll learn about in the second half of this chapter.

Causes for System Failure

An enterprise data center or a cloud service provider is a complex system of interrelated hardware and software. As the complexity of these systems continues to increase, so does the threat of a single device or software application failing and causing a chain reaction to bring down the system.

For example, if you look at the risks associated with integrating the Internet and web into a system, such as is the case with a cloud service provider, there are numerous *failure points*, some of which include other failure points. Some of the more common Internet failure points are:

> **End user**: The end user enters the wrong URL; the end user's computer has a virus; or the end user's Internet service provider (ISP) connection is down.

> **Internet service**: The Internet service provider (ISP) cannot connect the end user to the Internet; the Domain Name System (DNS) is not working; the domain name is incorrect; or there is a routing failure point on the Internet.

> **Service provider**: There's a bad connection between the Internet and the service provider's web server; the server is down; or the website or user interface is corrupted or has errors.

Regardless of which of these areas are causing a problem, the end user sees it as the system being unavailable. What's that, you say? "Some of these problems are beyond the service provider's responsibility." Technically, you're right, but remember that to customers and users, IT services can never be too available. There are literally dozens, if not hundreds, of reasons why a service may not be available end to end; and, no, the service provider isn't normally held responsible for anything before the service data center's point of demarcation (where the Internet connects to the data center).

So, what's the answer? Availability. How do you ensure that? Read on.

Fault Tolerance

Other than scheduled downtime (typically excluded from Service Level Agreement [SLA] downtime), a primary cause for a system, network, or device to be unavailable is a system fault of one kind or another. This is especially true of the physical devices in the system or network; after all, they are mostly mechanical machinery with moving parts, heat-sensitive circuits, or electrical components.

The key to availability in this environment is to build up the system or network's *fault tolerance*, meaning its capability to withstand almost any kind of component, device, or system failure. A *fault-tolerant* computer, storage device, or networking device is able to continue operating to a defined level of function even after a fault or failure occurs. Understand that a "defined level of function" can mean the failed device or system continues to be available, but it can also mean that the failed component coasts to a stop without crashing, or it can be something in between these extremes.

> **Note**
>
> One class of failure condition often supersedes fault tolerance—catastrophic and disastrous natural phenomena, such as hurricanes and typhoons, tornadoes, fires, and tsunamis. Any of these conditions requires a disaster recovery plan.

HARDWARE FAULT TOLERANCE

Fault tolerance allows a system to continue processing, or at minimum close itself down, in a normal manner in the event of a failure in one or more of its components. Fault tolerance is a desired system design feature that describes computer systems able to continue operating in the event of a partial failure. An example is the small emergency-only spare tire in many cars, which allows you to continue on your trip, but at a much lower recommended speed. Because of its spare tire, your car is fault tolerant to tire failure (at least one at a time, anyway).

Hardware fault tolerance depends on fault detection procedures. Before you (or the system) can apply fault tolerance recovery, you need to know the nature of the fault. When a fault occurs, the following information is necessary to start recovery actions.

> ➤ **Fault identification**: When a failure occurs, the system must be able to identify the source of the hardware fault. The National Institute for Standards and Technology (NIST) identifies four identifying factors for fault detection:
>
> **Locality**: Where in the system does the fault occur, and what other components does the fault affect?
>
> **Cause**: What is the root cause of the fault? Power? Mechanical Failure? Volume?
>
> **Duration**: Has the fault persisted without relief? Or has it been regularly intermittent over a set period? Or did it occur once and never repeat?
>
> **Effect**: If not removed from the system, what effect could the fault have on the availability of its subsystem or the overall system?

Fault identification can be a manual process, meaning a human does it using the information at hand, but there are fault detection software tools available for which you define the thresholds or conditions of fault identification. Actually, this capability is built in to several of the system performance monitors discussed in Chapter 18.

> **Fault isolation**: Once you identify the root cause of a failure, it's best to isolate the failing component from the rest of the system to avoid causing a chain reaction of failures.

> **Fault containment**: In some cases, an entire subsystem must be isolated from the system to contain the effect of the failure. However, it's always better for overall system availability to separate the single component that fails, if that truly is the case.

Fault Recovery

There are several types of hardware fault detection and recovery. Static recovery and dynamic recovery are the most common, but there is also a hybrid method and those recovery schemes that employ replication.

Static Recovery *Static hardware recovery*, also called *passive fault tolerance*, uses *fault masking* to mitigate the occurrence of a fault by hiding the fault from the system. Typically, there is no action required by the system itself, because the fault tolerance technology in a device or its controller generally handles the issue.

Within a set of redundant identical devices, each of the devices processes the same instructions or functions and provides its results to a "voter," as Figure 19-1 illustrates. The *voter* compares the results from all the devices and votes on which of the results is the assumed correct result. The voter compares the results produced by the majority of the devices to any different results and assumes the majority result to be valid. Only the "correct" response goes back to the system or requestor. This action covers up or masks the fact that one of the devices had an error or fault.

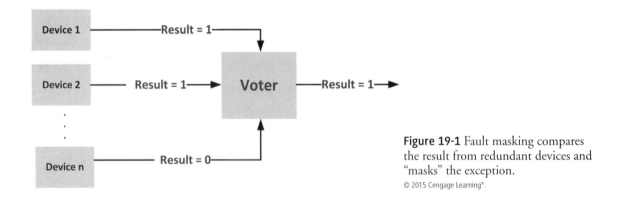

Figure 19-1 Fault masking compares the result from redundant devices and "masks" the exception.
© 2015 Cengage Learning®.

The illustration in Figure 19-1 also illustrates a process called *triple modular redundancy (TMR)*, if the redundant set of devices is held to three. However, as indicated in the figure, three is not a limit and there can be "n" devices in a modular redundancy. As is the case with the fault-masking example above, TMR uses the result of all three devices in agreement or two of the three devices in agreement. The downside to TMR is that if two of the devices produce an error, the error is the result forwarded.

Hardware Versus Software Voting The decision of whether to use *hardware voting* or *software voting* depends on several factors. These factors are:

> **Processor**: Does the processor have the capability to perform voting?

> **Voting speed**: Voting adds overhead to any process, regardless of the method. Hardware voting is faster, but you need to add hardware for it. Software voting is slower but avoids the need for additional hardware.

> **Flexibility**: Will the voting method chosen support future changes to the system?

> **Environment**: If space or power consumption is a major issue, software voting may have an advantage over hardware voting.

Dynamic Recovery *Dynamic fault recovery*, also called *active fault tolerance*, uses detection and diagnostics to identify a fault and affect a recovery. Its detection and recovery methods apply fault identification, fault location, and fault recovery actions to maintain a fault-tolerant system. Dynamic recovery must apply specific mechanisms to detect a fault, replace the faulty component, and either roll back or roll forward the associated data. Dynamic recovery is common in high-performance systems, like a cloud service provider, where the active components are in maximum use. However, dynamic recovery can cause slowdowns in throughput and processing speeds during a recovery. Figure 19-2 (a) depicts a local area network (LAN) with redundancy in switches and routers. Each of the workstation groups connects primarily to one switch with an inactive secondary link to the other switch. For example, the upper workgroup in section a (top) has an active connection to Switch 1 with a secondary link to Switch 2. Switch 1 connects to Router 1, with a secondary link to Router 2, and so on.

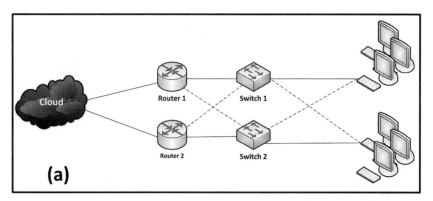

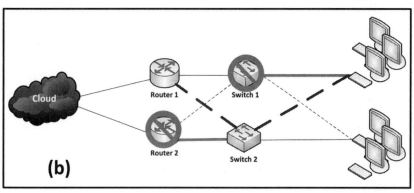

Figure 19-2 Before (a) and after (b) images of a network with redundancy in its networking devices.

© 2015 Cengage Learning®.

Figure 19-2 (b) depicts the situation on this network in which both a switch (Switch 1) and a router (Router 2) have failed. The redundancy configured into the system alerts the workstations to connect to the active switch, and the active switch enables the now active link to the active router.

Hybrid Recovery A *hybrid fault tolerance* incorporates both the static and the dynamic fault recovery techniques. The hybrid method uses fault masking until it can complete its fault diagnostics and then move the redundant components into the active role. This method is perhaps the most reliable, but it is also the most expensive.

Failover and Failback Two concepts that apply to both static and dynamic recovery techniques are failover and failback. *Failover* is the action of a redundant device taking over for a failing device. Typically, the two devices connect with a *heartbeat cable*, which synchronizes the two devices through a regularly transmitted signal. Should the redundant device, based on an algorithm to determine an unacceptable interval, not receive the signal, the redundant device comes online and begins processing. The devices could be hard disk drives, servers, switches, or routers. Failback is the reverse of failover. *Failback* is the process that restores the primary device to operations after a failover action removes the primary device from operations.

Replication *Replication* is a fault-tolerant approach that incorporates several identification and recovery methods. Multiple instances of the same system process tasks or requests in parallel, and a voter chooses the forwarded response or result based on the most common response from the system's devices or processes, which is a voting process. Replication also involves redundancy, in that with multiple instances of the same devices running in parallel, one could fail and the others could continue processing.

Fault-Tolerant Design

If all the hardware in a data center and network could be fault tolerant, the ultimate in high availability, at least from the hardware perspective, would be possible. However, it isn't always economically prudent or even possible to provide this level of fault tolerance. Therefore, you must make choices when designing a fault-tolerant system.

Achieving fault tolerance in a system requires the anticipation of all or at least most of the potential failure events that could happen to the system, components, and environment. After you've identified the most-likely-to-fail and the most-costly-to-lose components, you should decide on the most efficient way to prevent, remediate, or work around each of the failures identified. The decision may be to put fault tolerance in place on only the top most damaging failures because they best satisfy the needs of the organization and are worth their investment. Is a stereo system in a car a better investment than airbags and seatbelts?

The single most important design consideration in a fault-tolerant system is the elimination of as many *single points of failure* as possible. The objective is that when a component failure occurs, the system must continue to operate as normally as possible until a permanent repair is affected. Although there are several recommended approaches to achieving fault tolerance, the most common approach is redundancy.

Redundancy

Redundancy simply means that a system has components installed that are not required for the system to function normally. Figure 19-2 (a) shows redundant equipment in a network. The network shown in the figure could certainly operate with only one pair of router and switch.

There are two types of redundancy: *space redundancy* and *time redundancy*. However, in the context of hardware fault tolerance, the focus is on space redundancy. Adding extra devices, functions, and storage space, including the possible duplication of data to a system, creates space redundancy. Space redundancy consists of extra resources in a system that would be unnecessary if the system were completely fault free. Space redundancy consists of hardware redundancy, software redundancy, and data or information redundancy.

One form of space redundancy is *standby sparing*. In this method, as illustrated in Figure 19-2, one component is operational and one (or more) identical components are standbys (spares). When a detected, identified, and located fault occurs, a standby component replaces the faulty operational module. In hot standby sparing, the standby component operates synchronously with the operational component and can go into service immediately. Hot standby sparing is better for environments in which any reconfiguration time must be minimal.

In *cold standby sparing*, the standby components are idle, and perhaps without power. When a fault occurs, a cold standby component replaces the faulty component. Obviously, cold standby sparing typically requires some downtime. Cold standby sparing is more appropriate where power consumption is an issue.

Time redundancy is more about ensuring the correctness of an action. Time redundancy involves the repetition of every action, such as a computation or a data transmission, and comparing the results of the repeated action to a stored copy of the original action. If the two results differ, the action repeats. The administrator's configuration settings determine how long this goes on before the system issues an alert.

Component Diversity

When it was first implemented into systems, *component diversity* was an attempt to reduce faults in software applications. Since then, this approach to fault tolerance has become a hardware fault tolerance method as well. The basic concept of component diversity is to have two (or more) teams develop the same application and run them in parallel. Should a processing error occur (due to a programming or specification error), the other application version is put into service. This concept assumes that the two teams, working independently, would not create the same errors.

In a hardware fault tolerance usage, this approach calls for the installation of two identical systems, each using different manufacturers, vendors, brands, or models, along with two versions of the software (in-house versus licensed or two licensed packages from different vendors) on two redundant channels. Obviously, this is an expensive approach to fault tolerance and is rare in computing. However, depending on the criticality of a system and its resources, the cost may not be the primary consideration.

SOFTWARE FAULT TOLERANCE

The approaches to creating fault tolerance in software are similar to those applied in hardware fault tolerance, in that they are primarily static and dynamic redundancy and recovery methods. Software fault tolerance is more about avoiding programming errors through real-time redundancy or standby subprograms or modules that replace all or part of a program that crashes. The two primary fault tolerance approaches for software are N-version programming and recovery blocks (RBs).

N-Version Programming

N-version programming (NVP) is a static fault-masking form of fault tolerance that is similar in concept to the TMR approach, but typically with only two modules. This approach is *dual modular redundancy (DMR)*. NVP involves two (or more) independent versions of an application running concurrently and performing the same functions to produce the same output. A voter checkpoint with the capability to identify and reject faulty versions while identifying and passing along good versions votes on their outputs. Figure 19-3 illustrates this model.

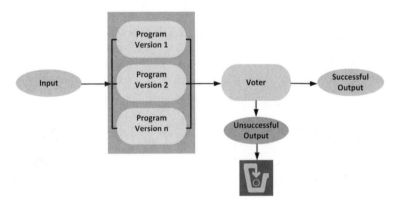

Figure 19-3 In NVP software fault tolerance, multiple versions of a program or program block execute the same actions. A voter adjudicates the results, passing along the successful result.
© 2015 Cengage Learning®.

Note

You've learned about TMR and now DMR as approaches to hardware and software redundancy and fault recovery. There is an overriding concept called n-Modular Redundancy (NMR), in which "n" represents any integer number of components, programs, or modules included in the setup.

NVP incorporates component diversity concepts. Two independently developed versions of a software system, commonly written in different programming languages, run concurrently. Each program produces a set of vectors or indicators that help the voter determine the faulty/not-faulty decision. These indicators include comparison vectors (c-vectors), comparison status indicators (cs-indicators), crosscheck points (cc-points), a comparison algorithm, and a set of responses to the entity performing the comparison.

At design-specified points in each program, built-in coding passes control of the programs to an *N-version execution environment (NVX)*, which compare the vectors and indicators of each program.

Recovery Blocks

The *recovery blocks (RB)* approach to software fault tolerance is a dynamic fault recovery model that uses redundant programming blocks or modules to replace faulty blocks in a program. The RB approach divides executable programming into blocks of coding. After each block executes, RB performs an acceptance test of the results of that block. If the acceptance test fails, a redundant block of programming associated with the failed block executes in its place.

RD requires at least one other version of a programming block to be available to perform the same functions and produce the same output. The backup or standby modules, when there is more than one, are secondary. The secondary modules are only there when the primary module's output is unacceptable. After the primary module executes, an acceptance test determines if the output is reasonable. Don't think of a report as the output of a module; it could very well be a hash total, a checksum, or the like. If the output is not acceptable, meaning that it's not within a range of acceptable values or has not changed within an allowed rate of change, a secondary module reprocesses the inputs to produce its output, and the process repeats. If all the secondary modules available produce the same result, the RB process generates a fault alert and the system halts.

High Availability

High availability (HA) is the desired condition of a system or component to be operational without fault or maintenance for an extended length of time. The ultimate uptime for a highly available component or system is 100 percent, but most data center or cloud service operators understand the difficulty in achieving that virtually impossible goal. Most administrators accept a slightly lower standard for HA, settling on a "five 9s" or "four 9s" percentage of availability.

To achieve any definition of HA, the design and implementation of the data center must include fault prevention and detection, redundancy, and a backup or failover scheme. For example, the inclusion of a Redundant Array of Independent Disks (RAID) or a storage area network (SAN) for the storage system can add to the availability of the system.

RELIABILITY, AVAILABILITY, AND SERVICEABILITY

Reliability, availability, and serviceability (RAS) is a computer design concept in which computer hardware contains redundant systems, high-quality components, and a modular design that facilitates serviceability. Each of the components of this design concept contributes to the overall goal of HA.

Reliability

Reliability defines the amount of time a computer system or component part will continue to perform, as it should, before requiring maintenance or replacement. Typically, an end user must depend on the reliability specifications of products supplied by their manufacturers or vendors. There is a definite relationship between cost and reliability, but if cost is the only criterion for a purchase, you may get just what you paid for.

The common measurements of reliability are *early life failure rate (ELFR)*, *mean time between failures (MTBF)*, *mean time to repair (MTTR)*, and *mean time to failure (MTTF)*. Table 19-1 lists these measurements and their meanings.

Measurement	Meaning
Table 19-1	**Reliability Measures**
ELFR	The average time for new products to fail in their early life
MTBF	The average length of service time before a component fails and needs repair
MTTR	The average length of time required to repair a failed component
MTTF	The average length of time before a component needs replacement

There are slight differences between these reliability measures. ELFR is a percentage of components that fail in their early life. The MTBF is the most commonly referenced measurement for repairable items. If the time stated in an MTBF is 100,000 hours, understand that this means service hours (the device is powered on and operating); you should expect the device to continue operating for approximately 100,000 hours. You should also understand that this is an average, and the average of 1 hour and 200,000 hours is approximately 100,000 hours. Figure 19-4 shows the "bathtub curve" of a component's life cycle. Some new components fail early in the life cycle (ELFR), and others deteriorate only much later in their service life and approach the MTBF.

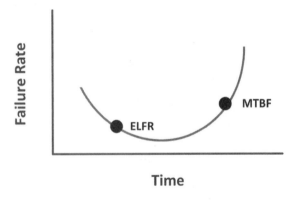

Figure 19-4 Components have a u-shaped or "bathtub curve" life cycle.

The MTTR measurement states how long it should take to fix a failed component. This measure is typically a projection based on repairs made under the manufacturer's factory conditions. However, for a product that has been in the market for a while, the manufacturer may have actual experience upon which to base this measurement. If the MTTR is anything over 24 hours, consider its overall value carefully. The MTTF measurement is important for unrepairable component parts. This measure indicates that should the component fail, it will require replacement.

Component Availability

In the context of RAS, availability is the probability that a component or system will remain operational over a set time period, which also states the percentage of time the component or system will be up and running (and available) in that time frame. An availability of 95 percent indicates that the system was not available to end users only 5 percent of a given time period. Availability is often a key metric in an SLA.

In addition to uptime, recovery time is important to availability. When a system or component fails, it is unavailable, and the clock is ticking. Therefore, it's extremely important how fast the system recovers. This is one reason why the MTTR metric discussed in the preceding section is so important when considering component purchases. Another time metric related to recovery is the *recovery time objective (RTO)*.

RTO is the total time allowed for making a repair, replacement, or whatever needs to be done to get the component or system back up and running. In other words, the RTO states the time allowed to affect a recovery. The RTO is in the operational rules or policies of an organization and absolutely included in its disaster recovery plan. The RTO links to the *recovery point objective (RPO)*. The RPO states the operational point to which the system or component is to be returned. The RPO could be in hours, as in an RPO of 6 hours before the failure, or time milestones, such as end-of-business the day before the failure. Figure 19-5 illustrates the relationship between the RPO and the RTO. Typically, the restoration point for the system is at the failure point. This is then the RPO. The disaster recovery plan (DRP) defines a set amount of time required to restore the system to the RPO, based on trial runs and vendor commitments. This is the RTO.

Figure 19-5 The RPO is commonly at the point of a failure, and the RTO is the time needed to restore the system.
© 2015 Cengage Learning®.

Serviceability

Serviceability is the ease and speed of repairing or maintaining a system. It directly relates to availability. The more time it takes to service a system, the less time the system is available. Serviceability includes the diagnostic time to troubleshoot and determine the cause and location of a failure and to affect its correction.

Larger enterprise or cloud service centers have systems installed that will automatically send a service alert to a manufacturer's service center when a system failure or fault occurs. This type of system reduces downtime and increases availability.

Disaster Recovery

Disaster recovery is a process that no IT manager ever wants to implement. However, should the need to recover from a catastrophic event be necessary, the processes, policies, and procedures specifically for the preparation, performance, and assurance of the recovery from a total loss of IT functionality should be in place. In today's computing environment, a disaster recovery plan should focus on more than just the recovery of the IT resources. Disaster recovery must be inherent in a company's business continuity plans.

Disaster Types

There are essentially two general types of disasters: natural disasters and man-made disasters. *Natural disasters*, often called "acts of God," include such weather-related events as hurricanes, typhoons, tornadoes, cyclones, floods, tsunamis, and earthquakes. An event of this type is not typically preventable, so an organization must develop planning on how the organization will react to reduce an event's impact on the business and to restore the business to a functioning level.

Man-made disasters are generally more preventable. This type of disaster includes industrial accidents, like hazardous material spills or leakage, regional or localized infrastructure failures, acts of terrorism, criminal activities, hacker attacks, and possibly acts of war. The preparedness for man-made disasters should include surveillance equipment, physical and logical intrusion detection and prevention, fire suppression systems, emergency shutdown procedures, and emergency services notification.

Disaster Recovery Planning

There are several levels of disaster recovery, which in general refers to data recovery. It should be safe to assume that every IT department makes regular backups of its system applications, images, and data. Therefore, with equipment in place to run on, restoring the processing environment shouldn't be that difficult. However, bringing the stored data and the currency of the stored data back to the desired point of recovery is by far the most important part of any disaster recovery.

LEVELS OF DISASTER RECOVERY PLANNING

Unfortunately, not every organization plans for the recovery from a disaster. Some have no disaster plan at all, and they don't take regular backups. Others really don't have a *disaster recovery plan (DRP)* and rely on the fact that they take good backups. This could be enough for some very small organizations, provided they store the backups offsite. The third level of no real disaster plan in place is an organization that created a DRP but has never acted on its policies, procedures, or requirements. These organizations have a DRP somewhere getting dusty. However, they haven't made an effort to acquire the resources required in the DRP.

Some organizations have made either a *cold site* or a *hot site* arrangement. A cold site is one that provides the services, facilities, and computing equipment needed for an organization to recover its operations. However, because this may take some time to set up, using a cold site may take longer for an organization to get back into operation. A hot site is a company that specializes in disaster recovery services. There are levels of hot sites, ranging from running mirrors to just idle copies of an organization's technology that can be ready to use in a few hours, also called *warm sites*.

An organization with a cold site agreement can expect to have to wait until the cold site operator acquires all the required resources and puts them in place before beginning their restoration of business activities, including their IT functions. An organization with a warm site agreement has a site that contains all the equipment needed to restore its operations; it only needs to make a bare-metal restore on the computers to get running again. The organization with a hot site agreement can move its operations to the new site, maybe restore a backup to bring the system to its RTO, and then proceed.

Another approach that can be internal to larger companies is to divide the IT operations into separate facilities of a city or state to create a *split-site* approach. The disaster to one location may not affect the operations of the other locations, and processing can shift to the sites still in operation.

DISASTER PLANNING CONTROL MEASURES

Business continuity plans (BCPs) and DRPs should be in lockstep on not only the processes, policies, responsibilities, and actions of a disaster recovery, but on the *control measures* (called loss control measures also) that can reduce or eliminate threats to an organization.

There are three general categories of control measures: preventive, detective, and corrective.

Preventive control measures avoid or prevent a threat event from occurring. Whether embedding posts in cement in front of the main doors of the headquarters building, storing backups offsite, using power conditioning or surge suppression, or running periodic audits, these methods are marked as preventive.

Detective control measures look for and discover threats and threatening events. The control measures included under detective controls are smoke and fire alarms, anti-virus software, and fire safety and first-aid training for employees.

Corrective measures are those that restore or fix the results of a threat or disaster. However, beyond the things discussed in this section of the chapter regarding restoring the IT systems, corrective measures also include insurance policies and restorative services contracts.

Disaster Recovery in the Cloud

Cloud services can also be part of a DRP. Cloud services provide several on-demand services that can replace contracted in-place services to assist an organization in its recovery. Some cloud service providers have begun to package these services under "Recover as a Service (RaaS)," "Disaster Recovery as a Service (DRaaS)," and "Cloud Recovery Services (CRS)," all of which are interchangeable to describe these services.

These services, which are also cloud DRPs, include backup services, such as server images and data, Infrastructure as a Service (IaaS) that provides a failover backup for an organization's in-house computing resources, and the opportunity to customize an environment through Platform as a Service (PaaS).

Chapter Summary

> ➤ Availability means that a system, service, communications link, or device works properly at the time it is required. Downtime is the opposite of availability.

> ➤ The common Internet failure points are end user, Internet service, and service provider.

> ➤ The key to availability is fault tolerance. A fault-tolerant system is able to continue operating at a defined level of function after a fault or failure occurs.

- The information necessary to start recovery actions is fault identification, including locality, cause, duration, and effect; fault isolation; and fault containment.

- Static hardware recovery uses fault masking to mitigate a fault. A voter compares the results from all the devices and votes on which of the results is the assumed correct result. Only the "correct" response goes back to the system or requestor. The decision to use hardware voting or software voting depends on several factors.

- Dynamic fault recovery uses detection and diagnostics to identify a fault and affect a recovery. Dynamic recovery is common in high-performance systems, but it can cause slowdowns in throughput and processing speeds during a recovery.

- A hybrid fault tolerance incorporates both the static and the dynamic fault recovery techniques.

- Failover is the action of a redundant device taking over for a failing device. Failback is the process that restores the primary device to operations after a failover action removed the primary device from operations.

- Replication incorporates identification and recovery methods. Multiple instances of the same system process tasks or requests in parallel, and a voter chooses the most common response.

- An important design consideration in fault-tolerant systems is the elimination of as many single points of failure as possible.

- Redundancy means that a system has components installed that are not required for the system to function normally. There are two types of redundancy: space redundancy and time redundancy.

- Space redundancy consists of extra resources in a system that would be unnecessary if the system were completely fault free.

- A form of space redundancy is standby sparing. In hot standby sparing, the standby component operates synchronously with the operational component. In cold standby sparing, the standby components are idle, and perhaps without power.

- Time redundancy repeats every action, such as a computation or a data transmission, and compares the results of the repeated action to a stored copy of the original action.

- Component diversity is a hardware fault tolerance method.

- NVP is a static fault-masking form of fault tolerance that uses DMR. NVP incorporates component diversity concepts in that two independently developed versions of a software system, commonly written in two different programming languages, run concurrently passing a set of vectors and indicators.

- The RB approach to software fault tolerance is a dynamic fault recovery model that uses redundant programming blocks or modules to replace faulty blocks in a program.

- High availability is the desired condition of a system or component to be operational without fault or maintenance for an extended length of time.

> Reliability, availability, and serviceability (RAS) is a computer design concept in which computer hardware contains redundant systems, high-quality components, and a modular design that facilitates serviceability.

> Reliability defines the amount of time a computer system or component part will continue to perform, as it should, before requiring maintenance or replacement. The common measurements of reliability are MTBF, MTTR, and MTTF.

> RTO is the total amount of time allowed for making a repair, replacement, or whatever needs to be done to get the component or system back up and running. The RPO states the operational point to which the system or component is to be returned.

> Serviceability is the ease and speed of repairing or maintaining a system.

> Natural disasters are weather-related events such as hurricanes, typhoons, tornadoes, cyclones, floods, tsunamis, and earthquakes. Man-made disasters include industrial accidents, like hazardous material spills or leakage, regional or localized infrastructure failures, acts of terrorism, criminal activities, hacker attacks, and possibly acts of war.

> Every organization needs a DRP. A cold site is one that provides the services, facilities, and computing equipment needed for an organization to recover its operations. A hot site is a company that specializes in disaster recovery services.

> BCPs and DRPs should be in lockstep on not only the processes, policies, responsibilities, and actions of a disaster recovery, but the control measures (also called loss control measures) that can reduce or eliminate threats to an organization.

> There are three general categories of control measures: preventive, detective, and corrective.

> Cloud services provide RaaS, DRaaS, and CRS. IaaS provides a failover backup service.

Key Terms

Active fault tolerance

Availability

Cold site

Cold standby sparing

Component diversity

Control measures

Corrective measures

Detective control measures

Disaster recovery

Disaster recovery plan (DRP)

Downtime

Dual modular redundancy (DMR)

Dynamic fault recovery

Early life failure rate (ELFR)

Failback

Failover

Failure points

Fault masking

Fault tolerance

Fault tolerant

Hardware voting

Heartbeat cable

High availability (HA)

Hot site

Hybrid fault tolerance

Man-made disasters

Mean time between failures (MTBF)

Mean time to failure (MTTF)

Mean time to repair (MTTR)

Natural disasters

N-version execution environment (NVX)

N-version programming (NVP)

Passive fault tolerance

Preventive control measures

Recovery blocks (RB)

Recovery point objective (RPO)

Recovery time objective (RTO)

Redundancy

Reliability

Replication

Serviceability

Single point of failure

Software voting

Space redundancy

Split-site

Standby sparing

Static hardware recovery

Time redundancy

Triple modular redundancy (TMR)

Voter

Warm site

Review Questions

1. A system, service, or device that works properly at the time it is required is said to have _____.

2. True or False? A fault-tolerant system is one that never fails.

3. What type of hardware recovery uses fault masking to mitigate a fault?

   a. Dynamic

   b. Fault isolation

   c. Failover

   d. Static

4. A _____ fault tolerance incorporates both the static and dynamic fault recovery techniques.

5. True or False? There are two types of redundancy: space redundancy and device redundancy.

6. Which of the following is not a common measurement of reliability?

   a. MTBC

   b. MTBF

   c. MTTF

   d. MTTR

7. _____ is the action of a redundant device replacing a failing device.

8. True or False? Component diversity is a hardware fault tolerance method.

9. Which of the following is the form of space redundancy in which a standby component operates synchronously with the operational component?

   a. Cold sparing

   b. Hot sparing

   c. Warm sparing

   d. Failover

10. _____ is a static fault-masking form of fault tolerance that uses DMR.

11. True or False? Failback is the process that restores a primary device to the operational level.

12. What is the characteristic quantified by the amount of time a component will continue to perform before requiring maintenance or replacement?

    a. Availability

    b. Dependability

    c. Reliability

    d. Serviceability

13. The _____ approach to software fault tolerance uses redundant programming blocks or modules to replace faulty blocks in a program.

14. True or False? The three categories of control measures are preventive, redundant, and corrective.

15. A disaster recovery plan should specify the objective goal for the amount of time to restore a system to operational status, which is the _____.

    a. RPO

    b. DRP

    c. RTO

    d. BCP

Answers to Review Questions

1. availability

2. False

3. d

4. hybrid

5. False

6. a

7. Failover

8. True

9. b

10. N-version programming or NVP

11. True

12. c

13. recovery blocks or RB

14. False

15. c

Cloud+ Examination Objectives

This book covers material related to all the exam objectives of the CompTIA Cloud+ Cloud Essentials exam (CV0-001). The official list of objectives is available from the CompTIA certification website at www.comptia.org. For your reference, the following tables list each exam objective and the chapter of this book where you can find information relating to that objective. Each of the individual exam objectives belongs to an exam domain. On the Cloud+ exam, each of the domains contributes a set percentage of the exam total questions, which also helps you direct your studies where you think you need the most help.

Exam Domain	% of Examination
1.0 Cloud Concepts and Models	12%
2.0 Virtualization	19%
3.0 Infrastructure	21%
4.0 Network Management	13%
5.0 Security	16%
6.0 Systems Management	11%
7.0 Business Continuity in the Cloud	8%
Total	**100%**

Objectives	Chapter(s)
1.0 Cloud Concepts and Models	
1.1 Compare and contrast cloud services	2
· SaaS (according to NIST)	2
· IaaS (according to NIST)	2
· CaaS (according to NIST)	2
· PaaS (according to NIST)	2
· XaaS (according to NIST)	2
· DaaS (according to NIST)	2
· BPaaS	2
· Accountability and responsibility based on service models	1
1.2 Compare and contrast cloud delivery models and services	1
· Private	1
· Public	1
· Hybrid	1
· Community	1
· On-premise versus off-premise hosting	1
· Accountability and responsibility based on delivery models	1
· Security differences between models	1
o Multitenancy issues	1
o Data segregation	1
o Network isolation	1
o Check laws and regulations	1
· Functionality and performance validation based on chosen delivery model	1
· Orchestration platforms	1

Objectives	Chapter(s)
1.3 Summarize cloud characteristics and terms	1, 4
· Elasticity	1
· On-demand self-serve/just in time service	1
· Pay-as-you-grow	1
· Chargeback	1
· Ubiquitous access	1
· Metering resource pooling	1
· Multitenancy	1
· Cloud bursting	1
· Rapid deployment	1
· Automation	1
1.4 Explain object storage concepts	3, 13
· Object ID	3, 17
· Metadata	3
· Data/blob	17
· Extended metadata	3
· Policies	3
· Replicas	15
· Access control	3
2.0 Virtualization	
2.1 Explain the differences between hypervisor types	5
· Type I and Type II	5, 7
o Bare metal versus OS dependent	5
o Performance and overhead considerations	5
o Hypervisor-specific system requirements	5
· Proprietary versus open source	5
· Consumer versus enterprise use	5
o Workstation versus infrastructure	5
2.2 Install, configure, and manage virtual machines and devices	5, 6, 18
· Creating, importing, and exporting template and virtual machines	6
· Installing guest tools	6
o Drives	6
o Management tools	4, 6
· Snapshots and cloning	6
· Image backups versus file backups	5, 6, 11
· Virtual NIC	5, 6
o Virtual network	16
o IP address	6

Objectives	Chapter(s)
2.5 Compare and contrast virtual components used to construct a cloud environment	5
· Virtual network components	5, 6, 11
o Virtual NIC	5
o Virtual HBA	5, 6
o Virtual router	5, 11
· Shared memory	11, 14
· Virtual CPU	4
· Storage virtualization	9
o Shared storage	9
o Clustered storage	5
o NPIV	5
3.0 Infrastructure	
3.1 Compare and contrast various storage technologies	3, 8
· Network attached storage (NAS)	8
o File-level access	8
o Shared storage	8
· Direct attached storage (DAS)	3, 8
o Block level access	3, 8
o Dedicated storage	3, 4, 8, 10
· Storage area network (SAN)	3, 8
o Block-level access	8
o Shared storage	5, 6, 8, 17
o HBAs	8
o LUN masking	6, 8
o Zoning	8
o WWN	8, 10
o Fiber channel protocols	10
· Different access protocols	10
o FCoE	10
o FC	10
o Ethernet	10
o iSCSI	10
· Protocols and applications	10, 16
o IP	10
o FCP	10
o iSCSI	10
· Management differences	10

Objectives	Chapter(s)
4.3 Given a scenario, appropriately allocate virtual (guest) resources using best practices	5, 11, 14
· Virtual CPU	11
· Memory	14
· Storage and network allocation	13
· Entitlement/quotas (shares)	14
· Hard limit, soft limit	14
· Reservations, licensing	14
· Dynamic resource allocation	4, 14
· Resource pooling	14
· CPU affinity	14
· Physical resource redirection and mapping to virtual resources	14
o Serial	14
o USB	14
o Parallel port mapping	14
4.4 Given a scenario, use appropriate tools for remote access	4, 14
· Remote hypervisor access	14
· RDP	10, 14
· SSH	14
· Console port	3, 10, 14
· HTTP	3
5.0 Security	
5.1 Explain network security concepts, tools, and best practices	15
· ACLs	5, 6, 15
· VPNs	15
· IDS/IPS hardware/software-based firewalls	15
· DMZ	15
· Review/audit logs	15
· Attacks	15
o DDoS	15
o Ping of death	15
o Ping flood	15
5.2 Explain storage security concepts, methods, and best practices	15
· Obfuscation	15
· Access control lists	6, 8
· Zoning	8
· LUN masking	1, 5, 15
· User and host authentication	15
· Review/audit logs	15

Cloud+ Practice Exam

The following questions cover nearly all the exam objectives of the Cloud+ Cloud Essentials (CV0-001) certification exam. To maximize your studies for the exam, be sure that you know why an answer is wrong just as you know why an answer is correct. You'll find the answers to these questions in Appendix D.

CompTIA Cloud+: Cloud Essentials CV0-001 Exam Domains	
Domain	**% of Examination**
1.0 Cloud Concepts and Models	12%
2.0 Virtualization	19%
3.0 Infrastructure	21%
4.0 Network Management	13%
5.0 Security	16%
6.0 Systems Management	11%
7.0 Business Continuity in the Cloud	8%
Total	**100%**

© 2015 Cengage Learning®

1.0 Cloud Concepts and Models

1. Jeffrey is an IT manager who needs to add development capacity to accommodate a large programming project that requires resources that are different from those in his data center. In addition, he doesn't believe he has existing capacity to support his users' needs. What form of a cloud service should Jeffrey consider acquiring?

   a. SaaS

   b. PaaS

   c. IaaS

   d. DCaaS

   e. None of the above

2. What type of cloud service provides essentially the same services as a colocation provider?

   a. CaaS

   b. DaaS

   c. IaaS

   d. XaaS

3. Who assumes the accountability and responsibility in an agreement and use of a cloud service?

   a. Cloud service provider

   b. Cloud service subscriber

   c. Both the cloud service provider and the cloud service subscriber

   d. A third-party assurance provider

4. What type of cloud computing service is implemented completely behind a company's firewall and under the complete control of the company's IT department?

    a. Community

    b. Hybrid

    c. Private

    d. Public

5. Which cloud computing service model is most likely to incorporate multitenancy?

    a. SaaS

    b. IaaS

    c. PaaS

    d. DCaaS

6. In which type of cloud computing model does a service provider make resources, such as applications and storage, available to anyone via the Internet?

    a. Private

    b. Public

    c. Hybrid

    d. Community

7. What is the action performed by specialized software that involves the management of the interconnections and interactions of cloud-based and on-premises processes?

    a. Elasticity

    b. Resource pooling

    c. Cloud bursting

    d. Orchestration

8. What is the name of the application deployment model in which an application runs in a private cloud and expands into a public cloud only when additional resources are needed?

    a. Elasticity

    b. Resource pooling

    c. Cloud bursting

    d. Orchestration

9. What is the storage method that stores discrete data units in a flat address space on the same addressing level?

   a. File storage

   b. Object storage

   c. Database storage

   d. Hierarchical storage

10. What stored data feature contains information about a stored data unit that is NOT intended for use by a file system?

   a. Metadata

   b. Policies

   c. Extended metadata

   d. Digital signature

11. What is the name of a collection of binary data stored as a single data object?

   a. Metadata

   b. BLOB

   c. CLOB

   d. Replicas

12. In object storage, an object consists of three parts: data, metadata, and _____.

   a. Object map

   b. Object header

   c. Object signature

   d. Object identifier

2.0 Virtualization

13. What is the type classification of a hypervisor that doesn't require an underlying operating system? (Choose all that apply.)

   a. Type I

   b. Type II

   c. Bare metal

   d. OS dependent

14. In a Type II hypervisor implementation, virtual machines interact with what system management software for resource requests?

    a. Operating system

    b. Hypervisor

    c. Physical device controllers

    d. Virtual switch

15. What standardized group of hardware and software settings can be used repeatedly to create new virtual machines configured with those settings?

    a. Snapshot

    b. Clone

    c. Image

    d. Template

16. What backup method captures the state of a system or virtual machine at a particular point in time?

    a. Snapshot

    b. Clone

    c. Image

    d. Incremental backup

17. What replication method captures a virtual machine completely to create a separate new virtual machine that may share virtual disks with the original virtual machine?

    a. Snapshot

    b. Clone

    c. Image

    d. Template

18. What are the two types of virtual networks implemented in a virtual environment? (Choose two.)

    a. Operating system based

    b. Protocol based

    c. Device based

    d. Hypervisor based

19. A backup method that copies the operating system and the data associated with an entire computer or an individual virtual machine, including its state and application configurations, is a(n)

    a. Incremental backup

    b. File backup

    c. Clone

    d. Image

20. What virtualized device facilitates one virtual machine to communicate with another virtual machine?

    a. Virtual NIC

    b. Virtual router

    c. Virtual switch

    d. Virtual bridge

21. What is the logical storage device supported by the hardware or firmware of a storage system with which a computer or application can interact for I/O operations?

    a. SAN

    b. NAS

    c. DAS

    d. Vdisk

22. Kristal wants to secure the virtual machines inside a virtualized environment in which the virtual machines connect directly to the physical network. What immediate action can she take without adding additional hardware? (Choose all that apply.)

    a. Segregate virtual machines on separate hardware

    b. Implement VLANs

    c. Implement virtual network adapters

    d. Implement virtual switches

23. What is the logical partition in an SAN that isolates I/O traffic to specific portions of the SAN?

    a. VSAN

    b. Zoning

    c. Binding

    d. NAS

24. What logical partitioning method divides an SAN into multiple, isolated subnetworks?

    a. VSAN

    b. Zoning

    c. Binding

    d. DAS

25. What is the term that refers to the migration of a computer's disk storage to a virtual machine or disk partition?

    a. P2V

    b. V2P

    c. V2V

    d. P2P

26. Which of the following is a benefit of implementing a virtualized environment in a cloud service system? (Choose all that apply.)

    a. Resource pooling

    b. Scalability

    c. Application isolation

    d. Time to service

    e. All of the above

    f. None of the above

27. What software feature enables HBA virtualization and the assignment of different WWNs to virtual servers so they are limited to accessing only the storage volumes assigned to them?

    a. LUN

    b. Fibre Channel

    c. NPIV

    d. WWN

28. What is the memory structure that allows multiple programs to access memory for the purpose of sharing data and avoiding redundant copies of data in memory?

    a. Virtual memory

    b. Clustered memory

    c. Cached memory

    d. Shared memory

29. What element of a virtualized environment creates an association between a multicore processor and a virtual machine?

    a. Virtual CPU

    b. SMP

    c. Virtual router

    d. Hyperthreading

30. What virtualization entity emulates a physical computing environment that passes its requests for system resources through a managed virtualization layer?

    a. Virtual NIC

    b. Virtual router

    c. Virtual switch

    d. Virtual machine

31. Which of the following is NOT a component in a virtualized environment?

    a. Virtual NIC

    b. Virtual operating system

    c. Virtual machine

    d. Virtual server

3.0 Infrastructure

32. Which of the following are characteristics, features, or components of SAN?
    (Choose all that apply.)

    a. Fibre Channel

    b. TCP/IP

    c. Block-level data

    d. File-level data

    e. RAID

    f. All of the above

33. The data storage technology in which the storage devices attach directly to a computer is
    _____.

    a. NAS

    b. SAN

    c. DAS

    d. SSD

34. NAS technology accesses data using what level of access?

    a. Block level

    b. File level

    c. Object level

    d. Field level

35. Which of the following data storage technologies provide shared access to data resources?
    (Choose all that apply.)

    a. NAS

    b. SAN

    c. DAS

    d. XFS

36. What is the device identity assigned to a SCSI logical component that supports I/O operations?

    a. LUN

    b. HBA

    c. WWN

    d. NAT

37. What is the network technology that allows Fibre Channel to utilize 10 Gigabit Ethernet with
    FC protocols?

    a. iSCSI

    b. FCP

    c. SNMP

    d. FCoE

38. What Network Layer protocol allows SCSI commands to be transmitted over IP networks to perform data transfers and manage remote storage devices?

    a. CDB

    b. SAN

    c. iSCSI

    d. FCP

39. Which of the following is a data storage technology that uses integrated circuit assemblies to store data persistently?

    a. HDD

    b. SSD

    c. Fibre Channel

    d. USB

40. Ted wants to reduce the total storage costs in his company's IT data center and to segregate the data based on its security requirements. Which of the following storage techniques would best accomplish Ted's goals?

    a. RAID

    b. Zoning

    c. Tiering

    d. iSCSI

41. Which of the following RAID levels does NOT implement striping? (Choose all that apply.)

    a. RAID 0

    b. RAID 1

    c. RAID 1+0

    d. RAID 5

    e. RAID 6

42. Which of the following RAID levels incorporate parity blocks? (Choose all that apply.)

    a. RAID 0

    b. RAID 1

    c. RAID 4

    d. RAID 5

    e. RAID 6

43. When calculating the IOPS rate for a RAID 5 system, what must be included in the calculation to portray this performance metric realistically?

    a. Mirroring

    b. Striping

    c. Parity

    d. Write penalty

44. What protocol effectively "hides" an entire private address space behind a single public IP address?

    a. NAT

    b. PAT

    c. Subnetting

    d. Supernetting

45. What protocol variation translates IP addresses using a pool of routable IP addresses?

    a. Subnetting

    b. Supernetting

    c. Dynamic PAT

    d. Dynamic NAT

46. What file system stores virtual machine disk images and allows multiple virtual servers to request I/O operations simultaneously as an alternative to the NFS?

    a. NTFS

    b. VMFS

    c. ZFS

    d. UFS

47. What is the IP addressing technique that combines several networks into a single network with a common network prefix?

    a. Subnetting

    b. Supernetting

    c. CIDR

    d. VLAN

48. What is the network ID of the IPv4 address 192.168.204.15/21?

    a. 192.168.200.0

    b. 192.168.192.0

    c. 192.168.204.0

    d. 192.168.0.0

49. What is the process that adds information to an Ethernet frame to identify it to a specific VLAN?

    a. VLAN bridging

    b. VLAN switching

    c. VLAN tagging

    d. VLAN prioritization

50. What is the assigned well-known port number of HTTP?

    a. 20

    b. 80

    c. 443

    d. 1120

51. What is the general category of technologies and techniques used to maximize the efficiency of data flow across a network?

    a. Compression

    b. Latency

    c. Load balancing

    d. Optimization

52. Which of the following troubleshooting utilities is used to solely verify the existence of a network connection?

    a. Ping

    b. Traceroute

    c. Dig

    d. Netstat

4.0 Network Management

53. Which of the following is the standard for computer message logging?

    a. WMI

    b. IPMI

    c. Web services

    d. Syslog

54. Jerry needs to manage a remote computer that may be powered off or may have a faulty network interface. What standardized computer interface can he use to connect to this computer?

    a. WMI

    b. Telnet

    c. IPMI

    d. Web services

55. When implementing a performance monitoring system, what must be defined before alert notifications can be configured? (Choose all that apply.)

    a. Baselines and thresholds

    b. Monitored devices

    c. Methods of transmission of alerts

    d. All of the above

56. In a virtual environment in which some device or component allocations are dynamic, what allocation threshold may be exceeded by a virtual machine for a short period?

    a. Hard limit

    b. Soft limit

    c. Reservation

    d. Share

57. When you aggregate the resources of a host or computer cluster so control over the resources can be delegated to certain users or departments, what action have you taken?

    a. Pooling

    b. Aggregation

    c. Clustering

    d. Allocation

58. A system administrator is allocating the CPU resources on a host server in a virtualized environment. The server has a single multicore processor installed in a single socket that has eight cores. Hyperthreading is enabled. What is the number of logical processors, the administrator can allocate?

    a. 8

    b. 12

    c. 16

    d. 32

59. When the Finance department is running its accounting period closing process, it needs to block all other access to certain volumes in the storage system. What type of access policy is required to grant the exclusive access to this data?

    a. Quota

    b. Hard limit

    c. Reservation

    d. Entitlement

60. What allocation method can be used to bind an application process to a particular CPU or group of CPUs so that the process will only run on that particular CPU or group of CPUs?

    a. Port mapping

    b. Affinity

    c. Entitlement

    d. Reservation

61. What encrypting network protocol can be used for secure communications to a remote command-line login that facilitates remote access to a hypervisor or other system components?

    a. RDP

    b. Telnet

    c. SSH

    d. FTP

62. Connie needs to connect to a remote router to change its configuration. Using a secure remote connection protocol, what router port should she connect to so she has administrative access to the router's operating system?

    a. Ethernet port

    b. Parallel port

c. Console port

d. Any router port

63. What is the network protocol that can be used for network management and network monitoring of network devices for conditions or performance that deserve an administrator's attention?

a. SMTP

b. SNMP

c. ICMP

d. Netstat

64. Under what form of resource allocation are resources assigned to processes based on the priority of each process?

a. Static

b. Dynamic

c. Round-robin

d. Affinity

65. True or False? Software licensing agreements extend to virtual machines, and each instance of a software application running in a virtual machine must have its own license.

a. True

b. False

5.0 Security

66. Evan is a security administrator for a cloud service provider. A subscriber of an IaaS service wants to restrict access to its data files as part of authentication and authorization on an SAN provided by the cloud service provider. On a non-windows bare-metal virtualized environment, what possible methods are appropriate to this situation as approaches to restricting users' access and their rights after accessing it? (Choose all that apply.)

a. Individual file permissions

b. ACL

c. RBAC

d. Multiple login credentials for users

67. What is the common name of the perimeter network that adds an additional layer of security to a company's LAN and serves to provide access to the company's public information to external requests?

    a. Proxy server

    b. DMZ

    c. Honey pot

    d. IDS

68. What network security application or appliance monitors the network or system for suspicious and malicious activities to identify, log, block, and report the activity?

    a. IDS/IPS

    b. IPsec

    c. TLS

    d. SSH

69. What network service technology allows remote users to access a private network through a tunneling protocol over a public network to gain access to the private network's resources and service?

    a. VLAN

    b. P2P

    c. VPN

    d. RAS

70. What is the type of attack launched from multiple sites on a single site to render the attacked site unable to process requests from its users and possibly crash?

    a. DoS

    b. Ping of death

    c. DDoS

    d. Ping flood

71. What is the type of DoS attack that overwhelms a targeted system with an overabundance of ICMP Echo Request packets?

    a. DoS

    b. Ping of death

    c. DDoS

    d. Ping flood

72. What is the type of attack that attempts to crash a system by sending it a malformed ICMP Echo Request packet?

    a. DoS

    b. Ping of death

    c. DDoS

    d. Ping flood

73. The term *obfuscation* refers to _____.

    a. Obscuring an attack payload from inspection by network protection systems

    b. Encryption

    c. Digital signatures

    d. Correcting a muddled or corrupted datagram's payload

74. What is the security arrangement that binds shared encryption keys with user identities using the services of a certificate authority?

    a. One-way encryption

    b. Private key encryption

    c. Public key encryption

    d. Symmetric encryption

75. Which of the following is NOT a commonly used encryption cipher algorithm?

    a. AES

    b. DES

    c. 3DES

    d. RC5

    e. None of the above

76. The TLS/SSL encryption protocols are best used for which of the following?

    a. Data at rest

    b. Data in archival

    c. Data in motion

    d. None of the above

77. Which of the following are encryption methods that can protect data at rest in a computer system?

    a. Full disk encryption

    b. File encryption

    c. Password protection

    d. All of the above

78. What is the type of authentication that may require a knowledge factor, a possession factor, and an inherence factor?

    a. Role-based authentication

    b. Mandatory access control

    c. Discretionary access control

    d. Multifactor authentication

79. Which of the following is NOT a technique for hardening a host computer?

    a. Disable unused ports and services

    b. Change passwords frequently

    c. Reinstall the operating system and applications

    d. Run antivirus software

    e. Install host-based firewall

80. What is the Layer 3 security protocol that provides end-to-end security for network packets?

    a. TLS/SSL

    b. SSH

    c. IPsec

    d. L2TP

81. What is the authentication method that links a user's identity and attributes, which can be stored on different identification systems, into a single identity token? (Choose all that apply.)

    a. Discretionary access control

    b. Mandatory access control

    c. Federation

    d. Single sign-on

6.0 Systems Management

82. What term describes the use of CIDR notation to combine several networks into a single network-addressing scheme?

    a. Resource pooling

    b. Subnetting

    c. Supernetting

    d. I/O throttling

83. Which of the following is an example of an IPv6 address?

    a. 192.168.32.240/24

    b. fd9b:7da8:4a66:63b1::/64

    c. 01:23:45:67:89:ab

    d. s2:4.126l4

84. What ITIL configuration management feature contains information about configuration items, including their location, status, and interchangeability with other configuration items as a means to improve configuration control on a system?

    a. SCM

    b. CMDB

    c. ITSM

    d. CMS

85. The users of the network that Jon manages have begun to complain that response time is increasing. What general network performance issue should Jon look at first to determine the increasing delay?

    a. Latency

    b. IOPS

    c. Throughput

    d. Hops

86. Jon suspects that the hard disk drives in the NAS arrangement of his network may be causing a significant portion of user complaints about system slowness. He obtained the rotation speed and seek time for each of his drives. What performance metric can he calculate using these drive characteristics?

    a. Delay

    b. Latency

    c. IOPS

    d. Transfer rate

87. What is the software that runs between the physical hardware and virtual machines and manages all virtual devices in the virtual environment?

    a. Host operating system

    b. Guest operating system

    c. Hypervisor/VMM

    d. All of the above

88. The act of moving a virtual machine from one physical server to another without stopping either physical server is called _____.

    a. High availability

    b. Fault tolerance

    c. Server provisioning

    d. Live migration

89. What is the virtual memory technique that frees unused memory from one virtual machine so it can be temporarily assigned to another?

    a. Memory ballooning

    b. Dynamic allocation

    c. Static allocation

    d. Heap allocation

90. During low-memory conditions, a system can slow down the read/write requests from memory by processing only one request at a time. This action is _____.

    a. Memory ballooning

    b. LUN throttling

    c. Request queuing

    d. I/O throttling

91. Disk storage manufacturers commonly publish this disk performance metric as a guideline for buyers on the general performance of their disk drives, including HDD, SSD, and SAN. What is the abbreviation for this metric?

    a. RAID

    b. IOSTAT

    c. IOPS

    d. QAPM

92. What is the action that groups several NICs so that they function as one logical NIC?

    a. Bonding

    b. Virtualizing

    c. Clustering

    d. Teaming

93. What is the action that combines the NICs on a single host to gain redundancy and improved throughput?

    a. Bonding

    b. Virtualizing

    c. Clustering

    d. Teaming

7.0 Business Continuity in the Cloud

94. A program in which business-critical systems and data are backed up securely to a secondary server is a form of disaster recovery, especially the process called _____.

    a. Failover

    b. Cold site

    c. Redundancy

    d. Backup

95. A site that completely mirrors a production site in real-time synchronization is an example of what type of disaster recovery site?

    a. Cold site

    b. Warm site

    c. Hot site

    d. High availability

96. The process that copies data over a WAN to a backup site so that data is written to a primary and a secondary site simultaneously to ensure multiple copies of up-to-date data exists is called

    a. Asynchronous replication

    b. Distributed redundancy

    c. Distributed replication

    d. Synchronous replication

97. What is the point that a disaster recovery program should specify as the time it should take to restore an organization to an operational point, including its IT operations?

    a. MTBF

    b. RTO

    c. MTTR

    d. RPO

98. What is the term that describes the use of geographically disperse computing resources to create a highly available system that provides for business continuity in the event of a catastrophic disaster?

    a. Geoclustering

    b. Multipathing

    c. Load balancing

    d. Failback

99. What is the system configuration mode that enables a system to continue operating in the event of one or more component failures?

    a. Multipathing

    b. Fault tolerance

    c. Self-stabilization

    d. Roll-forward

100. In the Service Level Agreements of the Apple SaaS cloud service provider, system uptime is stated as being "5 nines." This level of uptime commitment indicates what characteristic has been configured into Apple SaaS systems?

    a. Fault tolerance

    b. Self-stabilization

    c. High availability

    d. Over-commitment

Glossary

5-3-2 principle of cloud computing The "5" represents the five essential attributes of cloud computing: on-demand/self-service, anywhere network access, location transparent resource pooling, rapid elasticity, and pay-per-use service. The "3" represents the three basic service models: SaaS, PaaS, and IaaS. The "2" represents the two primary deployment methods for cloud computing: private cloud and public cloud.

10 Gigabit Ethernet An Ethernet technology that transmits data across a network at 10 Gigabits per second (Gbps).

10BASE-T The IEEE 802.3 nomenclature for a twisted-pair copper cable with baseband bandwidth of 10 Megabits per second (Mbps).

Acceptance testing Typically associated with software development but also included in environmental or system tests. Attempts to replicate the "real-life" use of a product, system, or entire computing environment.

Access control entry (ACE) An element in an access control list (ACL) that specifies the access to a particular system resource for a specific authorized entity.

Access control list (ACL) An access control mechanism that contains zero to multiple access control entries (ACEs) that specify a list of privileges and permissions to a system object.

Access protocols The standardized rules for conducting communication sessions over a network.

Accountability The responsibility for the outcome of an action, task, or project.

Active attack An attempt to gain access to system resources to alter their contents or change how they operate.

Address prefix The network identification portion of an IPv6 address.

Address Resolution Protocol (ARP) Converts logical addresses into physical or MAC addresses on a Layer 2 network.

Administrative metadata Data on the management, use, and retention of an object.

Advanced Encryption Standard (AES) A standard for the encryption of electronic data established by NIST.

Alert notification An alert message generated after an administrator-defined threshold is reached or detected by performance or system monitoring software.

American National Standards Institute (ANSI) The agency that oversees the creation, promulgation, and use of standards, norms, and guidelines that impact businesses in every sector.

Anomaly-based detection Detects unusual changes in the usage or consumption of network resources by users, nodes, connectivity devices, or server-based applications.

Anycast addressing An IPv6 addressing scheme that combines unicast and multicast.

Any-to-any network connection Because of its capability to connect and interact with a network using switches, an SAN creates a no-limit to no-limit network connection.

Apple Filing Protocol (AFP) Formerly the AppleTalk Filing Protocol, AFP is a proprietary network protocol that provides file services for Mac OS.

Application layer The layer in the Open Systems Interconnection (OSI) model on which communications protocols and process-to-process communications across a computer network take place.

Application programming interface (API) Defines the interactions between software components and provides a standard coding block for interfaces between application programs and other components, such as device drivers, database systems, and video/graphics cards.

Application streaming Downloads some or all of an application to your desktop and allows you to run the application locally.

Application virtualization A software technology that creates application software encapsulation under the control of the native operating system.

Arbitrated Loop Physical Address (ALPA) Each device on a Fibre Channel Arbitrated Loop (FC-AL) is assigned an 8-bit identity, which is limited to one of 134 possible values.

Asynchronous Transfer Mode (ATM) A high-speed networking standard that supports both voice and data communications.

Attack surface The general vulnerability of a computer that may be exploited by attacks.

Authentication The verification of at least one type of identifying information, such as a username or a passcode.

Authentication, authorization, and accounting (AAA) A combined method for controlling user access to computing resources, enforcing access policies, and gathering billing information.

Authentication Header (AH) One of the security protocols under IPsec. Its primary function is to provide authentication for the contents of a packet.

Authentication token A digital code issued by an authentication process that must accompany all requests for object storage actions.

Availability The characteristic of a system, service, communications link, or device that can be accessed and will work properly when required.

Availability class Using the "nines" metric to indicate availability, the number of nines in the metric indicates its class of availability.

Backout plan A plan that specifies the actions and processes required to restore a system back to a specific known-good point in the event of an improper or nonfunctioning implementation.

Balloon driver A virtual machine process that shares the unused memory of one virtual machine with another virtual machine that needs additional memory.

Bare metal A type of installation that creates a server by installing a server image on a blank computer or building it up from "bare metal" with its operating system, networking, and major applications.

Baseline An agreed-to description, depiction, or diagram of the attributes of a system, network, or application at a specific point in time that serves as a basis for defining change.

Basic Input-Output System (BIOS) A standard firmware configuration interface that initializes and tests system hardware components at start-up and loads the operating system.

Basic journaling This method of journaling writes both the file metadata and the file contents to the journal before writing them to the file system.

Berkeley Internet Name Domain (BIND) Allows for the creation and management of DNS servers.

Bidirectional mode Also called byte mode, this is a half-duplex parallel communications mode that transmits in both directions, but in only one direction at a time.

Binary large object (BLOB) A group of binary data stored as a single entity, such as images, audio, and multimedia objects.

Bind Allows a resource to be sent or received by binding requests to a protocol to indicate that it is ready to receive or send information.

Binding Linking two network resources so they are able to communicate with each other.

Black box A penetration test type that provides no information about the organization, except maybe its name to the attacker, who simulates a brute-force attack.

Block cipher Converts a fixed-length number of bits at a time, typically on large data blocks or bulk data. *See* Advanced Encryption Standard (AES) or Data Encryption Standard (DES).

Block storage device Hard disk drives read and write data in fixed-length blocks.

Block virtualization Creates a logical structure of the physical storage that is transparent to applications and users at the data-block level.

Bounds checking A preventive measure against buffer overflow, this process compares the length of incoming input against the size of the allocated memory and stops the input process should the input exceed the length of the buffer.

Branch to Headquarters (branch) WAN Connects a remote operation with a main or intermediate data center.

Branching snapshot Also called a read-write snapshot, the snapshot type used in most virtualized environments.

Bring Your Own Device (BYOD) An enterprise policy that permits its employees to bring personally owned mobile devices (laptops, tablets, and smartphones) to the workplace and use them to access the company network, applications, and information.

Broadcast The method used to transmit a message to one or more destination addresses.

Broadcast domain A logical division of a computer network, in which all nodes can reach each other by broadcast on the Data Link layer.

Buffer A fixed size space in memory allocated to a program to accept inputs.

Buffer overflow attack An exploit of a weakness in programs written in C or C++ in which input data exceeds the program's memory allocation to write over other data or instructors in memory.

Business continuity plan (BCP) The overall planning for the capacity needs of a business. Within computing services, it derives from service-level commitments, organizational plans, and configuration management.

Business Process as a Service (BPaaS) Contracted cloud services to provide business processes, such as payroll or CRM.

Business process outsourcing (BPO) Contracting operations and responsibilities for specific business functions or processes to a third-party service provider.

Capacity management The process that ensures a computing environment has the processing and resource capacity to service the existing and defined plans of an organization effectively and efficiently.

Carrier Ethernet Telecommunications technology deployed by common carriers to extend Ethernet services beyond local area networks (LANs).

Carrier Ethernet Transport (CET) An enhancement of conventional Ethernet that incorporates multiple technology components that provide scalability, secure demarcation, traffic engineering, and a carrier-grade transmission medium.

Carrier Sense Multiple Access with Collision Detection (CSMA/CD) An Ethernet technology that detects if the carrier is in use and if so, if a signal collision has occurred.

Central processing unit (CPU) The hardware inside a computer that executes instructions through the performance of basic arithmetic, logic, and input/output (I/O) operations.

Centralized metadata architecture The more commonly used of the three metadata architectures. All data and object metadata are placed in one repository.

Chain of trust A logical security structure that is created by validating each component of hardware and software to ensure that only trusted software and hardware are used.

Change control Controls the submission, recording, analysis, decision-making, and approval of changes.

Change management Manages changes to a computing environment to improve the value of the system and to minimize potential disruptions to the organization.

Character large object (CLOB) A collection of character data stored as an object in a database management system.

Child partition In a virtualized environment, this partition type contains a virtual machine, its guest operating system, and any applications running in the virtual machine.

CHKDSK (Check Disk) A Windows operating system command-line utility that checks an NTFS (or FAT) hard disk volume for errors.

Cipher An algorithm that performs encryption or decryption.

Ciphertext Plaintext that has been encrypted by a cipher.

Classful A type of subnetting that considers the IPv4 address class.

Classful IP addressing A protocol standard that preassigns the number of network IDs and hosts per network of specified address classes.

Classless Inter-Domain Routing (CIDR) Designates the number of bits in an IPv4 address used to represent the network ID. In CIDR notation, an IPv4 address appears as 192.168.4.20/24, with the "/24" indicating that 24 bits of the address represent the network ID.

Classless IP addressing A variable number of bits is specified with an address to indicate the number of bits used to identify the network ID without regard to address classes.

Client hypervisor A hypervisor installed on a client device, such as a notebook, a desktop PC, or the like.

Clock skew A form of device fingerprint that allows a servicing host to identify a remote host.

Clone A copy of an existing VM.

Close-in attack A type of attack from someone physically gaining access to modify, steal, or destroy resources.

Cloud computing Delivering and receiving hosted services over the Internet.

Cloud orchestration Provides the capability to manage, apply, and facilitate elements in a cloud infrastructure in real time to meet the computing needs of an organization.

Cloud service provider (CSP) A company that provides one or more cloud services to subscribers.

Cluster The smallest allocation unit managed by a file system for storing files, directories, and folders.

Clustered file system Allows an individual file system to mount to multiple servers at the same time.

Cold site A redundant system that provides the services, facilities, and computing equipment needed for an organization to recover its operations, although it must be powered up and restored to an operational point.

Cold standby sparing A component or system in which the standby components are idle and without power.

Command Descriptor Block (CDB) A message sent by a SCSI/iSCSI initiator to request service from a SCSI/iSCSI target.

Common Information/Interface Model (CIM) A standard for providing data about network devices and software applications that is used for management and control actions.

Common Internet File System (CIFS) A protocol that defines a standard for remote file access on multiple computers at a time. Users on different computers can share files without having to install new software.

Communications as a Service (CaaS) Contracted cloud services to provide a communications solution.

Community cloud A shared environment in which several subscribers gain the benefits of a public cloud with private cloud control and security.

Compatibility testing A testing type that evaluates whether hardware or software is compatible with other hardware, software, the operating system, a virtual environment, or a network.

Component capacity planning Analyzes each component's utilization to ensure it's sufficient for the component as well as the aggregate capacity for a multicomponent configuration in which the component is a member.

Component diversity An approach to fault tolerance for hardware and software in which two (or more) versions, or models of a component or system, run in parallel.

Component Object Model (COM) A binary-interface standard for software components used to enable inter-process communication and dynamic object creation in programming languages.

Computing resources Includes all CPU-related functions of a data service center.

Configuration management Ensures that a system maintains its integrity and value to the organization before, during, and after applying changes to it.

Configuration standardization The part of configuration management that controls the consistency of a system configuration in terms of performance, compatibility, and planned modifications.

Connection-less mode No communication is established and data packets may be routed independently and delivered in a different order than they were sent.

Connection-mode A network communication mode in which a communication session is established before data is transferred and the transmitted data is delivered in the same order as sent.

Console port A connection interface that connects an administrator to the operating system of a networking device or the hypervisor of a virtual environment.

Console server Provides serial ports that interconnect to the serial ports on other devices, such as servers, routers, or switches.

Container A storage container holds the data, metadata, and even some associated files of an object.

Content delivery network (CDN) A distributed network of servers, dispersed in multiple data centers across the Internet, that provide content to users as well as high availability and performance.

Control measures Processes and procedures that attempt to reduce or eliminate threats to an organization.

Convergence Enhanced Ethernet (CEE) A single interconnect Ethernet technology that combines multiple applications in one or more data centers to reduce the number of cables and network adapters connected to the servers.

Cooperative Association for Internet Data Analysis (CAIDA) A standard that provides the basis for hardware device fingerprinting as a value produced by an algorithm that uniquely identifies every remote device interacting with a server.

Counter In performance monitoring software, a specifically identified condition or action that is tallied.

CPU affinity Associates a process or thread to one or more specific CPUs.

CPU socket The mounting frame into which a microprocessor assembly installs on a computer motherboard.

Customer relationship management (CRM) A software system that manages interactions with customers, including the automation of sales, marketing, customer service, and technical support.

Cyclic redundancy check (CRC) An error-detection code used on digital networks and storage devices to detect incidental or accidental changes to raw data.

Cylinder A virtual construction that includes all the same numbered tracks on each of the platters of a hard disk drive.

Data at rest Data stored on storage devices.

Data Center Management Interface (DCMI) A system management standard based on Intelligent Platform Management Interface (IPMI) for use in data center environments.

Data Center to Data Center (DC2DC) WAN A WAN that covers a longer distance and has greater dependence on routing and switching in the cloud compared to a Branch WAN.

Data classification A designation of the security, restrictions, access speed, availability, and retention for each defined level of data.

Data compression The use of encoding algorithms that store data with fewer bits than their original characters or values. Compression algorithms are lossy or lossless.

Data deduplication A software-driven compression technique that eliminates duplicate instances of repeated data from a data store.

Data Encryption Standard (DES) At one time this was the data encryption standard with a 56-bit key length and 64-bit symmetrical block encryption.

Data in motion Data in transmission from one point to another.

Data integrity Maintaining and ensuring the accuracy and consistency of data over its entire life cycle.

Data masking *See* Obfuscation.

Data origin authentication Verifies that no alterations occurred to a message in transit and that the message originated from an expected or accepted sender.

Data storage policy Defines the specifics of data collection, storage, access, retention, integrity, and security.

Data transfer rate (DTR) A measurement of the time required to move data from one location to another.

Datagram The message unit transported by User Datagram Protocol (UDP).

Defragmentation Reduces the amount of fragmentation on a disk by physically rearranging and organizing the data blocks on a disk drive or other types of mass storage.

Demilitarized zone (DMZ) A physical or logical subnetwork that provides access to an organization's public information, such as an extranet or a web server, blocking access to the organization's primary internal network.

Denial of service (DoS) attack An attempt to consume all the processing capability of a server or network connectivity device so that the server or device is unavailable to its associated network.

Descriptive metadata The most commonly used form of metadata that may store an object title, the creator's name, dates, subject matter titles and keyword tags, or a descriptive abstract of the object content.

Desktop as a Service (DaaS) Contracted cloud services to provide virtual desktop infrastructure (VDI).

Desktop virtualization A software-based technology in which the physical desktop computer is separated from the computer's operating system and its applications, creating a standalone virtual environment.

Device fingerprinting The action of generating a device identity through an algorithm. *See* Cooperative Association for Internet Data Analysis (CAIDA).

DHCP version 6 (DHCPv6) The DHCP version that works with IPv6 is a stateful process as opposed to the IPv6 auto-configuration process in which a host configures itself without regard for its state.

Differencing hard disk On this type of disk drive, each file has a parent and a child image. The parent image contains the original data content of the file, and the child image contains the changes made to the file.

Differential backup Captures only the data that changed since the last full backup.

Dig (domain information groper) The new utility that replaced the nslookup utility.

Digital signature Provides a "proof of origin" and proof against tampering of a transmitted document or email.

Digital signature algorithm (DSA) Converts two large numbers into a value that can confirm the authenticity of the signatory.

Digital Signature Standard (DSS) A digital signature algorithm (DSA) developed by the U.S. National Security Agency (NSA) to provide a digital signature for authenticating electronic documents.

Direct attached storage (DAS) One or more unshared storage devices attached to a single computer.

Direct memory access (DMA) Allows some hardware within a computer to access system memory independent of the CPU.

Directory files These files mark the branches of the root directory in the hierarchical tree structure.

Disaster recovery The restoration of business operations, including computing functions following a catastrophic event.

Disaster Recovery as a Service (DRaaS) Hosted, redundant physical or virtual servers supported by a cloud service provider to provide failover in the event of a catastrophic event.

Disaster recovery plan (DRP) A detailed plan on the processes and procedures to recover a business from a catastrophic event, including the policies and procedures for the preparation, performance, and assurance of the recovery from a total loss of IT functionality.

Discretionary access control (DAC) An ACL under the control of the owner of an object that lists who can access a data object and what they can do with it.

Disk cache An area of main memory or a segregated portion of a disk drive used to hold data recently read from or written to storage, in an attempt to prevent the need for a storage I/O to access this same data.

Disk mirroring The replication of logical disk volumes to another physical hard disk drive.

Disk optimization A process that involves running software that collects fragmented files and rebuilding them into a single entity.

Disk striping Divides data into smaller blocks that it stores on different partitions on multiple hard disks.

Disk striping with parity Creates parity files along with a data stripe using error correction and detection algorithms.

Disk-to-disk (dd) A command on Linux/UNIX operating systems that converts and copies files.

Distributed DoS (DDoS) attack Two or more attackers collaborate on a single target simultaneously.

Distributed Management Task Force (DMTF) An information technology organization that creates and maintains standards that enable effective management of IT environments.

Distributed metadata architecture A collection of the metadata from various system metadata stores in real time to provide the most up-to-date information about the content in each system.

Distributed Resource Scheduler (DRS) A VMware subsystem that pools resources based on allocations that the system administrator designs.

Domain A Windows feature that consists of a super-group, which is a set of user accounts and host accounts grouped so that administrators can manage them as a single entity.

Domain controller (DC) A Windows feature that facilitates the central management of the domains and Active Directory.

Domain Name System (DNS) A hierarchical system of databases that associate IP addresses with URLs.

Dotted decimal notation The notation for the decimal value equivalent of an IPv4 address, such as 192.168.32.247.

Downtime The time periods when a system or service is unavailable to users or subscribers.

Dual modular redundancy (DMR) A fault tolerance approach in which components of a system are duplicated to provide redundancy in case one should fail.

Dynamic fault recovery The application of specific mechanisms to detect a fault, replace the faulty component, and either roll back or roll forward the associated data.

Dynamic hard disk Files are dynamically sized to the data they contain at any one time, plus a VHD header and footer.

Dynamic Host Configuration Protocol (DHCP) A standard networking protocol that distributes IP network configuration data to host computers.

Dynamic NAT Network address translation that uses a pool of external addresses to map internal addresses to external addresses.

Dynamic RAM (DRAM) A type of RAM that stores a data bit in an individual capacitor within an integrated circuit. Because the capacitors slowly discharge, DRAM's charge must be refreshed periodically, hence "dynamic."

Dynamic resource allocation The categorization and managing of common resources under a single point of control and allocation.

Dynamic routing A routing process that uses routing information to determine the better next hop decision.

Eager Zero thick provisioning A VMware thick provisioning method that creates a pre-zeroed VM disk in thick format.

Early life failure rate (ELFR) When a product is "young" or new, its failure rate is high but then decreases as defective products are removed from service.

E-LAN A multipoint-to-multipoint communication service that connects two or more customer interfaces on an Ethernet network.

Elasticity In cloud computing, the automatic reprovisioning or configuring of an infrastructure to meet the storage and computing resource needs of a subscriber.

Electrically erasable programmable read-only memory (EEPROM) A type of nonvolatile memory used in computers to store small amounts of data, such as device configurations. Data stored on an EEPROM can be read, erased, and rewritten.

Electronic codebook (ECB) A symmetric key encryption process that divides variable-length messages into cipher-length blocks with padding bits added to short blocks.

E-Line A point-to-point communication link that connects two Ethernet ports/interfaces over a WAN service.

Encapsulating protocol This type of protocol encrypts the original packet and encapsulates it in a second packet. Protocols of this type are IPsec, L2TP, PPTP, and GRE.

Encapsulating Security Payload (ESP) Similar to IPsec AH. Operates in two modes: transport mode and tunnel mode. Transport mode encrypts only the payload of the packet. Tunnel mode encrypts the entire packet.

Encryption A method of encoding transmitted messages or stored data so that only authorized individuals have access to its original values.

End user licensing agreement (EULA) The user licensing conditions regarding the ownership, usage, and disposition of a particular software program or system issued by its publisher.

End-to-end availability A stipulation in a Service Level Agreement that states the performance and availability responsibilities of the cloud service provider and the cloud service subscriber.

End-to-end testing Includes connectivity testing, latency testing, network monitoring, monitoring of key computing services including data storage system performance, and the configuration of VMs and virtual network devices, if applicable.

Enhanced Interior Gateway Routing Protocol (EIGRP) An advanced distance-vector routing protocol used to automate routing decisions and configuration on a network.

Enhanced Parallel Port (EPP) A fast parallel communication mode that has the ability to transmit larger amounts of data than older modes.

Entitlement A guaranteed hardware or virtual resource reservation.

EtherChannel A link aggregation specified in the IEEE 802.3ad standard.

Ethernet A Physical and Data Link layer transmission and media access technology used to create a network.

E-Tree A multipoint communication service that connects a host root endpoint to a subscriber's endpoint.

Evacuating Migrating virtual machines during maintenance mode of a host computer.

Everything as a Service (XaaS) A cloud service model that may combine SaaS, PaaS, IaaS, and possibly CaaS, DaaS, and NaaS.

Exploit attack An attacker launches an attack on a known vulnerability.

Extended Capability Port (ECP) A parallel communication mode that uses DMA to transfer data, removing this burden from the CPU.

Extended FAT (exFAT) A Microsoft operating system that is usable when NTFS is not appropriate because of NTFS's data structure overhead requirements or when the file size limit of the standard FAT32 file system is too small.

Extended file system (ext) A file system developed specifically for the Linux kernel that extended the physical disk size for partitions and files and added VFS.

Extended unique identifier (EUI-64) The IPv6 equivalent of a MAC address that contains the 24-bit OUI and expands the 24-bit serial number to 40 bits. *See* Organizationally unique identifier (OUI).

Extensible Markup Language (XML) A markup language that defines a set of rules for encoding documents in a format that is both human readable and machine readable.

External Serial Advanced Technology Attachment (eSATA) An extension of the Serial ATA (SATA) standard that enables drives to be externally connected.

External switch tagging (EST) The VLAN tagging that a physical switch performs.

External transfer time The time required for the disk controller to transfer data to the host system.

Failback A process that restores a primary device to operations after a failover action removes the primary device from operations.

Failover The action that takes place when a component fails and a hot-swap or active backup component is put into service automatically.

Failover testing Tests a system's capability to continue operating if an extreme event occurs. Also tests a system's ability to add resources during a component or system failure or if the system reaches a preset performance threshold.

Failure points Any component, process, communication, or interface point that could fail and jeopardize the availability of a system.

Family Educational Rights and Privacy Act (FERPA) A Federal law that protects the content and disclosure of educational records.

Fan-in ratio The ratio of oversubscribed source ports to target ports within a storage network.

Fan-out ratio The ratio of storage network ports to source ports within a storage network.

Fast Ethernet A version of Ethernet implemented on 100 Mbps media.

Fat provisioning *See* Thick provisioning.

Fault masking Mitigates the occurrence of a fault by absorbing or hiding the fault from the system.

Fault tolerance The capability of a component, process, or system to withstand a failure.

Fault tolerant *See* Fault tolerance.

FC fabric *See* Fibre Channel Cross-point Switched (FC-SW) topology.

Federal Information Processing Standards (FIPS) Public standards of the United States government for use in computer systems by government agencies and contractors.

Fiber Distributed Data Interface (FDDI) A data transmission standard for LANs that uses fiber optics as its physical medium.

Fibre Channel (FC) One of two primary connection methods on an SAN.

Fibre Channel Arbitrated Loop (FC-AL) topology A network configuration in which the devices linked into a loop equally share the available bandwidth and the management of the entire loop.

Fibre Channel Cross-point Switched (FC-SW) topology A network configuration, commonly referred to as fabric, to which the FC-AL topology can link.

Fibre Channel over Ethernet (FCoE) Technology that enables data frames to travel on 10 Gigabit or faster Ethernet networks.

Fibre Channel Protocol (FCP) A Transport layer protocol that carries SCSI commands over a Fibre Channel network.

File Allocation Table (FAT) A Microsoft file system that constructs and maintains a table containing a map of the location and allocation of files on a disk.

File system Provides a definition for the naming convention for data files and the logical file and directory/folder organization on the physical hard disk.

File Transfer Protocol (FTP) Transfers files from one network host to another over TCP.

File virtualization A method of storage virtualization that is similar to block virtualization, except the logical mapping occurs at the file level.

Five-nines availability A commitment level for high availability of services that limits downtime to less than 5.26 minutes per year.

Fixed hard disk One or more files with an allocated space equal to the configured size of a virtual disk.

Fixed-scope multicast address Also known as well-known multicast addresses, these addresses are permanently set for the IPv6 address space.

Formatting Adds the logical data elements required by a file system to allocate and manage the disk.

Four-nines availability A commitment level for high availability of services that limits downtime to less than 52.56 minutes per year.

FTP Secure (FTPS) Applies TLS/SSL security at the client through security services requested from an FTPS server.

Full backup Similar to an image-based backup that captures an entire data store.

Full clone A complete and independent copy of a VM that shares nothing with its parent after its creation.

Full hexadecimal notation The expression of an IPv6 address in hexadecimal form.

Full virtualization A hypervisor that creates and controls a simulated virtual environment.

Full zero suppression notation Suppresses all leading zeroes in address segments and removes any address elements that are all zeroes with a double colon symbol ("::").

Full-stroke The slowest seek time for a storage device.

Fully qualified domain name (FQDN) A domain name that specifies all domain levels and can only be interpreted one way.

Generic bonding On a Linux system, a network adapter aggregation method that allows all the bonded adapters to use one MAC address.

Generic Routing Encapsulation (GRE) A proprietary tunneling protocol that encapsulates a variety of Network layer protocols on virtual point-to-point links on an IP network.

Generic segmentation offload (GSO) Queues up large outbound message buffers and allows the network adapter to divide them into separate Layer 2 frames.

Gigabit Ethernet A version of Ethernet implemented on 1 Gbps media.

Gigabit Fibre Channel (GFC) The line rate given for FC protocols for those with gigabit speeds is appended with "GFC."

Global File System (GFS) A file system that treats all nodes of a cluster as peers, regardless of their actual roles as servers or clients.

Globally scoped A multicast address that is universally unique across the entire Internet.

Globally unique identifier (GUID) A unique 128-bit identification number used in computer software.

Gramm-Leach-Bliley Act (GLBA) A mandatory compliance regulation in the banking industry that requires protection for financial information from threats to data integrity and security breaches.

Graphical user interface (GUI) A type of user interface that allows users to interact with electronic devices through graphical icons and visual indicators.

Hard disk drive (HDD) A spinning platter mechanical storage device that has been the standard for permanent secondary storage in virtually all personal computers.

Hard limit A guaranteed maximum fixed share of hardware resources.

Hard zoning An SAN is divided into access zones. This type of zoning restricts requests from flowing to a restricted zone.

Hardening The process of increasing the security level of a host or server while lowering its vulnerability to attack.

Hardware as a Service (HaaS) A cloud service model for hardware that is essentially a license in a managed service. In a grid computing service, it's a pay-as-you-go model that provides a complete end-to-end managed service solution.

Hardware voting A redundancy and fault tolerance approach in which performance monitoring is used to determine how to reconfigure individual components so that a component continues operating.

Hardware-assisted memory virtualization The operating system has direct access to resources without emulation or operating system modification.

Hardware-assisted virtualization Processor-based virtualization assistance.

Hash message authentication code (hmac) A specific algorithm that calculates a message authentication code (MAC) using a hash function and a secret key.

Hashing A hashing function is an algorithm that converts text and data into a fixed-length string of digits.

HBA queue depth The number of pending storage I/Os waiting for processing by the HBA.

Health Insurance Portability and Accountability Act (HIPAA) Under Title II of this law, keepers of medical records must comply with the national data storage, security, and privacy standards of electronic health care transactions.

Heap A dynamic area of primary memory that a program can request space in to perform data-handling functions under the total control and addressing of the program.

Heap overflow attack Occurs when incoming data corrupts the heap and possibly modifies internal address and program pointers.

Heartbeat cable A cable connection over which two devices are able to synchronize through regularly transmitted signals.

Hexadecimal (Base 16) A positional numeral system with a base of 16. It uses sixteen distinct symbols, 0 to 9 to represent values zero to nine and A to F to represent values ten to fifteen.

Hierarchical file system (HFS) A file system in which directories and files are arranged in a directory tree structure with its root at the top.

High availability (HA) A system or component that is continuously operational for a desirably long length of time.

High-Performance Parallel Interface (HIPPI) A legacy computer bus that has been replaced by SCSI and Fibre Channel.

Host bus adapter (HBA) Connects the physical host server to storage devices or other devices in a network.

Host header buffer overflow attack An attack that exploits a flaw in the Apache web server.

Hosted hypervisor A Type II hypervisor that operates on top of a host operating system.

Hot site A duplicate of an organization's IT operations, with full computer systems as well as near-complete backups of user data.

Hot swappable The capability of a system component to be replaced without shutting down the system.

HTTP Secure (HTTPS) This is not a protocol; it is HTTP layered on top of TLS/SSL.

Hybrid cloud Contains at least one private cloud service and at least one public cloud service.

Hybrid fault tolerance Combines the processes of static and the dynamic fault recovery techniques. Uses fault masking until it can complete its fault diagnostics and then move the redundant components into the active role.

Hybrid metadata architecture   A metadata architecture that combines centralized and distributed architectures and includes real-time updates into a centralized repository.

Hybrid zones   Zones that combine names and ports.

Hypercalls   Short for hypervisor calls.

Hypertext Markup Language (HTML)   The standard markup language used to create web pages.

Hypertext Transfer Protocol (HTTP)   An Application layer protocol for distributed, collaborative, hypermedia information and the foundation of data communication on the web.

Hypertext Transfer Protocol Secure (HTTPS)   A communications protocol for secure communication over a computer network or the web. HTTPS communicates on port 443.

Hyperthreading   A technique that allows a multicore CPU to support multiple virtual CPUs, such as a single physical core supports two logical cores.

Hyper-V Enlightened I/O   Device drivers in the Hyper-V virtual environment that allow direct access to the VMBus virtual network adapter.

Hypervisor   Computer software, firmware, or hardware that creates, manages, controls, and runs virtual machines.

Hypervisor-aware VM   A virtual machine type that can interact directly with the hypervisor for device and control functions.

I/O throttling   A technique used to slow down I/O memory requests during low memory conditions.

IEEE 1284   This standard defines five parallel communication modes through a standard parallel port.

IEEE 802.1Q   Defines and supports VLANs on Ethernet networks.

IEEE 802.3ad   A subsection of the IEEE 802.3 standard that specifies link aggregation on bonded NICs.

Ifconfig   The Linux/UNIX version of ipconfig.

Image-based backup   Captures the entirety of a computer or VM, including its operating system, applications, and all associated data.

Incremental backup   Captures only data that changed since the last backup of any kind.

Information Technology Infrastructure Library (ITIL)   A set of practices for IT service management focusing on the alignment of IT services with the needs of business.

Infrastructure as a Service (IaaS)   Contracted cloud services that can provide an on-demand complete computing infrastructure.

Infrastructure consolidation   The centralization of networking resources to gain more effective and efficient use of resources, including physical, logical, and human resources.

Initiator   A host that requests services from an SAN.

Inode   A file system identifier that contains control information for the operating system regarding an individual file.

Input/output operations per second (IOPS) Measures the number of disk operations (input or output) per second on a storage system.

Institute of Electrical and Electronics Engineers (IEEE) A professional trade and standards organization that is dedicated to advancing technological innovation and excellence.

Integration testing A testing approach that verifies the functional performance and reliability of an integrated set of related system components.

Integrity Check Value (ICV) A calculation that uses symmetric keys to generate a hash total of the Authentication Header.

Intelligent Peripheral Interface (IPI-3) A channel protocol supported by Fibre Channel.

Intelligent Platform Management Interface (IPMI) A standard computer system interface that allows network administrators to access network devices that may be powered off or unresponsive for other reasons.

Interface In IPv6 context, the rightmost 84 bits of the address represent the host ID, also called the interface.

Interior Gateway Protocol (IGP) A routing protocol that exchanges routing information between routers within an organization's networking structure.

Internal transfer time The amount of time that elapses from when the hard disk drive's read/write head begins reading data and completes the transfer of the data to the disk controller.

Internet Assigned Numbers Authority (IANA) The agency responsible for global coordination of the DNS Root, IP addressing, and other Internet protocol resources.

Internet Control Message Protocol (ICMP) Used to send error and query messages between hosts or routers and in some diagnostic tools like ping and traceroute.

Internet Engineering Task Force (IETF) An international community of network designers, operators, vendors, and researchers focused on the evolution of the Internet architecture and its smooth operation.

Internet Header Length (IHL) The number of 32-bit words in an IPv4 packet header.

Internet Protocol (IP) Defines logical network addressing and routing.

Internet Protocol Security (IPsec) An encryption method that uses strong algorithms and provides a robust authentication. IPsec contains two encryption methods: tunnel and transport.

Internet service provider (ISP) A service organization that provides a link between an end user and the Internet via dial-up modems, cable, or digital subscriber lines (DSLs).

Internet Small Computer System Interface (iSCSI) Storage device protocol that facilitates storing and retrieving data from location-independent data storage facilities.

Internetwork Packet Exchange (IPX) A Network layer protocol in the IPX/SPX protocol suite that can also act as a Transport layer protocol as well. IPX is primarily used by the Novell NetWare network operating system.

Inter-process communication (IPC) The communication links between the elements of shared memory.

Inter-switch link (ISL) In a storage arrangement, the interconnects between switches.

Intrusion Any action on the part of an unauthorized network user that violates the security and acceptable use policies or the standard security practices of an organization.

Intrusion detection and prevention system (IDPS) Monitor network traffic on hard-wired network segments and their connectivity devices and analyze the protocol activity on the network to identify suspicious-looking activities.

IP version 4 (IPv4) The primary protocol on the Internet that defines a 32-bit, 4-octet address and the standards for forwarding IP packets across the internetwork.

IP version 6 (IPv6) A Network layer addressing scheme that uses 128 bits to extend the possible addresses on the Internet to more than 340 undecillion (2^{128}).

Ipconfig Displays the current TCP/IP configuration of a host and can be used for the management of a host's DHCP settings.

IPv4-compatible IPv6 address An IPv6 address that has all zeroes for its leading 96 bits, with the rightmost 32 bits containing the 32-bit IPv4 address.

IPv4-mapped addresses An IPv6 address in which the rightmost 32 bits are an IPv4 address, the first 80 bits contain zeroes, and the middle 16 bits receive all ones.

IPv6 Stateless Address Autoconfiguration This IPv6 feature allows devices to perform a stateless configuration of their IP configuration settings automatically.

Isolation The separation of a computer, network, or service from other of the same to restrict access to it as a security measure.

Java Message Service (JMS) An API for sending messages between two or more clients on a Java platform.

Journaling A file system action that logs all transactions performed against individual files, such as reads, writes, and deletes.

Just a Bunch of Disks (JBOD) An array of hard disks without configuration as a RAID mode.

Keystream A random seed number used by a symmetric key to decode ciphertext.

Kin processor The association of a process or thread to a specific CPU.

L_port An I/O device or a processor-based system on an FC-AL topology.

L1 cache Located on the same integrated circuit as the processor to be close to the processor. It ranges in size from 8 KB to 64 KB of SRAM.

L2 cache The backup buffer for L1 cache that can range from 64 KB to 4 MB of DRAM.

L2TP Access Concentrator (LAC) The client end of an L2TP tunnel session that initiates the connection to the LNS.

L2TP Network Server (LNS) The server end of an L2TP tunnel session.

L2TP/IPsec Transmits data over a secure channel and tunnel. IPsec establishes a secure channel, and L2TP provides a tunnel.

L3 cache Not included on all processors, this cache uses DRAM and is commonly twice as large as L2 cache on a system.

Large receive offload (LRO) Queues up large inbound message buffers and allows the network to divide them into separate Layer 2 frames.

Large segment offloading (LSO) *See* generic segmentation offload (GSO).

Latency Delay as an element of the throughput and turnaround times experienced by subscribers.

Launch Code Policy (LCP) A set of security rules configured by an administrator that guides the start-up of a hypervisor under an MLE.

Layer 2 Forwarding (L2F) Uses only Ethernet headers to forward frames to their MAC address destinations.

Layer 2 Tunneling Protocol (L2TP) Common on VPNs; ISPs use it to deliver content to users.

Layer 2 Tunneling Protocol (L2TP)/IPsec Combines PPTP with Layer 2 Forwarding (L2F) technology to create a secure tunneling protocol.

Lazy Zero thick provisioning In virtual machine provisioning, a hypervisor writes zeroes to a virtual disk file to erase any data from an earlier use.

Leading zero suppression notation An IPv6 address notation that removes any zeroes found in the first digit of any address element.

Lightweight Directory Access Protocol (LDAP) A set of protocols for accessing information directories.

Limit A virtual machine setting that sets the maximum amount of a physical resource a guest operating system can allocate at start-up.

Link aggregation The logical combination of two or more network adapters into a single and larger interface.

Linked clone A copy of a virtual machine parent that shares virtual disks with the parent, allowing several virtual machines to use the same software configuration.

Linked hard disk A file that contains a logical link to a physical drive.

Link-local unicast address An IPv6 address format that indicates a packet intended only for the local network.

Live Migration A utility available in both Microsoft and VMware virtual environments in which network nodes are completely independent.

Load balancing with failover (LBFO) A logical teaming of multiple network adapters to provide bandwidth aggregation and traffic failover to maintain connectivity in the event of a network component failure.

Load testing A testing approach that determines how a system performs under low, average, and high load conditions.

Local area network (LAN) A computer network connecting computers within a limited area on a common network media.

Locally scoped A type of IPv6 multicast address that only needs to be unique within its local network.

Logical unit number (LUN) On Fibre Channel and SCSI storage devices, each device is identified with this number.

Loopback address An IPv4 or IPv6 address that indicates to switches and routers that a message is to return to its source.

Lossless compression A compression technique that retains the full image of data by removing redundancy.

Lossy compression A compression technique that may lose some of a data stream's original content by attempting to remove unnecessary information.

LUN masking Restricts access to SAN devices by hiding certain LUNs from certain initiators.

Maintenance mode When a host computer goes into maintenance mode, its virtual machines either migrate to another active host or go into a saved or idled state, for the duration of the host's maintenance mode suspension.

Managed devices *See* Managed switch.

Managed runtime environment (MRE) A dynamic runtime environment that provides a platform that abstracts the operating system and the hardware and software architecture running on a host computer.

Managed switch A switch that a network administrator can access for configuration, function, and interface assignment.

Management information base (MIB) Contains entries that list the statistical and control values for each SNMP-managed element on a network.

Mandatory access control (MAC) An access control method that applies a confidentiality stamp to each asset.

Man-made disasters This type of disaster includes industrial accidents, like hazardous material spills or leakage, regional or localized infrastructure failures, acts of terrorism, criminal activities, hacker attacks, and acts of war.

Mapping file A file created by a virtual environment's hypervisor that maps the virtual and physical components, devices, and services and stores it as metadata.

Mashup Software or web application created by combining existing coding, web applications, or other blocks of programming.

Maximum Message Unit (MMU) *See* Maximum Transmission Unit (MTU).

Maximum Transmission Unit (MTU) The maximum datagram length an interface is able to accommodate.

Mean time between failures (MTBF) The average amount of time that should elapse between failures on a component, device, or system.

Mean time to failure (MTTF) The average amount of time before a system component fails for the first time.

Mean time to implement (MTTI) The average amount of time required to implement a system component.

Mean time to repair (MTTR) The time required to fix or replace a failed component.

Mean time to restore service (MTRS) The average time to restore service after a fault, including the time to identify, isolate, and locate the fault.

Measured Launch Environment (MLE) An Intel Corporation feature within TPM technology that creates a start-up environment in which an operating system or hypervisor is measured against a standard to detect possible changes.

Media Access Control (MAC) A sublayer of Layer 2 that provides addressing and channel access control and allows network nodes to communicate within a network on a shared medium.

Memory ballooning A virtual memory management technique that frees unused memory of one virtual machine and assigns it temporarily to another virtual machine to resolve memory shortages.

Memory cache A performance enhancement that attempts to eliminate reading data from storage.

Memory management unit (MMU) A computer hardware unit that translates virtual memory addresses to physical addresses.

Memory reservation A virtual machine setting that specifies the guaranteed minimum amount of physical memory the virtual machine needs to run efficiently.

Memory virtualization Uncouples physical RAM on one or more computers to create a memory pool that the computers contributing to the pool can share.

Message authentication Applies PKI encryption to create a digital signature that allows a recipient to verify the identity of the sender using the sender's public key.

Message authentication code (MAC) A hash total added to a message by a one-way hashing algorithm.

Message priority code Indicates the severity and the facility of the message. This code and the message severity code are numerical values stored in an 8-bit field in a system log entry.

Message severity code Along with the message priority code, this code occupies the high-order three bits of an 8-bit field on a system log entry to indicate the severity of the event.

Metadata "Data about data." There are two types of metadata: structural metadata and descriptive metadata.

Metropolitan area network (MAN) An interconnection of networks in a city into a single larger network that may then connect to a WAN.

Micro-kernelized hypervisor A thin hypervisor implementation that includes only a bare minimum of the coding necessary to perform basic functions. Any device drivers, memory managers, and virtualized services are loaded to the parent partition.

Microsoft Hyper-V The Microsoft virtualization software that installs on Windows Server 2012.

Mixed mode notation An IPv6 address notation in which the last two elements convert to their decimal equivalents using the dotted decimal notation.

Monolithic hypervisor This type of hypervisor contains its control, management, and interface software on board.

Mount   On Linux/UNIX systems, this command is used to link a file system into the active system.

Multicast   Transmits a specific data block from one or more originators to multiple destinations.

Multicast addressing   An allocation of the IPv6 address space in which addresses with the hex value "FF" in the first 8 bits are multicast addresses.

Multicast DNS version 6 (mDNSv6)   A version of DNS configured to access IPv6 addressing.

Multicore processor   A single computing component that has two or more independent CPUs (cores) that can independently read and execute program instructions.

Multipath I/O   Facilitates fault tolerance and performance improvement by providing more than one link between the server's CPU and the storage system using the system buses, storage device controllers, and storage switches along the connecting links.

Multipathing   A failover protection technique that ensures that an SAN stays up and functioning.

Multiprocessing computer   On SMP systems, the multiprocessor that contains two or more independent processors.

Multiprotocol Label Switching (MPLS)   A switching method used in telecommunications networks that directs data from one node to the next using short path labels in place of network addresses and eliminating the need for routing tables.

Multitenancy   Multiple consumers share a computing resource; the core structure of a community cloud service.

Multithreaded processors   Processors or cores that multiplex two or more streams of instructions, alternatively processing instructions from each thread.

N_port   A general node on a Fibre Channel topology.

N_Port_ID Virtualization (NPIV)   Virtual HBAs incorporate this feature that permits each virtual server to have a unique WWN.

Name zoning   The use of WWNs.

Named pipe   A system entity that remains available after a process completes.

NAND flash memory   Flash memory with NAND (not and) circuitry.

National Institute for Standards and Technology (NIST)   The federal technology agency that develops and applies technology, measurements, and standards.

Natural disasters   This type of disaster is generally weather related and includes hurricanes, typhoons, tornadoes, cyclones, floods, tsunamis, and earthquakes.

Neighbor Discovery Protocol (NDP)   A protocol used with IPv6 that facilitates autoconfiguration of nodes, discovery of other nodes on a link, determination of the EUI-64 addresses of other nodes, duplicate address detection, discovery of available routers and DNS servers, address prefix detection, and the paths to other active neighbor nodes.

Netstat   Displays the listening ports on a computer and any active network connections.

Network address translation (NAT) A network management method that replaces the private source address in an outbound IP packet header with a common public address to protect the internal addressing.

Network as a Service (NaaS) Contracted cloud services that provide network, transport, and cloud service model connectivity available on-demand to a consumer via the Internet.

Network attached storage (NAS) A file-level data storage arrangement that is directly connected to a computer network to provide access to data to network-attached clients. NAS is implemented through hardware, software, or a combination of both.

Network baseline *See* Baseline.

Network behavior analysis (NBA) Monitors network traffic for unusual flows of traffic, such as repeating transactions, flooding, DDoS attacks, malware, and violations of local security policies.

Network documentation A formal representation of the configuration, maintenance history, and performance of a network.

Network File System (NFS) A file-level data storage arrangement accessed by network clients over a computer network.

Network Information Service (NIS) A client-server directory service protocol for distributing user and host names between computers on a network.

Network monitoring Detects or prevents problems to avoid the risk of losing crucial network-accessed resources and business continuity.

Network number Represents the network ID portion of the public IP address of a network gateway.

Network optimization The processes and actions that ensure that a network operates at its highest availability and efficiency.

Network port A unique number identifier that allows specific applications, services, and protocols to share network resources concurrently. *See* Port.

Network protocol Defines a convention or a standard set of formats and rules to use in establishing a connection, communicating, and moving data between linked endpoints.

Network Service Access Point (NSAP) An IPv6 address space that links the Network layer functions of a network to its Transport layer functions.

Network service provider (NSP) A company that provides backbone services to an Internet service provider (ISP).

Network share On an SAN, the network structure shares data storage and retrieval among network storage devices.

Network switch Physical or virtual network device that connects network nodes on the same network to create access to shared resources.

Network Time Protocol (NTP) A networking protocol that provides clock synchronization between systems on packet-switched data networks.

Network-based IDPS *See* Intrusion detection and prevention system (IDPS).

Networking resources Includes the pooling of the physical network devices and software services that connect, segment, and isolate network services performed at the OSI Network layer and below.

New Technology File System (NTFS) A journaling Microsoft file system that allows for the recovery of parts or all of the file system.

Nibble mode A legacy parallel communication mode that transmits only 4 bits at a time.

NIC bonding Logically combines two or more network adapters into a single interface.

NIC teaming Logically combines multiple network adapters into a team of interfaces that provide backup and failover insurance to each other.

Non-hypervisor-aware VM An older version of Hyper-V virtualization software includes support for virtual machines that do not include hypercall capabilities.

Nonvolatile A type of data storage circuit that is able to retain its data content without a power source, such as nonvolatile memory or SSD drives.

Not and (NAND) An electronic logic gate that produces an output that is `false` if all inputs are `true`.

Not or (NOR) A digital electronic logic gate that returns `true` when both inputs are `true` or `false` and returns `false` when either input is `true` or `false`, but not both.

Nslookup Displays the DNS information for a URL or domain name.

N-version execution environment (NVX) A fault tolerance process that compares the vectors and indicators of each program to determine which result is the correct response.

N-version programming (NVP) Two independently developed versions of software running concurrently, with each producing a set of vectors or indicators that are used by the software voter to determine the fault/nonfault decision.

Obfuscation Changes out the characters of a data block in a way that is meaningful to only the applications that access the data.

Object A data entity stored on an object storage device that contains the data and all related metadata.

Object storage This storage method stores objects on an object storage device that contains the data and all its related metadata.

Object storage device (OSD) Arranges data into variable-length objects or containers.

Octet A set of 8 bits used together as one of four sections of an IP address.

One-way hashing Creates a message digest value that is impossible to decode and is used for comparison purposes only.

Open Shortest Path First (OSPF) A link-state, interior routing protocol that operates within a single autonomous system (AS).

Open Systems Interconnection (OSI) Model A standardized computer networking model by the International Organization for Standardization (ISO).

OpenStack Object Storage An object storage API that defines core components and functions that provide specific sets of functions in support of user interactions.

Operating system virtualization A form of virtualization common for virtual hosting environments, multiple virtual web servers, and load balancing.

Oracle Clustered File System (OCFS) A file-sharing system that allows the nodes of a computer cluster to share data files.

Ordered journaling This journaling method only journals the file metadata. It is the default journaling method for Linux systems.

Ordinary files These files contain data, strings of executable scripts in text form, audio, video, or other forms of text or binary data.

Organizationally unique identifier (OUI) An element of a MAC address that identifies the manufacturer of a computer or network component.

Originating protocol Provides the formatting of the original data packet.

Overallocation A common pooling of storage resources shared by multiple virtual machines. *See* Oversubscription.

Oversubscription A common pooling of storage resources shared by multiple virtual machines. *See* Overallocation.

P2V capacity planning A planning function performed by a P2V migration system.

Pagefile *See* Swap space.

Paging The memory swapping process on Windows systems, where memory blocks are called pages.

Parallel port Transmits an entire byte at a time over individual internal wires in the connecting cable.

Para-virtualization In this form of virtualization, a guest operating system must work with the hypervisor for the nonvirtualizable instructions of the guest operating system. The guest operating system's kernel is modified to remove the nonvirtualizable instructions and replace them with compatible hypercalls.

Parent partition This type of partitioning contains the host operating system and the software services required to interact with the hypervisor and other virtual machines.

Partition A logical disk drive. Partitioning a disk into multiple partitions allows one physical hard disk drive to appear to be two or more logical disk drives.

Passive attack An attempt to gain information by observing or stealing the data for outside use.

Passive fault-tolerance *See* Static hardware recovery.

Pass-through mode A RAID controller mode used in VSAN implementations.

Payment Card Industry Data Security Standard (PCI DSS) Standard that defines the secure data storage requirements for all companies that process, store, or transmit credit card information.

Penetration testing This testing approach simulates an attack on a system or network with the purpose of identifying any security weaknesses or vulnerabilities that hackers could exploit to gain access to resources or corrupt or crash the system.

Perfmon A Windows utility that monitors the disk performance on a single computer.

Performance baseline *See* Baseline.

Peripheral Component Interconnect (PCI) A local bus standard that provides a 64-bit bus, although typically implemented as a 32-bit bus.

Personal digital assistant (PDA) A mobile or palmtop device that serves as a personal information manager.

Personally identifiable information (PII) Information that on its own or with other information can be used to identify, contact, or locate a single person.

Phishing attack An attempt to capture information through an unauthorized replica website presented to be the actual website of a financial or retail company.

Physical consolidation *See* Infrastructure consolidation.

Physical NICs (pNICs) A physical network adapter that can be associated with a number of virtual NICS.

Physical to virtual (P2V) A migration of a physical nonvirtualized environment's files to a virtual environment.

Ping A standard command-line utility used to test a network connection.

Ping flood attack A form of DoS attack that sends a high volume of ICMP Echo requests, which saturate the target computer and prevent it from processing normal traffic from its associated network.

Ping of death (PoD) attack An attack that sends an oversized ping packet to a target computer.

Pipe file A temporary file that links commands so that the data produced by one command is available for another command.

Plaintext Data that is the input to a cryptographic algorithm.

Platform as a Service (PaaS) Contracted cloud services that provide virtual or cloud servers and an array of operating systems, IDEs, and mashup tools.

Platform Configuration Register (PCR) Special-purpose registers with extensions that store a variety of measurements that are encrypted using SHA-1 hashing to create a chain of trust.

Pointer-snapshot A snapshot type that starts with a full copy of a data set and then captures only changes made to the data after that, using pointers to reference the data changes to the initial snapshot.

Point-to-point (FC-P2P) topology A direct connection between two devices using an FC link.

Point-to-Point Protocol (PPP) An encapsulating protocol that operates on Layer 2 and sets up direct connections between two nodes.

Point-to-Point Tunneling Protocol (PPTP) A protocol used for VPNs that uses a TCP control channel and a GRE tunnel to encapsulate PPP packets.

Port Transport layer protocols identify assigned logical ports that allow outbound and inbound traffic to share a single IP address and the identification of an arriving service request or response. Port also refers to interface connections on network devices.

Port address translation (PAT) Modifies internal addressing into multiple unique addresses by appending TCP/UDP port numbers.

Port forwarding Used by a remote computer to establish a connection to a specific node or service on a private LAN.

Port group Clusters virtual switch ports under a common configuration.

Port triggering Allows applications or services to set up temporary port forwarding to itself.

Port zoning In an SAN, limits the access to data to only designated authorized ports.

Pretty Good Privacy (PGP) A data encryption and decryption utility that provides privacy and authentication for data communication.

Preventive control measures This type of control measures, avoids, or prevents a threat event from occurring, including storing backups offsite, using power conditioning or surge suppression, or running periodic audits.

Private cloud Completely proprietary computing architecture located behind a single firewall.

Private key In asymmetrical encryption, this key decrypts the data encrypted with a public key. Only the holder of the private key can decrypt the data.

Private loop FC-AL topologies that consist of only local nodes or NL_ports.

Process identifier (PID) A number assigned by an operating system to temporarily and uniquely identify a process running on a host.

Process VM Runs only a single process in support of program portability.

Processor core A multicore CPU has two or more processors (cores).

Program/erase (P/E) cycle A sequence of actions that writes data to solid-state NAND flash memory, which is immediately erased and then rewritten.

PS/2 A legacy serial interface method that uses a 6-pin mini-DIN connector for keyboards and mouse units.

Public cloud Cloud services over the Internet.

Public key In asymmetrical encryption, this key encrypts the original data or is used to create a digital signature.

Public key infrastructure (PKI) encryption Asymmetric encryption that requires two encryption keys: a private (secret) key and a public (shared) key.

Pushdown stack A stack mode in which the last item placed on the stack is the first item available for use.

PuTTY An open source SSH and Telnet client originally developed for the Windows platform.

Quality control A testing and verification method that involves testing the quality of an application or other system component.

Quality of Service (QoS) A general term that measures the performance of a computing system quantitatively to established performance metrics.

Quota Limits the amount of time a subscriber can exceed the soft limit without going over the hard limit.

RAID 0 Striping divides a body of data into several stripes and writes each stripe to a different hard disk.

RAID 0+1 A hybrid combination of RAID 0 and RAID 1 that implements disk striping and disk mirroring of the data stripes.

RAID 1 Applies disk mirroring only.

RAID 1+0 A hybrid combination that mirrors the data and then stripes the mirrored sets across additional disks.

RAID 5 Implements parity blocks and then stripes them across at least three hard disk drives along with the data.

RAID 6 Enhances RAID 5 by adding duplicated distributed parity blocks.

RAID write penalty In the calculation of IOPS, this number accounts for the multiple disk writes of a RAID system.

RAM-based SSD Stores data electronically on DRAM or SRAM integrated circuits.

Read-only snapshot Uses an exception table to track changed data blocks.

Read-write snapshot *See* Branching snapshot.

Real Time Streaming Protocol (RTSP) A network control protocol used to control streaming media servers.

Recovery blocks (RB) An approach to software fault tolerance that applies the dynamic fault recovery model to use redundant programming blocks or modules to replace faulty blocks in a program.

Recovery point objective (RPO) The point in business or IT operations to which a system is to be restored by a disaster recovery plan.

Recovery testing A testing approach that measures the capability of a component, integrated set, or system to determine how fast it can recover from some form of failure or catastrophic event.

Recovery time objective (RTO) The time objective for accomplishing a system restoration after a disaster recovery.

Redundancy In the context of computing, a system with components or software installed that are not required for the system to function normally.

Redundant Array of Independent Disks (RAID) A data storage technology that combines multiple disk drive components into a single logical unit for data redundancy.

Reliability The amount of time a computer system or component will continue to perform before requiring maintenance or replacement.

Reliability testing This testing approach measures the consistency of an application to perform the same functions repeatedly and produce the same results.

Remote Desktop Protocol (RDP) A Microsoft proprietary protocol that gives a user a GUI to connect to another computer over a network connection.

Remote Desktop Services (RDS) Also known as Terminal Services, RDS is one of the components of Microsoft Windows that allows a user to take control of a remote computer or virtual machine over a network connection.

Remote Desktop Web Connection (RDWC) A Microsoft web application consisting of an ActiveX control and a sample connection page.

Remote-access VPN Establishes a secure, encrypted connection between a private network and a remote user over third-party communication lines.

Replication The sharing of information to ensure consistency between redundant resources to improve reliability, fault tolerance, and availability.

Representational State Transfer (REST) Defines a set of structure rules that allow the transmission of data over a standard transport protocol, typically HTTP.

Reservation A guaranteed CPU resource allocation to a virtual machine. *See* Entitlement.

Resilient File System (ReFS) A Microsoft file system intended for file servers only.

Resource allocation The configuration of a physical or virtual resource or device shares to provide baseline resources to virtual machines.

Resource pooling A grouping of computer and network resources to provide throughput, availability, reliability, and fault tolerance.

Resource sharing *See* Share.

Response rate The amount of time required for a disk storage system to process, access, and return or write data from or to a hard disk drive, start to finish.

Reverse delta backup Combines a full backup with continuous synchronization with live data and records the data needed to restore the storage system to a previous version.

Ring 0 x86 processors define four rings of protection that allow only software with specific privileges to execute on any one of the rings. The innermost ring with the highest protection and the highest level of program privilege. Software executing in Ring 0 is running in system space.

Ring −1 Created by the virtualization technology on Intel VT and AMD-V processors, this ring allows a virtual machine's guest operating system to run in system space without affecting any other VMs or the host computer's operating system.

Rivest Cipher 4 (RC4) An encryption stream cipher developed by Ron Rivest that uses variable-key-size encryption algorithms.

Rivest Cipher 5 (RC5) An encryption block cipher developed by Ron Rivest that uses variable-key-size encryption algorithms.

Rivest-Shamir-Adleman (RSA) The encryption algorithm that is the most frequently used algorithm in web browsers and many applications.

Role-based access control (RBAC)   An access control method that defines access to all members of a role-based group.

Root partition   The foundation partition of a Hyper-V installation.

Rotational latency   The amount of time required for the desired disk sector on a given track of a hard disk drive to rotate to a position under the read/write head.

Rotational speeds   The number of times per minute that the disk spindle rotates.

Route   An available pathway on the internetwork on which a router can forward a packet.

Routing   The process of moving data across a network to its destination address.

Routing table   Stores the metrics and route information used in dynamic routing.

RS-232C   The registered standard for the connectors and communications of serial devices.

Sarbanes-Oxley Act (SOX)   Federal law that establishes management, reporting, and data accuracy standards for U.S. public company boards of directors, company management, and public accounting firms.

Scalability   The capability to quickly increase or decrease available resources as needed.

Scalability testing   A testing approach commonly used to test a cloud service to determine the system's capabilities to scale itself to the demands of the subscriber.

Second extended file system (ext2)   Replaced the ext file system and was the file system for flash storage media. ext2 doesn't include journaling, and flash devices have a limited number of write cycles.

Sector   The smallest addressable unit that a hard disk drive can read or write in a single operation.

Secure FTP (SFTP)   FTP extension of SSH that provides secure file transfer capabilities.

Secure Shell (SSH)   A cryptographic network protocol for secure data communication.

Secure Sockets Layer (SSL)   Uses sockets to pass data between clients and servers. Employs both PKI and symmetric key encryption, including the use of digital certificates.

Secure Sockets Layer/Transport Layer Security (SSL/TLS)   Provides three services: validating website identity, creating an encrypted connection (tunnel), and ensuring the transmitted data is error free.

Security association (SA)   A set of values that indicate the authentication of the recipient of a message. *See* Encapsulating Security Payload (ESP).

Security controls   The policies and rules relating to the control, access, and integrity of stored data, financial documents, sensitive information, and financial processes to ensure that data, document, and process risks are minimized.

Security Parameter Index (SPI)   A value that combines with the destination IP address to indicate the security association (SA) of the intended recipient in an IPsec ESP header.

Security testing   A testing approach that attempts to identify security flaws and vulnerabilities in an application or system that may defeat the defined security policies of an organization.

Seek time   The time required for a read/write head to travel to the track and sector where data is to be read or written.

Separation of duties An accounting control that directs an organization to separate the financial-related tasks in a process to two or more individuals.

Serial Advanced Technology Attachment (SATA) A computer bus interface that connects HBAs to mass storage devices such as hard disk drives.

Serial Attached SCSI (SAS) A point-to-point serial protocol that moves data to and from computer storage devices such as hard drives.

Serial port An interface that conforms to the RS-232C standard and communicates by transmitting one bit at a time.

Server Manager A management console utility of Windows Server 2012 that allows administrators to configure and manage local and remote Windows servers without enabling RDP connections on either computer.

Server Message Block (SMB) An Application layer protocol used for providing shared access to files, printers, serial ports, and miscellaneous communications between nodes on a network.

Server virtualization Also known as hardware virtualization and platform virtualization, creates one or more logically isolated execution partitions on a single physical server.

Service As defined by NIST, contractible operations available on demand and for a fee.

Service capacity planning Planning that addresses the capacity needs of services like email, Internet, intranet, telephony, instant messaging, and teleconferencing.

Service Level Agreement (SLA) A formal agreement that spells out in specific terms, metrics, and quantities what a service delivered to a customer provides.

Serviceability The ease and speed of repairing or maintaining a system.

Service-oriented architecture (SOA) The structure that supports the communications between cloud-based services.

Share The percentage of a physical or virtual device or resource's capacity that a virtual machine is allocated and can consume.

Shared disk The managing file system replicates the underlying file system in real time to another storage device and maintains enough copies to provide multiple accesses to a file, although each request goes against a different copy of the data.

Shared memory Memory that can be accessed by multiple programs simultaneously to provide communication, pass data, and avoid redundant data copies.

Shared nothing (SN) Nodes that don't share memory or disk storage.

Shareware A form of proprietary software provided to users on a limited or trial basis, subject to a license that restricts the use, resale, or other commercial use of the software.

Short Message Service (SMS) A text messaging service on telephone, the web, or mobile communication systems.

Short stroking A characteristic of smaller physical drives that reduces seek time.

Signature-based detection A detection method that looks for a consistent pattern of characters or data in data objects of any type.

Simple Mail Transfer Protocol (SMTP) A TCP/IP protocol standard for email transmission.

Simple Network Management Protocol (SNMP) A TCP/IP suite protocol that manages and monitors network devices.

Simple Object Access Protocol (SOAP) A web service standard that defines the rules for transferring XML messages using the WSDL standard.

Simple Storage Service (S3) A proprietary web-based data storage service from Amazon, through which users can store and retrieve any amount of data at any time.

Simultaneous multithreading (SMT) Hardware multithreading is used to improve the efficiency of CPUs by permitting multiple independent execution threads to utilize processor resources.

Single Byte Command Code Set (SBCCS) A Fibre Channel code set that is transmitted in segments consisting only of a header, the command byte, and a checksum on replies.

Single point of failure A component or software in a system that is no longer available if the component fails.

Site-local unicast address An IPv6 address format that doesn't include an address prefix because any packet with this address type stays within a local site.

Site-to-site VPN A VPN that communicates over dedicated lines applying large-scale encryption.

Small Computer System Interface (SCSI) A primary interconnection standard implemented by an SAN. This parallel interface provides data speeds of up to 160 MBps for up to 16 devices.

Snapshot The capture of the state of a system, virtual environment, or virtual machine at a particular point in time.

SNMP agent Managed devices have a built-in agent that communicates with an SNMP manager to alert of issues, status, or data.

SNMP manager Communicates with SNMP agents to send queries, processes responses from agents, configures agents, and interacts with agents about triggered events.

Social engineering A type of attack in which an attacker engages a user through email or phone to learn security information.

Socket A logical addressing entity consisting of an ID for the Transport layer protocol in use, the TCP/UDP port number associated with a specific process, and an IP address.

Soft limit In a virtual machine, the amount of a resource's allocation as specified in a reservation.

Soft zoning Requests to an SAN may query all storage devices or partitions but can only view the permissioned subset of the SAN.

Software as a Service (SaaS) Cloud-based services that provide access via the Internet to software applications hosted in the cloud.

Software, platform, infrastructure (SPI) A model that encompasses the three primary types of cloud computing services: Software as a Service (SaaS), Platform as a Service (PaaS), and Infrastructure as a Service (IaaS).

Software voting *See* Hardware voting.

Software-based memory virtualization A hypervisor uses either paravirtualization or binary translation to allow the host operating system to function as if it is accessing physical memory directly.

Solid state drive (SSD) A storage medium type that uses integrated circuit assemblies as memory to store data.

Space redundancy Extra resources in a system that would be unnecessary if the system were completely fault free.

Special files These files link to physical devices, like printers, external storage devices, or any other I/O device attached to the computer.

SPI model The NIST cloud services model that defines the use of hardware and software to provide client/server services via the Internet.

Split-site An approach to redundancy and availability in which IT operations are separated onto facilities in geographically separate locations.

Spoof attack A type of attack in which an attacker intercepts message packets and modifies the source address so that the packet appears to have originated from a different location.

SSD controller Performs the operations required to read or write data to the flash memory components of the drive.

Stack An area of primary memory in which a program can store variable data values. The CPU controls the stack.

Stack overflow attack This attack occurs when a program is induced to place data onto the stack that exceeds the size of a stack entry.

Standard Parallel Port (SPP) Also called the Centronics standard, this parallel communication mode is a one-direction interface designed specifically for printers.

Standby pairing A form of redundancy in which a component is operational and one or more identical components are standbys.

Stateful The processing condition that considers an object and all its data.

Stateful protocol analysis An IDPS method that compares the activity it sees with established profiles provided by device and software vendors.

Stateless The processing condition that treats all requests independently without regard to their status.

Static hardware recovery The use of fault masking to mitigate the occurrence of a fault by hiding the fault from the system.

Static NAT Replaces the internal IP address in a message with an external IP address and recalculates any checksums, including the internal IP address.

Static RAM (SRAM)   A type of semiconductor memory that retains its contents without power for longer periods than dynamic RAM (DRAM).

Static route   A fixed administrator-entered destination address for a particular interface.

Storage area network (SAN)   A high-speed network of storage devices that connects with servers to provide access to block-level storage by applications running on network servers.

Storage as a service (SaaS)   A cloud service model that provides on-demand storage space to subscribers.

Storage migration   Moving virtual data storage from one storage device or volume to another in the same file format or into a new file format on a target device.

Storage Networking Industry Association (SNIA)   The developer and publisher of the OSD standard.

Storage provisioning   A step-by-step sequence of configuration and specification activities by an SAN administrator.

Storage resources   Includes storage devices and the physical and logical resources that enable resource availability, security, and elasticity.

Storage virtualization   A consolidation of multiple network storage devices into a single virtual device.

Stress testing   This testing approach determines if defined specifications are met, what the safe usage limits are, and what potential failure points of a system or application exist.

Structural metadata   This metadata type contains descriptive information about the formatting, processing, and dependencies of an object's data.

Structured data   Data associated with an event, such as a transaction, that is stored in groups of related data, commonly in a database system.

Subnet mask   A binary filter used to extract the network ID from an IPv4 address.

Subnetting   Dividing a network into two or more network subnets, each of which is a separate collision domain.

Superblock   Contains control information for the operating system regarding a disk partition.

Supernet   Using a number of bits other than the standard IPv4 classful standards to indicate the network ID in an IPv4 address, aggregates subnets into supernets.

Sustained DTR   The data transfer rate at a disk drive's highest peak or burst load.

Swap file   The receiving space for memory swapped out to virtual memory.

Swap space   A reserved portion of a hard disk drive that extends a computer's internal memory as part of the system's virtual memory function.

Symmetric key encryption   This encryption method uses the same encryption key for both encoding and decoding.

Symmetric multiprocessing (SMP)   A microprocessor hardware and software architecture in which two or more identical processors share memory and have access to I/O devices under the control of a single operating system.

Syslog A standard for logging computer system messages. A syslog packet has three parts: message priority, message header, and message content.

Sysprep A Windows utility that prepares a virtual image for transfer to a physical machine.

System Center Virtual Machine Manager (SCVMM) Performs P2V migration in either online or offline modes.

System development life cycle (SDLC) The general term used in software and hardware engineering to describe a process for planning, creating, testing, and deploying a system.

System life cycle management The planning, measurement, and monitoring of a computing entity's useful life.

System space *See* Ring 0.

System testing This testing approach measures the capability of an entire system, such as a virtualized system or network, a cloud service data center, or perhaps a localized network, to functionally produce the predefined expectations of its test plan.

System VM Provides an operating platform that supports the system elements of a physical machine, including an operating system and device drivers.

Target A servicing device on an SAN.

TCP segmentation offloading (TSO) *See* Generic segmentation offload (GSO).

Test strategy Documents the why, what, and how of the testing approach before actual testing begins.

Thick provisioning The traditional approach to storage provisioning that allocates the same amount of resource capacity as a process actually uses.

Thin provisioning A type of storage provisioning that allocates only the resources needed by a virtual machine.

Third extended file system (ext3) Added journaling to the ext2 file system.

Thread An ordered stream of instructions.

Threshold A quantified performance metric against which actual performance measurements are measured.

Throughput time The slower of either internal transfer time or external transfer time.

Tiered storage Data storage is separated into categories of descending need and stored on storage devices of descending speed and capabilities.

Time redundancy In this form of redundancy, every action is repeated, and the results of the original and the repeated action are compared.

Time to Live (TTL) A counter or timestamp attached to or embedded in a data packet that specifies the event count or timespan at which the packet is to be discarded to prevent a packet from circulating indefinitely.

Time to service (TTS) The amount of time required to start up a new implementation or the amount of time required to restore service after a system failure.

TLS Handshake Protocol Within TLS, this protocol provides the capability for a client and a server to authenticate each other and to agree on an encryption method and its associated keys prior to the transmission of data.

TLS Record Protocol Within TLS, this protocol provides security on communication links, running on a transport protocol, and applying or omitting an encryption method as desired.

Top-level domain (TLD) Identifies the highest domain level for a URL, such as cengagelearning.com, where ".com" is the TLD.

Traceroute/Tracert A command-line utility that displays the route between a local host and a remote IP address or domain name along with the transit time of the ICMP message exchange.

Track Concentric logical circles of equal size on the surface of an HDD platter.

Track-to-track time The time required to move a hard disk read/write head to an adjacent track, typically between 0.2 and 1.0 ms.

Translation look-aside buffer (TLB) In the two-layer memory page table approach of software-based memory virtualization, the second layer contains the mappings of host physical page addresses to machine page addresses. The TLB caches the more active mappings.

Transmission Control Protocol (TCP) The TCP/IP protocol that tracks individual packets and fragments to ensure their integrity and guarantee their arrival at their destinations. TCP is a connection-mode protocol that manages and ensures the existence of a connection throughout the exchange of messages between two endpoints.

Transmission Control Protocol/Internet Protocol (TCP/IP) The suite of communications protocols used to connect hosts on the Internet.

Transport encryption Encrypts only the payload in each data packet.

Transport Layer Security (TLS) A secure transport protocol that provides encrypted privacy of data between clients and servers on the Internet with a guarantee that no third party can access or tamper with encoded messages.

Transport mode One of the two IPsec ESP modes that encrypt only the payload of the packet.

Transport protocol Carries an encapsulated packet across a network.

Triple DES (3DES) Applies the DES algorithm three times to encrypt data and make it secure.

Triple modular redundancy (TMR) A fault-tolerant form of N-modular redundancy in which three systems perform a process and the results are processed by a software voting system to produce a single output. If any one of the three systems fails, the other two systems can correct and mask the fault.

Trunk port A communication link that is able to receive and process two or more signals at the same time. Connects switching centers or multiple nodes in a communication system, such as the telephone system, video distribution, or the like.

Trusted Execution Technology (TXT) Provides assurances at start-up (boot) that the computer and its operating system are authentic and that the operating system is trusted.

Trusted Platform Module (TPM) Provides security features through PCRs and works with TXT to ensure a secure start-up.

Tunnel encryption Encrypts the header and payload of each data packet.

Tunnel mode One of the two IPsec ESP modes that encrypts an entire packet.

Tunneling protocol Encapsulate and encrypt data at one end of a transmission and decrypt and remove the encapsulation at the other end.

Type I hypervisor A hypervisor that runs directly on the physical hardware of a host computer, also called a bare metal hypervisor.

Type II hypervisor *See* Hosted hypervisor.

U.S. National Institute for Science and Technology (NIST) Publishes the authoritative and definitive standard for cloud computing in a document titled "NIST Cloud Computing Reference Architecture."

UNetbootin An open-source utility that can be used to create a boot disk for Linux, Windows, and Mac OS computers.

Unicast A network datagram from a single source addressed to a single destination.

Unicast address The dominant addressing scheme used in IPv4 and IPv6 in which a packet has a single destination address and a single source address.

Unified communications (UC) The integration of two or more real-time communication services, such as IM, chat, presence information, VoIP, video conferencing, data sharing, and unified messaging.

Uniform Naming Convention (UNC) A method of identifying a shared file without specifying its storage device.

Uniform Resource Identifier (URI) A string of characters used to assign a name or identity to a web or network resource.

Uniform Resource Locator (URL) A logical human-readable web address that consists of three sections, back to front: a top-level domain (TLD), a second-level domain, and a subdomain.

Unit testing This testing approach focuses on the smallest unit of the tested item to isolate it from the remainder of the system.

Uniting and Strengthening America by Providing Appropriate Tools Required to Intercept and Obstruct Terrorism Act of 2001 (USA PATRIOT Act) Defines the standards for business record searches and counter-terrorism surveillance.

Universal Plug and Play (UPnP) A set of networking protocols that allow networked devices to automatically establish network services for data sharing and communications.

Universal serial bus (USB) A computing industry standard that defines the interconnections of a bus structure to automatically detect and establish connection, communication, and power between computers and peripheral devices.

UNIX file system (UFS) An HFS, in which directories and files are in a directory tree structure with its root at the top.

Unmanaged switch A preconfigured, plug-and-play device that network devices communicate with using a fixed configuration, with no provision for reconfiguration by local administrators.

Unspecified address An IPv6 address that indicates a message sent from a host to itself. This message has the format of 0:0:0:0:0:0:0:0 or "::".

Unstructured data Data without a predefined data model or a predefined organization that is typically text but may also be dates or numbers.

Update sequence number (USN) A sequential count that indicates how up-to-date a domain controller is on a Windows system.

Uptime The opposite of downtime. It measures the time a system is available.

User acceptance test (UAT) The process for verifying whether a system fulfills user expectations. Also called Beta testing.

User Datagram Protocol (UDP) A connectionless Transport layer protocol that provides no connection management or guarantee for messages arriving error free, in sequence, or without duplication.

USN rollback An action that takes place when too many domain controllers become uncoordinated on a Windows system.

Variable-length subnet masking (VLSM) Allows for creating subnets of various sizes by adjusting the number of bits representing the network ID in an IP address.

Variable-scope multicast address This type of IPv6 multicast address has the same basic format as fixed-scope multicast but can be reserved to a specific organization, group, protocol, or service.

VHDTool A Windows command used to convert data volumes to a virtual environment.

Virtual bridge (vbridge) A virtual network device that connects a VM to the physical LAN of the host server.

Virtual central processing unit (vCPU) A component of a CPU with a symmetric multiprocessing (SMP), multithreaded, and multicore design.

Virtual CPUs (vCPUs) A VM's virtual processor that is associated with one or more cores on a physical CPU. Each VM can have four to eight vCPUs, depending on the virtualization software in use and the number of processors and cores of the multicore processor.

Virtual data center (VDC) A service that virtually constructs an environment that optimally meets a subscriber's existing IT needs of the consumer with the ability to scale.

Virtual desktop infrastructure (VDI) A desktop service that hosts user desktop environments on remote servers accessed over a network using a remote display protocol.

Virtual disk (vdisk) A logical disk storage device that provides data I/O support for systems or applications running in a VM or in native mode on a host computer.

Virtual disk drive In VMware, one or more .vmdk files that contain addressing and access information of the partitions the VM can access.

Virtual File System (VFS) Allows applications to access various formal file systems in a consistent manner.

Virtual firewall (vfirewall) A network firewall service or appliance running entirely within a virtualized environment that provides packet filtering and monitoring like a physical firewall.

Virtual guest tagging (VGT) A virtual switch performs VLAN tagging under the IEEE 802.1q standard inside a VM.

Virtual hard disk (VHD) A file format that allows multiple operating systems to run on a single computer through the implementation of virtual machines providing transparent movement of files between the VHD and a host file system.

Virtual host base adapter (vHBA) A virtual network interface device that limits virtual servers and VMs to only their assigned virtual data storage.

Virtual local area network (VLAN) A logical LAN that is set up in a physical network switch or a virtual switch by partitioning the LAN into two or more logical LANs.

Virtual machine (VM) A software-created computer emulation that takes on the characteristics of the computer it runs on, with its configuration controlled by the hypervisor that creates it.

Virtual Machine Bus (VMBus) In Hyper-V, a logical channel that enables inter-partition communication.

Virtual machine connection A VM can connect to multiple vNICs through a port group. In a VM connection, many vNICs can associate with one port group.

Virtual Machine File System (VMFS) A clustered file system for virtual machines.

Virtual machine lifecycle management (VMLM) A set of processes that allow administrators to monitor, manage, and control the implementation, delivery, operation, and maintenance of a virtual machine (VM) throughout its existence.

Virtual machine manager (VMM) Also virtual machine monitor. *See* Hypervisor.

Virtual memory A hardware and a software memory management technique that increases the memory allocation of a running application by extending memory storage to a disk drive.

Virtual network A computer network that creates connections between two or more virtual devices.

Virtual network interface card (vNIC) A software-based abstraction of a physical network adapter (NIC).

Virtual private LAN service (VPLS) Provides Ethernet-based multipoint-to-multipoint communication over IP or MPLS networks.

Virtual private network (VPN) Extends a private network across a public network, such as the Internet.

Virtual router (vrouter) A software program that provides the capability to route network traffic over a LAN in the same way as a hardware router.

Virtual Router Redundancy Protocol (VRRP) Implements one or more vrouters on a network to improve its reliability.

Virtual socket An abstract virtual mounting for a processor core.

Virtual storage area network (VSAN) A part of an SAN system or a virtualized environment as a software-created entity controlled by the hypervisor.

Virtual storage console (VSC) A proprietary software application that gives administrators the ability to manage NetApp storage from the VMware vCenter client.

Virtual switch (vswitch) A software program through which one VM communicates with another under control of the hypervisor.

Virtual switch tagging (VST) The type of VLAN tagging that a vswitch performs before the frame leaves the hypervisor.

Virtual to physical (V2P) The migration of a virtual system to a physical, nonvirtualized system.

Virtual to virtual (V2V) The migration of one virtual system to another virtual system.

Virtualization Creates an abstracted version of computer hardware, operating systems, storage devices, or computer network resources.

Virtualization Technology (VT) A set of hardware enhancements to Intel server and client platforms that provide software-based virtualization solutions.

Virtualized environment A computing environment in which users, applications, and devices see virtualized resources as one logical resource.

VLAN tagging Identifies frames transmitted on a trunk line.

VM template A captured copy of a virtual machine state that can be used to create additional independent virtual machines.

VMKernel In a VMware virtual environment, this is the liaison between virtual machines (VMs) and the physical hardware.

VMKernel connection A special-purpose port connection of a VMKernal.

vMotion A VMware tool that allows administrators to move files between hosts without scheduling downtime.

VMware Consolidated Backup A centralized fast backup utility for virtual machines that runs on proxy servers to avoid affecting the load on hypervisor servers.

VMware ESX Server The virtualization layer that runs on physical servers and manages the virtualization of processors, memory, storage, and networking resources and their provisioning to virtual machines.

VMware vCenter Management Server Controls the configuration, provisioning, and management of the virtualized infrastructure.

VMware Virtual Machine Disk (VMDK) A disk drive for a virtual machine consists of two .vmdk files, with the first a text file containing metadata about the virtual hard disk and the second containing the actual content of the disk.

Voice over IP (VoIP) A group of technologies for the delivery of voice communications and multimedia sessions over IP networks.

Volume shadow service (VSS) A snapshot of connected storage devices on a Windows system as part of a P2V migration.

Volume snapshot service (VSS) *See* Volume shadow service (VSS).

Volume testing This testing approach measures the capability of an application or system to function under a variable-sized set of data.

Voter A hardware or software process that compares the results produced by a majority of devices/ programs to any different results and assumes the majority result to be valid.

Vulnerability assessment This analysis reviews the results of penetration testing to identify, quantify, and prioritize or rank any vulnerability found in an IT system.

WAN optimization Improves the efficiencies of Layer 3 operations of an extended network, including throughput, bandwidth, latency, protocol efficiencies, and areas of congestion.

Warm site A form of redundancy or disaster recovery site that contains all the equipment needed to restore IT operations after a bare-metal restore.

Web Services Description Language (WSDL) An XML-based interface description language used for describing the function of a web service.

Web Services-Management (WS-Management) A DMTF open standard that defines a SOAP-based protocol for the management of servers, devices, applications, and various web services.

Web-Based Enterprise Management (WBEM) A standard that defines the management of distributed and networked computing environments.

Well-known multicast address *See* Fixed-scope multicast address.

White box A form of penetration testing in which a hacker has all the information needed to penetrate access, authentication, authorization, and manipulation controls.

Wide area network (WAN) A computer network that connects to network devices over metropolitan, regional, national, or international boundaries over telecommunication lines.

Windows Management Instrumentation (WMI) Also called Windows Management Interface (WMI). A management standard that interchanges with SNMP. WMI is the Microsoft implementation of the WBEM.

Windows Performance Monitor (WPM) A Windows system utility that determines CPU or processor utilization on a local server or remotely on a host or server.

Windows PowerShell A command-line shell and configuration management tool built on the Microsoft .NET Framework.

Workload categorization Considers the end user, the type of work, and the processes to categorize the capacity requirements of different workload categories.

Workstation Server A VMware subsystem that enables remote access to shared VMs.

World Wide Identifier (WWID) *See* World Wide Name (WWN).

World Wide Name (WWN) A serial number or an addressable locator code, such as a WWPN or a WWNN.

World Wide Node Name (WWNN) A WWNN assigned to an endpoint device on a Fibre Channel system.

World Wide Port Name (WWPN) A WWN assigned to a Fibre Channel port to identify an interface uniquely.

Wrapper The data put in front of or around a transmission that may encapsulate it.

Write caching Allows a system to transfer data into a cache, which releases the processor to move to its next operation without waiting for the write operation to complete.

Write-back caching This operation writes the contents of the write cache to the disk as a background process.

ZFS Formally known as Zettabyte File System. A proprietary 128-bit file system that has a maximum volume size of 2^{64} and a maximum files per directory of 2^{48}.

Zoneset A zoning configuration file for an SAN that contains the configuration of each separate zone.

Zoning Divides a physical SAN into a number of separate subnets, which create a storage environment similar to a VLAN.

Cloud+ Practice Exam Answers

1. B PaaS

2. C IaaS

3. C Both the cloud service provider and the cloud service subscriber

4. C Private

5. A SaaS

6. B Public

7. D Orchestration

8. C Cloud bursting

9. B Object storage

10. C Extended metadata

11. B BLOB

12. D Object identifier

13. A and C Type I and Bare metal

14. B Hypervisor

15. D Template

16. A Snapshot

17. B Clone

18. B and C Protocol based and Device based

19. D Image

20. C Virtual switch

21. D Vdisk

22. B, C, and D Implement VLANs, Implement virtual network adapters, and Implement virtual switches

23. A VSAN

24. B Zoning

25. A P2V

26. E All of the above

27. C NPIV

28. D Shared memory

29. A Virtual CPU

30. D Virtual machine

31. B Virtual operating system

32. A, C, and E Fibre Channel, Block-level data, and RAID

33. C DAS

34. B File level

35. A and B NAS and SAN

36. B HBA

37. D FCoE

38. C iSCSI

39. B SSD

40. C Tiering

41. B RAID 1

42. C, D, and E RAID 4, RAID 5, and RAID 6

43. D Write penalty

44. A NAT

45. D Dynamic NAT

46. B VMFS

47. B Supernetting

48. A 192.168.200.0

49. C VLAN tagging

50. B 80

51. D Optimization

52. A Ping

53. D Syslog

54. C IPMI

55. D All of the above

56. B Soft limit

57. A Pooling

58. C 16

59. D Entitlement

60. B Affinity

61. C SSH

62. C Console port

63. B SNMP

64. B Dynamic

65. A True

66. B and C ACL and RBAC

67. B DMZ

68. A IDS/IPS

69. C VPN

70. C DDoS

71. D Ping flood

72. B Ping of death

73. A Obscuring an attack payload from inspection by network protection systems

74. C Public key encryption

75. E None of the above

76. C Data in motion

77. D All of the above

78. D Multifactor authentication

79. C Reinstall the operating system and applications

80. C IPsec

81. C and D Federation and Single sign-on

82. C Supernetting

83. B fd9b:7da8:4a66:63b1::/64

84. B CMDB

85. C Throughput

86. B Latency

87. C Hypervisor/VMM

88. D Live migration

89. A Memory ballooning

90. D I/O throttling

91. C IOPS

92. D Teaming

93. A Bonding

94. C Redundancy

95. C Hot site

96. D Synchronous replication

97. B RTO

98. A Geoclustering

99. B Fault tolerance

100. C High availability

Index